Society and Culture in Qajar Iran

Hafez Farmayan

Society and Culture in

Qajar Iran

Studies in Honor of Hafez Farmayan

Edited by
Elton L. Daniel

MAZDA PUBLISHERS, Inc. ◆ Costa Mesa, California ◆ 2002

The publication of this volume was made possible by a grant from the Iranica Institute, Irvine California, and with the cooperation of the University of Texas at Austin and the Friends of Iranian Studies, Houston, Texas

Mazda Publishers, Inc.
Academic Publishers since 1980
P.O. Box 2603
Costa Mesa, California 92628 U.S.A.
www.mazdapub.com

Library of Congress Cataloging-in-Publication Data

Society and Culture in Qajar Iran: Studies in Honor of Hafez Farmayan/
Edited by Elton L. Daniel.
p.cm.
Includes bibliographical references.

ISBN: 1-56859-138-1
(Cloth, alk. paper)

1. Iran—Civilization—19th century. 2. Iran—Intellectual life—19th century. 3. Travelers' writings, Persian—History and criticism. 4. Travelers—Iran—History. 5. Iran—History—Qajar dynasty, 1794-1925. I. Daniel L., II. Farmayan, Hafez.
DS300.S43 2002
955'.04—dc21
2002021893

Photograph of Hafez Farmayan by Diane Watts, Center for Middle East Studies, University of Texas.

CONTENTS

Preface
Hafez Farmayan and Qajar Studies

This volume of essays is dedicated to Professor Hafez Farmayan on the occasion of his retirement from teaching at the Department of History of the University of Texas at Austin. It is offered as a tribute to an active and accomplished scholar who was a founding father of modern Iranian studies in the United States.

Professor Farmayan, or Hafez as he insists on being called by friends and colleagues alike, was born in Tehran on 7 October 1927 into one of the most distinguished families of modern Iran. His father was Prince ʿAbd-al-Ḥosayn Mīrzā Farmānfarmā (1858-1940), the great-grandson of Fatḥ-ʿAlī Shah Qājār, through the lineage of the crown prince ʿAbbās Mīrzā. By the time Hafez was born, his father had already retired from a long life of active public service, during which he was governor of southern and western provinces of Iran, served as commander-in-chief of the Constitutional armies (1911), and held various ministerial posts including that of prime minister (1915). With the rise of the Pahlavi regime in 1926, Prince Farmānfarmā devoted himself completely to philanthropic activities and the upbringing of his numerous sons and daughters, who received a thorough traditional and Western education under the most qualified teachers.

Hafez's education, with an early emphasis on Persian literature and history, began with private tutors at home and continued at public schools in Tehran. In the summer of 1944, at the age of seventeen, Hafez left Iran for the United States to receive his university education. Traveling alone and under harsh wartime conditions, he went overland by trucks and railways through Baluchestan, Afghanistan, and northwestern India to Bombay and from there by an American ship to southern California, arriving in December 1944. In the fall of 1945, he enrolled as a freshman at Stanford University. He was at first interested in a career in engineering, but, after completing the university's general requirements for lower division students, he became inspired by Stanford's program in Western Civilization and decided to study history instead. He received his B.A. in 1949 and his M.A. in 1950, with both degrees in history. During this time, he took courses with well-known Stanford professors in many fields of history: American, Russian, and European. He enjoyed studying historiography and paid particular attention to questions of methodology and differing approaches to the study of history.

Shortly before completing his M.A. degree, Hafez married Jody Hambrick, a talented artist who had graduated with honors from the Chicago Art Institute at the age of nineteen and afterwards acquired an M.A. degree in art education from Colorado State College of Education. Hafez and Jody lived in Palo Alto for a year and then moved to Washington, D.C., where Hafez had been admitted to the Ph.D. program in history at Georgetown University.

Since graduate classes were held in the evening, Hafez studied during the day at the Library of Congress, and Jody taught art in the District of Columbia School System. Life was pleasant and exciting for both of them, and they had the opportunity to make friendships with many interesting people. Among these friends were two very distinguished scholars at Georgetown, Professors Richard Ettinghausen and Cyrille Toumanoff. Ettinghausen was at that time also curator of Islamic and Persian art at the Smithsonian. Hafez and Jody met with Ettinghausen on numerous occasions at both the Smithsonian and his farm in Maryland, and in the course of their visits Ettinghausen helped unlock the inner aspects of Persian art for them. Toumanoff, a specialist in Sasanian and Byzantine history, supervised Hafez's studies at Georgetown. Among the many other friends who enriched the lives of Hafez and Jody during their stay in Washington were Hajji Mohammad Nemazi, the well-known philanthropist; Dr. Walter Maurer, a distinguished Sanskrit scholar; and Mr. Allahyar Saleh, the great Iranian nationalist who was at that time (1952) the ambassador of Iran to the United States (not to be confused with his brother Jahanshah Saleh, the arch-royalist who was later chancellor of the University of Tehran, where he became Hafez's adversary and caused him to become alienated from the institution he had served enthusiastically for fifteen years).

As a student at Georgetown, Hafez compiled, at the request of the Library of Congress, what was one of the first and is still one of the most useful systematic and critical bibliographies of scholarship on Iran.[1] He completed his dissertation, entitled "The Fall of the Qajar Dynasty," and received the Ph.D. degree in history in 1953. The

[1] *Iran: A Selected and Annotated Bibliography* (Washington, D.C., 1951).

dissertation dealt with the end of the Qajar dynasty and the rise of the Pahlavis; it remains a standard account of these events.

Like many Iranians in that tumultuous year, Hafez had been enthralled by Dr. Moḥammad Moṣaddeq, whom he met during the latter's visit to Washington, as well as by Moṣaddeq's program for nationalizing Iran's oil industry and other progressive policies. Hafez returned to Iran a few months after Dr. Moṣaddeq's overthrow, determined to make his own contribution to the development of his country. One opportunity that presented itself in this respect arose from the efforts of the Point Four aid program to introduce modernized public administration in Iran. As a result of a highly competitive exam, Hafez was selected as one of a small group of Iranians to be sent to study public administration at the University of Southern California. He received the D.P.A. degree from USC in 1957 and returned to Iran, where he was appointed assistant professor of public administration at the University of Tehran in 1958 and served as director of the University's new Library and Research Program of the Institute of Public Administration (1958-60).

While carrying out these duties, Hafez was stimulated to continue his interest in history and the humanities by one of the greatest of modern Iranian scholars, Professor Saʿīd Nafīsī. Nafīsī, impressed by Hafez's mastery of modern historical methodology, was one of the examiners who recommended that he be given an academic post as associate professor in the Department of History at the University of Tehran in 1959. The position was in European history, and Hafez eventually published a book in that field in order to be promoted to full professor.[2] Nonetheless, Nafīsī soon persuaded Hafez to change the focus of his interests from European to Iranian and Islamic history.

During the years that followed, Hafez served as director of the University of Tehran Press (1960-62), as a founding member of the *Journal of the Book Society of Persia* (1957-76), as founder and editor of the *Journal of Iranian Studies* of the Faculty of Letters and Humanities of the University of Tehran (1963-70), and as the founder and editor of the Persian Historical Text Series (1960-76). He lectured on Iran and represented the University of Tehran at many major international conferences and congresses from Shiraz to Peshawar, New Delhi, Montreal, Jerusalem, and Chicago. He also became the founder and first director of the Center for Middle Eastern Studies of the University of Tehran in 1960 and a full professor in its Department of History in 1965.

---

[2] *Europe in the Age of Revolution* (Tehran, 1965).

These accomplishments notwithstanding, Hafez was becoming increasingly disenchanted with the politicization and bureaucratization of the University of Tehran that had resulted from Moḥammad-Reżā Shah's so-called "Educational Revolution." He was also beginning to feel stifled by his many administrative, publishing, and library duties, particularly since they limited his opportunities for teaching and working with students. After much soul-searching, and despite great reluctance to leave his country and extended family, he decided to accept one of the many offers he was receiving to return to the United States and teach there. He held visiting professorships at Columbia University (1966-67), the University of Utah (1967-69), and the University of Texas at Austin (1967-69), where he then accepted a permanent position as Associate Professor in the Department of History. The University of Texas was in the process of establishing a Center for Middle East Studies, and Hafez was instrumental in its development. Unlike many such centers then being developed in the United States, the Texas program made Iran rather than Turkey or the Arab world its primary geographic focus and emphasized degree programs pursued in the context of traditional disciplines such as history or geography, rather than in conventional area studies on the Orientalist model. Able at last to devote himself to teaching and helping to train a new generation of historians of Iran, his true professional passion, Hafez remained a highly active member of the program at Texas until his retirement in the year 2000.

An enthusiastic and charming teacher in the classroom, Hafez has been responsible for introducing a host of students to Iranian history and inspiring many of them to pursue careers in that field. His students invariably found that Hafez was not only an exemplary scholar, he was also one of the rare academics who was absolutely devoted to teaching and his students, always accessible, and willing to pour hours of his time into mentoring them. Thanks to his guidance, they are established today in universities from Beirut to Costa Rica and across the United States, as well as in government service and business.

Moreover, Hafez and his wife Jody have welcomed countless visitors and guests into their home, where their graciousness, generosity, wit, and insight made them true ambassadors for the finest traditions of Iranian hospitality and culture. Hafez will thus long be remembered and cherished by his students and his numerous friends and colleagues for his tireless and selfless efforts over the years in assisting them with their studies, research, and careers.

Qajar history has often been neglected, not only for historical studies in general but even in the specialized field of Iranian history, itself a relatively underdeveloped discipline. There were a variety of reasons—and motivations—for ignoring or dismissing the historical importance of the Qajar period, mostly stemming from the preconception that it was a backward, dull, parochial, weak, and hopelessly corrupt time during which Iran slipped inexorably into internal disarray and foreign domination. More recently, this pejorative view has given way to the recognition that the Qajars came to power and governed under extremely adverse conditions, and yet they managed to hold Iran together, sponsor a significant cultural revival, fend off the worst of colonialism as long as possible, and lay the foundations for a modern nation-state with a constitution and permanent institutions of government. With this recognition has come a new, and much deserved, interest in the historical, literary, artistic, and religious accomplishments of the Qajars.

The work of Hafez Farmayan contributed to this reappraisal of the Qajar period in three key respects. First, he recognized the critical importance of methodology and the identification of new sources of information for improving the quality of Qajar studies. At the beginning of his academic career, he lamented the narrow scope and often jaundiced vision of Qajar history found in both traditional Persian histories and early European studies, but he also emphasized the legitimate need for a fair and balanced history of that period.[3] In an important interpretative essay in 1974, he went on to argue that the writing of Qajar history was still far too restricted in perspective and tended to produce either "shallow, narrow, cliché-littered imitations" of older works or "official glorifications of Iran's present, not always consistent with the truth."[4] At the same time, he emphasized and described the treasure trove of untapped sources awaiting exploitation by scholars to rectify this deficiency. Earlier in his career, he himself had helped compensate for an over-dependence on European (almost exclusively British) archival and narrative sources by locating, editing, and publishing several of the important Qajar historical manuscripts then languishing in obscurity in various private and public libraries in Iran. Among the many now classic texts he resurrected in this way were the political memoirs of the prime minister Amīn-al-Dawla, the travelogue of Ḥājjī Pīrzāda, and Vazīrī Kermānī's history of Kermān.[5]

---

[3] "Neqāṭ-e čand dar barā-ye moškelāt-e tārīḵnevīsī dar Īrān," *Barrasīhā-ye tārīḵī* 1/5-6(1967):165-79.

[4] "Observations on Sources for the Study of Nineteenth and Twentieth Century Iranian History," *International Journal of Middle East Studies* 5(1974):32-49.

[5] *Ḵāṭerāt-e sīāsī-e Mīrzā ʿAlī Ḵān Amīn-al-Dawla* (Tehran, 1962); *Safar-nāma-ye Ḥājjī Pīrzāda*. 2 vols., (Tehran, 1963-65); *Tārīḵ-e Kermān* (Tehran, 1962).

Second, Hafez realized that much was being written about Qajar history not only on the basis of a narrow and rather biased range of sources but also with a very shallow and prejudiced understanding of the concerns and aspirations of the Qajar political and social elite responsible for the country's affairs. He therefore emphasized the importance of biography in Qajar studies, particularly the need for careful, comprehensive, and impartial biographies of Qajar rulers and statesmen. This was exemplified in his own keen interest in Mīrzā ʿAlī Khan Amīn-al-Dawla and the publication of what is still the most sober and reliable assessment of that minister's life and career.[6] Third, Hafez was keenly aware of the crucial social, intellectual, and cultural innovations that had in fact taken place in Iran under the auspices and with the encouragement of the Qajar elite. One of his earliest and most influential articles drew attention to the process of modernization and Westernization in Qajar Iran, examining in detail the individuals, writings, and institutions that contributed to this.[7] Later, his interest focused in particular on the role of travel and travel literature during the Qajar period in broadening Iranian awareness of the non-Iranian world and as a vehicle for social, intellectual, economic, and technological change. He had edited several memoirs by Qajar travelers, including Moḥammad-Ḥosayn Farāhānī, whose account of a pilgrimage to Mecca was subsequently translated into English.[8] The theme of travel and travel literature was also the subject of a conference he organized at the University of Texas in April 1994, where several of the papers in this volume originated.

The articles offered here in appreciation of Hafez's career all reflect the influence of these ideas and the direction Hafez has helped give to the study of Qajar history.

Roger Savory (University of Toronto) cuts through the extremely complex tribal politics of the late Safavid period to provide a comprehensive account of the establishment of the Qajar dynasty. His essay elucidates the complex and difficult political situation the Qajars had to overcome to restore unified rule to Iran; by tracing the roots of the

---

[6] "Portrait of a Nineteenth Century Iranian Statesman," *International Journal of Middle East Studies* 15(1983):337-51. He has also authored the useful short article "Amīn-al-Dawla," *Encyclopaedia Iranica* (London, etc. 1985-), 1:943-45.

[7] "The Forces of Modernization in Nineteenth-Century Iran: A Historical Survey," in W. R. Polk and R. L. Chambers, *Beginnings of Modernization in the Middle East* (Chicago, 1968), 119-51.

[8] *Safar-nāma* (Tehran, 1964); ed. and tr. Hafez Farmayan and Elton L. Daniel as *A Shiʿite Pilgrimage to Mecca 1885-1886* (Austin, 1990).

Qajar dynasty in the Safavid period, it also serves as a useful reminder of the Qajar success in keeping alive the Safavid experiment in nation-building that created modern Iran.

Four articles examine the nature of social and cultural change during the Qajar period. Layla S. Diba (independent curator, New York) identifies a key source for the study and appreciation of Qajar accomplishments in art and particularly the role of court and sub-royal patronage in making that art possible. Maryam Ekhtiar (independent scholar, New York) surveys developments in music following the introduction of European-style music instruction at the most important institution of secular education in Qajar Iran, the Dār al-Fonūn, and reveals the interplay between tradition and innovation at the heart of so much cultural creativity during the Qajar period. Every element of society was affected by the changes taking place during the Qajar period, but perhaps none so dramatically as women: Mansureh Ettehadieh (Našr-e Tārīḵ, Tehran) shows both how far women progressed during this time and how far they still had to go in constructing a new political and social role for themselves. Farzin Vahdat (Tufts University) examines the ways major Qajar intellectuals in the late nineteenth century dealt with the ambivalent and contradictory concept of modernism and shows how their philosophical insights anticipated or shaped the political dynamics and dialectics of Iran in the following century.

The remaining articles take up the theme of travel and travel literature in the Qajar period—a topic which gives great interdisciplinary significance to Qajar studies not only by drawing on both history and literature but because of the central importance the analysis of the phenomenon of travel writing has acquired in recent scholarship on imperialism, modernism, and colonial and post-colonial societies. There was unquestionably a boom in travel and in writing about travel, both by Europeans to Iran and Iranians abroad, which took place in the nineteenth century, and this phenomenon was of tremendous importance in many respects—shaping the Western view of Iran, popularizing an Iranian view of the West, contributing to cultural interactions, and serving as a vector for the introduction of changes in both material and intellectual culture.

Iraj Afshar (University of Tehran) provides a comprehensive survey of the travel books written during the Qajar period, the sheer quantity of which serves as a useful index of the exploding popularity of travel within Iran and abroad. William Hanaway (University of Pennsylvania) raises the question of whether these travel narratives constitute a new and distinct literary genre in Persian and the extent to which their literary characteristics evolved during the Qajar period.

In terms of the impact of travel to Europe, Shireen Mahdavi (independent scholar, Salt Lake City) uses the carefully archived correspondence of one of the most successful Qajar entrepreneurs,

Amīn-al-Żarb, to show how he was simultaneously attracted to the commercial, technological, and institutional aspects of European culture but repelled by other aspects of its lifestyle that conflicted with his traditional Iranian values. Few subjects so fascinated travelers, whether European or Iranian, as the question of gender relations in the areas they visited. Mohammad Tavakoli-Targhi (Illinois State University-Normal) explores how various Qajar travelers frequently used this issue as a symbolic or psychological way of expressing their deepest fears (or hopes) about the seductive yet threatening and potentially corrupting attractions of Western culture.

Three articles deal with literature relating to travel between Qajar Iran and Russia. Anna Vanzan (Università IULM, Milano-Feltre) discusses the narrative of the ambassador Abu'l-Ḥasan Khan Šīrāzī's stay in Russia, a work which combines judicious admiration of Russian military and economic prowess with the most prejudiced and misogynistic appraisal of its moral life. Elena Andreeva (Virginia Military Institute) examines an account of travel to Iran by an eminent Russian scholar and dissects the ways in which his book, however much it may have been intended as a source of factual data, reflects the ideological presuppositions of its authors and emerges as an illustrative example of the "discourse" of Orientalism in its Russian form. The situation is somewhat reversed in an article by James Clark (American Institute of Iranian Studies) dealing with the memoirs of ʿAbd-Allāh Mostawfī. A Qajar diplomat in turn-of-the-century Russia, Mostawfī often mixes observations of Russian society with views colored by the dramatic events then taking place in Iran and the world.

Qajar travel and travel accounts were by no means confined to Europe. Elton Daniel (University of Hawaii) points out that Qajar travelers also took a great interest in visiting neighboring Muslim countries and that Qajar accounts of the pilgrimage to Mecca reveal dramatic changes in intellectual perspective as well as material conditions. Other Qajar travelers ventured much further from home. M. R. Ghanoonparvar (University of Texas) looks at narratives of travel to the United States and what they reveal about Iranian perceptions of the New World. Hashem Rajabzadeh (Osaka University of Foreign Studies) shows how Japan, particularly after its victory over Russia in 1905, captured the imagination of some Qajar statesmen, who were able to use accounts of travel to Japan to suggest potential models of development for their own country.

Finally, Denis Wright (British Institute of Persian Studies) provides a survey and bibliographical listing of the very considerable corpus of writings by British travelers to Qajar Iran.

Editorial Note

Transliteration of foreign languages is perhaps the most vexing problem involved in editing a book of this type. There is, in short, no completely satisfactory or universally accepted method for representing Persian names and expressions in the Latin alphabet. In this volume, a system has been adopted that follows closely the one used by the *Encyclopaedia Iranica*, which has emerged as a standard reference work on Iranian subjects for both specialists and general readers, in order to facilitate the work of readers wishing to turn to it for further information. However, its practice of transliterating certain consonants differently according to whether they occur in Persian words or words of Arabic origin has been discarded: s̱, ẕ, ż, and v are used throughout (not ṯ, ḏ, ḍ, w). Some Turkish words and names transliterated from Persian script are also given with the Turkish rather than the Persian vowels. A few common place names (Tehran, Isfahan, Khorasan, Azerbaijan, etc.), as well as the names of most places outside Iran, are not transliterated. Anglicized forms for some technical terms are also used in preference to transliterated forms (e.g., ulema rather than *ʿolamāʾ*). The names of dynasties are anglicized, and Qajar is transliterated as Qājār only when it appears as part of a personal name.

Dates using the Islamic lunar calendar are followed by a backslash (/) and the C.E. equivalent. Dates according to the Persian solar calendar are indicated by "Š." (*šamsī*), followed by a backslash and the C.E. equivalent.

Part One
Historical Origins

The Qajars: "Last of the Qezelbāš"[1]

Roger Savory

In the summer of 906-7/1501, Esmāʿīl entered Tabrīz and was crowned shah, thus founding the Safavid dynasty which was to rule Iran for more than two and a quarter centuries. This event marked a new era in the history of Iran in at least two important ways. First, the whole of the heartland of Iran was reunited under Persian rule for the first time since the Arab conquest of Iran in the first/seventh century.[2] Second, the Es̱nā-ʿašarī rite of Shiʿi Islam was proclaimed to be the official religion of the Safavid state. The ideological bases of the Safavid dynasty were threefold. First, during the rise of the Safavids to power, the Safavid leaders, by virtue of their position as *moršed-e kāmel* (spiritual directors) of the Ṣafavīya or Safavid Sufi order, demanded the unquestioning obedience of their followers or *morīd*s. Loyalty to the leader was termed *ṣūfīgarī* ("conduct appropriate to a Sufi"). Its converse, *nā-ṣūfīgarī* ("deviationism"), was tantamount to treason and was punishable by death. As the charismatic aspect of Safavid leadership declined, *šāhī-sevanī* or "love of the shah" became the touchstone of loyalty to the ruler. Second, up to the time of the disastrous defeat at the hands of the Ottomans at the battle of Čālderān in 920/1514, many Safavid followers believed that their leader was the living emanation of the godhead.[3] Third, the Safavid shahs claimed

---

[1] I have borrowed this pregnant phrase from J. R. Perry, "The Last Ṣafavids, 1772-1773," *Iran* 4(1971):68.

[2] Only once during the intervening eight and a half centuries had a Persian dynasty (the Buyids/Bowayhids) ruled over much of Iran (334-447/945-1055)—a period felicitously termed "the Iranian intermezzo" by V. F. Minorsky—but Iran did not constitute an independent political entity during that period.

[3] See M. M. Mazzaoui, *The Origins of the Ṣafawids* (Wiesbaden, 1972), 73; R. M. Savory, "Some Reflections on Totalitarian Tendencies in the Safavid State," in *Studies on the History of Safawid Iran* (London, 1987), no. X, 231-32.

to be the representatives on earth of the Twelfth Imam or Mahdi. These three elements together made up the potent Safavid *daʿwa*, or religious propaganda, which fired the imaginations of the Turkoman tribesmen of Syria, Anatolia, Azerbaijan and ʿErāq-e ʿAjam, and caused them to flock to the banners of the early Safavid leaders.

It was the fighting qualities of these Turkoman tribesmen[4] that brought the Safavids to power, and which remained the mainstay of the Safavid state until the policies of Shah ʿAbbās I (996-1038/1588-1629) eroded the power of the Turkoman tribes. From an early stage in the development of the Safavid revolutionary movement, the militant Turkoman supporters of the Safavid cause had been known as Qezelbāš, "redheads," a derogatory term applied to them by the Ottomans[5] but adopted as a mark of pride by them. The name derived from the distinctive headgear worn by the Qezelbāš, known as the "Sufi *tāj*." This was said to have been devised by Shaikh Ḥaydar, leader of the Safavid order (*ṭarīqa*) from 864-93/1460-88 as the result of instructions communicated to him in a dream by the Imam ʿAlī. This headgear consisted of a turban or hat (*kolāh*) with twelve gores surmounted by a scarlet or crimson spike or baton.[6] The term Qezelbāš should properly be applied only to the Turkoman followers of the Safavids,[7] but it came to be used also of various non-Turkish speaking Iranian tribes which supported the Safavids, such as the tribes of Ṭāleš and Qarāja-dāḡ (Sīāh-kūh), and some of the Kurdish and Lur tribes.[8]

This essay is concerned only with the Qezelbāš tribes properly so called, and its purpose is to trace the history of one of these tribes, the Qajars, in Safavid times and to suggest some reasons why it was the Qajar tribe in particular that, after the overthrow of the Safavids, the Afghan inter-regnum, and the struggle for power that followed the assassination of Nāder Shah Afšār, succeeded in establishing a new

---

[4] Described by Jean Chardin, *Voyages*, ed. L. Langlès, 10 vols. (Paris, 1811), 5:299-300 as "une vieille race de bon soldats, gens robustes et économes"; quoted by V. Minorsky, tr., *Tadhkirat al-Mulūk: A Manual of Safavid Administration* (London, 1943), 188.

[5] Compare the use of the abusive term "Roundheads" to designate the parliamentary forces in the English Civil War.

[6] For a detailed account of the evolution of the Qezelbāš hat, see Barbara Schmitz, "On a Special Hat Introduced During the Reign of Shah ʿAbbās the Great," in *Iran* 22(1984):103-12.

[7] Chardin, *Voyages*, 5:299-300 as quoted in Minorsky, *Tadhkirat*, 188: "Ce sont eux proprement qu'on appelle Qizilbash, ou têtes rouges."

[8] See R. M. Savory, "Ḳizil-bāsh," in *The Encyclopaedia of Islam: New Edition* (Leiden, 1960-), 5:243-45.

dynasty which ruled Iran for a century and a quarter (1210-1342/1796-1925).

Background History of the Qajar Tribe

A betting man, had he been asked in 1501, the year of the establishment of the Safavid dynasty, to predict which of the Qezelbāš tribes would eventually form a new ruling dynasty in Iran, would have been prescient indeed had he laid his wager on the Qajars. It is true that, when the future Shah Esmāʿīl mobilized his supporters at Arzenjān in the late summer of 1500, Qajar tribesmen were among their number.[9] It is also true that a Qajar officer, Pīrī Beg, fought at the decisive battle of Šarūr early in 1501 against the army of the Āq Qoyunlū ruler Alvand.[10] His valor in that battle was such that Esmāʿīl bestowed on him the *laqab* (soubriquet) of *toz koparan* ("whirlwind of dust").[11] All in all, however, the Qajars played only a small part in the establishment of the Safavid state. Apart from Pīrī Beg, only one other Qajar amir is mentioned in the sources during the reign of Esmāʿīl I: Ače (Eçe)-Solṭān, governor of Urfa, who rejoiced in the *laqab* of Qudurmoš ("mad dog"). Neither he nor Pīrī Beg was an amir of the first rank in the sense of holding high office in the early Safavid administration.

The origins of the Qajar tribe, like those of the Safavids themselves, are obscure. Most authorities reject the claims to be found in nineteenth century sources that the Qajars were of either Mongol or Timurid ancestry.[12] Even the origin of the name of the tribe is in dispute. A. K. S. Lambton, quoting Solaymān Efendī's *Loğat Čağatay* and Pelliot, suggests the derivation from the Turkish *kaçar*, "marching quickly," but Sümer prefers to derive it from a certain leader named Qarāčar or Qarčar.[13] At all events, by the ninth/fifteenth century the Qajar tribe seems to have been living in the Kayseri/Sivas region of Anatolia as

---

[9] Untitled MS London, British Library, Or. 3248, fol. 53b.

[10] Faruk Sümer, *Safevi Devletinin Kurulušu ve Gelišmesinde Anadolu Türklerinin Rolü* (Ankara, 1976), 21.

[11] From *toz koparmak*, "to kick up dust"; see Sümer, *Rolü*, 54.

[12] See, for example, Mīrzā Jamāl Javānšīr Qarābāğī, *Tārīḵ-e Qarābāg*, tr. George A. Bournoutian as *A History of Qarabagh: An Annotated Translation of Mirza Jamal Jayanshir Qarabaghi's Tarikh-e Qarabagh* (Costa Mesa, Calif., 1994), 70, footnote 168; Faruk Sümer, "Ḳādjār," in *The Encyclopaedia of Islam: New Edition* (Leiden, 1960-), 4:87; A. K. S. Lambton, "Ḳādjār," in *The Encyclopaedia of Islam: New Edition* (Leiden, 1960-), 4:387.

[13] Lambton, "Ḳādjār," 387.

part of the Boz Ok ("Grey Arrow") branch of the Turkomans that recognized the suzerainty of the Ḏu'l-Qadr rulers of Marʿaš and Elbestān.[14] At that time, the tribe was divided into four *oba* ("tents," i.e. families): Āqča Qoyunlū; Āḡčalū; Šām-bayātī; and Yīva.[15] At least some of the Qajars seem to have moved into Azerbaijan after the overthrow of the Qara Qoyunlū by the Āq Qoyunlū (872/1467), and to have entered the service first of the Āq Qoyunlū rulers and then of the Safavid leader Shaikh Ḥaydar. A number of scholars have noted what is possibly the first mention of Qajar tribesmen in Iran, in 897/1491-92, in the service of Ayba/Ībe-Solṭān Āq Qoyunlū.[16] By that time, the Qajar tribe had established itself in the region of Qarābāḡ, which remained its power base until that area was overrun by Ottoman forces under Farhād Pasha in 997/1588-89.

The region of Qarābāḡ (Turko-Persian "black garden," supposedly from the fertility of its mountain valleys, though this may be a case of popular etymology),[17] constituted the southern part of the mediæval Islamic province of Arrān. Prior to Islam, the region was considered part of Armenia. In Safavid times, the chief cities of Qarābāḡ were Ganja and Barḏaʿa/Bardaʿa; the latter was "strategically located on the edge of the lowlands of the lower Kor-Araxes (Aras) valley, adjacent to the mountains of eastern Transcaucasia."[18] Qarābāḡ is divided into three geographical regions: the highlands west of the Aqdam mountains, which range from 2,000 to 12,000 ft.; the central valleys; and the steppeland in the southeast adjoining the Moḡān/Moqān steppe.[19] Qarābāḡ was famous for its mild climate (*laṭāfat-e havā*), the abundance of its vegetation (*rayāḥīn*), its advantages for nomads, and its special qualities for summer and winter quarters.[20]

---

[14] See J. H. Mordtmann [V. L. Ménage], "Dhu'l-Ḳadr," in *The Encyclopaedia of Islam: New Edition* (Leiden, 1960-), 2:239-40.

[15] Sümer, "Ḳād̲j̲ār," 387. The Yīva *oba* had Oḡuz roots: See John E. Woods, *The Aqquyunlu: Clan, Confederation, Empire* (Minneapolis and Chicago, 1976), 39.

[16] Lambton, "Kād̲j̲ār," 387; Sümer, *Rolü*, 53-54; Woods, *Aqquyunlu*, 164.

[17] C. E. Bosworth, "Ḳarā Bāg̲h̲," in *The Encyclopaedia of Islam: New Edition* (Leiden, 1960-), 4:573.

[18] C. E. Bosworth, "Bardaʿa," in *The Encyclopaedia Iranica* (London, etc., 1985-), 3:779.

[19] Bournoutian, *Qarabagh*, 16, n. 58. For a map of the area, see V. Minorsky, *A History of Shirvan and Darband* (Cambridge 1958), 174.

[20] Eskandar Beg Monšī, *Tārīḵ-e ʿālamārā-ye ʿabbāsī*, ed. Īraj Afšār, 2 vols. (Tehran, 1334-35 Š./1955-56), 2:415.

These rich lands were given to the Qajar tribe in recognition of their services to the Safavid house. No wonder they were loath to abandon them even after the region was overrun by the Ottomans in 996/1588.

Faruk Sümer, in his work *Safevi Devletinin Kuruluşu ve Gelişmesinde Anadolu Türklerinin Rolü* ["The Role of the Anatolian Turks in the Foundation and Development of the Safavid State"], divides the Qezelbāš tribes into "great tribes" (*büyük oymaklar*) and "lesser tribes" (*küçük oymaklar*). Most of the tribes were divided into sub-tribes or septs.[21] Few, if any, of the Qezelbāš tribes in Safavid times could trace their genealogy back to a common ancestor. Rather, they consisted of an "amalgamation of nomads made up of fragments not only of different families but also of different tribes."[22] Of course, this did not prevent historians from concocting genealogies of a greater or lesser degree of credibility as was the case with the Safavid family itself. In the case of the Qajars, nineteenth-century historians in particular traced the Qajars back to a certain Qājār Noyān b. Sertāq Noyān, who was *atābak* to Argūn[23] but, as already mentioned, most historians today reject the idea of an Il-Khanid or Timurid ancestry for the Qajars.

The First Qezelbāš Civil War (932-940/1526-33)

During the reign of Shah Esmāʿīl I (907-30/1501-24), Sümer does not list the Qajar tribe among either the "great" or the "lesser" Qezelbāš tribes, and, as we have seen, only two Qajar amirs are mentioned during this period. During the reign of Shah Ṭahmāsp (930-84/1524-76), however, the status of the Qajar tribe was greatly enhanced. No fewer than ten Qajar amirs are mentioned in the

---

[21] Minorsky uses the word "sept" occasionally in the sense of "a division of a tribe"; see *Tadhkirat,* 191, n. 3. I shall use it in preference to the word "clan" used by many historians in order to avoid the confusion caused by the fact that in English usage "tribe" and "clan" are often used as synonyms. Similarly, in Persian chronicles, the words *ṭāyefa/ṭawā'ef*, *īl/īlāt*; and *oymaq/oymaqlar* are used interchangeably both in the sense of tribe and subtribe. The words *ulus, ʿašīra/ʿašāʾer,* and *qabīla/qabāʾel* are also used without any precise definition. As R. D. McChesney has noted, there was "no precisely and strictly established terminology" in Safavid sources to denote "tribe"; see his article "Comments on 'The Qajar Uymaq in the Safavid Period, 1500-1722'," *Iranian Studies* 14(1981):88.

[22] McChesney, "Comments," 88.

[23] Lambton, "Ḳādjār," 387.

Tārīḵ-e ʿālamārā-ye ʿabbāsī during the reign of Ṭahmāsp,[24] and the Qajar tribe is now listed by Sümer among the "great tribes."[25] Ṭahmāsp was only ten and a half years old when he came to the throne, and the first part of his reign was marked by civil war as rival factions of Qezelbāš tribes fought for supremacy.[26] After some preliminary maneuvering and the establishment of a short-lived triumvirate in 931-32/1525 consisting of a Rūmlū, a Takkalū, and an Ostājlū amir, civil war broke out in 932/1526 and raged for some seven years. All the Qezelbāš tribes accorded the status of "great tribes" by Sümer during the reign of Esmāʿīl I,[27] namely, the Rūmlūs, the Ostājlūs, the Takkalūs, the Šāmlūs, and the Ḏu'l-Qadrs, were heavily involved in this civil war.

The accession of Shah Ṭahmāsp was followed almost immediately by the establishment of a de facto Qezelbāš state (*dawlat-e Qezelbāš*), as the Qezelbāš amirs asserted their hegemony. Initially, Dīv-Solṭān Rūmlū, who held the positions of *atābak* to the young Ṭahmāsp and *amīr al-omarāʾ*, tried to take over the administration of the state (*daḵl dar omūr-e salṭanat va żabṭ-e mamlekat mīnamūd*),[28] but the Ostājlūs in particular refused to acknowledge his sole authority, buttressed though it was by a testamentary disposition of the late Shah Esmāʿīl I, and Dīv-Solṭān was forced to set up a triumvirate consisting of himself, Köpek-Solṭān Ostājlū and Čūha-Solṭān Takkalū. Historically speaking, triumvirates have not been notably successful,[29] and this one was no exception. Köpek-Solṭān was rapidly excluded from the affairs of state by his two fellow-triumvirs, and the Ostājlūs withdrew to Erevan and Nakhchivan, which was Köpek-Solṭān's province.[30] With the Ostājlūs out of the way, Dīv-Solṭān and his supporters canceled their *toyūl*s[31]

---

[24] They are: Būdāq Khan Qājār; Ebrāhīm Beg Zīādoḡlū Qājār; Gökče-Solṭān Qājār; Šāhverdī-Solṭān Zīādoḡlū Qājār; Qarā-Ḥasan Zīādoḡlū Qājār; Solaymān Beg Zīādoḡlū Qājār; Yūsuf-Ḵalīfa Zīādoḡlū Qājār; Mīrzā ʿAlī-Solṭān Qājār; Ṭabghūn/Ṭūyqūn/Toykun Beg Qājār; and Yaʿqūb-Solṭān Qājār.

[25] Sümer, *Rolü*, 96-8.

[26] See Savory, *Studies,* no. V, 67-71

[27] Sümer, *Rolü,* 43-49.

[28] *Tārīḵ-e īlčī-e Neẓāmšāh*, MS London, British Library, Add. 23,513, fol. 465a.

[29] Cf., for example, the fate of the two triumvirates established during the period of the Roman Republic: that of. Pompey, Caesar and Crassus in 60 B.C., and that of Antony, Octavian, and Lepidus in 43 B.C.

[30] *Tārīḵ-e īlčī*, fol. 466a: *keh velāyat-e ū būd.*

[31] The *toyūl/tīūl* was an assignment on the revenue of a stated district. In many cases, the actual revenue was in excess of the official valuation. The *toyūl* system was one of the principal methods of paying the Qezelbāš troops.

and alienated much of the land held by the Ostājlūs in the form of *eqṭāʿ*s.[32] This act provoked the Ostājlūs into open rebellion, and in the spring of 932/1526 the rival forces fought a pitched battle near Solṭāniyya. When the Ostājlūs initially gained the upper hand, Dīv-Solṭān played his trump card and brought the young shah on to the battlefield.

> When the Ostājlū amirs saw the royal standard, they observed the rules governing the relationship between the spiritual director and disciple and between master and servant, and all desisted from conflict, placed the swords of strife in their sheaths, and galloped from the battlefield.[33]

Köpek-Solṭān and the other Ostājlū chiefs fled to Gīlān. The following year (933/1526-27) they took the field again, but were defeated in a battle with the Rūmlūs and Takkalūs at Šarūr, and Köpek-Solṭān was killed; the surviving Ostājlūs again took refuge in Gīlān.

The two remaining triumvirs, Dīv-Solṭān Rūmlū and Čūha-Solṭān Takkalū, then turned on each other. Čūha-Solṭān succeeded in persuading the shah that Dīv-Solṭān was the principal cause of the civil war, and the latter was executed on the shah's order. For four years (933-37/1527-31), Čūha-Solṭān wielded supreme power in the state. Then a new rival appeared on the scene in the form of the Šāmlū chief Ḥosayn Khan, governor of Herat. After the latter was forewarned of a plot by Čūha-Solṭān to murder him, an armed struggle ensued between the Šāmlūs, aided by the Ḏu'l-Qadrs, and the Takkalūs. When the combatants carried their conflict right into the royal tent, and the Takkalūs subsequently attempted to abduct the shah, Ṭahmāsp decided that the time had come for drastic action. He gave the order for the slaughter of the Takkalūs, whose leader, Čūha-Solṭān, had been killed in the course of the struggle. The survivors of the massacre escaped to Baghdad, and some of the amirs defected to the Ottomans. The chronogram *āfat-e Takkalū* ("the Takkalū disaster") gives the date for the event: 937/1530-31. All three of the triumvirs now being dead, Ḥosayn Khan, the Šāmlū chief, was able to assert his hegemony

---

[32] *Tārīḵ-e īlčī*, fol. 466a.

[33] *Tārīḵ-e īlčī*, fol. 466a: *omarā-ye ostājlū-rā, čūn čašm bar rāyat-e ẓafar-āyat-e šāhī oftād qavānīn-e pīr-o-morīdī va qavā'ed-e ṣāḥebī va čākerī-rā reʾāyat namūda majmūʿ rūy az vādī-ye kelāf bar tāfta šamšīr-e kīn dar ḡelāf kardand va ʿenān-e yakrān-rā az maʿreka bar tāfta.* On the *pīr-o-morīdī* relationship, see Savory, "Reflections," in *Studies*, no. X, 228-29.

between 937-40/1530-33. In 940/1533, Shah Ṭahmāsp, who had a number of grounds for getting rid of Ḥosayn Khan, put him to death, thereby bringing to an end the first Qezelbāš civil war and signaling his intention to exercise his royal authority to the full.

The Role of the Qajars in the First Qezelbāš Civil War

The available evidence suggests that the Qajar tribe was not involved in the actual fighting at all. Immediately after the accession of the young Ṭahmāsp, when Dīv-Solṭān called on the Qezelbāš tribes to obey the *ḥokm* of the late shah appointing him the guardian of Ṭahmāsp, it was the Ostājlūs who were the ringleaders in opposing his authority—no doubt because they surpassed the other Turkoman tribes in power and number of tribesmen (*kos̱rat-e qabāʾel*).[34] In the autumn of 931/1525, Dīv-Solṭān made another appeal to the Ostājlūs, and the latter, reflecting on the dishonor which would attach to their name if they refused, initially decided to respond favorably to this appeal, and, as mentioned above, a triumvirate was set up which included the Ostājlū leader, Köpek-Solṭān. At this point Dīv-Solṭān put to death two amirs whom he accused of being the instigators (*ḵamīr-māya*) of this discord. One of these amirs was Nārīn Beg Qājār.[35] It is worth noting that he was executed at a time when the Qezelbāš tribes were still jockeying for position and actual fighting had not yet broken out. It does not seem too unreasonable to conjecture that it was the virtual non-involvement of the Qajars in this civil war, coupled with the (in the case of the Takkalūs, severe) setbacks suffered by some of the tribes which had up to that point held "great tribe" status, that led to the dramatic rise of the Qajars to "great tribe" status and to the recording of the names of no fewer than ten Qajar amirs of note after the civil war, as mentioned above. This proposition is supported by the concomitant rise in importance of the Afšār tribe under Ṭahmāsp. Like the Qajars, the Afšārs are not listed by Sümer among either the "great" or the "lesser" Qezelbāš tribes during the reign of Shah Esmāʿīl, but, again like the Qajars, vaulted into prominence after the civil war. The Afšārs are listed by Sümer among the *büyük oymaklar* during the reign of Ṭahmāsp,[36] and seven Afšār amirs of note are recorded by the *Tārīḵ-e*

---

[34] *Tārīḵ-e īlčī*, fol. 466a.

[35] Būdāq Monšī Qazvīnī, *Javāher al-aḵbār*, MS Leningrad, Academy of Sciences, Dorn 288, fol. 298b; Ḥasan-e Rūmlū, *Aḥsan al-tavārīḵ*, ed. C. M. Seddon as *A Chronicle of the Early Safawis: Being the Ahsanu't-Tawarikh of Hasan-i-Rumlu* (Baroda, 1934), 189.

[36] Sümer, *Rolü*, 98-100.

ʿālamārā-ye ʿabbāsī at the time of the death of Ṭahmāsp in 984/1576.[37] As in the case of the Qajars, the involvement of the Afšārs in the civil war appears to have been minimal. The sources record only their participation in a combined force of Ostājlūs, Rūmlūs, and D̲u'l-Qadrs in action against the rebel Takkalūs at the *emāmzāda* of Sahl ʿAlī near Hamadan.[38]

In contrast, the fortunes of the five tribes listed by Sümer as *büyük oymaklar* during the reign of Shah Esmāʿīl (Rūmlūs, Ostājlūs, Takkalūs, Šāmlūs, D̲u'l-Qadrs) were affected to a greater or lesser degree by their involvement in the first Qezelbāš civil war or by other factors. The most obvious losers were the Takkalūs. Those of their leaders who were not killed during the insurrection of 937/1530-31 fled to Ottoman territory, and many of them entered Ottoman service and fought alongside Ottoman forces during the four Ottoman invasions of Iran between 940/1534 and 961/1554. Their *eqṭāʿ*s in the Hamadan area were alienated and transferred to the Ostājlūs and Šāmlūs some time before 994/1586, and, after the events of the second Qezelbāš civil war (988-96/1581-88), they were reduced to the status of a second-class tribe.[39] Of the sixty-five Qezelbāš amirs listed by the *Tārīḵ-e ʿālamārā-ye ʿabbāsī* as being still active at the time of the death of Shah ʿAbbās I (1038/1629), not one came from the Takkalū tribe.[40]

Of the other "great tribes," the Šāmlūs and Ostājlūs were unique in that they possessed no specific tribal territory.[41] The Šāmlūs lost their former position of trust after the execution of their chief Ḥosayn Khan in 940/1533-34,[42] but nevertheless continued to play a significant part in the Safavid administration.[43] The Ostājlūs, although initially outmaneuvered by the Rūmlūs and Takkalūs and forced to flee to Armenia or Gīlān, were subsequently restored to royal favor and, between 1532 and 1576, the year of Shah Ṭahmāsp's death, had more than thirty amirs holding the rank of khan or sultan.[44] The Rūmlūs

---

[37] Eskandar Beg, *Tārīḵ*, 1:140; tr. R. M. Savory as *History of Shah ʿAbbas the Great*, 2 vols. (Boulder, Colo., 1978), 1:225.

[38] Ḥasan-e Rūmlū, *Aḥsan*, 236.

[39] Sümer, *Rolü*, 144.

[40] Eskandar Beg, *Tārīḵ*, 2:1084 ff. (Savory, *History*, 2:1309 ff.)

[41] Sümer, *Rolü*, 144.

[42] Sümer, *Rolü*, 92.

[43] Five Šāmlū amirs are listed by the *Tārīḵ-e ʿālamārā-ye ʿābbāsī* at the death of Ṭahmāsp (984/1576) and seven at the death of ʿAbbās I (1038/1629); see Eskandar Beg, *Tārīḵ*, 1:138 and 2:1084 (Savory, *History*, 1:222, 2:1309).

[44] Sümer, *Rolü*, 107.

suffered a decline in status during the reign of Ṭahmāsp not so much because of their part in the civil war, but rather because of their lack of an effective tribal organization.[45] The Rūmlūs, who were mostly town and village dwellers[46] rather than nomads, and were concentrated to a large extent in Šīrvān, suffered great losses in both men and property as a result of the devastating Ottoman campaigns in Šīrvān.[47]

The fifth "great tribe" of the reign of Esmāʿīl I, the Ḏu'l-Qadrs,[48] was involved in the intertribal fighting of the civil war period, but always as defenders of the shah against the rebellious tribes. In fact, during the reign of Shah Ṭahmāsp, the Ḏu'l-Qadrs were noted as one of the most obedient[49] of the Qezelbāš tribes. They had no leader who was hungry for political power. They seem not to have experienced the fluctuating fortunes of the other "great tribes," but to have maintained a state of equilibrium, six amirs being listed by the *Tārīḵ-e ʿālamārā-ye ʿabbāsī* in 984/1576, and six in 1038/1629.[50]

Finally, it should be noted that, during the reign of Ṭahmāsp, another Qezelbāš tribe, the Torkmāns, entered the ranks of the "great tribes," making eight in all. The Torkmāns were of Āq Qoyunlū origin, and their most important septs, the Mawṣellūs and the Pornāks, had been connected by marriage with the Safavid royal house since the early days of the Safavid revolutionary movement.

The Qezelbāš Factionalism of 982-84/1574-76

As already stated, in 940/1533 Shah Ṭahmāsp had brought the first Qezelbāš civil war to an end and had signaled his determination henceforth to rule *de facto* as well as *de jure* by putting to death the powerful leader of the Šāmlū tribe, Ḥosayn Khan. Qezelbāš factionalism remained dormant until the shah's serious illness in 982/1574. Various factions then promoted the candidacy for the succession of no less than four sons of Ṭahmāsp: Solṭān-Moḥammad Mīrzā, his eldest son; Esmāʿīl Mīrzā, his second son; Ḥaydar Mīrzā, his third son; and Solaymān Mīrzā, his fourth son. A new force had now appeared on the political scene, namely, the "third force" of Georgians

---

[45] Sümer, *Rolü*, 158-60.

[46] Sümer, *Rolü*, 85.

[47] Sümer, *Rolü*, 143.

[48] The form Ḏu'l-Qadr is a fanciful Arab etymology for the original Turkish form Dulqadır or Dulğadır.

[49] Sümer, Rolü, 94 calls them "itaatkâr."

[50] Eskandar Beg, *Tārīḵ*, 1:140, 2:1085 (Savory, *History*, 1:225, 2:1310).

and Circassians, known as *ǧolāms*, who had been introduced into the Safavid political and military institution by Ṭahmāsp.[51] In the maneuverings for political power which followed the death of Ṭahmāsp in 984/1576, Georgian and Circassian women in the royal harem who were the mothers of Safavid princes played an important role. Solṭān-Moḥammad Mīrzā was initially not considered as a possible successor to Ṭahmāsp because of his defective eyesight, and the two serious candidates in the period between Ṭahmāsp's illness in 982/1574 and his death two years later were Esmāʿīl and Ḥaydar.

A striking feature of this period is that the loyalties of the Qezelbāš tribes were divided. Some tribes supported Esmāʿīl, others Ḥaydar. The Qezelbāš seem not to have initially realized that the accession of a prince whose mother was not a Turkoman might seriously threaten the Turk-Tājīk condominium that had ruled the Safavid state since its establishment in 907/1501. Thus the supporters of Ḥaydar, whose mother was a Georgian, included not only Georgians but Ostājlūs. It was only after a coup by this faction to place Ḥaydar on the throne had failed, and Ḥaydar had been killed, that the majority of the Qezelbāš tribes, including Afšārs, Rūmlūs, Bayāts, and Torkmāns, joined now by some Ostājlūs,[52] rallied round Esmāʿīl Mīrzā, released him from the state prison of Qahqaha, proclaimed him shah at Qazvīn on 24 Ṣafar 984/23 May 1576, and crowned him as Shah Esmāʿīl II on 27 Jomādā I, 984/22 August 1576.[53]

The Qezelbāš thus had a Turkoman candidate on the throne, but he did not fulfill their expectations. His long years of incarceration had engendered a morbid suspicion of all those around him. Fearing further attempted coups by one faction or another, this time directed against himself, he killed or blinded no less than nine Safavid royal princes. Even more disquieting to the Qezelbāš were clear signs of pro-Sunni proclivities on the part of the shah. This trend caused increasing discontent among the Qezelbāš, the ulema, and the populace at large. The Qezelbāš elders at first hesitated to question the actions of their *moršed* ("spiritual director"), on the grounds that to do so would be tantamount to unbelief (*kofr*),[54] but an unfounded rumor reached the ears of the shah that some of the Takkalū and Torkmān amirs planned to murder him and place Ḥasan Mīrzā, the son of Solṭān-Moḥammad

---

[51] See R. M. Savory, *Iran under the Safavids* (Cambridge, 1980), 66-67, 78-79.

[52] Sümer, *Rolü*, 101 ff.

[53] Eskandar Beg, *Tārīḵ*, 1:196 ff. (Savory, *History*, 1:290 ff.)

[54] Eskandar Beg, *Tārīḵ*, 1:215 (Savory, *History*, 1:321).

Mīrzā, on the throne. The shah at once ordered these amirs to do away with Ḥasan Mīrzā as proof of their loyalty. In the midst of this turmoil, the shah was found poisoned on 13 Ramażān 985/24 November 1577. Esmāʿīl's sister, Parī Khan Ḵānom, was alleged to have inserted the poison into an electuary consisting of a mixture of hemp and opium which the shah was in the habit of consuming.[55] The Qezelbāš then turned to Esmāʿīl's elder brother Solṭān-Moḥammad Mīrzā, whom they had previously disregarded, and placed him on the throne (5 Ḏu'l-Ḥejja 985/13 February 1578)[56] with the title of Solṭān-Moḥammad Shah. His accession ushered in a period of Tājīk dominance, as the shah's powerful mother Mahd-e ʿOlyā, directed the affairs of state with and on behalf of her favourite son, Ḥamza Mīrzā. In 988/1580-81 a confrontation occurred between Mahd-e ʿOlyā and the Qezelbāš amirs. Mahd-e ʿOlyā's power and influence, they said, was unacceptable to all the Qezelbāš tribes. The Queen Mother rebuffed the amirs, and refused to change her pro-Tājīk policies or make any concessions to the Qezelbāš. As a result, she was murdered by a group of Qezelbāš amirs, and this act precipitated the second Qezelbāš civil war, which raged for eight years until the accession of ʿAbbās I.

The Second Qezelbāš Civil War (988-96/1580-88)

The second Qezelbāš civil war divided the loyalties of the Qezelbāš tribes even more than the first one had done. Ḥamza Mīrzā remained in control at the capital, Qazvīn, and was supported mainly by Takkalūs and Torkmāns, but some of his boon-companions were Ostājlūs. Ḥamza's principal rival was his younger brother ʿAbbās Mīrzā, who was also the son of Mahd-e ʿOlyā. In Khorasan, a coalition of Ostājlūs and Šāmlūs raised the banner of revolt and proclaimed ʿAbbās Mīrzā shah. Solṭān-Moḥammad Shah tried in vain to suppress the revolt, while Ḥamza Mīrzā tried desperately to stem the tide of Ottoman invasion in Azerbaijan. In 994/1586, Ḥamza Mīrzā was murdered in mysterious circumstances, and a triumvirate of two Ostājlū amirs and one Šāmlū amir took the reins of government from the weak hands of Solṭān-Moḥammad Shah; one of the amirs, ʿAlīqolī Khan Fatḥoḡlū Ostājlū, assumed the title of *vakīl*, or vice-gerent of the shah.[57] The triumvirs

[55] Naṣr-Allāh Falsafī, *Zendegānī-ye Šāh ʿAbbās-e Avval* (Tehran, 1334-41 Š./ 1955-62), 1:32. Felūnyā is from the Greek φιλώνιον, "électuaire calmant," according to R. Dozy, *Supplément aux Dictionnaires Arabes* (Paris, 1927), 2:282.

[56] Ḥasan-e Rūmlū, *Aḥsan*, 502. Some sources give 11 February.

[57] Eskandar Beg, *Tārīḵ*, 1:349-50 (Savory, *History*, 1:486-87). For the significance of this title see Savory, *Studies*, no. IV, 93-99 and no. V, 71 ff.

declared as heir-apparent Abū Ṭāleb Mīrzā, another son of Mahd-e ʿOlyā; Abū Ṭāleb was two years old at the time of the death of Shah Ṭahmāsp. After the murder of Ḥamza Mīrzā, Solṭān-Moḥammad Shah exhorted the amirs to set aside their differences and end the civil war, but the feuding between the "ʿErāq amirs," who were based on Qazvīn and supported Abū Ṭāleb Mīrzā, and the "Khorasan amirs," who supported ʿAbbās Mīrzā, intensified. Divided loyalties, not only between tribe and tribe, but within tribes, continued. Some Afšārs and Ḏu'l-Qadrs joined the ʿAbbās camp,[58] but some Šāmlūs, Afšārs, and Bayāts were members of the Abū Ṭāleb camp, the core of which consisted of Takkalūs and Torkmāns.[59]

Among the "Khorasan amirs," the powerful Moršedqolī Khan Ostājlū had emerged as a kingmaker. In 995/1587, the "ʿErāq amirs" made the fatal mistake of moving against the Afšārs and Ḏu'l-Qadrs of Fārs, Yazd, and Kermān, who had declared their allegiance to ʿAbbās Mīrzā; by making this move, they left undefended the road to Qazvīn. Moršedqolī Khan at once began his advance on the capital from Khorasan. As he proceeded, he made a number of appeals to the "ʿErāq amirs" to unite round the standard of ʿAbbās Mīrzā. At Qazvīn, his rival kingmaker ʿAlīqolī Khan Fatḥoḡlu Ostājlū was maneuvered into responding favorably to Moršedqolī Khan's overtures, even though each knew that whichever gained the upper hand would not allow his rival to draw another single breath.[60] Support for Abū Ṭāleb Mīrzā began to melt away, and his camp was in utter disarray. A few miles outside the capital, Solṭān-Moḥammad Shah divested himself of his royal authority and placed the crown upon the head of his son ʿAbbās.[61] One of the new shah's first acts was to put to death the triumvirs and others charged with complicity in the murder of Ḥamza Mīrzā.

To what extent was the Qajar tribe involved in the factionalism and civil war between rival Qezelbāš tribes which had gone on for more than a decade? The answer seems to be, very little. Qajars were not involved at all in the political maneuvering which preceded the death of Shah Ṭahmāsp and the accession of Esmāʿīl II. The Qajars joined neither the pro-Esmāʿīl nor the pro-Ḥaydar camp. We are specifically told that one of the leading Qajar amirs, Mīrzā ʿAlī-Solṭān Qājār, with some others, stayed in his own house all day, and did not go to the

---

[58] Eskandar Beg, *Tārīḵ*, 1:362 (Savory, *History*, 1:501).

[59] Eskandar Beg, *Tārīḵ*, 1:368-69 (Savory, *History*, 1:508-9)

[60] Both amirs dubbed themselves *vakīl al-salṭana* and were "kingmakers" (*pādešāh-nešān*). See Eskandar Beg, *Tārīḵ*, 1:369 (Savory, *History*, 1:510)

[61] Eskandar Beg, *Tārīḵ*, 1:371-72 (Savory, *History*, 1:513).

rendezvous of either faction.[62] The Qajars might have been expected to throw their support behind Esmāʿīl Mīrzā, since the latter had grown up among the Yīva/Yūva sept of the Qajar tribe,[63] and, when Esmāʿīl had been appointed governor of Šīrvān in 954/1547, a Qajar amir, Gökče-Solṭān, was appointed his *lala* or guardian.[64] The Qajars were not involved in the murder of the Queen Mother Mahd-e ʿOlyā, in 988/1580-81. The Qajars were not the prime movers in the revolt by the "Khorasan amirs" in 989/1581, when ʿAbbās Mīrzā was declared to be king in Khorasan with the title of Shah ʿAbbās, although there is mention of one Qajar amir who was a supporter of ʿAbbās Mīrzā. This was Qobād Khan Qājār, the governor of Sabzavār in 986/1578. Qobād Khan was ejected from Sabzavār by Mortażāqolī Khan Pornāk, an amir opposed to the pro-ʿAbbās faction, in 988/1580-81.[65] When royalist forces marched into Khorasan in 991/1583, Qobād Khan was killed in action at the battle between them and the Šāmlū and Ostājlū supporters of ʿAbbās Mīrzā.[66]

The non-involvement of the Qajars in the Qezelbāš factionalism of 982-84/1574-76, or in the second Qezelbāš civil war of 988-96/1580-88, together with their support of ʿAbbās Mīrzā in 991/1583, left the Qajars well placed to increase their power and influence after the accession of Shah ʿAbbās in 996/1588. They seem to have made good use of this opportunity, since no less than eighteen Qajar amirs of note are mentioned by the *Tārīḵ-e ʿālamārā-ye ʿabbāsī* during the reign of Shah ʿAbbās I.[67] The only other tribe with a comparable number of amirs at the beginning of the reign of Shah ʿAbbās I was the Torkmān tribe, with fourteen.[68] The Torkmāns who, as already noted, had achieved the status of *büyük oymak* during the reign of Ṭahmāsp, and had initially been supporters of Solṭān-Moḥammad Shah and Ḥamza Mīrzā. In 992/1584, however, after Ḥamza Mīrzā adopted ʿAlīqolī

[62] Eskandar Beg, *Tārīḵ*, 1:193 (Savory, *History*, 1:285).

[63] Sümer, *Rolü*, 145.

[64] Ḥasan-e Rūmlū, *Aḥsan*, 323.

[65] Eskandar Beg, *Tārīḵ*, 1:255 (Savory, *History*, 1:376).

[66] Eskandar Beg, *Tārīḵ*, 1:285 (Savory, *History*, 1:416).

[67] They are: Alpān Beg; ʿAbd-al-Solṭān; Besṭām Āqā; Amīr Güne Beg; Ṭahmāspqolī Beg/Khan; Budāq Khan II; Čelebī Beg; Moḥammad Khan Zīādoğlū; Emāmqolī Khan II; Ḥosayn Khan Moṣāḥeb; Ḥosayn Khan Zīādoğlū Qarābāğī; Moršedqolī Beg Zīādoğlū; Moḥammadqolī Khan Zīādoğlū; Ḥosaynqolī Beg; Laṭīf Khan Beg/Khan; Meḥrāb Khan; Šarīf Khan; Mīrzā Khan Beg.

[68] Sümer, *Rolü*, 219.

Khan Fatḥoḡlū Ostājlū as his favourite, the Torkmāns, along with the Takkalūs, plotted to dislodge the Ostājlūs and Šāmlūs from their positions of power at court, and were accused by Ḥamza Mīrzā of sedition. This schism in the ranks of the Qezelbāš seriously hampered the ability of Ḥamza Mīrzā to deal with a major invasion of Azerbaijan by the Ottomans, and Ḥamza Mīrzā determined to crush the Torkmān/Takkalū rebellion. After a number of Qezelbāš had been wounded in skirmishing, Emāmqolī Khan Qājār, the *beglerbeg* of Qarābāḡ, was one of a group of amirs who offered their services as mediators to Ḥamza Mīrzā, but without success.[69] After the murder of Ḥamza Mīrzā in 994/1586, the Torkmāns espoused the cause of Abū Ṭāleb Mīrzā and opposed the pro-ʿAbbās Mīrzā faction. After the accession of Shah ʿAbbās, therefore, despite their various marriage connections with the Safavid royal family, their power rapidly waned, and by the time of the death of Shah ʿAbbās only two Torkmān amirs are listed by the *Tārīḵ-e ʿālamārā-ye ʿabbāsī*.[70]

The Ottoman Occupation of Qarābāḡ and Subsequent Dispersal of the Qajar Oymak

Shah ʿAbbās came to the throne convinced that drastic changes had to be made in the existing organization of the Safavid state. Born in 978/1571, almost the whole of his life up to his accession had been lived in the shadow of Qezelbāš factionalism and outright civil war between rival Qezelbāš tribes. He had seen that Qezelbāš chiefs would stop at nothing in the furtherance of their ambitions. His own mother had been assassinated by the Qezelbāš. He had seen how the rivalries between Qezelbāš tribes had seriously impaired the efforts of his father, Solṭān-Moḥammad Shah, and his elder brother, Ḥamza, to stem the tide of Ottoman invasion in Azerbaijan and Safavid territories north of the river Aras. He himself had been used as a pawn in the struggles between various would-be kingmakers among the Qezelbāš chiefs, and, when he was only ten year of age, and through no wish of his own, he had been proclaimed shah in Khorasan in open revolt against his father. After his accession, therefore, he put into effect a number of policies designed to curb the power of the Qezelbāš.[71] These included the transfer of groups of Qezelbāš to different parts of the country, thus dissociating them in some instances from their traditional *olka* or tribal lands, often held in fief. Another policy was to appoint as head of one

---

[69] Eskandar Beg, *Tārīḵ*, 1:326-27 (Savory, *History*, 1:460-61).

[70] Eskandar Beg, *Tārīḵ*, 2:1085 (Savory, *History*, 2:1311).

[71] See Savory, *Iran under the Safavids*, 77 ff.

tribe a Qezelbāš officer from another tribe, or even to appoint a non-Qezelbāš officer from one of the *ğolām* regiments created by him; such officers might be Georgians, Armenians or Circassians. It is arguable that the long-term consequence of these policies was fatally to weaken the military strength of the state. In the short term, law and order were restored and the authority of the shah as the head of the ruling institution was reaffirmed.

The immediate cause of the decline in the power of the Qajar tribe, however, was not the policies of Shah ʿAbbās, but the loss through Ottoman conquest of the tribe's ancestral lands in Qarābāğ. In 996-97/1588-89 strong Ottoman forces under Farhād Pasha overran Qarābāğ and established a garrison at Ganja.[72] From the time of Shah Ṭahmāsp, a succession of Qajar amirs had held the office of *beglerbeg/amīr al-omarā*ʾ of Qarābāğ and had been entrusted with the security of the north-west frontier.[73] Under the three shahs Ṭahmāsp, Esmāʿīl II, and Solṭān-Moḥammad Shah, five Qajar amirs had held this office; four of them belonged to the powerful Zīādoğlū sept of the Qajar tribe.

At the time of the Ottoman invasion of Qarābāğ, Emāmqolī Khan Qājār was still *beglerbeg* of Qarābāğ. He was unable to check the Ottoman advance, and fell back to Arasbār, where he died. Shah ʿAbbās, who had but recently come to the throne, appointed Moḥammad Khan Zīādoğlū Qājār in his place,[74] but the latter was unable to restore the

---

[72] Eskandar Beg, *Tārīḵ*, 1:403 (Savory, *History*, 2:580).

[73] The first Qajar officer so appointed (ca. 963/1555-56) was (1) Šāhverdī-Solṭān; see Eskandar Beg, *Tārīḵ*, 1:88 (Savory, *History*, 1:147). He was succeeded in this office by (2) Yūsof-Ḵalīfa Zīādoğlū, "an amir of the first rank" (*ṭerāz-e avval*), who was appointed *lala* of Ṭahmāsp's eighth son Solṭān-ʿAlī Mīrzā, born ca. 970/1562-63. After the accession of Shah Esmāʿīl II (22 August 1576), the new shah appointed Yūsof-Ḵalīfa's nephew, (3) Paykar-Solṭān as *amīr al-omarā*ʾ of Qarābāğ. Shortly afterwards, Paykar-Solṭān, hoping to ingratiate himself further with Shah Esmāʿīl II, murdered his uncle; see Eskandar Beg, *Tārīḵ*, 1:212-13 (Savory, *History*, 1:316 where Paykar-Solṭān is erroneously referred to as Shah Ṭahmāsp's nephew). However, Esmāʿīl II disapproved of Paykar-Solṭān's action, dismissed him, and appointed (4) Ebrāhīm Beg Zīādoğlū governor of Qarābāğ and *lala* of Solṭān-ʿAlī Mīrzā. Subsequently, Esmāʿīl II replaced him by another Qajar amir, (5) Emāmqolī Khan, who was confirmed in office by Solṭān-Moḥammad Shah in 985/1578 (Eskandar Beg, *Tārīḵ*, 1:227; Savory, *History*, 1:339) and held the office for ten years until his death in 996/1587-88 (Eskandar Beg, *Tārīḵ*, 1:385; Savory, *History*, 1:555).

[74] Sümer, *Rolü*, 145.

situation in Qarābāḡ, and the Qajar forces again retreated across the river Aras to Arasbār, leaving many of their possessions to be plundered by the Ottomans.[75] Moḥammad Khan regrouped his forces, and marched back into Qarābāḡ with an army consisting of Qajar *ḡāzīs* and assorted troops from other tribes and the Turkomans of Qarābāḡ.[76] Moḥammad Khan's aim was to recapture Ganja, and thus establish a claim to continuing Safavid suzerainty over Qarābāḡ before the Safavid ambassadors reached Istanbul. Shortly after his accession, Shah ʿAbbās had opened peace negotiations with the Ottoman sultan, in order not to have to fight major campaigns simultaneously on two fronts—against the Ottomans in the north-west and against the Özbegs, who had overrun a large part of Khorasan and Sīstān, in the east.

The Qajar siege of Ganja raised a storm of protest from the Ottomans. Jaʿfar Pasha, the Ottoman commander at Tabriz, where the citadel had been in Ottoman hands since its capture by ʿO̱smān Pasha in 993/1585 during an earlier invasion of Azerbaijan by the armies of Sultan Morād III, sent a letter to Shah ʿAbbās complaining that it was improper to conduct military operations while peace negotiations were in progress. Faced by Jaʿfar Pasha's protests, the shah, anxious above all to conclude a peace treaty with the Ottomans, ordered Moḥammad Khan Qājār to raise the siege, but the Qajars "refused to abandon so easily the rich province of Qarābāḡ, which had been their tribal territory, and where they had established estates and flourishing gardens, and they disobeyed the shah's order." Farhād Pasha, the supreme Ottoman commander in the region, and the officer who had initiated the peace negotiations, added his protests to those of Jaʿfar Pasha. Shah ʿAbbās then sent a Qajar officer, Šāhverdī Beg, to Moḥammad Khan with the following message:

> Your forefathers, as a reward for their loyal services to the Safavid house, received the province of Qarābāḡ from my forefathers. Policy now dictates that I should not at this moment contest this province with the Ottomans. If you are truly loyal to me, you will cease military operations and return, and I will give you fiefs elsewhere in the kingdom in lieu of Qarābāḡ. Qarābāḡ will not run away (*qarābāḡ jā-ī namīravad*). God willing, it will be recovered easily; if not, one cannot fight against fate. I hope that, with God's help, right will shortly triumph.[77]

---

[75] Eskandar Beg, *Tārīḵ*, 1:406 (Savory, *History*, 1:583).

[76] Eskandar Beg, *Tārīḵ*, 1:416 (Savory, *History*, 1:592).

[77] Eskandar Beg, *Tārīḵ*, 1:416-17 (Savory, *History*, 1:592-93).

This message from the shah, redolent at once of the recognition by the shah of the exigencies of *realpolitik* and of his compassionate understanding of the Qajar attachment to Qarābāḡ, reached its destination by a roundabout route. Šāhverdī Beg, too frightened to deliver this message direct to Moḥammad Khan, took the extraordinary step of showing the shah's order to the Ottoman garrison in the citadel at Tabriz, and the Ottomans forwarded it to Moḥammad Khan. The latter, "being a loyal Sufi" (*ṣūfī-ye dawlatḵᵛāh*), obeyed orders, raised the siege, and his troops dispersed. Some of the Qezelbāš tribesmen, such as the Šams al-Dīnlūs, the Qazāqs, and the Qarāmānlūs,[78] deserted (*dönük gašta*), and scattered to their own territories. Other Qezelbāš defected to the Ottomans. Moḥammad Khan found his line of retreat cut off by hostile deserters and was forced to take refuge with Alexander, who had succeeded his father as ruler of the Kakheti district of Georgia in 982/1574. Alexander treacherously handed Moḥammad Khan over to the Ottomans, who imprisoned him at Istanbul but eventually repatriated him after the peace treaty had been signed (14 Jomādā I, 998/21 March 1590).[79]

After the recapture of Tabriz by Shah ʿAbbās in 1012/late 1603, a Qajar officer, Amir Güne Beg, "who had not yet been promoted to the status of amir but was trusted by the shah," was despatched to the Arasbār area with a force of Söklen[80] and Ṭavāleš tribesmen to serve as a rallying-point for any Qajar and Torkmān refugees who might still be left in Qarābāḡ.[81] Appointed governor of Erevan (Čoḵūr-e Saʿd) after its recapture from the Ottomans in 1012-13/1604,[82] Amir Güne Beg did succeed in establishing a bridgehead across the river Aras into Qarābāḡ, where he was joined by numbers of Qajars and Otuz-iki Turkomans.[83] For the next twenty years, until his death from wounds

---

[78] The Šams-al-Dīnlū were a sept of the Ḏu'l-Qadr tribe. The Qarāmānlūs originated from Qarābāḡ and had given their allegiance succcessively to the rulers of Qarāmān and the Āq Qoyunlū. After throwing in their lot with the Safavids, they remained a minor tribe among the Qezelbāš tribes of lesser rank (*küçük oymaklar*) during the reign of Shah Ṭahmāsp. They achieved greater prominence under Shah ʿAbbās I but still remained in the *küçük oymaklar* category (Sümer, *Rolü*, 130-31, 230-31).

[79] Eskandar Beg, *Tārīḵ*, 1:416-17 (Savory, *History*, 1:592-93).

[80] A sept of the Ḏu'l-Qadr tribe.

[81] Eskandar Beg, *Tārīḵ*, 2:643 (Savory, *History*, 2:883).

[82] Eskandar Beg, *Tārīḵ*, 2:652 (Savory, *History*, 2:843).

[83] Eskandar Beg, *Tārīḵ*, 2:657 (Savory, *History*, 2:848). On the "Thirty-Two" clans of the Javānšīr-Turkoman confederation of Qarābāḡ, see

incurred in battle against the Georgians in 1034/1624-25 Amir Güne, now promoted to the rank of khan and *amīr al-omarā'* of Čokūr-e Saʿd, acted as Lord Marcher along the whole of the disputed north-west border from Erzurum in the west, north to Āḵesqa (Akhaltzikhé) in the Meskhia district of Georgia, and east to Erevan near Lake Van. Fending off successive Ottoman attacks, his valor earned him the respect of his foes and the admiration of Shah ʿAbbās, who dubbed him Sārū Aṣlān ("Yellow Lion").

The Reconquest of Qarābāḡ

After the eviction of the Qajars from Qarābāḡ in 997/1588-89, Shah ʿAbbās relocated the bulk of the Qajar tribe along the northeast frontier of Iran in the region of Astarābād, and in 1007/1598 he appointed Ḥosayn Khan Zīādoḡlū Qājār governor of that province.[84] Ḥosayn Khan had already made his mark in 999/1590-91, when he suppressed a serious revolt by Ḏu'l-Qadrs in Fārs and Afšārs at Kermān, and he is described as "one of the amirs whom the Shah trusted."[85] The shah had not forgotten his promise to the Qajars to reconquer their ancestral lands in Qarābāḡ if this became possible. In Ḥosayn Khan, the shah must have thought he had found the man capable of achieving this goal, because Ḥosayn Khan, who seems to have risen rapidly in the shah's favour and to have been given the sobriquet of "Qarābāḡi," was dispatched in the direction of the river Aras sometime in 1012-13/1604 while the shah was engaged in the siege of Erevan. As already noted, Ḥosayn Khan's fellow-Qajar officer Amir Güne Khan had succeeded in establishing a bridgehead across the Ḵodā-āfarīn bridge into Qarābāḡ, and the plan seems to have been that Ḥosayn Khan would take command of operations in Qarābāḡ while Amir Güne Khan was involved in operations elsewhere. Ḥosayn Khan, however, was an arrogant and self-willed officer of unpredictable moods. His arrogance led him to underestimate the capabilities of the Ottoman governor of Qarābāḡ, Dāwūd Pasha. In addition, Ḥosayn Khan proved to be an incompetent field commander. Although he redeemed his reputation somewhat by a fighting withdrawal to the river Aras, he was nevertheless driven back across the river with the loss of all his baggage and supplies. He asked Shah ʿAbbās permission to "make amends" by attacking Ganja. The shah took the news of his defeat philosophically, but ordered Ḥosayn Khan to remain where he was until further orders.

Minorsky, *Tadhkirat al-Mulūk*, 167 and Eskandar Beg, *Tārīḵ*, 2:857 (Savory, *History*, 2:1068).

[84] Eskandar Beg, *Tārīḵ*, 1:581 (Savory, *History*, 2:768).

[85] Eskandar Beg, *Tārīḵ*, 1:435 (Savory, *History*, 2:610).

Shah ʿAbbās, following his crushing defeat of the Ottoman army at the battle of Ṣūfīān on 24 Jomādā II 1014/6 November 1605,[86] moved his headquarters to Arasbār and began preparations for a spring offensive in Qarābāḡ. The Ottoman garrison at Ganja having rejected his call to surrender, the shah advanced into Qarābāḡ, reaching Ganja in Šavvāl 1014/towards the end of February 1606.[87] After an arduous siege, the fort finally surrendered on 28 Ṣafar 1015/5 July 1606.[88] Perhaps this was the moment when the shah appointed Ḥosayn Khan governor of Qarābāḡ. At all events, his tenure of office was short; he was dismissed from office the same year after complaints from the people of Qarābāḡ about his "unbridled behaviour" *(aṭvār-e nā-hanjār)* and his "unbecoming conduct" (*solūk-e nā-hamvār*).[89]

The shah reappointed to the post of governor of Qarābāḡ Moḥammad Khan Zīādoḡlū Qājār, who, as noted earlier, had been driven out of the province by the Ottomans in 996/1588 before he had been able to exercise jurisdiction there. After his release from Ottoman imprisonment in 998/1590, he had taken up residence at Ardabīl. He used to say that, through the power of the holy spirit of Shaikh Ṣafī, Ganja would one day return to Safavid hands, and he would once again be appointed governor of the province of Qarābāḡ.[90] Moḥammad Khan Zīādoḡlū Qājār seems to have retained his position as governor of Qarābāḡ until 1024/1615, in which year he was killed in action against the Georgians,[91] and he was succeeded by the ninth and last Qajar to govern that region: Moḥammadqolī Khan Zīādoḡlū.[92] Moḥammadqolī Khan was dismissed from office in 1036/1626-27 for dereliction of duty in leaving the Ganja region defenseless against the ravages of Morāv, the *atālīq* ("guardian") of Simon, ruler of the Kartlia district of Georgia.[93]

Qarābāḡ Becomes a Ḵāṣṣa Province

The dismissal of Moḥammadqolī Khan marks the end of Qarābāḡ's status as a *mamālek* province governed by a Qezelbāš amir.[94] In his

---

[86] Savory, *Iran under the Safavids*, 87.

[87] Eskandar Beg, *Tārīḵ*, 2:710 (Savory, *History*, 2:902).

[88] Eskandar Beg, *Tārīḵ*, 2:715 (Savory, *History*, 2:906).

[89] Eskandar Beg, *Tārīḵ*, 1:716 (Savory, *History*, 2:907).

[90] Eskandar Beg, *Tārīḵ*, 1:417 (Savory, *History*, 2:593-94).

[91] Eskandar Beg, *Tārīḵ*, 2:892 (Savory, *History*, 2:1108).

[92] Sümer, *Rolü*, 184.

[93] Eskandar Beg, *Tārīḵ*, 2:1065 (Savory, *History*, 2:1289).

[94] On Shah ʿAbbās's policy of converting *mamālek* to *ḵāṣṣa* provinces, see Savory, *Iran under the Safavids*, 77-79.

place, Shah ʿAbbās appointed a *ḡolām*, Dāwūd Khan, the son of the famous Allāhverdī Khan, an Armenian Christian from Georgia who had risen to the rank of commander-in-chief of the Safavid armies.[95] Dāwūd Khan was also appointed chief of the Qajar tribe (*mīr-e īl va oymaq-e qājār*).[96] The conversion of Qarābāḡ to a *ḵāṣṣa* province, and the appointment of a *ḡolām* to be the nominal head of a Qezelbāš tribe, did not bode well for the continuance of Qezelbāš influence in Qarābāḡ in general and of the power of the Qajar tribe there in particular. However, at the time of the death of Shah ʿAbbās (1038/1629), a Qajar amir, Paykar Khan Igirmi-dört, is described as "one of the amirs of Qarābāḡ and governor of Bardaʿ."[97]

Mashashi Haneda has argued that ʿAbbās's policy of centralizing military power by appointing either a *ḡolām* or a *qūrčī* from his own bodyguard to provincial governorships, gave the shah complete control of the army, but did not act to the detriment of the tribal system:

> Certes, le gouverneur arrivait de la capitale avec la dignité royale, mais les tribus turkmènes et leur organisation restaient intactes sous le commandement de ce personnage.

When royal power at the center weakened, he says, it was natural that the Turkoman tribes "réapparussent en première ligue." Such was the case, he says, with the Afšārs and the Qajars. In this regard, he concludes, the reforms of Shah ʿAbbās I did not greatly modify traditional Iranian society.[98]

In reality, the extent to which the Qajar tribe was able to enjoy the usufruct of their lands in Qarābāḡ after the Ottoman occupation of the province in 996/1588 is problematical. Shah ʿAbbās, when he called on the Qajars to abandon the province to the Ottomans at that time, specifically promised to allocate the Qajar tribe a place of residence elsewhere within the Safavid dominions (*dar ʿevāż-e qarābāḡ dar sāʾer-e mamālek jā va maqām be-īšān ʿenāyat mīfarmāʾīm*). The shah also said that if the Qajars were of one accord in their support of the Safavid state (*yakjehat-e īn dawlatand*) they would obey his orders.[99]

---

[95] R. M. Savory, "The Office of Sipahsālār (Commander-in-Chief) in the Safavid State," in *Proceedings of the Second European Conference of Iranian Studies* (Rome, 1995), 603-5.

[96] Eskandar Beg, *Tārīḵ*, 2:1088 (Savory, *History*, 2:1316).

[97] Eskandar Beg, *Tārīḵ*, 2:1085 (Savory, *History*, 2:1311).

[98] Mashashi Haneda, *Le Chāh et les Qizilbāš: le système militaire Safavide* (Berlin, 1987), 219-20.

[99] Eskandar Beg, *Tārīḵ*, 1:417 (Savory, *History*, 2:593).

As stated earlier, some of the troops from other Qezelbāš tribes deserted, or even defected to the Ottomans However, all those tribesmen who possessed a measure of loyalty, put the king's pleasure before land and property, and left the province (*az īl va oymaqat nīz har kas bahra'ī az iḵlāṣ dāšt rešā-jū'ī-ye ḵāṭer-e mobārak-e ašrāf-rā bar melk va māl tarjīḥ dāda tark-e ān velāyat karda*). The author of the *Tārīḵ-e ʿālamārā-ye ʿabbāsī* then adds a very significant phrase: "that province [i.e., Qarābāḡ] became the touchstone of loyalty" [among the Qezelbāš].[100] Unfortunately, we have no means of knowing what proportion of the Qezelbāš in general, and of the Qajars in particular, passed this test. Undoubtedly, many inhabitants took refuge in neighboring Georgia, hoping to return to their homes in due course. What is certain is that Shah ʿAbbās was not speaking lightly when he made Qarābāḡ a touchstone of Qezelbāš loyalty. Nearly twenty years later, when the shah reconquered Qarābāḡ, it is clear that he regarded the loyalty of all those, whether Qezelbāš or civilians, who had remained behind in Ottoman occupied territory as suspect. Some had entered Ottoman service, had collaborated with the Ottomans, had been granted privileges by them, or had held office under them. The shah decided that it was not in the best interests of the state to leave such persons in a frontier area, and a Qajar officer, Laṭīf Khan Beg, was placed in charge of moving to Faraḥābād in Māzandarān all those who were Muslims, Jews, or Christians. Some fifteen thousand families in all were moved, and the chronicler comments that "their exile was a punishment for disloyalty to the crown" (*dar īn jalā mokāfāt-e namak-ḥarāmī yāftand*).[101] It is probable that the great majority of the Qajars did answer the shah's call to leave Qarābāḡ in 996/1588, and that they gradually established new power bases in Astarābād, Khorasan and Māzandarān.

The Qajars on the Northeast Frontier

It has been suggested by James J. Reid that the vulnerable state of the Qajars after the loss of their tribal base in Qarābāḡ was "attractive" to ʿAbbās because he sought to elevate the weaker Qezelbāš groups at the expense of the more powerful *oymaq*s.[102] Another interpretation might be that Shah ʿAbbās I always rewarded loyal service, that there are many instances of his placing his trust in individual Qajar amirs,

---

[100] Eskandar Beg, *Tārīḵ*, 1:417 (Savory, *History*, 2:593).

[101] Eskandar Beg, *Tārīḵ*, 2:881 (Savory, *History*, 2:1095-96).

[102] James J. Reid, "The Qajar Uymaq in the Safavid Period, 1500-1722," *Iranian Studies* 11(1978):134.

and that he genuinely regretted the loss of the Qajar tribal lands in Qarābāḡ and did his best to make amends. If the defense of the north-west frontier against the Ottomans had been a major responsibility and an onerous task, the defense of the north-east frontier against the Özbegs was no sinecure. The Qajars served with equal distinction in Khorasan. One of their leading amirs was Meḥrāb Khan, who had been appointed governor of Ṭabas in 1002/1593-94,[103] a few years before the Ottoman occupation of Qarābāḡ. He was governor successively of Ḵᵛāf and Bāḵarz (1007/1598-99),[104] Mašhad (1011/1602-3),[105] and Marv (1017-18/1608-10).[106] In addition to his celebrated military exploits against the Özbegs, he made the notable discovery that the burial place of Shah Ṭahmāsp within the precincts of the shrine of the Emām Reżā at Mašhad had not been desecrated by the Özbeg chief ʿAbd al-Moʾmen, as had been thought, on the occasion of his capture of Mašhad in 997/1589. Meḥrāb Khan had the remains sent to Shah ʿAbbās, who reinterred them at Isfahan, and subsequently transferred them to a site within the shrine complex at Ardabīl.[107] Meḥrāb Khan retained the shah's favor until his death in 1032/1622-23, and was accorded the signal honor of himself being buried within the shrine precincts.[108]

Although some nineteen Qajar amirs are mentioned in the sources as having served under ʿAbbās I, only two are mentioned as holding high office at the time of his death in 1038/1629.[109] There are two principal reasons for this: First, of the other seventeen, six had died and two had been dismissed from office prior to the death of Shah ʿAbbās; eight had been active either during the early part of ʿAbbās's reign or at any rate prior to 1025/1616; only one, Mīrzā Khan Beg Qājār, was active within five years of the death of the shah. Second, as mentioned earlier, an important part of Shah ʿAbbās's plan to increase the power of the central administration was to curb the influence of the Qezelbāš. The results of this policy are clearly shown

---

[103] Eskandar Beg, *Tārīḵ*, 1:490 (Savory, *History*, 2:615-16).

[104] Savory, *History*, 2:762 (the notice of appointment is missing in the text).

[105] Eskandar Beg, *Tārīḵ*, 2:630 (Savory, *History*, 2:821).

[106] Eskandar Beg, *Tārīḵ*, 2:804 (Savory, *History*, 2:1006).

[107] Shah Ṭahmāsp had originally been buried at Qazvīn, where he died in May 1576, but his remains were transferred to Mašhad in the autumn of that year by Shah Esmāʿīl II; see Eskandar Beg, *Tārīḵ*, 1:526-28 (Savory, *History*, 2:701-5).

[108] Eskandar Beg, *Tārīḵ*, 2:1005 (Savory, *History*, 2:1230).

[109] Eskandar Beg, *Tārīḵ*, 2:1085 (Savory, *History*, 2:1311).

by Eskandar Beg Monšī. The eight "great" Qezelbāš tribes had more than sixty-nine amirs of standing during the reign of Ṭahmāsp. By the end of the reign of Shah ʿAbbās, these same eight tribes had only twenty-four amirs of standing; the total was raised to twenty-seven by the inclusion of three amirs of the Bayāt tribe, which had acquired the status of a "great" tribe during the reign of ʿAbbās. By the death of ʿAbbās I, the only "great" tribes which had more than three amirs of note were the Šāmlūs and the D̲u'l-Qadrs, with seven and six respectively. According to Eskandar Beg, the Šāmlūs were accounted "the chief of the Qezelbāš tribes" (*sar-daftar-e oymaqat-e qezelbāš*).[110]

A. K. S. Lambton was the first to call attention to the unique nature of the biographical material in the *Tārīk̲-e ʿālamārā-ye ʿabbāsī*: Eskandar Beg's "principles of selection," she says, "are clearly different from those followed by earlier writers. In general only those whose work is important in the light of the state appear to have been included."[111] The Safavid chroniclers who followed Eskandar Beg did not follow his principles of selection either, and the information they give on the appointment and dismissal of both civil and military officials is sparse. One is not, therefore, able to draw anything like such a clear or detailed picture of the relative standing of the Qezelbāš tribes in the later Safavid period as is possible for the earlier period. It seems that, in the reign of Shah ʿAbbās II (1052-77/1642-66), there were still two Qajar amirs of note. One of them, Mortażāqolī Khan Qājār, the son of the Meḥrāb Khan mentioned above, rose to the highest positions in the Safavid administration. He held successively the posts of *īšīk-āqāsī-bāšī, dīvānbegī, qūrčī-bāšī,* and, finally, *sepahsālār*, or commander-in-chief of all Safavid forces, both Qezelbāš and non-Qezelbāš. He seems to have held the last-named office for only a year (1057-58/1648). About the year 1074/1663-64, he was executed by ʿAbbās II; his property was confiscated, and his sons jailed.[112] The other Qajar amir of note was Meḥrāb Khan, governor of Qandahār, who was killed in 1057/1647-48 during a Mughal siege of that city.[113] ʿAbbās II, who had continued and extended his great-grandfather's policy of converting "state" (*mamālek*) provinces into "crown" (*k̲āṣṣa*)

---

110 Eskandar Beg, *Tārīk̲*, 2:1084 (Savory, *History*, 2:1309).

111 A. K. S. Lambton, "Persian Biographical Literature," in B. Lewis and P. M. Holt (eds.), *Historians of the Middle East* (Oxford, 1962), 147-48.

112 Savory, "Office of Sipahsālār," 609-10.

113 Moḥammad Ṭāher Vaḥīd Qazvīnī, *ʿAbbās-nāma* (edited by Ebrāhīm Dehqān; Arāk, 1329 Š./1950), 137.

ones, took this opportunity to remove yet another governorate from the control of the Qezelbāš and appointed a *ḡolām* in his place.[114]

The Position of the Qajars at the End of the Safavid Period

The reigns of the last two Safavid shahs, Solaymān (1077-1105/1666-94) and Solṭān-Ḥosayn (1105-35/1694-1722), mark the decline of the Safavid dynasty and state. Little or no specific information regarding offices held by Qajar amirs during this period is available. What is certain is that, during these reigns there was a total breakdown of military discipline and morale, and a decline in the fighting qualities of the Safavid forces with the exception of small detachments of Qezelbāš. The military weakness of Iran was starkly illustrated in 1110/1698-99, when a force of Balūčīs ravaged Kermān, nearly reached Yazd, and threatened Bandar ʿAbbās. Although the Balūčīs were subsequently defeated by a Safavid force led by Georgian officers, the fact that they had been able to penetrate unopposed so far into Iran should have alerted the shah to the need for drastic measures to ensure the defense of the realm.[115]

Throughout this period, the Qajars seem to have retained their fighting qualities and a significant degree of tribal cohesiveness in their new bases in the Astarābād and Marv regions. At some point, probably during the eleventh/seventeenth century,[116] the Qajar tribe split into two main branches, the Ašāḡī-bāš or Ašāqa-bāš, and the Yūḵārī-bāš or Yūqārī-bāš, each of which was sub-divided into septs.[117] About the year 1132/1719-20, Fatḥ ʿAlī Khan Qājār became chief of the Ašāḡī-bāš branch and played a prominent and somewhat ambiguous role during the turbulent period that both preceded and followed the overthrow of the Safavids by the Afghans in 1135/1722.[118] After the Afghan capture of Isfahan in that year, the Qajars and the Afšārs emerged as the most numerous and the strongest of the Qezelbāš tribes, and each initially competed for the position of defenders of the Safavid cause. The third son of Shah Solṭān-Ḥosayn, Ṭahmāsp Mīrzā, escaped from the Afghan blockade of Isfahan, had himself proclaimed shah at

[114] Qazvīnī, *ʿAbbās-nāma*, 140 footnote 2.

[115] See Laurence Lockhart, *The Fall of the Ṣafavī Dynasty and the Afghan Occupation of Persia* (Cambridge, 1958), 46-47.

[116] Bournoutian, *History of Qarabagh*, 70 n. 168 claims that the division of the Qajars into Yūḵārī-bāš and Ašāḡī-bāš occurred in the early tenth/sixteenth century, but this is extremely doubtful.

[117] For their names, see Sümer, "Ḳādjār," 387.

[118] For details, see Lockhart, *Fall*, 280-81.

Qazvīn with the title of Ṭahmāsp II, and subsequently took refuge with the Qajars at Astarābād, where he received a "warm welcome"; he hoped the Qajars would provide him with "the military force he so badly needed."[119]

Fatḥ ʿAlī Khan Qājār, however, was unable to hold his own against a rival Qezelbāš chief, Nāder Khan Afšār, who steadily supplanted him in the favor of Ṭahmāsp II, dubbed himself Ṭahmāspqolī Khan, claimed to have as his goal the restoration of the Safavid monarch, and, finally, in 1139/1726, was complicit in the execution of Fatḥ-ʿAlī Khan Qājār.[120] Fatḥ-ʿAlī's eleven-year old son, Moḥammad-Ḥasan Khan Qājār, sought asylum among the Yomut Turkomans. A few Qajars were arrested, but were released a few days later upon payment of a ransom by some of the prisoners. According to Laurence Lockhart, neither Ṭahmāsp nor Nāder "had any wish further to antagonise this powerful tribe, and so treated them leniently."[121] In 1142/1730 Nāder Khan Afšār routed the Afghan usurper Ašraf, entered Isfahan in triumph, and placed Ṭahmāsp II on the throne. Our hypothetical betting man, to whom we were introduced at the beginning of this paper, would have concluded at this point that it was odds on the Afšārs to win the battle for hegemony among the Qezelbāš, and the probability that this would be the case must have seemed a certainty by 1148/1736. In 1145/1732, Nāder had deposed Ṭahmāsp II, and had placed the latter's infant son on the throne as ʿAbbās III. In 1748/1736, Nāder abandoned all pretense of ruling on behalf of a Safavid *roi-fainéant*, and had himself crowned as the first ruler of the new Afsharid dynasty. Four years later, his son Reżāqolī Khan, fearful of a pro-Safavid coup in Iran during his father's absence in India, had Ṭahmāsp II, ʿAbbās III, and ʿAbbās's younger brother Esmāʿīl, put to death.[122] This dastardly deed appears to have been committed by that "execrable Qajar"[123] Moḥammad-Ḥosayn Khan of the Develū sept of the Yūḵārī-bāš branch of the Qajars.

After his accession to the throne in 1148/1736, Nāder Shah Afšār's power seemed unassailable. The rule of the Afsharid dynasty over the

---

[119] Peter Avery, "Nādir Shāh and the Afsharid Legacy," in *The Cambridge History of Iran* VII: *From Nadir Shah to the Islamic Republic* (Cambridge, 1991), 26. Avery quotes the *Tārīḵ-e ʿālamārā-ye nāderī* of Moḥammad Kāẓem as saying that thirty thousand Qajars rallied to Ṭahmāsp Mīrzā.

[120] See Lockhart, *Fall*, 309 ff.; Avery, "Nādir Shāh," 26.

[121] Lockhart, *Fall*, 310.

[122] Laurence Lockhart, *Nadir Shah* (London, 1938), 177-78, 180.

[123] Lockhart, *Nadir Shah*, 177.

whole of Iran, however, lasted a mere twelve years (1148-61/1736-48). His grandson, Šāhrok̲, continued to rule in Khorasan only until 1210/1795.[124] Why did Nāder Shah, who had already driven the Afghan usurpers and the Russian invaders from Persian soil before he came to the throne; who subsequently weakened the power of the Mughal empire by his invasion of India in 1151-52/1738-39; and who had inflicted a number of defeats, inconclusive though they were, on the Ottomans, fail both to consolidate his own position on the throne of Iran and to bequeath to his successors a stable inheritance?

The Final Phase: Afšārs, Qajars, and Zands

A number of factors seem to have played a part in the failure of the Afšārs. Avery has made a shrewd assessment of these.[125] Initially, Nāder Shah was praised for "restoring" the Safavid monarchy and expelling foreign invaders. As time went on, however, Nāder Shah found it increasingly difficult to rid himself of the Safavid "aura." Safavid pretenders appeared in various parts of the country,[126] and these pretenders were seen as "representatives of an Iranian need for unity, continuity, hierarchy and well-ordered government sanctified by tradition."[127] Mistaken policies on the part of Nāder increasingly strengthened the perception that it was the Qajars, not the Afšārs, who were concerned about the unity of Iran. First, Nāder was perceived as attempting to water down the Es̱nā-ʿašarī Shiʿi tradition which was one of the mainstays of the Safavid state. At a council of ulema in 1156/1743, Nāder Shah deplored "the extremist policies of the Safavids."[128] Second, in recruiting men for his armies, he relied heavily on (Sunni) Afghans and (Sunni) Özbeg tribesmen in preference to (Shiʿi) Qezelbāš and men from other Shiʿi Turkoman tribes.[129] Third, he moved the center of gravity in Iran away from the centrally located Isfahan, the Safavid capital, to the northeastern city of Mašhad in Khorasan, which he clearly regarded as his capital from about 1153/1741 onwards.[130] This move conduced to the perpetuation of Tīmūr's

---

[124] Shāhrok̲ had connections with the Safavid royal family; his mother was a daughter of the last Safavid shah, Solṭān Ḥosayn; see Avery, "Nādir Shāh," 53.

[125] See Avery, "Nādir Shāh," 53 ff.

[126] As late as 1187/1773; see Perry, "The Last Ṣafavids," 59-69.

[127] Avery, "Nādir Shāh," 57.

[128] J. R. Perry, "Nādir Shāh Afs̲h̲ār," *in Encyclopaedia of Islam: New Edition* (Leiden, 1960-), 7:855.

[129] Lockhart, *Nadir*, 54, 96.

[130] Lockhart, *Nadir*, 197.

Central Asian-Khorasan imperium—an east-west split in Iran which was eventually healed by the Safavids. Such a policy was entirely in conformity with Nāder's fairly obvious desire to model himself on Tīmūr. Finally, the progressively more harsh, tyrannical and extortionary nature of Nāder's rule brought disenchantment, and in 1160/1747 he was assassinated by a group of his own officers. Among their number was the Qajar chief Moḥammad Beg Qājār Erevānī.

In the Nāder Shah and post-Nāder periods, which were marked by constantly shifting alliances and capricious loyalties, the actions of the Qajars were no more and no less Machiavellian than those of their Qezelbāš rivals, the Afšārs, and those of the leaders of the new faction on the political scene, the Zands. Both Afšārs and Zands recognized that the Qajars "posed a serious threat to their own ambitions."[131] The Zands, a pastoral people belonging to a minor branch of the Lak tribes centred on the Malāyer district in the Zagros foothills,[132] took advantage of the enormous vacuum in central and southern Persia caused by the collapse of Afšārid rule, and, under their leader Karīm Khan Zand, rapidly increased their power in those areas, cleverly making use of the Safavid ethos, which remained strong. Just as Nāder had initially posed as the regent of the Safavid princes Ṭahmāsp II and ʿAbbās III, in 1165/1751-52 Karīm Khan Zand posed as the *vakīl* (vice-gerent) of the Safavid pretender Esmāʿīl III. The expansion of Zand power was facilitated by the fact that Afšār jurisdiction was confined to Khorasan after 1161/1748, while the center of Qajar power was also in the north-east, in Astarābād, and in the Caspian province of Māzandarān. Moḥammad-Ḥasan Khan Qājār, who had been a wanderer in the deserts of Dašt-e Qepčāq for over twenty years, emerged after the death of Nāder Shah (1160/1747) as the chief of the Ašāgī-bāš branch of the Qajars. Gavin Hambly is of the opinion that Moḥammad-Ḥasan Khan "behaved as more than a mere tribal khan," and that for some years, between 1164-65 and 1172-73/1751-59, he ruled over considerable areas of northern, western, and central Iran. He seems to have acquired part of Nāder Shah's treasure after the latter's death, and to have held court at Ašraf in Māzandarān, where he struck coins, evidence of a claim to sovereignty."[133] Karīm Khan Zand astutely exploited the

---

[131] Gavin Hambly, "Āghā Muḥammad Khān and the Establishment of the Qājār Dynasty," in *The Cambridge History of Iran* VII: *From Nadir Shah to the Islamic Republic* (Cambridge, 1991), 113.

[132] J. R. Perry, *Karīm Khan Zand: A History of Iran 1747-1779* (Chicago, 1979), 17.

[133] Hambly, "Āghā Muḥammad Khān," 113.

rivalry between the Ašāḡī-bāš and the Yūḵārī-bāš Qajars by supporting the latter, and in 1172/ 1759 the Zand chief routed Moḥammad-Ḥasan Khan Qājār and seized Astarābād.[134] The Qajar leader was treacherously murdered by some of his own followers.[135] Most of Moḥammad-Ḥasan Khan's nine sons fled to the Dašt-i Qepčāq, "the traditional Qajar refuge."[136] Among them were Āqā Moḥammad Khan, the future founder of the Qajar dynasty (1211/1796), and Ḥosaynqolī Khan, both of whom were subsequently captured by the Zands and taken to Shiraz. Karīm Khan Zand had spoken of Shiraz as his capital since 1169/1756,[137] and from 1179/1765 onwards he definitely considered that city to be his capital. He was now the "undisputed ruler of most of Iran,"[138] and the odds on the eventual triumph of the Qajars had lengthened immensely.

In 1182/1769, Karīm Khan Zand took the extraordinary step of appointing Ḥosaynqolī Khan, one of the Ašāḡī-bāš Qajar chiefs held hostage at Shiraz, governor of Dāmḡān.[139] Ḥosaynqolī Khan was then twenty years of age. This enabled Ḥosaynqolī Khan, over the next eight years, skillfully to build up the power of the Ašāḡī-bāš branch of the Qajars while simultaneously reducing that of the rival Yūḵārī-bāš branch, which had already demonstrated its hostility to the Safavid house by being party to the murder of the Safavid princes, as mentioned above. During this period, Ḥosaynqolī Khan tried not to incur the wrath of Karīm Khan Zand, the protector of the Yūḵārī-bāš Qajars, but in 1190/1776 his destruction of the Develū stronghold provoked a punitive expedition led by Karīm Khan's brutal cousin Zakī Khan Zand, and the following year Ḥosaynqolī Khan was murdered near Astarābād by some Yomut Turkomans.[140] However, the death in 1193/1779 of both Karīm Khan Zand and Zakī Khan, the latter assassinated by his own men, plunged the Zands into the same kind of internecine factionalism that had plagued the Qajars for many years.[141] In the confusion, Āqā Moḥammad Khan Qājār escaped from Shiraz and made his way to the Qajar base in Māzandarān. The odds on the Qajars inheriting the mantle

---

[134] J. R. Perry, "The Zand Dynasty," in *The Cambridge History of Iran* VII: *From Nadir Shah to the Islamic Republic* (Cambridge, 1991), 76-77.

[135] Bournoutian, *History of Qarabagh*, 74 footnote 183.

[136] Perry, "Zand Dynasty," 85

[137] Perry, *Karīm Khan*, 74.

[138] Perry, *Karīm Khan*, 243.

[139] For the possible reasons for this action, see Perry, "Zand Dynasty," 85-86.

[140] Hambly, "Āghā Muḥammad Khān," 113.

[141] Perry, *Karim Khan*, 297 ff.

of the Safavids as rulers of the whole of Iran had now shortened dramatically. Āqā Moḥammad Khan entered Tehran on 11 Jomādā I 1200/12 March 1786, and from then on regarded himself as ruler of Iran, although he refrained from assuming the title of shah.[142] Formidable Zand forces still challenged Qajar supremacy, and Āqā Moḥammad Khan's own position as chief of the Qajar tribe was still contested intermittently by some of his brothers and half-brothers.[143] His capture of Kermān in 1208-9/1794, the atrocities committed against the civilian population of that city after the Zand chief Loṭf-ʿAlī Khan escaped to Bam, and his subsequent brutal treatment of Loṭf-ʿAlī Khan, finally crushed Zand resistance. In the spring of 1210/1796, Āqā Moḥammad Khan was crowned at Tehran shah of Iran and the first ruler of the new Qajar dynasty. His single-minded ambition and ruthlessness[144] had made him the ruler of the whole of Iran. In keeping with Safavid tradition, the sword of Shah Esmāʿīl, the founder of the Safavid dynasty had been suspended for one night above the tomb of Shaikh Ṣafī in the shrine at Ardabīl, which was sacred to the Safavid family. At Āqā Moḥammad Shah's coronation in Tehran, after the crown of the Kayānids had been placed on his head, "the sword, which was imbued with the blessing of the shrine of [Shaikh] Ṣafī at Ardabīl, was girded round his waist."[145] Nothing could have been more symbolic of the fact that the Qajars saw themselves as the heirs of the Safavids, and the designation of the Qajars as "the last of the Qezelbāš" is therefore entirely fitting.

---

[142] Hambly, "Āghā Muḥammad Khān," 118.

[143] Hambly, "Āghā Muḥammad Khān," 114 ff.

[144] No doubt his implacable vindictiveness is attributable in part to the fact that, when he was only five years old, he had been castrated by ʿĀdel Shah Afšār, hence his soubriquet of Āqā, "eunuch."

[145] Ḥasan-e Fasāʾī, *Fārs-nāma-ye nāṣerī*, tr. Heribert Busse as *History of Persia under Qajar Rule* (New York, 1972), 68.

Part Two
Cultural Change

Dūst-ʿAlī Moʿayyer's *Painters of the Nāṣerī and Moẓaffarī Period*: A Little Known Document for the Study of Artists and Patrons of the Qajar Period

Layla S. Diba

Documentation for late nineteenth-century Persian art and culture is unusually rich for a society which has left otherwise few textual records of its achievements in this field. This evidence has been extensively utilized in recent years by Iranian scholars. However, few, if any, of these sources have been translated or made easily accessible to Western art historians.

A frequently cited memoir of the period is the *Rejāl-e ʿaṣr-e nāṣerī* (Notables of the Nāṣerī Period; henceforth *RAN*) by Dūst-ʿAlī Khan Moʿayyer, a compendium of essays on the late Qajar period written from 1955 to 1960 for the journal *Yağmā* and published in book form in 1982. The work includes an essay on the artistic life of the court entitled "Naqqāšān-e ʿaṣr-e nāṣerī va moẓaffarī." Given the dearth of information on Qajar painting and the importance of painting in the social and cultural life of the period, even a preliminary introduction to this little known document should prove useful to the study of the Qajar period.[1]

The Author and His Family

Dūst-ʿAlī Khan was descended from a family of Safavid ministers and statesmen that rose to particular prominence during the latter part of Moḥammad Shah's reign (1834-48) and the reign of his successor Nāṣer-al-Dīn (1848-96). The family was related to the dynasty through

[1] The author is planning a facsimile publication of this document in its entirety with a translation of the complete text.

the marriage of Ḥosayn-ʿAlī Khan II (d. 1274/1857) to Farzāna K̲ānom, thirty-ninth daughter of Fatḥ-ʿAlī Shah. He was the first of three family members to bear the title Moʿayyer-al-Mamālek (Assayer of the Realm) and began both to amass the fortune and to display the artistic interests which were to characterize this family for the next three generations.

His son Dūst-ʿAlī Khan II (1819-73), was appointed to numerous court posts, including that of Supervisor of Royal Buildings, which culminated in his appointment as Assayer of the Realm in 1283/1866-67.[2] The celebration of the marriage of Dūst-ʿAlī Khan's son, Dūst-Moḥammad, to Fātema K̲ānom, second daughter of Nāṣer-al-Dīn Shah in the same year, was described as unequalled in pomp and sumptuousness since the time of the Barmakids and Buyids by the principal chronicler of Qajar court life, Mahdī Bamdād.[3] Dūst-ʿAlī's death in 1873 marked the beginning of the decline of the political importance of the family.

While the Moʿayyerī family's genealogy and history are well documented,[4] their contribution to the arts, inasmuch as it clearly underlies Dūst-ʿAlī Khan's interest in recording the artistic as well as the political life of his time, is what concerns us here. This interest was undoubtedly inherited from his father.

Dūst-ʿAlī Khan II was a leading patron of the arts and architecture of his time: As would have been expected of a statesman of his stature, he commissioned both residential and religious buildings and formed a notable personal library. Dūst-ʿAlī Khan's pride in his achievement is conveyed by a superb watercolor portrait, now in the Louvre Museum, depicting him standing in a landscape with his Šemrān residence, the Bāḡ-e Ferdows, in the distance (Figure 1).[5]

The Bāḡ-e Ferdows, described in 1865 by A. H. Mounsey,[6] is one of the few Qajar private mansions in Tehran extant. The residence

---

[2] The preceding biographical information has been culled from the comprehensive study by Klaus Dieter Streicher, *Die Männer der Era Nasir* (Frankfurt, 1989); see especially the genealogical chart (p. 47) and pp. 20-33.

[3] Mahdī Bamdād, *Šarḥ-e ḥāl-e rejāl-e Īrān,* 6 vols. (Tehran, 1968-73), 1:495-500. See also A. H. Mounsey, *A Journey Through the Caucasus and the Interior of Persia* (London, 1872), 285 ff.

[4] Bamdād, *Rejāl*, loc. cit., note 2 and Mohammad Tavakoli-Targhi, "Dūst-ʿAlī Khan Moʿayyer-al-Mamālek," *Encyclopaedia Iranica*, forthcoming (s.v. Moʿayyer-al-Mamālek). I wish to thank the author for making this article available to me.

[5] See *Arabesques et Jardins du Paradis* (Paris, 1989), 259.

[6] Mounsey, *Journey*, 286 maintains that the residence was so magnificent that Dūst-ʿAlī Khan felt it advisable to offer it to Nāṣer-al-Dīn Shah.

Figure 1: Portrait of Dūst-ʿAlī Khan at the age of twenty-one. Watercolor, signed Mīrzā Bābā Ḥosaynī and dated 1263/1846. Louvre Museum, MAO 774.

evoked the unequivocal admiration of the American minister to Persia, S. G. W. Benjamin, who visited it in the early 1880's and recorded its appearance and the name of the architect, Ostād Ḥosayn. A two-storied building of great elegance, the interior decoration of the Bāḡ-e Ferdows included inlaid wooden doors, colored glass windows, magnificent plaster *moqarnas* (honeycomb) ceilings, and wall paintings of women dancers.[7] Twenty-six paintings known to have been commissioned for the mansion have been assigned to Bahrām Kermānšāhī, a little-known painter who worked in a highly Europeanized style.[8] While the paintings no longer survive, the complex system of *moqarnas* decoration bears testimony to the lavishness of his patronage and the refinement of his taste.

A more cynical observer of Qajar life, the Comte de Rochechouart, notes in his *Souvenirs* that Dūst-ʿAlī Khan collected erotic European paintings of Venuses of questionable aesthetic value for the decoration of one of his reception rooms.[9]

Among his other accomplishments as supervisor of royal buildings may be cited the construction for Nāṣer-al-Dīn Shah of two of the most celebrated architectural projects of the time, the Šāms-ol-ʿEmāra palace, completed in 1285/1865-66, and the Takya Dawlat theatre, both in the Golestān Palace complex.[10] Dūst-ʿAlī Khan also endowed a *madrasa* in Tehran at which the eminent theologian Ḥājj Mollā Moḥammad Ṭehrānī preached.[11]

Dūst-ʿAlī Khan was also put in charge of the Persian participation at the Paris World's Fair of 1867.[12] The World's Fair provided an international forum for the promotion of the arts and crafts of non-Western countries. The appointment to such a post carried with it both great responsibilities as well as considerable prestige.

As we have seen, contemporary European observes took note of Dūst-ʿAlī Khan's artistic patronage. In addition to Rochechouart's caustic commentary cited above, Benjamin records that he was a

---

[7] S. G. W. Benjamin, *Persia and the Persians* (Boston, 1886), 279.

[8] Moḥammad-ʿAlī Karīmzāda, *Aḥvāl va āṯār-e naqqāšān-e qadīm-e Īrān* (Tehran, 1985-91), 1:105-6.

[9] C. de Rochechouart, *Souvenirs d'un voyage en Perse* (Paris, 1867), 261.

[10] Moḥammad-Ḥasan Khan Eʿtemād-al-Salṭana, *al-Maʾāṯer va'l-āṯār*, ed. Īraj Afšār as *Čehel sāl-e tārīḵ-i Īrān*, 3 vols. (Tehran, 1363 Š./1984), 1:84; cited in Tavakoli-Targhi, "Dūst-ʿAlī," and *RAN*, 42 and 83.

[11] Streicher, *Die Männer*, 33; Bamdād, *Rejāl*, 2:317; Tavakoli, "Dūst-ʿAlī."

[12] Moḥammad-Ḥasan Khan Eʿtemād-al-Salṭana, *Merʾāt al-boldān*, 4 vols. (repr. Tehran, 1978-79), 3:66.

collector of drawings, calligraphy, engravings, and manuscripts and had formed one of the largest libraries in the Middle East.[13] Dūst-ʿAlī Khan's influence also extended directly to the shah's entourage since Persian sources note that Nāṣer-al-Dīn Shah's doctor, Mīrzā Sayyed ʿAlī Moʿayyerī, was a former protégé.[14]

Dūst-ʿAlī Khan II's interest in the arts was inherited: According to the *RAN,* his father supervised the production of six volumes of *Alf layla va layla* (The Thousand and One Nights)—the most ambitious manuscript project of the late Qajar period—illustrated by Abu'l-Ḥasan Khan Ḡāffārī Ṣanīʿ-al-Molk and his pupils. Dūst-ʿAlī Khan must have taken over the project, since he is credited with its completion in 1259/ 1852-53,[15] four years before his father's death.

While the fate of his library is unknown, a number of watercolors and calligraphies commissioned by the family were used to illustrate the *RAN*. The album of watercolors, calligraphies, and *farmān*s in which they were mounted is still held in a private collection.

Although married to a daughter of Nāṣer-al-Dīn Shah, Dūst-ʿAlī Khan II's son, Dūst-Moḥammad Khan (1272-1330/1855-1913), was ousted by rivals from important court sinecures during the latter part of the reign of Nāṣer-al-Dīn and the reign of Moẓaffar-al-Dīn. He absented himself from the capital for long sojourns in Europe, although he did complete the decoration of the Bāḡ-e Ferdows. On his return, he retired from active life and devoted his attentions to raising pigeons, a not inexpensive hobby as practiced by Dūst-Moḥammad, the subject of one of the articles for *Yaḡmā* written by his son Dūst-ʿAlī Khan III.

Dūst-ʿAlī Khan III, the author of the text under discussion, was born in 1293/1876 into court life and was soon in attendance on his grandfather Nāṣer-al-Dīn Shah. He received a traditional education with emphasis on military arts, painting, calligraphy, and French. His career was typical of the time. After marriage to a daughter of the Grand Vizier, Mīrzā ʿAlī-Aṣḡar Khan Atābak Amīn-al-Solṭān, he was

---

[13] Benjamin, *Persia*, 206-7.

[14] Eʿtemād-al-Salṭana, *Maʾāser*, 1:273; cited by Tavakoli-Targhi, "Dūst-ʿAlī."

[15] Yaḥyā Ẕokā, "Mīrzā Abu'l-Ḥasan Khan Ṣanīʿ-al-Molk Ḡaffārī," *Honar o Mardom*, no. 9-10(1963):27. The project was doubtless completed during Dūst-ʿAlī Khan's tenure as supervisor of the Majmaʿ-al-ṣanāyeʿ; see Eʿtemād-al-Salṭana, *Montaẓam-e nāṣerī*, 3 vols. (repr. Tehran, n. d.), 3:224. I wish to thank Maryam Ekhtiar for this reference. See her study "From Workshop and Bazar to Academy: Art Training and Production in Qajar Iran" in Layla S. Diba, ed., *Royal Persian Paintings: The Qajar Epoch, 1785-1925* (London, 1998).

appointed a general while still in his teens and later treasurer. However, after the fall of Amīn-al-Solṭān in 1907, his career declined. Nevertheless, Dūst-ʿAlī Khan still lived comfortably on a pension from Reżā Shah Pahlavī in his later years.[16] Dūst-ʿAlī Khan authored three monographs, including his own autobiography, the *RAN*, the *Memoirs of Nāṣer-al-Dīn Shah's Private Life,* and numerous articles on the Qajar period. He died in 1966.[17]

Description and Content of the Document

This essay first appeared in two parts in *Yaḡmā*.[18] It was illustrated with three nineteenth-century photographs of the artists and patrons mentioned in the text: Mīrzā Mostašār with attendants; a group portrait including Esmāʿīl Jalāyer and Mīrzā Mūsā with Dūst-ʿAlī Khan II; and another group portrait with Dūst-ʿAlī Khan II and his son Dūst-Moḥammad. In the 1982 publication, the article is unillustrated, although one of the paintings described therein, a watercolor portrait of Dūst-ʿAlī Khan by the painter Mīrzā Bābā Eṣfahānī Emāmī, is used to illustrate the essay on the author's grandfather.[19]

Dūst-ʿAlī Khan presents short notices of sixteen of the court painters of the late nineteenth and early twentieth centuries. The contents are organized in chronological fashion and in accordance with the prominence of the personalities. Most entries are relatively short, running only a few lines, with the longest descriptions of a page to a page and a half being accorded to the painters Abu'l-Ḥasan Ḡaffārī, Mīrzā Moḥammad Khan Ḡaffār, Kemāl-al-Molk, Āqā Mīrzā Esmāʿīl Jalāyer, and Mīrzā Mahdī Moṣawwer-al-Molk. The entries include biographical details and discussions of the artists' works, techniques, subject matter, location of paintings, and patrons.

The information is organized informally with no attempt at consistency and is anecdotal and affectionate in tone. One keenly feels the author's personal interest in the subject since, like most members of the ruling class, Dūst-Moḥammad had received some training as a painter himself. The sources for the information are undoubtedly the author's personal acquaintance with a number of the painters and recollections and documents of the family. For instance, the painter Mīrzā Mūsā is recorded as having died in the author's home in 1319/1940.[20]

---

[16] The above account is distilled from Streicher, *Die Männer*, 34-41.

[17] See Streicher, *Die Männer*, 41 and Tavakoli-Targhi, "Dūst-ʿAlī."

[18] *Yaḡmā* 10(1336 Š./1957):158-75; 216-17.

[19] *RAN*, 37.

[20] *RAN*, 278.

Even more interesting is the entry on Kemāl-al-Molk, which records the author's visit to the artist's studio in Paris in 1900 and the paintings that Kemāl-al-Molk was working on at the time. In this touching passage, Dūst-ᶜAlī Khan refers to his "intoxication" with the paintings in the Louvre and their shared love for the art of painting. More tellingly, the author discusses seeing two portraits of a beautiful young Persian woman, daughter of a diplomat, of whom the painter was enamored. The terms he uses to describe these portraits reveal much more about the Qajar aesthetic: For Dūst-ᶜAlī Khan, the painter's love has transformed these paintings from mere canvases to love objects with which all viewers fell in love. This poetic metaphor is carried to its ultimate conclusion when Dūst-ᶜAlī Khan asserts that the painting was so life-like that he thought it would join in the conversation.[21]

As a whole, the tone is quite objective and factual. The author's terminology and criteria are informed, detailed and aesthetically sophisticated. While he seeks to enliven the narrative with amusing anecdotes, he refrains, on the whole, from value judgments, although his admiration for Kemāl-al-Molk and Ṣanīᶜ-al-Molk is readily apparent.

Significance: Value as a Historical Document

Painters' biographies are rarely referred to in other biographical sources of the Qajar period. Of those that do, Mahdī Bamdād records only seven of the most celebrated court painters. Scattered references are found in memoirs, such as those of Qāsem Ḡanī, in the biographical section on Kemāl-al-Molk, or in court chronicles, such as Eᶜtemād-al-Salṭana's *al-Maʾāṯer va'l-āṯār* which contains a short section on painting and photography.[22]

The court newspapers, the *Rūz-nāma dawlat-e ᶜalīya-ye Īrān* and *Šarāfat*, include biographical information on court painters associated with the Dār al-Fonūn, such as the appointment of Ṣanīᶜ-al-Molk to the office of editor of the court newspaper in 1861.[23]

While this document remains the most substantial evidence for the artistic life of the period yet known, it is far from comprehensive. It

---

[21] *RAN*, 277.

[22] Bamdād, *Rejāl*, s. v. Abu'l-Ḥasan Ḡaffārī Ṣanīᶜ-al-Molk; Moḥammad Ḡaffārī Kemāl-al-Molk; Āqā Mīrzā Esmāᶜīl Jalāyer and Moṣawwer-al-Molk; Mīrzā ᶜAbd-al-Ḵān Mozayyen-al-Dawla; Mīrzā ᶜAbd-al-Moṭṭaleb Mostašār; Loṭf-ᶜAlī Ṣūratgār; Maḥmūd Khan Malek-al-Šoᶜarā. See also Qāsem Ḡanī, *Yād-dāšthā,* 8 vols. (London, 1981), 5:38-162; Eᶜtemād-al-Salṭana, *Maʾāṯer*, 1:123.

[23] See *Rūz-nāma dawlat-e ᶜalīya-ye Īrān* (Tehran, 1992), 309-12 (no. 472).

lacks, for instance, any mention of enamel painters who were both numerous and extremely talented.[24] Lacquer painters, whether of the late Moḥammad Shah period who worked for the court, such as Moḥammad Esmāʿīl and Āqā Najaf and his studio, or even later lacquer painters of the author's own time, are given short shrift.[25] Curiously, a seminal figure of late nineteenth-century court painting, Maḥmūd Khan Malek-al-Šoʿarā is omitted altogether, while other painters much less well known to history, such as Ostād Bahrām or Mobārak Mīrzā, are recorded. The entry of Ostād Bahrām, while referring to the wall paintings he executed for the palaces of Nāṣer-al-Dīn Shah, omits to record the paintings described above, which may undoubtedly be assigned to him, commissioned for the reception room of the Bāḡ-e Ferdows.[26]

Factual errors, such as assigning two sons instead of three to Abu'l-Ḥasan Ṣanīʿ-al-Molk, while rare, do occur.[27] Nevertheless, it is possible to provide confirmation for much of the author's information from other sources of the period and extant works. For instance, his account that a penbox by Moḥammad-Ḥasan Afšār Orūmīya, whom he refers to only by his sobriquet of Qalamdān-e Lāl, decorated with a crowded scene of a battle of Sālār in Khorasan, was purchased by a European for 1,500 tomans is confirmed by the description of the same work given by the French traveler Hommaire de Hell,[28] and can be compared with the extant work itself.

In other cases, the author's attributions are supported by extant works: the portrait of Dūst-ʿAlī Khan by Mīrzā Bābā cited above; a calligraphy of Saʿdī's verses by Esmāʿīl Jalāyer; and portraits executed by Mahdī Khan Moṣawwer-al-Molk for the court newspaper *Šarāfat*.[29]

This essay documents the very active presence of court painters in the cultural life of the late nineteenth century. The detailed descriptions of artworks and painter-patronage relationships described are rarely recorded elsewhere. Thus, this essay fills an important lacuna in the historical records of the late Qajar period.

---

[24] Benjamin, *Persia*, 309-12.

[25] Benjamin, *Persia*, 322-31 and Rochechouart, *Souvenirs*, 260 ff.

[26] *RAN*, 279.

[27] *RAN*, 277. For a study of Yaḥyā, the third son, see Layla S. Diba, "The Qajar Court Painter Yahya Ghaffari: His Life and Times," in *Studies in Honor of Basil W. Robinson, Pembroke Papers*, forthcoming.

[28] Xavier Hommaire de Hell, *Voyage en Turquie et en Perse*, 4 vols. in 2 (Paris, 1854-60), 2:18 and Sotheby's *Catalogue of Islamic Works of Art Sale* (London, 9 October 1978), lot. No. 187 (illustrated in color).

[29] For Jalāyer, see S. J. Falk, ed., *Treasures of Islam* (Geneva, 1985), 190.

Value as a Document for the History of Art

The essay's significance has already been recognized by Klaus Streicher[30] and is evidenced by its inclusion in the publications of contemporary Iranian writers.[31] In assessing its importance, four points are of particular interest.

In the first place, documentation is given for paintings long since lost by leading court painters of the day, particularly Abu'l-Ḥasan Ṣanīʿ-al-Molk, and for the genesis and execution of the most important commission he was awarded, the illustration of the manuscripts of the translation of the *Thousand and One Nights*.

Secondly, the role of court patrons other than Nāṣer-al-Dīn Shah himself and the commissions executed for them are recorded, often with humorous anecdotes designed to reveal the painters' quick wit and the patrons' generosity. We may cite the case of the unfinished penbox commissioned by ʿAlīqolī Mīrzā ʿEteżād-al-Salṭana, the Minister of Education, from Šāzda Mobārak Mīrzā. ʿEteżād-al-Salṭana had ordered the penbox to be painted with battle scenes on three sides. When it was delivered, after a lengthy delay and numerous advances, it featured only landscapes. When called to account by ʿEteżād-al-Salṭana, the witty painter explained that he had not skimped on his duty since the principal action had taken place *behind* the mountainous landscape depicted![32]

Numerous specific references are given to a variety of architectural monuments, including palatial residences such as the Pārk-e Atābak and the residence of Moḵber-al-Salṭana, and most particularly the tombs of Mostawfī-al-Mamālek, Nāṣer-al-Dīn Shah, and Ḥosaynqolī Khan Baḵtīārī Sardar Asʿad and the paintings commissioned to decorate them. These references shed new light on the history of mural painting, both secular and religious, in the Qajar period. Taken together, they provide documentation for the prevalence of life-size painting for commemorative purposes in mausolea and shrines, and for the significant role of sub-royal patronage in this tradition.

Thirdly, the significance of this essay for the history of the literary genre of treatises on calligraphers and painters should not be underestimated.[33] The essay provides the first such account identified

---

[30] Streicher, *Die Männer*, 62.

[31] Karīmzāda, *Aḥwāl*, 438.

[32] *RAN*, 278.

[33] See Wheeler Thackston, *A Century of Princes: Sources on Timurid History and Art* (Cambridge, Mass., 1989) and Layla S. Diba, "Lacquerwork of Safavid Persia and Its Relationship to Persian Painting" (Ph.D. diss., New York University, 1994), 114-17.

since the heyday of this genre in the late Timurid and Safavid periods. Dūst-ʿAlī Khan's numerous references to artists' materials, fees, and mechanisms of production and the sophisticated vocabulary employed for the variety of painting techniques, constitute a valuable source for contemporary artistic production and criteria and will undoubtedly contribute to the comparative study of Persian painting of earlier periods as well.

Finally, the importance of this document for the history of taste needs to be recognized. Dūst-ʿAlī's text provides a welcome and original voice for our appreciation of the artistic achievements of this period, a crucial counterbalance to the often condescending and colonialist attitudes of European travelers of the time who have been up until only recently the principal sources for Western art historical scholarship. He affords a salutary correction to the disdainful views of a Rochechouart, who dismisses contemporary painters as mere decorators of apartments and penbox painters, only a dim reflection of their past glory as manuscript illustrators.[34]

---

[34] Rochechouart, *Souvenirs*, 264-66.

Harmony or Cacophony: Music Instruction at the Dār al-Fonūn

Maryam Ekhtiar

The establishment in 1856 of the department of military music at the Dār al-Fonūn, Iran's first European-style institution of higher learning, marks a new era in the history of Iranian martial music. This development was part of a comprehensive program of military and educational reform and was considered an integral component of an intensive course of military training. Military music in the European mode was, however, perceived in some circles as an alternative and a challenge to the music of the royal *naqqāra-ḵāna* (house of the kettledrum). For much of the nineteenth century the two forms of martial music coexisted, presenting an intriguing dynamic.

Military music or *mūzīqī-ye razmī* in Iran has a long history which predates the modern era. The loud echo of kettledrums and horns was considered by the ancient kings of Persia as a signal for maneuver, action, and alertness, symbolizing military solidarity, dynastic courage and victory. According to the ancient Greek historian Xenophon, the Achaemenid ruler Cyrus the Great ordered horns blown at sunrise, alerting soldiers to rise and stand guard,[1] and relied on his military musicians to heighten the spirit of his troops and instill fear in the enemy.

Military music had other functions as well, many of which carried over into the Islamic period. It was used to mark the passage of time. Horns and drums were sounded at specific times of the day and used in much the same way as the chiming of church bells or a clock. The

---

[1] Xenophon, *Cyropaedia,* tr. W. Miller (Cambridge, Mass., 1919, repr. 1989), 2:65, 215, 217; Rūḥ-Allāh Ḵāleqī, *Mūzīqī-e Īrānī* (Tehran, 1985), 7. For a more extensive discussion of the history of the *naqqāra-ḵāna*, see Yaḥyā Ẕokāʾ, "Āʾīn-e naqqāra-kūbī dar Īrān va pīsīna-ye ān," *Honar o mardom* no. 180(1976):29-50.

Figure 1. Yaḥyā b. Maḥmūd Vāṣeṭī, illustration of horsemen and camel drivers in a pilgrimage (*ḥajj*) caravan with horns, rattles, and kettledrums. From the *Maqāmāt* of Ḥarīrī commissioned by the Abbasid caliph al-Mostanṣer in Baghdad (634/1237). Thirty-first *maqāma*. MS Paris, Bibliothèque Nationale, Arabe 5847, folio 94v. By permission of the Bibliothèque Nationale.

Zoroastrians, who sounded drums and horns to signal the hour or *gāh* of prayer, originally practiced this usage of martial music. In the early Islamic period, the caliphs and the local governors and amirs also observed this practice. The band of the Buyid amir ʿAżod-al-Dawla (r. 338-72/949-83) was composed of various instruments such as kettledrums, horns, trumpets, and reed pipes, and it played three times a day at the time of prayer (*nawba*) exclusively at his residence.[2] A

[2] A. K. S. Lambton, "Naḳḳara-k͟hāna," *Encyclopaedia of Islam: New Edition* (Leiden, 1960-), 7:927-30.

painting by Yaḥyā b. Maḥmūd Vāṣeṭī from the 634/1236-37 manuscript of the *Maqāmāt* of Ḥarīrī, commissioned at the time of the caliph al-Mostanṣer in Baghdad (Figure 1), depicts horsemen and camel drivers carrying standards and playing horns, rattles, and kettledrums (*naqqāra*s) in a pilgrim caravan.

Throughout the early Islamic period and until well into the nineteenth century in Iran, the music of the *naqqāra-ḵāna* performed numerous ceremonial and military functions. It signaled troops with mutually understood sounds and rhythms, accompanied court ceremonials and weddings, led troops into battle, served as an essential emblem of sovereignty, celebrated victory (*naqqāra-ye šādmānī*), announced the accession of the ruler or his entrance or departure from the capital, announced the time of prayer, and marked sunrise and sunset during the holy month of Ramażān.

Aside from the introduction of a few new instruments, the practices of the *naqqāra-ḵāna* remained relatively unchanged throughout the centuries. The instruments included the *naqqāra* (kettledrums); *ṭabl, tabīra, dohol, tanbūr, kaws, sargīn* and *sanj* (larger drums and cymbals); *nāy, sornāy, kārnāy*, (wind instruments similar to hautboys, horns, and reed pipes); *nafīr, šaḵ, šāypūr* (horns, trumpets); *būq-e halazūnī* (shell horns); and *zang* (small bells with wide rims which were attached to the fingers). Sketches by ʿAlī-Akbar Mozayyen-al-Dawla, the instructor of painting and French interpreter at the Dār al-Fonūn, illustrate these traditional *naqqāra-ḵāna* percussion and wind instruments (Figures 2 and 3).[3] The poetry of Ferdowsī and Neẓāmī, as well as accounts by European travelers to Iran, historical narratives, and memoirs from the tenth to the early twentieth century[4] are replete

---

[3] However, Ḥosayn-ʿAlī Mallāḥ (see below, n. 18) believes that these sketches are not by Mozayyen-al-Dawla but by Victor Advielle himself.

[4] Abu'l-Qāsem Ferdowsī, *Šāh-nāma*, ed. Julius Mohl, 7 vols. in 4 (repr. Tehran, 1991), 1:95, 100, 203, 208, 2:289, 291, 300, 302, 349, 372, 578, 589-90, 603, 607, 615-16, 3:961, 990, 993, 998-99, 1015, 1028, 1040, 4:1773-75, 1882, 1885, 1890, 1925, 1981, 1896; Neẓāmī Ganjavī, *Ḵamsa: Šarāf-nāma,* ed. Behrūz Sarvatīān (Tehran, 1994), 130, 135, 142, 150, 215, 225, 336, 455, Abu'l-Fażl Bayhaqī, *Tārīḵ-e masʿūdī maʿrūf ba tārīḵ-e Bayhaqī,* ed. Saʿīd Nafīsī, 3 vols. (Tehran, 1980), 1:7, 566-67, 2:698; Eskandar Beg Torkamān Monšī, *Tārīk-e ʿālamāra-ye ʿabbāsī*, ed. Īraj Afšār (Tehran, 1956), 370. Moḥammad-Hāšem Mūsawī Āṣaf, *Rostam al-tawārīḵ*, ed. Moḥammad Mošīrī (Tehran, 1978), 95; ʿAbd-Allāh Mostawfī, *Šarḥ-e ḥāl-e zendagānī-e man,* 3 vols. (2nd ed., Tehran, 1964), 1:420-21; Dūst-ʿAlī Khan Moʿayyer-al-Mamālek, *Yad-dašthā-ī az zendagānī-e ḵoṣūsī-e Nāṣer-al-Dīn Šāh* (Tehran, 1982), 60, 61, 66; J. Chardin,

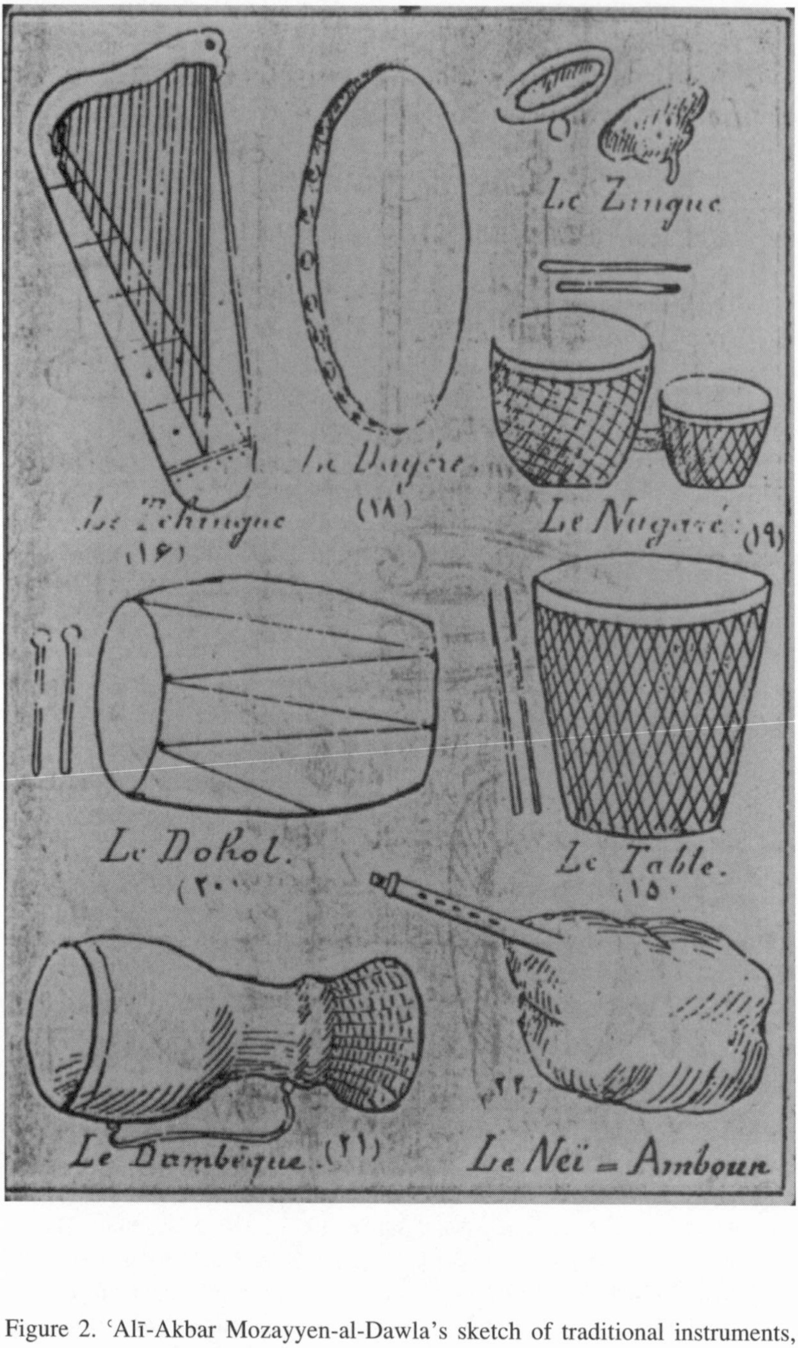

Figure 2. ʿAlī-Akbar Mozayyen-al-Dawla's sketch of traditional instruments, mostly percussion, used by the *naqqāračī*s.

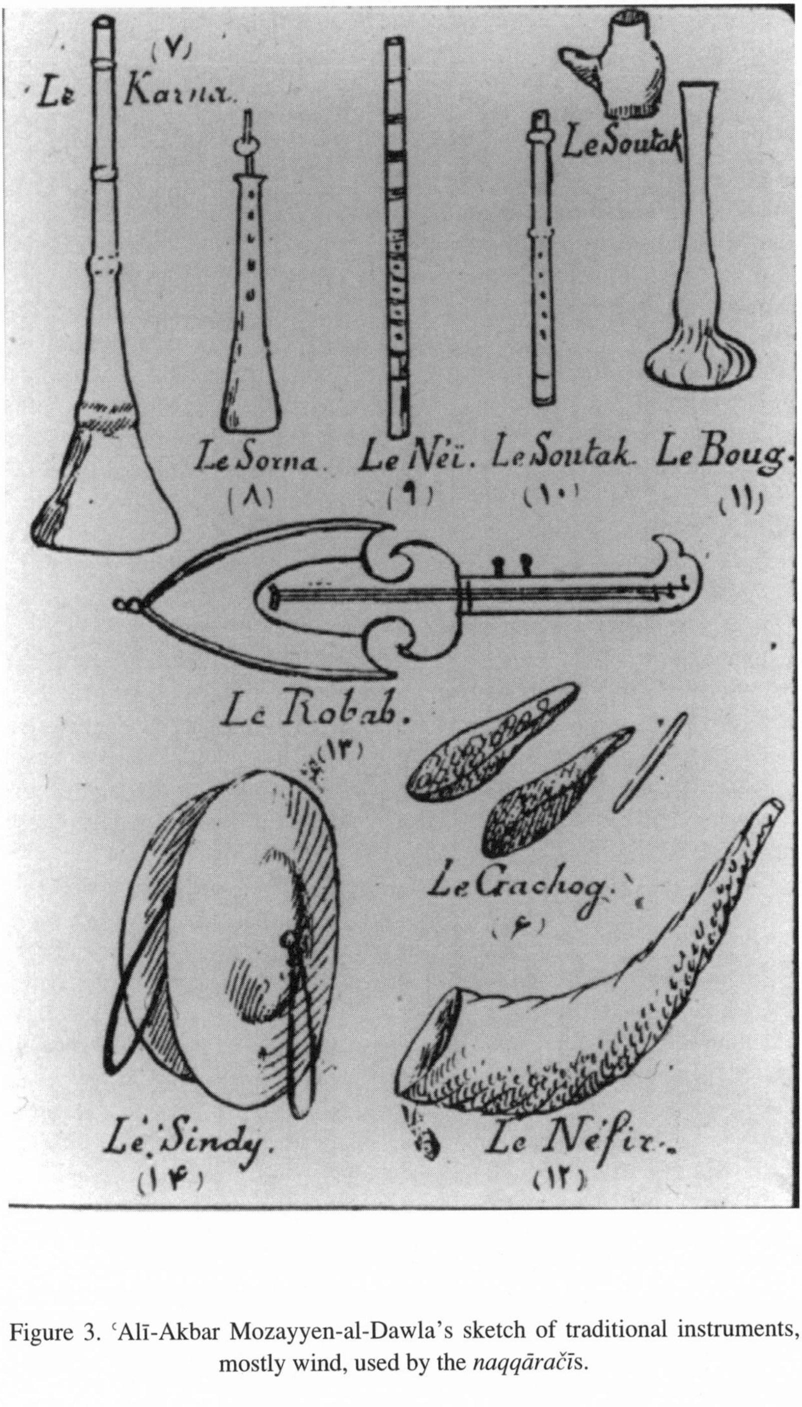

Figure 3. ʿAlī-Akbar Mozayyen-al-Dawla's sketch of traditional instruments, mostly wind, used by the *naqqāračīs*.

with references to the activities of the *naqqāra-ḵāna* and its instruments in descriptions of war, battle, and court ceremonials.

In Europe, horns and trumpets were the only instruments of martial music until the time of the Crusades. Henry Farmer, an authority on European military music, maintains that European military music did not assume any definite shape before then. According to Farmer, "'the military band' as we know it was undoubtedly copied from the Saracens .... One thing that especially took the Crusaders' fancy was the Saracen side drums and kettledrums, which were unknown in Europe at the time."[5] The Janissaries, the powerful soldiers of the Ottoman Empire, also exercised a prominent influence on the construction of the military bands of Europe in the eighteenth century.[6] Thus, the introduction of European music in the Islamic world was not a simple linear process; elements of military music of the Islamic world had been assimilated into European martial music well before the nineteenth century.

In Isfahan under the Safavids and often during the eighteenth and nineteenth centuries, the site of the *naqqāra-ḵāna* was an elevated place over the entrance of royal residences or over the city gates. According to the French jeweler, Jean Chardin, during the coronation of Shah Ṣafī II in 1668, the *naqqāra* was played from two balconies above the Qaysarīya in Isfahan (the bazaar entrance) and sounded "more like the noise of war than music, lasting twenty days and nights without interruption."[7] Chardin believed that the *naqqāra-ḵāna* was essentially an urban phenomenon whose presence was a distinguishing feature of a major city. He added that the *naqqāračī*s played at sunset and sunrise with horns and drums that were three times the size of European drums[8] and stated that the music of the *naqqāra-ḵāna* was frequently sounded at the shah's audiences with foreign ambassadors.[9] Jean-Baptiste Tavernier, who visited Persia several

---

Le courennement de Soleïmaan troisième, roy de Perse (repr. Tehran, 1976), 146-47; Père Raphael du Mans, *Estat de la Perse en 1660* (Paris, 1890), 23, 113, 151; Engelbert Kaempfer, *Am Hofe des persischen Grosskönigs, 1684-1685*, tr. Walther Hinz (Tübingen and Basel, 1977), 157; Gaspard Drouville, *Voyage en Perse pendant les années 1812 et 1813* (Paris, 1819), 47-48; Moritz von Kotzebue, *Narrative of a Journey into Persia in the Suite of the Imperial Russian Embassy in the Year 1817* (Philadelphia, 1820), 148-49.

5 Henry George Farmer, *The Rise and Development of Military Music* (New York, 1970), 12-13.

6 Farmer, *Military Music*, 12-13.

7 Chardin, *Couronnement*, 146-47.

8 Chardin, *Couronnement*, 146-47.

9 J. Chardin, *Travels in Persia* (repr. London, 1927), 87.

times between 1632 and 1668, maintained that the sound of these musicians echoed throughout the city; they played at midnight, sunrise, and sunset for a quarter of an hour in all towns where the ruler resided and those which had khans as governors. Although the observations of these European travelers provide valuable insight into the practices of the *naqqāra-ḵāna*, in many cases their remarks are tainted with a disturbing arrogance; many have little to say except that the sounds of the *naqqāra-ḵāna* were an annoying intrusion to a good night's sleep.

During the Safavid period the *naqqāra-ḵāna* was part of the shah's royal household (*boyūtāt-e salṭanatī*) and functioned under the auspices of the *mašʿal-ḵāna* (the royal lighting department).[10] Other low status occupations such as the dancers, singers, owners of gambling houses and wine shops, pigeon-trainers, and keepers of brothels were also under the control of the department of the *mašʿaldārbāšī* (chief torchbearer).[11] The inclusion of the *naqqāračī*s with such occupations is a reflection of the low esteem with which musicians of this period were regarded. Although somewhat marginalized, the practices and functions of the *naqqāra-ḵāna* under the Safavids continued into the eighteenth and nineteenth centuries.

During the early nineteenth century, the services of the *naqqāra-ḵāna* were used in battle, as well as in ceremonials and to signal the call for prayer. Gaspard Drouville, who visited Iran in 1812-13, recalls that the *naqqāračī*s were a distinguishing feature of every city that had a *beglerbegī* (governor); situated in front of the bazaar gate, they signaled the opening and closing hour of the shops, as well as the call for prayer.[12] In a painting in the State Hermitage Museum collection depicting a "Military Review with Fatḥ-ʿAlī Shah and ʿAbbās Mīrzā" (dated ca. 1815-16), the *naqqāračī*s accompany Fatḥ-ʿAlī Shah, ʿAbbās Mīrzā, and their troops, on foot or mounted on camels (Figure 4). Crown Prince ʿAbbās Mīrzā is shown kneeling in reverence before his father, Fatḥ-ʿAlī Shah. The ceremonial procession before the battle includes princes on horseback, *naqqāračī*s mounted on camels, young footmen (*šāṭer*s), and rows of soldiers clad in European military uniform. The *naqqāračī*s and the European-style musicians coexist, all playing their distinct roles, one group representing the established order and continuity, and the other representing a desire to modernize and measure up to the Russians and Western Europeans (Figure 4 detail).

---

[10] *Tazkerat al-Molūk*, facs. ed. and tr. V. Minorsky as *Tadhkirat al-mulūk: A Manual of Ṣafavid Administration* (London, 1943), 51a-51b.

[11] Du Mans, *Estat de la Perse*, 24; Kaempfer, *Am Hofe*, 87.

[12] Drouville, *Voyage en Perse*, 47-48.

During his tenure as the governor of Azarbaijan, ʿAbbās Mīrzā was one of the first proponents of Western-style military music in Iran.[13] Apart from the arrival of a piano and a few other European instruments as gifts from European rulers,[14] his attempts at setting up a military band in the European mode were only preliminary. Judging from the paintings and visual representations of ʿAbbās Mīrzā's army, a small group of European-style military musicians in military attire were frequently included (Figure 5). In another painting from the State Hermitage collection the European-style musicians are depicted playing flutes and drums in the center of the painting (Figure 5 detail).

During the reign of Moḥammad Shah (1834-48) the *naqqāračīs*, as well as the European-style military band, both figure prominently as accoutrements of battle and ceremony. A watercolor by the French colonel and artist F. Colombari, who served in Iran during the reign of Moḥammad Shah, depicts the *naqqāračīs* mounted on camels playing horns and rattles (Figure 6), while a drawing of the same period by the Russian prince Alexei Saltykov (Alexis Soltykoff) portrays a European-style uniformed military band greeting the Russian general as he enters the palace gates (Figure 7). Baron Feodor Korf, a Russian official who worked in the Russian mission in Iran in 1834-35, describes the *naqqāračīs* lining the side of the road to the battlefield playing long slender horns (probably the *kārnāy*) and refers to the sounds of both the European-style military band as well as the *naqqāra-ḵāna* ensemble as a "disorderly deafening racket."[15] The most faithful adaptations of European-style military bands in Iran, however, did not occur until the second half of the nineteenth century after the establishment of the Dār al-Fonūn.

A full military curriculum modeled on that of the French École Polytechnique required a program of study in music and a well-trained military band. The establishment of a European-style music department at the Dār al-Fonūn and the introduction of a systematic program of military music instruction were the first real attempts at introducing European-style military music in Iran, presenting a challenge to the centrality of the *naqqāra-ḵāna* and the court's reliance on its services.

---

[13] Kotzebue, *Narrative*, 148-49.

[14] An inscription on the first piano to arrive in Iran reveals that it was a gift from Napoleon to Fatḥ-ʿAlī Shah Qājār in 1806.

[15] Feodor Korf, *Vospominaniia o Persii*, tr. Eskandar Zabīhīān as *Safar-nāma-ye Baron Fīodor Korf, 1834-35* (Tehran, 1993), 164-92.

Figure 4. Painting and detail of "Military Review with Fatḥ-ʿAlī Shah and ʿAbbās Mīrzā," by an unknown artist, Iran, circa 1815-16. Oil on canvas, State Hermitage Museum, Saint Petersburg, VR-1121.

Figure 5. Painting and detail of "Battle of Prince ʿAbbās Mīrzā with Russian Troops," by an unknown artist, Iran, circa 1815-16. Oil on canvas, State Hermitage Museum, Saint Petersburg, VR-1122.

Figure 6. Colonel F. Colombari, watercolor of *zanbūrakčīs* mounted on camels. After Lynne Thornton, *Images de Perse: le voyage du Colonel F. Colombari à la cour du Chah de Perse de 1833 à 1848* (Paris, 1981), 13.

Figure 7. European-style band greeting the Russian general Alexsei Saltykov as he enters the palace gates. Drawing after Alexis Soltykoff, *Voyage en Perse* (Paris, 1851). Courtesy of the Brooklyn Museum of Art Library Collection.

The department of military music at the Dār al-Fonūn was instrumental in standardizing the instruction and performance of military music and introducing a variety of innovations, methodologies and a specialized terminology for the field. Terms such as *mūzīkčī, mūzīkānčī, orchestre, solfège* (scale singing), and *harmonie* became prevalent; European instruments were imported and introduced (the clarinet, trumpet, trombone, oboe, French horn etc.); music was taught and approached for the first time as a modern science (*ʿelm*); and textbooks were written.[16] Furthermore, Iranian music was transcribed for the first time according to a European system of notation,[17] while composition, orchestration, and conducting were taught following European methods and standards by European instructors.

In 1856, two Frenchmen, Messieurs Bousquet and Rouillon, were recruited to train musicians in the "new music" at the Dār al-Fonūn. However, Bousquet left Iran after two years, and Roullion's unstable health did not permit him to make any significant contribution. Since France had always taken the lead in military music in Europe, the Iranian government requested that the French Minister of War in Paris, Marshal Adolphe Neil, recommend a knowledgeable and experienced French music instructor. Alfred Jean-Baptiste Lemaire (1842-1909) was selected for this position. In 1868, Lemaire arrived in Tehran to supervise the military music department at the Dār al-Fonūn and serve as *mūzīkānčībāšī* (chief court musician). Upon his arrival, he found the department in a state of disarray and channeled all his energies to reviving it. Initially, Lemaire found himself in a frustrating situation; the students had had little exposure to music and could hardly read notes. Lemaire's inability to speak Persian exacerbated the situation. Most foreign instructors at the Dār al-Fonūn had personal interpreters; the French-educated Mozayyen-al-Dawla, the school's painting instructor, was assigned as Lemaire's interpreter. With great perseverance, Lemaire overcame obstacles and was able to train a band of considerable quality. By 1885, there were about eighteen organized military bands, all trained by Lemaire and his students.

In 1885, Victor Advielle, a French officer who came to Iran with Lemaire to teach military music, wrote a treatise entitled *La Musique*

---

[16] Moḥammad-Ḥasan Khan Eʿtemād-al-Salṭana, *al-Maʾāṯer vaʾl-āṯār*, ed. Īraj Afšār as *Čehel sāl-e tārīḵ-i Īrān,* 3 vols. (Tehran, 1984), 1:150.

[17] Iranian attempts at making notations of their music have been discussed in Forṣat-al-Dawla Šīrāzī's treatise on music and poetry written in 1904, ed. Moḥammad-Qāsem Ṣāleḥ Rāmsarī as *Boḥūr al-alḥān: dar ʿelm-e mūzīqī wa nesbat-e ān bā ʿarūż* (Tehran, 1988).

Figure 8. Alfred Jean-Baptiste Lemaire and ʿAlī-Akbar Mozayyen-al-Dawla surrounded by their students at the Dār al-Fonūn.

chez les Persans en 1885, which documents the details of Lemaire's curriculum at the Dār al-Fonūn.[18] This document contains the most comprehensive curriculum of instruction in any field of study at the school now extant.

Every year Lemaire was assigned a new group of roughly ten students. Thus, in the seventeen years Lemaire taught in Iran, he must have trained approximately two hundred students. When his students reached an acceptable level of proficiency, he allowed them to assist him as *ḵolafā-ye darsī* (teaching assistants) in teaching the elementary students. The use of teaching assistants was a common practice at the Dār al-Fonūn; it gave students a chance to consolidate their knowledge and relieved the instructor of his heavy teaching load. For example, students with three years of experience taught preliminary courses, while those with six years behind them were able to give lessons in a variety of wind instruments. Lemaire was also able to secure an appropriate outdoor space at the Dār

---

[18] Victor Advielle, *La Musique chez les Persans en 1885* (Paris, 1885), tr. Hosayṇ-ʿAlī Mallāḥ in "Mūzīqī nazd-e Īrānīān dar 1885 mīladī," *Honar o mardom* no. 147 (1975):20-27; no. 148 (1975):40-51. Copies of the original book may be found at the Scheide Music Library at Princeton Library and the Seeley Mudd Library at the Yale University.

al-Fonūn where the students could practice daily drills on a regular basis without disturbing their colleagues. A photograph shows Lemaire alongside his interpreter ʿAlī-Akbar Mozayyen-al-Dawla, surrounded by a group of his students (Figure 8).

As part of their eight-year program of training, students studied piano, wind instruments, scale-singing (*solfège*), harmony, orchestration, music theory, conducting, and composing. Since no suitable textbook was available, particularly in Persian, Lemaire and Mozayyen-al-Dawla collaborated on translating into Persian a text on music theory entitled *Taʿrīf-e ʿelm-e mūzīqī* (Theories in the Science of Music), which was originally written by Monsieur Kuhn of the Paris Academy of Music. Lemaire and Mozayyen-al-Dawla also translated a number of other books on music into Persian, all of which were printed by the Dār al-Fonūn Press in the 1880s and used in the classroom. According to Advielle, the program of study was as follows:

> Year 1—*solfège*, music theory, training in one wind instrument, Persian, and mathematics.
> Year 2—*solfège*, music theory, use of one wind instrument, Persian, and mathematics.
> Year 3—*solfège*, music theory, and history.
> Year 4—instruments, orchestration, harmony, French, and geography.
> Year 5—training in a second wind instrument, military music drills, and French language (at the end of the fifth year students would obtain a certificate in military band music).
> Year 6—harmony, piano, orchestration, math, and French.
> Year 7—harmony, piano, and French.
> Year 8—harmony, orchestration, piano, composition, conducting.

A close examination of the curriculum reveals Lemaire's belief in a well-rounded education, rather than one solely limited to military music instruction. For example, students also had the opportunity to study subjects such as Persian literature, mathematics, history, geography, and French. In this way, Lemaire academized and institutionalized European military music at the Dār al-Fonūn, placing it in the context of a larger educational institution.

The court's patronage was a determining factor in the development of the military music curriculum at the Dār al-Fonūn, which gradually came to include European classical music. In fact, on his 1873 trip to Europe, Nāṣer-al-Dīn Shah brought back a few pianos for the court, but since hardly anybody in Tehran knew how to play or tune them, Moḥammad Ṣādeq Khan, known as Sorūr-al-Molk, the famous *santūr* musician and an eminent member of the shah's military band, took advantage of this opportunity to learn how to play and was even able to tune the piano according to a system of quarter-tones that would suit the various modes of Persian music.[19] He was ordered by the shah to teach the women of the harem how to play the piano. Soon, a number were able to give private concerts for Nāṣer-al-Dīn Shah, for which he often rewarded them with jewels and gold coins.[20]

Although Nāṣer-al-Dīn Shah preferred traditional Persian music as entertainment, his fascination with novelty and his fascination with all things European prompted him to encourage the progress of Western-style music in Iran. In social gatherings, when Western music of his taste was performed, he never failed to reward the musicians. In 1871, a concert was organized for the European residents in the city by the Dār al-Fonūn's Director and Minister of Education, Mok̲ber-al-Dawla. This was considered an occasion for social interaction and a diversion from the pressures of the long winter nights. The proceeds of this concert were sent to help victims of the most recent drought.[21] Aside from the European residents, many court officials and members of the nobility attended.[22] In March 1882, Lemaire was also involved in organizing a second concert in which a few of his students performed as soloists. The program consisted predominantly of instrumental compositions adapted from European opera, such as *Rigoletto* and *La Traviata* by Verdi, *La Sonnambula* and *Norma* by Bellini, and *Lucia de Lammemoor* by Donizetti, with a few pseudo-Persian pieces thrown in.[23]

Lemaire also composed a number of pieces for the court, among them an Iranian national anthem and a coronation march; a copy of the score of the anthem is presently in the music collection of the New York Public Library.[24] In 1883, the government granted Lemaire the necessary resources to travel to Paris to purchase additional musical instruments and equipment for the school. This gesture was made by the minister of education, ʿAlīqolī Mīrzā

---

[19] Dūst-ʿAlī Khan Moʿayyer-al-Mamālek, *Rejāl-e ʿaṣr-e nāṣerī* (Tehran, 1361 Š./1982), 286; see also Sāsān Sepāntā, *Čašmandāz-e mūzīqī-e Īrān* (Tehran, 1990), 82.

[20] Moʿayyer-al-Mamālek, *Yād-dašthā-ī*, 21.

[21] *Īrān*, 11 Ẕu'l-Qaʿda 1288/26 January 1872.

[22] Fereydūn Ādamīyat, *Andīša-ye taraqqī wa ḥokūmat-e qānūn-ē ʿaṣr-e Sepahsalār* (Tehran, 1351 Š./1973), 452.

[23] Mallāḥ, "Mūzīqī," 40.

[24] MS New York, New York Public Library, Otto Kinkeldey Memorial Collection, music sheet 85-576.

Figure 9. Under glaze painted tile copied from a photograph of Nāṣer-al-Dīn Shah's European-style military band. From a frieze in the Golestān Palace installed in 1887.

Mok̲ber-al-Dawla, who personally oversaw the progress of the music students at the Dār al-Fonūn at this time and was present during their periodic examinations. The involvement of Mok̲ber-al-Dawla illustrates that music, like painting, was perceived as a science and an academic discipline and thus placed under the jurisdiction of the Ministry of Higher Education.

The *naqqāračī*s and the members of the "new" royal military band, however, continued to function side-by-side during this period. Both performed before the shah when summoned to court. A polychrome tile panel from the Golestān Palace depicts the shah's European-style military band performing on a palace porch, outfitted in European military uniform, playing European instruments (Figure 9). Occasionally Lemaire's students had the privilege of giving private concerts for the shah.[25] Another tile from the Golestān Palace shows Nāṣer-al-Dīn Shah attending a private piano concert (Figure 10). In fact, according to one source, on his yearly visits to the Dār al-Fonūn, the shah paid closer attention to

[25] The *Ketābča-ye madrasa-ye Dār al-fonūn*, 28 Ẕu'l-Ḥejja 1302/8 October 1885, records that the students of music went to the palace on Saturday evening and performed for the shah until Sunday morning.

Figure 10. Under-glaze painted tile copied from a photograph of Nāṣer-al-Dīn Shah listening to a piano recital. From a frieze in the Golestān Palace installed in 1887.

the activities of the music classes than to any of the other classes at the school.[26] The school's military band was also called upon to open and close *taʿzīa* (Shiʿite passion play) performances. According to the school's logbook, in 1884, the music students performed on the occasion of ʿĀšūrā; they participated in passion plays and mourned the tragedy of Imam Ḥosayn's martyrdom. The logbook records that during ʿĀšūrā, all the music students would be present every day at the school, and after practicing in the school courtyard and eating lunch, they would go to the *takya* (site for a

---

[26] Moḥammad-Ḥasan Khan Eʿtemād-al-Salṭana, *Rūz-nama-ye k̲aṭerāt-e Eʿtemad-al-Salṭana*, ed. Īraj Afšār (Tehran, 2536=1356 Š./1977), 304.

taʿzīa performance) accompanied by Mozayyen-al-Dawla, where they would be busy until sunset.[27] Dr. Joannès Feuvrier also recalls that at one *taʿzīa* performance a member of the royal band played the French march "Pompiers de Nanterre" as the band marched before the shah.[28] Dūst-ʿAlī Khan Moʿayyer-al-Mamālek describes in detail the procession of the *naqqāračī*s and European musicians led by Mozayyen-al-Dawla prior to the *taʿzīa* performance. He states that the first group of European military musicians carried the silver musical instruments sent to Nāṣer-al-Dīn Shah by Queen Victoria of England. Mounted on horses, the second group were the musicians of the Cossack Brigade led by Ḡolām-Reżā Khan Mīnbāšīān known as Salār Moʿazzez, while the third marched on foot. The ornately decorated camels of the royal *zanbūrak-ḵāna* and *naqqāra-ḵāna* followed with pomp and ceremony.[29]

An important reason for Nāṣer-al-Dīn Shah's support of band music at the Dār al-Fonūn stemmed from his frivolous desire to please his favorite protégé, Ḡolām-ʿAlī ʿAzīz-al-Solṭān, also known as Malījak. The shah ordered that a special music class be set up for Malījak's courtiers, so that they could learn how to perform exclusively for his entertainment. This class was first started in 1882 when Malījak was only five years old.[30] The shah's increased attention to music, painting, and drama at this time was symptomatic of the general state of affairs at the school in the last decades of the nineteenth century. By this time, he had already grown suspicious of the school's activities, thus shifting the emphasis from a hard-core military curriculum to one with a focus on the arts. The reason for this shift may have been that the shah felt more confident patronizing such subjects as music, photography, painting, and drama than military and scientific subjects. He appears to have perceived these subjects as being less prone to the penetration of dissident political activity at the school.

Probably Lemaire's most significant contribution during his long tenure at the Dār al-Fonūn was the introduction of note reading and writing. Before this, Iranians had transcribed their traditional music by writing down the various melodic references and rhythms (*gūša*s) and not through a commonly recognized set of symbols. Persian classical and traditional music was essentially passed on through imitation of a master, memorization, and repetition. Lemaire introduced

[27] *Ketābča-ye madrasa-ye Dār al-fonūn*, 28 Ẕu'l Ḥejja 1302/8 October 1885.

[28] J. Feuvrier, *Trois ans à la cour de Perse* (Paris, 1906), 127-31.

[29] Moʿayyer-al-Mamālek, *Rejāl*, 65-66.

[30] Mahdī Bamdād, *Tārīḵ-e rejāl-e Īrān,* 6 vols. (Tehran, 1968), 6:157.

a systematic method of note-writing and also managed to devise a notation system suitable for Persian music. In addition, he composed and transcribed adaptations of some Persian folkloric dances and songs for piano, the most famous of which is a piece in the *homāyūn* mode (*dastgāh*), entitled *Avaz et Tesnif Persans* which was published in Paris in 1883. In 1899, Lemaire accompanied Moẓaffar-al-Dīn Shah to Paris. In his account of his travels to Europe, Moẓaffar-al-Dīn Shah indicated that he was very impressed with Lemaire and his students' performance and was pleased that they had published scores of their works in Paris, achieving international recognition.[31]

Although it is not clear whether Lemaire's efforts had any significant impact on the traditional music of Iran, what is certain is that his curriculum provided some structure, organization, and a scientific methodology to music instruction and military music instruction in general. At first glance, the study of music at the Dār al-Fonūn seems to have been a passing phase with little long-term impact. A thorough investigation of the program's activities and attempts in promoting Western-style military and classical music in Iran, however, reveals that when judged by international standards, some very talented and successful musicians were trained at the school who were able to continue Lemaire's legacy. His efforts insured that the next *mūzīkānčībāšī* was not just another European, but a well trained Iranian. A tile panel commissioned by Lemaire in 1884 proudly pronounces one of his students, Mīrzā Abu'l-Ḥosayn Khan, as *mūzīkānčībāšī* (Figure 11). In fact, after Lemaire's death in 1909, his student Salār Moʿazzez was nominated chief of the royal orchestra and subsequently chief musician for the Cossack Brigades. The first Iranian to study music in Europe, Sālār Moʿazzez made sure his son did the same. Thereafter, with few exceptions military music was taught and administered by Iranians.

Sālār Moʿazzez revived Lemaire's legacy by establishing a new and independent center for the instruction of European military music in Tehran, which, like the Dār al-Fonūn, was closely affiliated with the Ministry of Higher Education. Thus, the music department at the Dār al-Fonūn can be considered a precursor to Iran's first Conservatory of Music and symphony orchestra, both inaugurated by Lemaire's circle of students and their successors, as well as the Music Department at the University of Tehran, established in 1925 (Figure 12).

---

[31] Moẓaffar-al-Dīn Shah Qājār, *Safarnāma-ye mobāraka-ye šāhanšāhī* (Tehran, 1900), 96. A copy of the score may be found at the National Conservatory of Music in Paris.

Figure 11. Tile panel commissioned by Lemaire in 1884, pronouncing his student Mīrzā Abu'l-Ḥosayn Khan *mūzīkānčībāšī*. 39 x 12 5/8 inches. Christies, Islamic Art and Indian Miniatures, Rugs and Carpets, 23 April 1996, lot 120.

Figure 12. European-style orchestra conducted by Ḡolām-Ḥosayn Mīnbāšīān.

Even though the introduction of European music may have marginalized the activities of the *naqqāra-ḵāna,* it did not replace it. The services of the *naqqāra-ḵāna* were in demand until the third decade of the twentieth century. Writing in 1877, Moḥammad-Ebrāhīm Taḥvīldār included the *ahl-e ṭarab* and the employees of the *naqqāra-ḵāna* among the various classes of the population of Isfahan.[32] An image from Jane Dieulafoy's *La Perse, La Chaldee et la Susiane* depicts the *naqqāračīs* greeting the dawn (Figure 13). George Curzon confirmed that in the 1880s the Tehran *naqqāra-ḵāna* was prominently located in the Meydān-e Šāh, outside the gardens of the Ministry of War and south of the palace enclosure, also the site of the famous Tūp-e Morvārīd (Cannon of Pearls), the symbol of the shah's preoccupation with military modernization[33] (Figure 14). The site and architectural form of the

---

[32] Ḥosayn b. Moḥammad-Ebrāhīm Tahvīldār, *Jogrāfīā-ye Eṣfahān*, ed. Manūčehr Sotūda (Isfahan, 1342 Š./1963), 126.

[33] George N. Curzon, *Persia and the Persian Question,* 2 vols.(London, 1892), 2:308-9.

Figure 13. Drawing of *naqqāračīs* greeting the dawn. After Jane Dieulafoy, *La Perse, La Chaldee et la Susiane* (Paris, 1887), 289.

Figure 14. Tehran *naqqāra-ḵāna* and the "Cannon of Pearls." After George N. Curzon, *Persia and the Persian Question*, 2 vols. (London, 1892), 2:308.

late Qajar *naqqāra-ḵāna* resembled those of the Safavid period and similar to their Safavid counterparts, the *naqqāračī*s in the 1880s played from the elevated balconies of a city gate.

Hence, the position and activities of the *naqqāra-ḵāna* remained unchanged even decades after the establishment of a European military band at the Dār al-Fonūn. According to ʿAbd-Allāh Mostawfī, there was an attempt after the granting of the Constitution to stop the activities of the *naqqāra-ḵāna*s and withhold its members' wages on the grounds that they were obsolete. These attempts proved fruitless; they remained undeterred and continued their daily celebrations without pay, until some months later the payment of their wages was reinstated.[34] When Reżā Shah Pahlavī came to power, he also relied on the *naqqāračī*s to mark his sovereignty at the time of his coronation in 1925, just as Shah Solaymān had done a few centuries earlier.[35] By the 1930s, however, the number of members of the *naqqāra-ḵāna* had dwindled to a band of less than a handful of musicians, and by the 1940s hardly any trace of them could be seen.[36]

Although the music of the *naqqāra-ḵāna* may have sounded cacophonous and even disturbing to European visitors and diplomats, it remained an auspicious emblem of dynastic power and solidarity throughout Iranian history. To the Iranians, it signified harmony and reassurance that the sovereign was strong and in command of his domain and people, and that the rhythms of daily life echoed loud and clear. However, the novelty and appeal of European military music at court eventually interrupted the beat of the ancient *naqqāra-ḵāna*. Today only occasional echoes of its music are heard in some Iranian cities.

---

[34] Mostawfī, *Šarḥ-e zendaganī*, 1:420-21.

[35] Mostawfī, *Šarḥ-e zendaganī*, 1:563-64.

[36] The only surviving and functioning *naqqāra-ḵāna* in Iran today is in Mašhad.

The Social Condition of Women in Qajar Society

Mansureh Ettehadieh (Nezam Mafi)

The history of women in Iran remains a largely unexplored field of research, and much needs to be done before the shape and voices of Qajar women can be distinguished behind the veil of oblivion and anonymity which surround them. As in most patriarchal societies, it has been the deeds of men which have been celebrated as the focal point of history, whereas the struggles and accomplishments of women have been ignored.

While the trips of Nāṣer-al-Dīn Shah to Europe, or the political treaties, or the opening of the Dār al-Fonūn, or the foundation of the Cossack Brigade were significant events, and the establishment of institutions such as the Dār al-Šūrā-ye Dawlat provided a basis for social change and development, is it not also important to ask ourselves what transpired in the households of the men of state responsible for them? If foreign concessions and foreign trade affected the position of the merchant class, threw artisans out of work and into poverty, and put small shopkeepers at the mercy of the brutal upheavals of international trade, should we not wish to know also about their impact on the relationship between the wives of the merchants and their husbands, or what effect male unemployment had on the welfare of the family? How did women who were for the most part illiterate cope with the education of their children? What effect did polygamy and families with numerous offspring have on society? One critic of Qajar society, Majd-al-Molk, wrote that Iran's problem was one of the tormentor and the tormented.[1] Should we not ask what happened to the poor members of society, particularly to poor women who were the weakest among the weak? Was injustice committed against women

[1] Moḥammad Khan Majd-al-Molk, *Resāla-ye majdīya,* ed. Fażl-Allāh Gorgānī as *Bīst sāl baʿd az Amīr Kabīr* (Tehran, 1358 Š./1979), 96.

equal to that against men, or was there a distinction? What differences were there in the case of upper class women and women of the middle and lower classes? In general, how did women perceive themselves in the male dominated Qajar society?

Omm-al-Ḵāqān, sister of ʿAbd-al-Ḥosayn Mīrzā Farmānfarmā (a prince and politician of great renown) and wife to Moẓaffar-al-Dīn Shah,[2] wrote a letter to her brother after the shah's death concerning her financial needs and her position as a woman in which she said:

> May I be your sacrifice. God willing, your dear self is in good health. I hear certain things from people, but I don't believe them, considering your intelligence. Jobs are worth nothing. Of course, you know better than me. I am only a woman. Well, you know the times and the conditions of the monarchy. For three months, Āḡābāšī has not paid me anything from that bankrupt customs [office]. To whomever I turn to borrow money, he only promises something tomorrow. In short, if it is possible, send me one or two hundred tomans. You paid me one hundred in the month of Ṣafar. I wish health for your dear self.

Literacy for women was not really valued. In a letter by Ḥosaynqolī Khan Neẓām-al-Salṭana,[3] a prominent politician of the late Nāṣerī period, to his nephew, Reżāqolī Khan, the author discusses the desirable qualities for women and the question of their literacy in particular:

> Upon my honor, I read the letter you wrote. You would have been amazed at how I laughed when I read your phrases and ideas. You wrote that all the wives in the world are wise and sage and can read and write except in your own unfortunate case, whose wife is illiterate. Wisdom and sagacity are God-given and not acquired. But reading and writing are learned, and it is necessary that I should reply and comment. I have no knowledge or acquaintance with all the women in the world, but in your tribe and family, for a hundred years till today, writing and reading were never the norm [for women]. Examples are easily found, for example the honorable *ḥājjīya*, your venerable aunt, the late

---

[2] The father of Omm-al-Ḵāqān and ʿAbd-al-Ḥosayn Mīrzā Farmānfarmā was Fīrūz Mīrzā, son of ʿAbbās Mīrzā, the crown prince in the time of Fatḥ-ʿAlī Shah.

[3] It should be kept in mind that Ḥosaynqolī Khan Neẓām-al-Salṭana died in 1908, and his title was inherited by his nephew Reżāqolī Khan.

> mother of the wife of Neẓām-al-Salṭana, the wife of the lieutenant-general, or the wife of Saʿd-al-Molk. So why is this destiny and bad luck only your lot and your fate? Since the dawn of time till today, modesty and chastity hasve been the virtues of women, not reading and writing. Good husbandry and domesticity were expected from women, not literacy … for women, writing is unholy, unholy, unholy (*ḥarām*). A little reading ability is not harmful.

Towards the end of the Qajar period, the position of women in society began to be discussed by some women. The first text written by a woman about the condition of life in male-dominated Qajar society was published before the Constitutional Revolution of 1906. The work was by Bībī K̲ānom (or Bībī Fāṭema K̲ānom) and was entitled *Maʿāyeb al-rejāl* (The Defects of Men). It was published in 1313/1896. It was written in reply to a text on correcting the faults of women, *Taʾdīb al-nesvān* (The Disciplining of Women), which was very derogatory to them. As Bībī K̲ānom wrote, "Pity women, who are attacked from all sides. Poets deride them, writers and thinkers lash out at them verbally and call it advice, but they all disparage them. At such a time … appears this book on disciplining women … it is a pain above all other pains."[4] Another text which might be mentioned here is the *K̲āṭerāt* (memoirs) of Tāj-al-Salṭana, the daughter of Nāṣer-al-Dīn Shah, who was a critic of the condition of women.[5] However this was not published in her lifetime.

It should be pointed out that the best and most important sources for the study of how women described their condition and expressed their wishes are to be found in the newspapers published during the Constitutional Revolution, especially in those newspapers published by women themselves.[6] For the first time women noticed that they

---

[4] *Rūyārūʾī -e zan va mard dar ʿaṣr-e Qājār, dō resāla: Taʾdīb al-nesvān va Maʿāyeb al-rejāl*, ed. Ḥasan Javādī, Manīža Marʿašī, and Sīmīn Šekarlū (Bethesda, Md. [Evanston, Il.], 1992).

[5] Tāj-al-Salṭana, *K̲āṭerāt-e Tāj-al-Salṭana*, ed. Manṣūra Etteḥādīya [Neẓām Māfī] (2nd ed., Tehran, 1371 Š./1992).

[6] The women's newspaper *Dāneš* was published by the wife of Dr. Ḥasan Kaḥḥālzāda in 1328/1910. It was a weekly magazine and wrote on women's character, their habits, and their awakening. Another was *Šokūfa*, published by the wife of Mozayyen-al-Salṭana in 1331/1913. The next one was *Zabān-e zanān* published by Ṣadīqa Dawlatābādī in Isfahan in 1337/1918. Other papers were *Nāma-ye banovān*, *ʿĀlam-e nesvān*, *Jahān-e zanān* (this was first published in Mašhad, then in Tehran), *Jahān-e nesvān-e vaṭānk̲ᵛāh,* and the magazines *Soʿādat-e nesvan-e šarq* and *Dok̲tarān-e Īrān*.

belonged to one social class, expressed themselves as women, organized societies, and claimed that they had "awakened." They made speeches. They founded schools for girls. They wrote articles and, little by little, asked the government to consider their problems. The interesting point made by these women was that not until women became educated and literate could they nurture good children for society nor would Iran advance. By thus expressing their patriotism and their enthusiasm and eagerness for liberty, they came gradually to discover their common problems and to express them vocally.

The most difficult problem for the study of the social position of women in the Qajar period is the lack of direct material about women.[7] However there are many sources which mention women indirectly and can be used. The main sources investigated in this article are:

1. *Rūz-nāma-ye ḵāṭerāt-e Eʿtemād-al-Salṭana*, a journal kept by a government official, Moḥammad-Ḥasan Khan Eʿtemād-al-Salṭana, which gives occasional information regarding the lives of upper class and aristocratic women and their treatment in society.[8]

2. The records from 1301-5/1883-87 of the Majles-e Taḥqīq-e Maẓālem (Council for the Investigation of Grievances). These consist of numerous complaints from ordinary people to the Council which were brought directly to the attention of the shah. Complaints by women and problems confronting them were included among these reports.[9]

3. The documents of the Āmār-e Dār al-Ḵelāfa-ye Tehrān (Statistics Bureau of the Capital Tehran), which have been published in three volumes.[10] They provide statistics about the population count and the number of buildings of Tehran during the Nāṣerī and early Moẓaffarī periods, and these include information about the number of women living in the capital as well as giving a count of the buildings in Tehran whose proprietors were women.

4. The archives of the municipality of Tehran (Maḥallāt-e Tehrān) for the years 1303-6/1885-88. These include police reports dealing with events in the capital, and they provide much interesting

[7] Surviving examples of women's correspondence from this period are especially rare. This article has been able to use letters from a private collection which preserves letters from the wife and daughter of Neẓām-al-Salṭana.

[8] Moḥammad-Ḥasan Khan Eʿtemād-al-Salṭana, *Rūznāma-ye ḵāṭerāt*, ed. Īraj Afšār (Tehran, 1345 Š./1966).

[9] These files are preserved at the Central Library of the University of Tehran.

[10] Āmār-e Dār al-Ḵelāfa-ye Tehran, *Asnād-ī az tārīḵ-e ejtemāʿī-e Tehrān dar ʻasr-e Qājār: 1269, 1286, 1317-20 H.Q.*, ed. Sīrūs Saʿdvandīān and Manṣūra Etteḥādīya [Neẓām Mafi] (Tehran, 1368 Š./1989).

information about middle and lower middle class people, including women.[11]

Although the value and consistency of these sources vary, they all cover roughly the same time period and in many cases corroborate the information in each other about the social position of women. Of course, one should not expect the ability to discover everything about all facets of women's lives, family relationships, judicial or social rights, and treatment. These documents by no means give us a complete picture of the position of women, but nonetheless they acquaint us in a general way about certain aspects of gender relations in the traditional and complex society of Iran.

The Memoirs of Eʿtemād-al-Salṭana

In his journal, Eʿtemād-al-Salṭana cast an ironic and reproving view on his contemporaries and the life of his time. His attention was first of all riveted on the king, then on the courtiers, and then on society. Thus he gives very perspicacious and interesting information about all classes of people. Nothing and no one escaped his sharp and vigilant eyes, and sometimes he gleefully derided and criticized what people said or he had heard. For instance, he wrote: "Today Malījak said the wives of the shah want to feed the shah the liver of a bear, so he could not procreate any more children. God only knows."[12]

Eʿtemād-al-Salṭana paid attention to women and, as his first object of interest was the shah, he had the most to say about the ruler's numerous wives as well as upper class women. However, other women and their lives did not escape his interest; he mentions, for example, the case of women who had been taken prisoner by Kurds in Kermānšāh, complaints by women to the shah, their superstitions, the dissipation of inheritances by women who had no husbands, an attack on a woman in the street by drunken soldiers, and other such problems.[13]

Eʿtemād-al-Salṭana was affectionate towards his mother and honored his wife Ašrāf-al-Salṭana even though she was barren. He had a *ṣīğa* (concubine), who bore him a daughter, ʿOẕrā, but he says he did not love her very much.[14] Nonetheless, he expressed considerable grief when ʿOẕrā died of diphtheria. Unlike most distinguished men of his time, it seems he did not have many relationships with women since

---

[11] MSS Tehran, Sazmān-e Asnād-e Mellī-e Īrān, Gozārešāt-e Maḥallāt-e Tehran.

[12] Eʿtemād-al-Salṭana, *Ḵāṭerāt*, 192.

[13] Eʿtemād-al-Salṭana, *Ḵāṭerāt*, 74, 91, 406, 437, 564, 557, 1106.

[14] Eʿtemād-al-Salṭana, *Ḵāṭerāt*, 78, 102.

he wrote: "No woman in this world has loved me."[15] He was aware of the harmfulness of the shah having a large number of wives, and deplored his lustfulness, and gave many details of the quarrels caused by hatred, jealousy, greed, and enmity among the shah's wives and their coteries, which involved some of the courtiers.[16] He pointed out, for instance, the enmity and rivalry between Anīs-al-Dawla and Amīn-e Aqdas, and the cliques each had formed against the other, and explained how this feud continued after Amīn-e Aqdas lost her eyesight, became paralyzed, and died. On another occasion he wrote:

> In actual fact, it was not a question of Anīs-al-Dawla, Oḡūl Beyga [a Turkoman concubine], and Baḡbānbāšī [Amīn-e Aqdas, the daughter of the keeper of the Aqdasīya garden], but of the prime minister [*ṣadr-e aʿẓam*] and Nāyeb-al-Salṭana [the shah's favorite son]. Just as their enmity has disrupted the public life of our sovereign and made it a hell, and puts the monarchy in jeopardy and discomfort, in the same manner the little comfort that our king has in his private life too, has been destroyed by these two people. I heard Anīs-al-Dawla had appointed Amīn-e Ḵāqān to spy on the shah.[17]

Of course, jealousy and spite was not only limited to the wives of the shah, but was rampant between women of other classes. As an example, one could cite the story told by Eʿtemād-al-Dawla about the eighty year-old *farrāš* (guard) of the shah's mother, Mahd-e ʿOlyā, who had taken a new bride, but had beaten her and thrown her out. This woman and another wife had then murdered him. The shah had ordered the woman to be put to death, but as the ulema had not found sufficient proof of her guilt, they had not given permission for her execution.[18]

Weddings were another item of news mentioned by Eʿtemād-al-Salṭana. Most marriages were arranged for financial, political, or family ends. The marriage age was low, and in this respect there was no difference between

---

[15] Eʿtemād-al-Salṭana, *Ḵāṭerāt*, 358.

[16] Jakob Polak, the shah's Austrian doctor and professor of medicine at the Dār al-Fonūn, who lived a number of years in Iran, discusses in his memoirs the issue of polygamy and the jealousies it engendered, which at times could be the psychosomatic cause of illnesses.

[17] Eʿtemād-al-Salṭana, *Ḵāṭerāt*, 13, 207, 233, 908, 1107. It is interesting to note that Nāṣer-al-Dīn Shah had a spy to keep him abreast of the events of the harem. Two of her reports were published by Ḵānbābā Bayānī, in *Panjāh sāl tārīḵ-e Īrān*, 5 vols (Tehran, 1375 Š./1996), 5:431-34.

[18] Eʿtemād-al-Salṭana, *Ḵāṭerāt*, 651.

classes (as is also noticeable in the police reports). For instance, Eʿtemād-al-Salṭana mentioned the wedding of the son of Qavām-al-Dawla, who married the twelve year-old daughter of Ẓahīr-al-Dawla, despite the fact that he already had five or six wives as well as five or six grown children.[19] He also reported the betrothal of the ten year-old Zarīn-Kolāh K̲ānom, daughter of the crown prince, to Morteżā Khan, the son of Mok̲ber-al-Dawla, and adds, "God willing, thanks to this wedding, Mok̲ber-al-Dawla will become minister of sciences when the crown prince becomes shah."[20]

Eʿtemād-al-Salṭana suffered from constant depression and saw evil in everything and everywhere, including the court circles. He thought women's behavior in and out of court was outrageous and deplored it. About the *taʿzīa* (a religious performance) staged by Malījak, he wrote that the mischief and evil was worse than a few years earlier: "They acted out the wedding of the holiest Ṣadīqa Kobrā [Fāṭema, the Prophet's daughter], and had that holy character wearing European-like clothes with a *farangī* hat. Woe to Islam! Woe to Moḥammad! What disrespect, particularly in a Shiʿite nation."[21]

The mother of the Nāyeb-al-Salṭana had also celebrated the birthday of the saintly Fāṭema as every year, and Eʿtemād-al-Salṭana wrote disapprovingly that "it was a very elaborate affair ... with Spanish [Espānyūlī, perhaps a mistake for Istānbūlī] musicians who had come to Tehran recently. They had dressed them up and had seated them on chairs, and the mother of Nāyeb-al-Salṭana had bejewelled herself."[22]

Another of the shah's concubines, Forūg-al-Dawla, "had painted up her face" to go on a pilgrimage (*zīārat*) to ʿAbd-al-ʿAẓīm,[23] and the wife of Amīn-al-Dawla, a courtier and statesman, had invited musicians to celebrate the circumcision of her nephews (the sons of Solṭān-Ebrāhīm Mīrzā). She had seated these crude people in her presence, and they had sung; "it was incredible," he concluded with disgust.[24] On the occasion of a horse race, a curtain had once been put on the roof of the harem so the women could watch the race from behind it, but some of them "were peeking out around it." After Eʿtemād-al-Salṭana noticed them and alerted the shah, the ruler got them back behind the curtain only by means of threats and cursing.[25]

---

[19] Eʿtemād-al-Salṭana, *K̲āṭerāt*, 104, 518. Four of Ẓell-al-Solṭān's daughters were married on the same night to four of Ṣārem-al-Dawla's sons (ibid., 178).

[20] Eʿtemād-al-Salṭana, *K̲āṭerāt*, 259.

[21] Eʿtemād-al-Salṭana, *K̲āṭerāt*, 1082.

[22] Eʿtemād-al-Salṭana, *K̲āṭerāt*, 550.

[23] Eʿtemād-al-Salṭana, *K̲āṭerāt*, 1202.

[24] Eʿtemād-al-Salṭana, *K̲āṭerāt*, 643.

[25] Eʿtemād-al-Salṭana, *K̲āṭerāt*, 995.

Eʿtemād-al-Salṭana also quotes Dr. Feuvrier, the French court physician, as being very upset because Mīrzā Neẓām had entered the harem on the pretext of translating for one of the shah's wives but then sat chatting with them for two hours when the person in question wasn't even sick. "I was very surprised at what Feuvrier had to say," concluded the outraged Eʿtemād-al-Salṭana, "for I remember that thirty years ago not even a child of ten would dare to enter the shah's harem."[26]

From what Eʿtemād-al-Saltana says, it can be surmised that the ordinary and traditional way of life was perhaps already changing amongst a certain class of women. Iran's expanding relationship with the West, the number of European missionary schools, the publication of books, etc. were no doubt bringing about certain changes. Also, there were growing connections with foreigners (as is evident from the police reports and in the memoirs of Eʿtemād-al-Salṭana), a factor which was no doubt instrumental in these changes. Iranian men met and became acquainted with European women in social gatherings, and women also met the foreign wives of Europeans residing in Tehran. It is interesting to note that Bībī Ḵānom, for instance, was well aware of the life style of foreign women.[27]

Perhaps these developments were a sign of the overall changes society was undergoing, rather than the sign of women's perversion and guile or the childish behavior of women, as Eʿtemād-al-Salṭana believed. At the upper level of society, traditional culture was changing.

No doubt, girls who were married by the age of eight or nine were mostly illiterate, for there had been little time for them to study.[28] But some women at this time were educated. As examples, we could cite two of the shah's daughters, Faḵr-al-Dawla and Tāj-al-Salṭana. Although Tāj-al-Salṭana married young, she continued her education and was familiar with French as well. She thought about the lot of women and expressed her opinions in her diary, which in many ways coincided with those expressed by Bībī Ḵānom, who was from a more modest background. They both wrote to say that women were in an

---

[26] Eʿtemād-al-Salṭana, *Ḵāṭerāt*, 940.

[27] *Rūyārūʾ-ī-e zan va mard.*

[28] Of 955 poets and writers known from the Qajar period, only seventy-five (8 percent) were women. Although it cannot be proven that the number of literate women in comparison to men was that small, this number could be more or less accurate. See Sayyed Aḥmad Dīvānbeygī Šīrāzī, *Ḥadīqat al-šoʿarāʾ: adab va farhang dar ʿaṣr-e Qājār*, ed. ʿAbd-al-Ḥosayn Navāʾī, 3 vols. (Tehran, 1366 Š./1987).

unstable position, that they had no freedom, and that they were illiterate and oppressed. This line of thought must have had some following in society amongst men and women, for as soon as the old order was overthrown in 1906, a number of women, with the encouragement and backing of men, or on their own initiative, began a movement about which a few examples are given at the end of this article.

The Council for the Investigation of Grievances

The second source for this study consists of the documents from the Majles-e Taḥqīq-e Maẓālem.[29] This Council received complaints from people from all over Iran about their problems, requesting compensation and justice. The society which is perceived through these letters is a society with undetermined laws, laws which remained out of the reach of ordinary people. Estates and land either did not have proper title deeds, or these were overlooked even if they existed. In many instances, disputes were caused because the area of the land was not clearly demarcated, and complaints were often useless or even dangerous. On occasion, even the direct order of the shah went unheeded, and both complaints to him and his orders had to be repeated until they became effective.

These complaints were sent either by telegram or post, and, if they were ineffective, the plaintiff came to Tehran, even though such journeys were expensive and difficult and not everyone could undertake them, nor were they always useful.

Towards the end of the nineteenth century, the influence of the central government did not reach out to all the corners of the kingdom, and insecurity was rampant. On many occasions the government was unable to put a stop to the injustices of the local governors or tribal leaders or the outlaws and brigands. In one letter, someone wrote to the shah from Sārī saying "they commit injustices, as we have no protection and no defender."[30]

The structure of society was paternalistic, and the shah was the head of society. The aristocrats benefited from a privileged position and could perform all kinds of unlawful acts and injustices, whereas the lower classes had only the means of filing complaints. A man from Sārī wrote to say that his belongings had been stolen, but as he had announced it in the telegraph office, Sāʾed-al-Dawla heard about it

---

[29] Mansoureh Ettehadieh Nezam-Mafi, "The Council for the Investigation of Grievances: A Case Study of Nineteenth Century Iranian Social History," *Iranian Studies* 22/1(1989):51-61.

[30] Majles-e Taḥqīq-e Maẓālem, Sārī.

and sent people who fined him forty tomans and beat him up. "Now my wife is obliged to work as a servant in people's houses." He concluded by adding that these two thieves worked for Sāʾed-al-Dawla.[31]

In a society where work was scarce and unemployment and poverty were the order of the day, many of the documents are demands to receive a salary or the continuation of a salary which had been paid to a member of the family before, in lieu of services.

Most complaints were from the poor and the feeble of society. Some 23 percent of all the complaints were addressed by people who were in a weaker position than their adversaries (tribal khans; governors and their employees; and outlaws and brigands, who committed unlawful deeds and oppressed ordinary people who had no protector). Of the 11,836 complaints, 91 percent are from men and only 9 percent are from women.[32] However, many of the complaints involved both men and women as they concerned a family. Some plaintiffs wrote that they had a wife and children and alluded to their family responsibilities. From Sārī, it was written that when one Mīrzā Moḥammad died, his salary was stopped; then the plaintiff added, "Only one, Moḥammad Khan, has gone, the other bread eaters are not gone. At least there should be some compassion about the condition of the population of this homeland. Why … should the bread of a number of young and old people be cut off?"[33] From Rašt, there was a demand for help for about thirty or forty young and old people. On several occasions, women mentioned they were in charge of a number of juveniles. Sometimes men made the complaint on behalf of women; from Zanjān, someone wrote that his wife was the daughter of the late Ḥaydarqolī Khan, and her brothers had refused to let her have her share of the inheritance.[34]

Perhaps one other reason for the scarcity of complaints by women was the fact that women did not consider themselves as having lawful rights and remained silent against the injustices committed against them. What is interesting, however, is the fact that both men and women had the courage to make complaints against the grandees of the land. No doubt this was with the approval and permission of the shah, as he wished to be in touch with all the events of his kingdom; indeed, he answered each complaint himself. Some were then referred to the court of a local *ʿālem* or molla, while others were referred to the governor of the province, ordering him to see that justice was done.

---

[31] Majles-e Taḥqīq-e Maẓālem, Sārī.

[32] Ettehadieh Nezam-Mafi, "Investigation of Grievances," 59.

[33] Majles-e Taḥqīq-e Maẓālem, Sārī.

[34] Majles-e Taḥqīq-e Maẓālem, Zanjān.

Women's complaints were generally of two kinds. Some were no different from those of the men and concerned general injustices and oppression suffered as the result of theft of property, etc. Salṭanat K̲ānom from Orūmīya complained against Hājjī Rajab-ʿAlī Mīrpanja and K̲osrowān Sartīp. They had refused to give up the property of the heir and had killed her sister, Ṭāvūs K̲ānom, with a dagger.[35] An old woman of eighty from Lārījān wrote that her husband and two sons had been servants of the state, and after their death, as she was too old and weak, she could not come to "embrace the dust under his [the shah's] feet "and asked to be given her husband and her sons' salary.[36] From Bījār, a woman wrote she was a poor woman who had no one to protect her, her property had been stolen, and the servants of the state did not carry out the orders of his majesty.[37]

The other type of complaints concerned women's affairs, especially injustices committed against them as women. For instance, a woman wrote from Nehāvand that her husband had two wives, and when he died they had thrown her and her daughter out of the house, and, as the other woman had a son, they had completely dispossessed them of all the property.[38] From Khorasan, it was reported that a woman and her servant had cut open the belly of her husband's other wife. In the report, it was added that the murderer had also died two days after.[39]

A woman from Kurdistan wrote that her husband had thrown her out of the house and paid her no support money, but he would not divorce her.[40] Several women from Ṭāleš and Gorgānrūd wrote that their husbands had been in Tehran for three years now, seeking redress for grievances, and that they were left homeless and poor and their children had perished.[41] From Semnān, a man complained that a richer man from the village had enticed his wife by saying he would marry her; she had taken about one hundred tomans worth of his goods and left the house. He then asked for his wife to be restored to him, as he could not afford to marry again.[42] From Sabzavār also, a man complained that when he was on duty in Kangāvar, he had divorced his wife, who had fallen in love with a younger man, and they had

---

[35] Majles-e Taḥqīq-e Maẓālem, Orūmīya.

[36] Majles-e Taḥqīq-e Maẓālem, Lārījān.

[37] Majles-e Taḥqīq-e Maẓālem, Bījār.

[38] Majles-e Taḥqīq-e Maẓālem, K̲orāsān

[39] Majles-e Taḥqīq-e Maẓālem, K̲orāsān.

[40] Majles-e Taḥqīq-e Maẓālem, Kordestān.

[41] Majles-e Taḥqīq-e Maẓālem, Ṭāleš.

[42] Majles-e Taḥqīq-e Maẓālem, Semnān.

stolen his goods.[43] From Sārī, a man wrote asking for redress, saying that for the last six months Mīrzā ʿAlī-Jūlā had taken his wife and daughter in law into his house, and claimed that they were not his and his son's real wedded wives. Even the ulema had tried to talk reason to him but to no avail.[44]

Some women were hard-working and despite many difficulties tried to keep their belongings and to control their property. One woman, for instance, wrote from Šāhrūd that she had 250 sheep and lamb, which grazed in Nardīn and Jājorm. This year, the Turkomans had taken all the herd and left her and her six young children destitute.[45] Women from Ūryaj in Besṭām wrote that from early autumn their menfolk went to Astarābād and Māzandarān to work, leaving the tasks of husbandry to the womènfolk, who had to pay taxes from the money sent to them. That year, a higher rate of taxes had been demanded of them, and they asked that this injustice be redressed.[46] One woman from Isfahan complained that her peasants were so ill treated, they could no longer work. From Rašt, the wife of Āqā Mīr-ʿAskar, the previous governor of Rašt, wrote that two people with the backing of the Beglerbegī had destroyed their once flourishing estates, ruined them, and seized possession of them.[47]

The information in these documents, whether they be about the general conditions of the country or about the situation of women, are of course very limited. No doubt there were other problems not echoed in these reports. However, they do help to give us a glimpse of the general condition of women in different provinces of Iran.

The Tehran Census

Āmār-e Dār al-Ḵelāfa is another source which gives interesting information about women. Compared to other parts of the country, our knowledge of Tehran is more substantial due to many factors: for instance, the court resided there, and the government took more interest in the improvement of the capital. Many foreigners came and went or lived there, some wrote their memoirs, so that we possess more information about the conditions of life in Tehran.

The first census of Tehran was compiled in 1269/1852. At the time Tehran was a small town with five quarters (*maḥalla*), 7,874 houses

---

[43] Majles-e Taḥqīq-e Maẓālem, Sabzavār.

[44] Majles-e Taḥqīq-e Maẓālem, Sārī.

[45] Majles-e Taḥqīq-e Maẓālem, Šāhrūd.

[46] Majles-e Taḥqīq-e Maẓālem, Besṭām.

[47] Majles-e Taḥqīq-e Maẓālem, Eṣfahān.

(*bāb-e ḵāna*), 4,220 shops (*bāb-e dokkān*), and a population of about 125,952.[48]

The five quarters were as follows: the Ark, where the shah and a number of courtiers resided; ʿŪdlājān and Čālmeydān in the east; Sangelaj in the west; and the Bāzār quarter in the south. The bazaar proper with 1,236 shops and a number of caravansaries, was positioned in the middle of the five *maḥalla*s. Most of the aristocrats and rich lived in Sangelaj and some in ʿŪdlājān; the *tojjār* (merchants) and *kasaba* (shopkeepers) lived mostly in the Bāzār quarter; and the lower classes were in Čālmeydān.

This particular statistic gives very precise information about the number of houses, which are divided according to class and their ownership. The different kinds of shops and shop owners are also enumerated and named. Women who are named as owners of houses are few, not more than one percent.[49] The number of shops owned by women is even fewer. It should be added that in general women owned less than men. The inheritance of daughters was half that of the sons. Women who bore no children inherited next to nothing from their husbands, and those who bore children, inherited an eighth of their husband's movable goods. The names of women who are mentioned as house owners are seldom given. They are usually referred to indirectly; for instance, it might be written "the house belonging to the Esfahani *żāʾefa* ["weakling," i.e. woman], who has no husband." Honorable women are referred to by such circumlocutions as "the shop of the princess possessed by (*moʿtaleqa*) the late Ḥājjī Sayyed ʿAlī, the custodian of the shrine (*motavalī-e emāmzāda*)."

Neẓām-al-Salṭana, the statesman mentioned earlier, in the letter addressed to his nephew about the status of his wife, wrote:

> The light of my eyes, you write 'to be opened and read by the mother of Ṣādeq.' With your quick mind and intelligence, why do you use such old fashioned terms? The system of the world has changed. You have heard from the older generation [such expressions as] the mother of Reżā, the mother of Aḥmad, the mother of Mahdī. What has this got to do with your world? The mothers of Reżā or Mahdī had reached a high status as mothers.

---

[48] ʿAbd-al-Ḡaffār Najm-al-Molk wrote that on average sixteen people lived in a house. The population of Tehran has thus been calculated on this basis. Āmār-e Dār-al-Ḵelāfa, *Asnād-ī az tārīḵ*, 345.

[49] Manṣūra Etteḥādīya (Neẓām Māfī), "Rošd va tawseʿa-ye šahr-e Tehrān dar dawra-ye nāṣerī, 1269-1320," in idem, *Īnjā Tehrān ast: majmūʿa-ye maqālātī dar bara-ye Tehrān* (Tehran, 1377 Š./1998), 27-51.

> Is this the right term to be used in the case of your possession (*moʿtaleqa*), who is fifteen years younger than you are?[50]

Some women of the lower classes whose names are mentioned, such as Golrūḵ or Zoleyḵā Kermānī, were probably prostitutes.[51] Few women were as rich as the wife of Ẓell-al-Solṭān, who owned the caravansary of the Armenians, or the sister of Pāšā Khan, who owned one and a half *dong* (measurement of property) of the goldsmith's bazaar. Some women were professionals or had a job, and worked as mollas, bath attendants, midwives, brokers, or teachers of small children. One woman's job was to put drops in peoples's eyes.[52] A few had made the pilgrimage to Mecca (*ḥajj*).

The first census of the population of Tehran was compiled in 1286/1869 by Najm-al-Molk. At that date, Tehran's population was 147,256. Of these 53,972 were men, and 46,603 were "the older and honorable women and wives of the merchants and shopkeepers." There were also 2,525 women slaves and 3,812 women servants and *gīsū safīd* (an older female servant more like a confidante). By then there were 9,571 houses in Tehran.[53]

Buying and selling of slaves was common. A certain Mīrzā Ḥosayn Khan wrote in a letter to his relative in Kāšān that because a servant received one toman cash a month and four dresses a year, he had bought a child at a high price, adding that right now she had to be looked after, but in two years she could be useful and work [private correspondence].

In 1285/1868, Najm-al-Molk began to draw the map of Tehran which took twenty years to complete. By the time it was finished in 1305/1887, the population of Tehran had increased to 250,000, according to him.[54]

The third statistic in this collection is again a count of the houses of Tehran, undertaken by one Aḵżar-ʿAlīšāh in 1317/1899 and completed in 1320/1902. According to Najm-al-Molk, there were sixteen people leaving in each house; in this case, the population of Tehran in 1902 was about 244,400. According to the map of Najm-al-Molk and the statistics of Aḵżar-ʿAlīšāh, the pace of the growth of Tehran, though

---

50 Letter from a private collection.

51 Āmār-e Dār-al-Ḵelāfa, *Asnād-ī az tārīḵ*, 78, 145, 216, 312.

52 Āmār-e Dār-al-Ḵelāfa, *Asnād-ī az tārīḵ*, 82, 95, 97, 100.

53 Āmār-e Dār-al-Ḵelāfa, *Asnād-ī az tārīḵ*, 343-50.

54 Map of Tehran drawn by Najm-al-Molk, Moʾassasa-ye jografīyā-ye Saḥāb.

not consistent, had quickened. In the north a large *maḥalla*, the Dawlat quarter, had come into existence and was the abode of the rich and foreigners and aristocrats.

Some of those who lived in Sangelaj and Dawlat were not so rich, such as Nāneh-Raʿnā the bath attendant, or the woman who was a *rawża-k̲ᵛān* (singer of religious chants), or the wife of Karbalāʾī Ḥasan the mat-knitter. However, these two *maḥalla*s were mainly where the rich lived, such as Navvāba (princess) Šawkat-al-Salṭana and Navvāba Monavvar-al-Salṭana. In fact, Tehran was becoming divided between the richer northern and western part and the poorer eastern and southern part, a characteristic still continuing today.[55]

Western fashions and foreign goods were beginning to be found in Tehran. Some parts of the city had electricity or gas lighting. Post and telegraph had been installed, and two banks, the Russian and British banks, were functioning. There were several hospitals and chemist shops, as well as several schools on the European model. A modern police force, headed by Count Monteforte, was established for the security of people and made a daily report of the events in the city. Not all the *maḥalla*s of the capital were safe. Thefts, however, were in general insignificant, but there were some professional thieves, whom the police wanted to arrest. The conditions of the streets were so bad that people and animals fell into wells and ditches. Eʿtemād-al-Salṭana often mentions the dirt of the streets and says that their maintenance was one of the duties of the police and of Nāyeb-al-Salṭana.[56] Lack of attention to braziers and oil lamps caused many fires. One winter it rained so much that the walls of many houses collapsed, and some people died of cold.

According to the statistics of Ak̲żar-ʿAlīšāh, it seems people had grown wealthier, for the number of people owing several houses or shops were more numerous. Women, too, seem to have benefited from the increase in wealth, and the number of women house owners had risen from 1 percent to 3.5 percent.[57] No doubt this increase in wealth gave some richer women more financial independence. Eʿtemād-al-Salṭana wrote that he once discussed with Amīn-al-Ḥożūr the wealth of the rich women of Iran and that of the private household of the shah.[58]

Some of the late Nāṣer-al-Dīn Shah's wives owned houses in various parts of the city. Amongst those mentioned, six lived in Sangelaj and

---

[55] Etteḥādīya, "Rošd va tawseʿa."

[56] Eʿtemād-al-Salṭana, *K̲āṭerāt*, 176.

[57] Etteḥādīya, "Rošd va tawseʿa."

[58] Eʿtemād-al-Salṭana, *K̲āṭerāt*, 3.

Dawlat, one in the Bāzār quarter, and one in ʿŪdlājān. Tāj-al-Salṭana bemoans the fate of those wives who suddenly were left without support, for a week after the shah died, the new ruler Moẓaffar-al-Dīn Shah declared that all the ladies should take their belongings and go, except those who had children. These were sent to the garden of Sarvestān, where the mother of Nāyeb-al-Salṭana had lived.[59] Tāj-al-Salṭana was right to deplore the fate of these women, for they were from mostly modest backgrounds and had no rich family to take care of them. Eʿtemād-al-Salṭana has named some of them, such as Fāṭema (Anīs-al-Dawla); Bāḡbānbāšī (Amin-e Aqdas), the daughter of the keeper of the Aqdasīya garden, who had several children; or Oḡūl Beyga (Oqūlbeyga), a Turkmen slave concubine.[60] One of these, Anīs-al-Dawla, who bore no child, came to own nine shops in the bazaar, but she had been a favorite with the shah.

Some other rich women were also named in these statistics such as Fāṭema-Solṭān Ḵānom who owned a caravanserai[61] and Ḥājjīya Maryam Ḵānom, who owned 26 shops in the *maḥalla* of Dawlat.[62] Some of the late shah's daughters were very rich, such as ʿEṣmat-al-Dawla, wife of Moʿayyer-al-Mamālek, who owned the Orosī Dūzhā Bāzār (the shoemakers' bazaar). Such properties might have been inherited by these women or they might have received them as *mehr* or dowry. Some women also invested in shops and property.

Some rich women performed charitable deeds, such as Qamar-al-Salṭana, who had given as *vaqf* or endowment a house and a *takya* (a place of worship) in the Dawlat quarter; or Mahd-e ʿOlyā, the mother of Nāṣer-al-Dīn Shah, who had had built a school in Almāsīya street.[63] ʿEzzat-al-Dawla, the sister of Nāṣer-al-Dīn Shah who had married the son of Mīrzā Āqā Khan Nūrī the Sadr-e Aʿẓam after her husband Amīr Kabīr had been murdered, had made a *vaqf* of a *takya* and a bath in ʿŪdlājān, where a street was still named after her in 1320/1902.[64] Of course many women were very poor, such as one Zaynab, who walked

[59] Tāj-al-Salṭana, *Ḵāṭerāt*, 66.

[60] Eʿtemād-al-Salṭana, *Ḵāṭerāt*, 490. According to Āmār-e Dār al-Ḵelāfa, *Asnād-ī az tārīḵ*, 370, 386, Oḡūlbeyga and Bāḡbānbašī lived in the Dawlat quarter.

[61] Āmār-e Dār-al-Ḵelāfa, *Asnād-ī az tārīk*, 51, 515.

[62] Āmār-e Dār-al-Ḵelāfa, *Asnād-ī az tārīk*, 397.

[63] Āmār-e Dār-al-Ḵelāfa, *Asnād-ī az tārīk*, 407.

[64] Amīr Kabīr owned two houses in the Bāzār quarter, which were sold after his death to Malek-al-Tojjār. Mīrzā Āqā Khan Nūrī lived in the ʿŪdlājān quarter, and according to Dr. Polak, when Mīrzā Āqā Khan became Ṣadr-e Aʿẓam in 1851, his family obtained part of that district and developed it by

geese, or Fāṭema, who washed the dead before burial. As before, the names of most women are omitted, and they are referred to as the possession of Mollā Bājī from Malāyer, or the wife of the sayyed, or the daughter (*ṣabīa*) of Moʿīn-al-Salṭana. Women with jobs and professions are also mentioned as brokers, teachers, musicians, and bath attendants. Some black slave women also owned houses, such as Dada Sīāh, in the *maḥalla* of Sangelaj, or Galīn Sīāh in the Bāzār quarter. Some of the wet nurses of the aristocrats owned houses, such as the wet nurses of ʿAzīz-al-Solṭān Malījak, Farmānfarmā, or Ẓell-al-Solṭān. Some, such as "Fat Zahrā" or "Mustachioed Kawkeb," were probably prostitutes.

The Police Reports

A fourth source of information may be found in the police reports of Tehran that were compiled for Count Monteforte, the Italian chief of police in Tehran. The count was in charge of the security of the city, and if one compares the conditions of people as stated in the complaints of the Majles-e Maẓālem with those of the inhabitants of Tehran as depicted in these reports, it may be noticed that the capital was in a relatively privileged position, though rioting did occur at times. However, according to the reports, the condition of women in other parts of the country were not very different from those depicted in these reports about Tehran.

The society depicted in these reports is a paternalistic one, and people lived under a tyrannical and cruel, but weak, government. Class differences were very marked. Religious beliefs and religious rites played a great role in people's lives. Perhaps because of these facts, there are only ten cases of murder but 288 cases of quarrels. Fights were generally about slight offences and were settled by the mediation of another party.

Besides being responsible for security, order, the prevention of corruption, quarrels, and thefts, the police also helped in case of fire, the loss of children, deception in the sale of goods, drunkenness, and misbehavior. In many instances, quarrels were referred to the headman of the quarter, who tried to make peace between the parties, and if he did not succeed, the case was referred to the religious court, Maḥżar-e Šarʿ.

---

building new palaces, but seven years later, when he fell from office, the houses became empty and ruined, and no care was taken of them. In 1320/ 1902, ʿEzzat-al-Dawla lived in the Dawlat quarter. Jakob Polak, *Persien: das Land und seine Bewohner* (Leipzig, 1865), tr. Kaykāvūs Jahāndārī as *Safar-nāma-ye Polak: Īrān va Īrānīān* (2nd ed., Tehran, 1368 Š./1989), 45.

The main complaints were about the non-payment of small debts or disputes which had financial reasons behind them or complaints about thefts. From among 3,846 cases, 387 concerned thefts, 145 were financial quarrels, 142 were family quarrels, 84 concerned drunkenness or debauchery and lewdness, and 52 cases were quarrels between landlords and tenants.

The police compiled reports of the events in the various districts of Tehran, and each day they were sent to Monteforte, who affixed his signature. Over a period of six months, 494 daily reports were made which are extant. These reports do not cover every day of the month, and some days are lacking from the reports. No doubt, news of some events did not reach the police. There is seldom news about the upper classes in these reports, which concern mostly their meetings or visits to each other or to foreigners and to religious ceremonies such as *rawża-k̲ᵛānī* or mourning ceremonies. News about births or marriages among this class is also rare, and only a few times is mention made about something like the great luxury of the bride's trousseau, as for example in the case of the wedding of the daughter of Naṣr-Allāh Mostawfī, when there were sixty tray-loads of silverware and fourteen mares carried the cases and the packs. The procession was accompanied by music and headed for the groom's house. On the other hand, there are many news items about the weddings of middle class people, saying, for instance, that the bride and been taken in an orderly fashion to the house of the groom. At times, some disorders did ensue. At the wedding of the daughter of a baker, the bride had been taken in the carriage of Sahām-al-Dawla to the groom's house. In Čerāḡ Gāz street, the bride's family had stopped the carriage, saying that the groom had to come to greet her, a quarrel had began, the carriage had overturned, some of the goods had broken, and the *yanga* (woman accompanying the bride) had been injured. Finally, the bride was taken to the groom's house, and the broken carriage was returned.

The plaintiffs, whether men or women, were generally referred to the headman of the district. In these reports, there are forty-six cases of complaints by wives against their husbands and twenty-four cases of complaints by men against their wives. However, all the complaints addressed to the headman of the district did not concern family quarrels; others concerned thefts, loss of children, the restitution of property and goods, etc.

Collecting news in a small city with a small population was not difficult, especially since most people from a district knew each other and met at weddings and in religious ceremonies and *rawża-k̲ᵛānī*s. The members of the police walked the streets of Tehran, and if they felt suspicious of someone, they interrogated him, but it seems they did not enter someone's house. If an individual was under suspicion, they followed him; if he took refuge in a house, they waited till he came out and then arrested him. Apparently the police had a number of spies, for on occasion it was written "as was reported." Eʿtemād-al-Salṭana, who was no friend of Monteforte, writes that the count made up secret reports of what went on in people's houses for the shah. Apparently the police were unpopular among people and took bribes, according to Bībī K̲ānom. In fact, Monteforte was unpopular, and Eʿtemād-al-Salṭana often mentions the brutality and chaotic behavior of the police.

Some examples of these reports are as follows: On 9 Jomādā I, the daughter of Amīn-e Ḥożūr was married to the brother of Amīn-al-Solṭān; the women were entertained in the house of Amīn-Homāyūn and the men in that of Amīn-al-Solṭān. On 25 Ẕu'l-Qaʿda 1303/25 August 1886, it was reported that the previous night one Ḥosayn, an army architect, had sent a message to the headman that Taqī, a builder from Qom, had a wife who was related to Ḥosayn. For some three years, he had left the woman (*żāʾefa*) alone in Tehran and had sent her no money, while he was somewhere in and around Qom. He had recently returned to the city, so Ḥosayn asked the headman to send the police to arrest him. The headman had thereby sent a person to bring Taqī in for questioning, so that justice should be done.

Among the middle classes, visiting, partying, and entertaining was quite frequent. There are 422 instances involving going to parties, sometimes with musicians, 113 cases of pilgrimages, and 628 cases of *rawża-k̲ᵛānī*. The social relations of the middle classes and shopkeepers were either among relatives or between people of the same trade or those who lived in the same quarter. In the *rawża-k̲ᵛānī*s, the religious class such as the *sādāt* and religious students (*ṭollāb*) were invited. Women also had their own parties, and there are many references to these in the reports as well as by Eʿtemād-al-Salṭana.

Women did commit thefts, and twenty-nine cases are recorded in these reports. On 26 Ẕu'l-Qaʿda 1303/26 August 1886, a woman named K̲ānom Jān had stolen a few insignificant items from someone named Ṣādeq. The police had arrested her and were questioning her. Fights also occurred between women or between women and men. On 2 Ṣafar 1304/29 October 1886, a report was made that "yesterday, ʿAbd-al-Ḥosayn quarreled with the 'weakling' Nana Esmāʿīl, and the two were going to brawl in the street, but the police intervened and settled it."

One woman complained on 2 Ẕu'l-Qaʿda 1304/23 July 1887 that she had rented a room to a *farrāš*, the bodyguard of Mošīr-al-Dawla, who had not paid his rent. In another case, a quarrel had begun between

Ḥājjīya K̲ānom, the wife of Mahdī Khan and Kāẓem Khan, about the rent of a house. Amīn-al-Solṭān had ordered that the house should be turned over to Kāẓem Khan, but Ḥājjīya K̲ānom had complained to the high court (ʿAdlīya Aʿẓam). At last ʿAżod-al-Molk had taken the house from Kāẓem Khan and locked it until its ownership could be decided.

Some 82 per cent of the reports concerned quarrels between husband and wife. Out of the 358 marriages mentioned in this collection of documents, 44 per cent were marriages between relatives, and 55.8 per cent were between members of the same trade, a practice which met with Bībī K̲ānom's approval.

To take a concubine (*ṣīga*), was cheap, only two *tomān*s, and divorce was easy. However, only twelve cases of divorce are recorded in the files. For instance, on 12 Ẕu'l-Qaʿda 1304/2 August 1887, it was reported that Rajab-ʿAlī had quarreled with his wife and complained to the headman, who sent them to the police office. After inquiries were made, they were referred to the *šarʿ* court, and the man divorced the woman there.

Marriage age was low, as explained earlier, and most sources corroborate this fact. On 19 Ẕu'l-Qaʿda 1303/19 August 1886, it was reported that a man had wedded a girl, but later he found out that, despite her young age, she had been married several times before. He had claimed the restitution of the cost of the wedding and a quarrel had ensued. On 8 Ẕu'l-Qaʿda it was reported that an old man had taken a young wife and had quarreled with his son, who had reproached him for it. There are references to the cost of weddings, and the dowry (*mehr*), which at times occasioned quarrels and fights. On 26 Ẕu'l-Qaʿda, at the wedding of a girl whose father had died, and who had thus inherited four hundred tomans, the aunts of the girl, wanting to keep her in the family, had beaten up the bride, the groom, and the bride's mother before the police arrived and mediated a settlement.

There is not much information in the reports about the relationship of husband and wife, since such questions about women were usually not discussed openly. However, in the correspondence between Mīrzā Ḥasan (an employee at the British embassy) with his kinsman Mīrzā Ḥosayn (the director of the customs of Kāšān), some mention of women is made since the men were close relatives. Apparently Mīrzā Ḥosayn wanted to divorce his *ṣīga*, who was the daughter of Ḥājjī Moḥammad-Reżā, but Mīrzā Ḥasan disapproved of this, saying she was "like buying gold," and recommended that he treat her kindly. The woman for a time had said she was pregnant, perhaps so that he would not divorce her. But later, in a letter from Mīrzā Ḥosayn, Mīrzā Ḥasan was instructed to go forward with the divorce. The account he gives of the procedure of the divorce is a witness to the inherent weakness of a woman's position.

> Yesterday I went to town especially in order to let the daughter of the late Mīrzā Reżā have her *mehr*. In the afternoon we went to the house of a molla. He was not at home. It is the month of Ṣafar and the mollas are busy morning, afternoons and nights, at *rawża-k̲ᵛānīs*. At last we found Āqā Sayyed ʿAlī-Akbar, who is a well known molla, and beseeched him to pay his attention to this question. But there was a difficulty, for we needed four witnesses who were known to the Āqā and to us, two on the Āqā's behalf and two on behalf of the daughter of the deceased. We had taken two people with us, but the Āqā did not know them, so they were useless. For a while we were left not knowing what to do. Luckily, the wife of the Āqā was an acquaintance of the wife of the late Mīrzā Reżā, and she was in the *andarūn* (women's quarters) at the time. This solved the problem; we gave her the sum, and the Āqā wrote out the certificate of conveyance (*qabāla*), and gave it to us.[65]

Mīrzā Ḥasan added that as soon as the daughter of Moḥammad-Reżā saw the money (which finalized the divorce), she began to cry like a spring shower.

Wife beating was a common practice. Out of 114 reports about the quarrels between husband and wife, twenty-eight cases were about wives who were beaten by their husbands, and in twenty-four cases women had taken opium to commit suicide as the result of such quarrels. Death did not generally ensue, no doubt because households were crowded, and someone would soon hear of it and begin a cure. However, it is clear that such desperate behavior was no doubt a sign of pressure, melancholy, and the dissatisfaction of women. On 26 Ẕu'l-Qaʿda 1303/26 August 1886, Šahāb-al-Molk divorced his *ṣīga* and ordered her daughter to be taken from her; the woman had taken opium to kill herself, but she had been treated, and recovered. The wife of one Mašhadī Raḥīm had quarreled with him because he had wedded a new wife; she also took opium. On 26 Jomādā II 1304/21 March 1887, the wives of Mollā Asad-Allāh the Schoolmaster quarreled, and one of them took opium.

Another reason for quarrels between husband and wife was that the wife had gone out of the house without her husband's permission; in such cases either the husband or his family punished her.

---

[65] Letter in a private collection, dated 18 Ṣafar 1307/13 October 1889.

Another cause for family quarrels arose when the husband did not pay the required *nafaqa*, daily expenses, to his wife. In such cases, women often complained to the headman. On 25 Jomādā II 1304/20 March 1887, the wife and mother of Esmāʿīl the Broker (*dallāl*), who had not bought the necessary things for the new year festivities (*haft sīn*), had quarreled with him: "The poor thing had been obliged to buy the garlic, the vinegar, etc., and she cursed Jamšīd-e Jam [the legendary shah] who had started this tradition." In Ẕu'l-Qaʿda 1303/August 1886, the wife of one Malek the Porter (*ḥamāl*) had complained to the headman that her husband did not pay her expenses and had beaten her for no reason. The headman mediated and made the man promise not to harm her in future.

In poor or middle class families, a great deal of harm often came to children. There are twenty-five cases of the loss of children reported by the police. A large number had fallen into pools or water reservoirs and drowned or fell from roofs and died painfully. Some lost their lives during fights between their parents or from neglect.

Of course, not all women were weak and feeble, and there are reports that some women beat their husbands; on one occasion, a man tried to commit suicide because of his wife. There is also a report about a woman who married a younger man, and others about those who had taken lovers, but such occurrences are rare. The general rule was for the woman to be the one oppressed. Once, on 14 Jomādā II 1304/9 March 1887, it was reported that a man had quarreled with his wife about her *nafaqa* and beat her even though she was pregnant. She had miscarried as a result, but he had then accused her of having killed the baby on purpose. When inquiries were made it was discovered that he wanted to divorce her and was seeking an excuse. Later they had made up.

After the Constitutional Revolution, newspapers carried many stories about women, the most famous example being those about the sale of girls from Qūčān to the Turkomans, a question raised several times in the Majles. The newspapers took a special interest in this case, notably *Ṣūr-e Esrāfīl*, which pursued the question until it was brought to trial. During the Second Majles, from 1909 to 1911, it was the newspaper *Īrān-e now* which paid attention to women and their problems, printing stories about men's unjustness to women, their poverty, their defenselessness, and their general inequality.

Conclusion

As we have seen, the situation of women in the lower echelons of Qajar society was an unenviable one. They had no social security and no freedom. They could be sold or abducted. They could easily be divorced, and the age for marriage was very low. Their fate depended on the kindness and humanity of their husband and his family. In the upper classes, women enjoyed the protection of their family and family connections. However, their social position does not seem to have been much more enviable. In fact, all women faced insecurity. There exist two letters by an upper class woman, the wife of Reżāqolī Khan Neẓām-al-Salṭana (who inherited the title when his uncle died in 1326/1908). She is the woman mentioned earlier whose husband had complained about her lack of literacy. The letters are addressed to her two sons, who were studying in Europe. Both letters concern the difficulties such a person faced because her husband had fallen politically foul of the government.

These letters were written in 1330/1912, when Reżāqolī Khan Neẓām-al-Salṭana was governor of Fārs. During his tenure, there had been a fight between Ṣawlat-al-Dawla, the great Qašqāʾī tribal leader, and one of the local magnates, Qavām-al-Molk. As the result of this fight, the son of Qavām-al-Molk had been killed, and all Fārs was in chaos. Reżāqolī Khan, who was considered responsible for the trouble, fled into exile to Europe. At the time, the government in Tehran was in the hands of the Bak̲tīārī chief Ṣamṣam-al-Salṭana, an enemy and rival of the Qašqāʾīs and Reżāqolī Khan. Ṣamṣām al-Salṭana vowed revenge and threatened to plunder the house of Reżāqolī Khan in Tehran. In the meantime, Reżāqolī Khan's daughter, Zahrā-Solṭān, was betrothed to be married to ʿAbbās Mīrzā, the son of Farmānfarmā. This is the subject of one of the letters by the wife of Reżāqolī Khan:

> Dear lights of my eyes, more dear than my life, may I be the sacrifice for both of you. I was sad yesterday, but when your two letters arrived I became really happy that at least you are together and live in a comfortable country. I and the lights of our eyes [the other brother and sisters] are well. But if you should want to hear the troubles I have suffered recently, it will be long as a book. I am going to make it short.
>
> Since the day Neẓām-al-Salṭana [her husband] went to Fārs and the son of Qavām got killed, I have not been at peace one day. For four months, I stayed in Zarganda [a summer resort] in a place that not even a dog would live in. I came to town twice so I could occupy myself with the affairs of Zahrā-Solṭān. Farmānfarmā sent word that it was not safe for me to stay in my house and that I should go back quickly to Zarganda. Ṣamṣām-al-Salṭana had said that "if Neẓām-al-Salṭana does not leave Fārs, I shall raze his house and not even spare his two year old son." You cannot imagine how I again left for Zarganda. After a few days, I heard they wanted to confiscate all the properties of Neẓām-al-

Salṭana. I wrote a request to Ṣamsām-al-Salṭana, the prime minister, saying that if Neẓām-al-Salṭana has committed a wrong, you have every power to punish him. But what have a few women and children done? We have committed no sin! Give us respite so we can return to our house and live there. I gave this request to Sālār Moḥtašem [her brother in law], who took it to the prime minister. He replied, "Rest assured; no one can do you harm." After receiving this letter we returned to town. I started to prepare Zahrā-Solṭān's trousseau. Every day I received requests from ʿAbbās Mīrzā saying, "I want to take my bride home." At the same time the government issued the order for the arrest of Neẓām-al-Salṭana. You can imagine what I felt. On the one hand, no merchant lends us any money because all our property is confiscated; on the other hand, the preparation of the trousseau for this girl is unfinished. It is with great difficulty that I completed some of the preparations.

We had agreed that they should take the bride on the fifteenth. On the morning of the tenth, Naṣr-Allāh came with the message that sixty gendarmes and several officers, together with the deputy of Mr. Shuster [the American serving as Treasurer-General] have come and say they have come to confiscate the house. They had surrounded the building and even entered the *andarūn* and the garden of the *bīrūnī* (common room). Now imagine what my poor self was going through. I sent a message to the deputy of Mr. Shuster that his men should step aside so we could make an inventory of the furniture and things and seal the doors and asked for an hour. Immediately, I wrote a letter to the Sardār Jang [another Baḵtīārī Chief] pleading with him to think of a solution for my plight. I gave it to Sālār Moḥtašem who took it to Sardār Jang. I also sent the original letter, which had promised me safety, to ʿAbbās Mīrzā to take to the prime minister to remind him that he had promised and written that no one had the right to Neẓām-al-Salṭana's house, so why had these people come to confiscate it? Sardār Jang ordered that no one should make a move for two hours and that he would remove these officials. He went to see the prime minister and started to shout at him, saying what kind of Islam is this? What kind of constitutionalism is this? What have these women and children done? Then the prime minister wrote a letter to Mr. Shuster, and they removed the soldiers from Neẓām-al-Salṭana's house. Now you can imagine what I went through till two hours before sundown.

On the one hand, there is the worry I feel for my own unsettled life; on the other hand, the worry I feel for Zahrā-Solṭān's things.

What would I have done if they had confiscated them? As soon as the soldiers were removed, I sent her mirror and Koran to Farmānfarmā's house to be placed in Zahrā-Solṭān's room. At night, I sent all her other things to be taken there by our own servants and those of Farmānfarmā. Two night later, on the 16th, two of ʿAbbās Mīrzā's relatives came and carried off the bride at the propitious hour, without any further ado.

Now think about it. You bring up a daughter with so much difficulty and give her away in such a miserable way! This is the result of your father's doing that has come down on my head. I have no more time, or else there would be much more to tell.

The other letter runs as follows:

Dear light of my eye, may I be your sacrifice. By the time this letter reaches you, you will have reached London and will see this historic event [the coronation of George V]. Unfortunately we did not hear of it in time; we could have arranged it so you could have participated as one of the embassy members. Still it is worth seeing. I hope wherever you are, that you are happy and well. I and the lights of our eyes [the other children] are well, thank God.

But you don't know the story of the son of Qavām and how I trembled. I was sick for about twenty days. I had barely risen from my sick bed when Farmānfarmā sent me a message: "Although I should not bother you at this time, I want to send ʿAbbās with the delegation of ʿAlāʾ-al-Salṭana to London for the coronation, and he says he will not go until he has seen his wife. Could you grant your permission for Zahrā-Solṭān to be married?" One evening, he came in person and talked to me for three hours in private in the *andarūn*. Although I had no mind for it, I had to accept. We arranged for the wedding to take place on the twenty-third. At first, ʿEzzat-al-Dawla [wife of Farmānfarmā] and I planned a big reception for the wedding and that she should invite all her relatives, but Farmānfarmā did not think it appropriate just now. The Baḵtīārīs had quieted down, and he said it was not good to make ourselves conspicuous, for their blood would boil again. So we agreed that only two of his sisters and two sisters of ʿEzzat-al-Dawla should come with her. For the men's part, Farmānfarmā would assist, along with two mollas. Still I wrote to all the members of his family so they couldn't say I had not invited them, but none came.

At three o'clock [i.e., after sunrise], the wedding took place, thank God. After the *ʿaqd* (religious ceremony) when the bride was brought in, you should have seen him [Farmānfarmā]. He left no time for the groom to kiss the bride; he had to take precedence. After the wedding, the guests stayed for about half an hour after sundown. I am sending you a list of the things that were brought from Farmānfarmā's house. He also sent me a message that for the few days that ʿAbbās is still in Tehran, I should grant him permission to visit her whenever he wished. I accepted. Every afternoon ʿAbbās Mīrzā came and walked in the garden with Zahrā-Solṭān and then took afternoon tea with her. The day he left, he took off from here, and we have already received his telegram from Baku. The journey is going to be about three or four months long. When he returns we will celebrate the wedding. You will meet him in London. He is a very reasonable young man and well educated. You and Taqī [her second son] are like a father to Zahrā-Solṭān, and if she has studied French and the piano so far, it is due to your insistence. Now she is busy day and night, and she has three teachers, one for piano, one for French, and everyday a French mademoiselle comes from Farmānfarmā's house for conversation. Farmānfarmā is very kind. Sometimes he visits his daughter in law...."

Towards the end of the reign of Nāṣer-al-Dīn Shah, because of a wider contact with the West and the criticism of a number of Iranian thinkers, people's knowledge of the world increased, the result of which became apparent during the Constitutional Revolution and which no doubt affected women's social awareness as well. Perhaps the period under review could be said to have been a preparatory time for the greater changes yet to come.

At the beginning of the Constitutional Revolution, some liberals and constitutionalists began to champion women's causes. They began to draw attention to their lowly social status and to deplore their simplicity and illiteracy. Women, too, began to take advantage of the newly found liberties by participating in political demonstrations and by taking an interest in the new developments.[66] Wives, sisters, and daughters of some of the constitutional leaders,[67] such as Moḥtaram

[66] Women addressed several letters to the Majles asking for schools and the organization of a society. One letter was read in the Majles by the women of Qazvīn in support of the foundation of a national bank; Moẕakerāt-e Majles-e avval, 14, 84; see also Mangol Bayat-Phillips, "Feminism and National Politics in Iran, 1905-1911," in Lois Beck and Nikki Keddie, eds., *Women in the Muslim World* (Cambridge, Mass., 1978), 295-306.

[67] Eliz Sanasarian, *The Women's Rights Movement in Iran: Mutiny, Appeasement, and Repression, 1900 to Khomeni* (New York, 1982), 42-44.

Eskandarī, Ṣadīqa Dawlatābādī, K̲ānom Kaḥḥālzāda, the daughters of Šams-al-Maʿālī, Madame Yeprem Khan, and the wife of Malek-al-Motakallemīn, took the first steps.

However there were also lesser known women whose names appear in the letters they wrote to newspapers and signed as "the servant of the homeland," or Šams-al-Nesāʾ, or the head-mistress Omm-al-Madāres, or the daughter of Ḥakīm-al-Ḥokamāʾ, or Šams-e Kasmāʾī.[68] The interesting point is the great enthusiasm and verve of these women, who had found an occasion to express themselves and perhaps to work. These women complained about their bad position because of the lack of healthcare, etc., and they tried to improve their lot, because the government and the majority of the people did nothing for them.

Of course it should be pointed out that this movement was neither large nor well organized, and it did not have a set agenda.[69] Furthermore most of the activity was limited to Tehran and a few other cities. However, there was contact and cooperation between these women and they had undeniably come to constitute a social class.

Before the Constitutional Revolution, at times of famine for instance, it had happened that, at the instigation of men, women demonstrated against the government. But political activity was a new phenomenon, no doubt due to the revolution and the nationalistic atmosphere of the times. The origin of women's political activity dates back to the time of the first Majles,[70] and despite the opposition of the deputies in the

---

This writer has prepared a list of twelve activist women who were from a comparatively well to do class. No doubt they had a better opportunity for political activity, though some of them later had to work for a living. They were all educated; eleven had literate fathers; most had married at an early age. Five came from cities other than Tehran, and they usually undertook more than one job.

[68] The women's movement during the Constitutional Revolution falls into two periods. During the first period, women followed the lead of the men. Men were dissatisfied for socio-political reasons, the weakness of their government before foreign imperial powers, and the tyranny of their own government. Women shared these sentiments and had no particular demands of their own. During the second period, women began to think about their own affairs and became aware of themselves as a social class.

[69] Sanasarian, *Women's Rights Movement*, 42-44. See also Janet Afary, "Grassroots Democracy, Social Democracy in the Iranian Constitutional Revolution, 1906-1911" (Ph.D. diss., University of Michigan, Ann Arbor, 1991).

[70] Nāẓem-al-Eslām Kermānī, *Tārīk̲-e bīdārī-e Īrānīān,* ed. Saʿīdī Sīrjānī, 2 vols. (repr. Tehran, 1362 Š./1983), 1:244.

Majles, women proceeded to organize *anjomāns*, societies, in order to continue their socio-political activities. In most of the meetings of these societies they discussed the need for women's education, the reform of the laws, and the knowledge of women's rights. They also undertook charitable deeds, founded a number of schools for girls, and undertook the publication of newspapers.[71]

Women's magazines and newspapers continued the same arguments and rationales, such as the need for healthcare for household management, the education of girls, etc. From the point of view of these women, the education of girls and the establishment of schools was one of their most important aims, and they took every pain with this goal in mind.[72] But these women did not always enjoy the support off all the men, and a large number of men opposed such activities, for no doubt at the time the presence and participation of women in social life was unacceptable and unsettling. For instance, there was a lot of opposition to the establishment of girls' schools at the beginning, and women did not obtain the right to vote.

During the second Majles in 1329/1911, when the question of the vote for women was discussed, Sayyed Ḥasan Modarres said:

> From the beginning of my life until today I have encountered many dangers, but I have never trembled as I have today. The problem of the Commission is first of all that it should not mention the name of women in connection with the right to election, as women do not have the right to vote. It is as if you said they were not mad or benighted. This is wrong on the part of the

---

[71] Moḥammad Ṣadr Hāšemī, *Tārīḵ-e jarā'ed va majallāt-e Īrān,* 4 vols. in 2 (Isfahan, 1327-32 Š./1948-53), passim.

[72] Article 19 of the Fundamental Laws dealt with the establishment of schools by the government and compulsory education. However, during the first Majles no step in this direction was taken. During the second Majles, once again a law was passed by the government about the preparation for primary and free education and also the need for secondary and higher education, and the budget for five schools for girls was discussed. Education for girls still remained in private hands and was undertaken by the women themselves. The first time the government took any initiative in this direction was in 1336/1918, i.e., twelve years after the Constitutional Revolution, when ten primary schools were established by the government in Tehran. *Majmūʿa-ye moṣavvabāt-e Majles-e šūrā-ye mellī dar 4 dawra-ye taqnīnīya* (Tehran, n. d.), pp 8, 20, 425; also *Sāl-nāma-ye Vezārat-e maʿāref va farhang va awqāf* (Tehran, 1297 Š./1918), 76.

> Commission. The answer that we must give should be a polite and reasonable one, and that is that God has not given them any worth that they should have the right to vote. The weak of mind, male and female, are among those who have no such a capacity.[73]

And this is the cry of a woman at the same time:

> Oh you brave brothers! the defenders of virtue! Oh you who seek knowledge and progress and civilization! ... Where did you test our abilities ? Which school did you found for us? Which teachers did you appoint for us ... to know that we have no ability and no capacity ...? What is the reason that you want all the comforts and joys and travels and science and industry for yourselves and forbid us all these good things, and then you say the class of women in our country have no capacity to improve and to learn science and industry? ... How sad and how strange! Oh dear brothers, come and make an effort to undo this injustice against women and help us to throw away our evil ways and to improve ourselves ....[74]

Eventually, all the excitement and enthusiasm engendered by the revolution dissipated, but women continued their efforts, especially in the educational field. However, on the whole, one must say that the social position of women did not change fundamentally during the period under review. What did change was perhaps the fact that men accepted the presence of women in public life, a development which was to bear fruit later.

---

[73] Moẕākerāt-e Majles-e Dovvom, 8 Shaʿbān 1329/3 August 1911, 1535.

[74] *Īrān-e now,* no. 65-92(1327/1910).

Iran's Early Intellectual Encounter with Modernity: A Dual Approach

Farzin Vahdat

Iran's intellectual encounter with modernity in the second half of the nineteenth century was characterized by the simultaneous appropriation of two closely related but opposite aspects of modernity: adoption of the potentially emancipatory moment of modernity, and the integration of the "darker" side of modernity, an aspect of the modern world that is more conducive to domination and reification. This dual appropriation of modernity is manifested in the theoretical discourses of the main intellectuals in Iran in the late nineteenth century, with important consequences for the development of the course of events in that country in the twentieth century. An analysis of this first requires some theoretical interpretation of the phenomena one may consider to be modernity.

This paper draws on critical theory for an evaluation and critique of the philosophy and phenomenon of modernity. In critical theory, the category of subjectivity has constituted a key feature of modernity.[1] Subjectivity can be viewed as the *property characterizing the autonomous, self-willing, self-defining, and self-conscious individual human agent*. Subjectivity, very much rooted in the humanist tradition, tends to view the human individual as the determinant of her or his own life-processes and is closely related to notions such as human freedom and volition, consciousness, reason, individuality, rights of

---

[1] Habermas has invoked Hegel to interpret the normative content of modern world mainly in terms of the principle of subjectivity: "The principle of the modern world is freedom of subjectivity, the principle that all the essential factors present in the intellectual whole are now coming into their right in the course of their development." G. W. F Hegel, *Hegel's Philosophy of Right* (Oxford, 1976), 286; cited in Jürgen Habermas, *The Philosophical Discourse of Modernity: Twelve Lectures* (Cambridge, Mass., 1987), 16.

various types, etc., but it is not reducible to any single one of these. An important aspect to keep in mind about subjectivity is that it is simultaneously the repository of emancipation as well as domination. While the Cartesian *cogito* as the modern detached subject is the source of liberation (for example, as the foundations of the rights of citizenship), it is also the responsible for the objectification of nature, the Other such as the colonized and women, as well as of the subject itself. Herein lies the very dialectical character of modernity and its emancipatory as well as dominative potential. For this reason, from Hegel to Habermas many social thinkers and philosophers have attempted to reconcile this subject of modernity and its Other.

Often this reconciliation has been attempted in terms of what might be described as universalization of subjectivity, approximating its emancipatory potential. Hegel conceptualized this reconciliation as a synthesis, to be achieved primarily in terms of universality. As such, universality, a somewhat more elusive category to analyze, may be perceived as the mutual recognition among the plurality of subjects of each other's subjectivity. In a strictly historical context, universality is often thought of as the elimination of restrictions based on privilege, status and/or other essential considerations. In a more restricted sense, universality is also considered as the bourgeois formal equality before the law. In this vein, Hegel interpreted the two concepts of subjectivity and universality as epitomized in the notion of civil society, but criticized it for what he called its formality and vacuity. For Hegel, the separation, or what he calls "diremption," from nature and society and the moral "chaos" that is the result of the process of subjectification and radical human autonomy associated with subjectivity cannot be healed by the universality of civil society in its Kantian formulation. Hegel was one of the first and most prominent thinkers to attempt to address this crisis of formality in modern society and to try to resolve the contradictions between subjectivity and universality in a substantive (as opposed to formal) synthesis of the two principles.[2]

---

[2] On the dialectical relations between the two categories of subjectivity and universality and Hegel's objection to Kant's "formality" and his own attempt at a substantive synthesis between them see Charles Taylor, *Hegel and Modern Society* (Cambridge, England, 1979). See also Lawrence E. Cahoone, *The Dilemma of Modernity: Philosophy, Culture, and Anti-Culture* (Albany, 1987); David Kolb, *The Critique of Pure Modernity: Hegel, Heidegger, and After* (Chicago, 1986) and Fred Dallmayr, *G.W.F Hegel: Modernity and Politics* (Newbury Park, Calif., 1993).

Expressed somewhat differently, the principle of subjectivity has given rise to freedom and the notion of individual and collective autonomy in the modern era. The unbridled subjectivity of modernity, however, also has been responsible for moral and political chaos and various types of the domination of the "Others." For this reason, much of the intellectual and political thought since Hegel in one way or another has attempted to address the abstract, monadic, and self-same subject of modernity and strived to embed it in a larger context.[3] The latest and one of the most comprehensive contemporary efforts at the synthesis between subjectivity and universality is elaborated in the works of Habermas and his attempt at shifting the ontological foundation of modernity from mere subjectivity to that of intersubjectivity through language, in his theory of communicative action.[4] Other critical theorists such as Adorno and Horkheimer have also elaborately discussed the dominative and reifying aspects of modern subjectivity. Categories such as positivism, instrumental rationality, bureaucracy, the advent of fascism, and what they called "culture industry," are among those constituting the dominative aspect of subjectivity and its destructive effects.

This article attempts to analyze the major philosophical and socio-political discourses of mid-nineteeth century Iranian thought, i. e., those articulated by Mīrzā Malkom Khan, Mīrzā Āqā Khan Kermānī, ʿAbd-al-Raḥīm Ṭālebof, Mīrzā Fatḥ-ʿAlī Āḵūndzāda, and Sayyid Jamāl-al-Dīn Afḡānī, in light of the theoretical insights culled from critical theory relating to two categories of subjectivity and universality and their reconciliation as universalizable subjectivity. It trys to demonstrate that in the discourses of these five figures two closely related but distinct strands of subjectivity, one more conducive to the emancipatory potential of a synthesis between subjectivity and universality and intersubjectivity and the other more conducive to domination and mastery grounded in positive subjectivity, emerge simultaneously.

---

[3] For a discussion of the debates regarding the efforts to embed the unbridled subject of modernity without compromising the freedom of subjectivity see, for example, Seyla Benhabib, *Critique, Norm, and Utopia* (New York, 1986); and idem, *Situating the Self: Gender, Community, and Postmodernism in Contemporary Ethics* (New York, 1992).

[4] See Jürgen Habermas, *The Theory of Communicative Action* I: *Reason and the Rationalization of the Society* (Boston, 1981) and II: *Lifeworld and System: Critique of Functionalist Reason* (Boston, 1984).

Dual Appropriation of Modernity: Positivist Subjectivity and Universalizable Subjectivity

Modernity struck Iran, as many other countries, in its most shocking and therefore awakening form, imperialism, at the beginning of the nineteenth century. The onslaught of modernity came in the form of military pressure and invasion, at first from the northern borders with imperial Russia and later, in the middle of the nineteenth century, from Britain. Russian expansionism, equipped with modern means of warfare, easily defeated the ill-prepared Iranian army, which relied for the most part on tribal military forces and methods. The result was the humiliating treaties of Golestān (1813) and Torkmānčāy (1828), according to which Iran lost territory and areas of suzerainty in Transcaucasia as well as navigational rights for its warships on the Caspian Sea.[5]

As a result, from the very beginning of Iran's encounter with the modern world, there was a dual approach to modernity. On the one hand, there was a strong interest in the appropriation of modern western "technique" in general, including military technology, and, on the other hand, there was some desire and curiosity for new ideas and institutions of civil society. To be sure, this duality in the appropriation of modernity in Iran reflected the very same duality that modernity had exhibited in its European birthplace.[6] Therefore, in Iran also, one may observe a positivist interpretation of subjectivity as well as, and side by side with, what can be designated as a "universalizable subjectivity." The notion of progress, for example, is of pivotal importance in both European and Iranian contexts. In the positivist interpretation of this concept by Iranian intellectuals, progress is codified as the development of science and technology and their application to the social sphere, whereas in universalizable subjectivity the notion of progress refers more to the possibility of democratic change and transformation of

---

[5] Firuz Kazemzadeh, "Iranian Relations with Russia and the Soviet Union, to 1921," in P. Avery, G. Hambley, and C. Melville, eds., *Cambridge History of Iran* VII: *From Nadir Shah to the Islamic Republic* (Cambridge, 1991), 334. One may imagine the shock and humiliation of defeat felt by the Iranians when a Russian force of merely 2,260 soldiers defeated the Iranian army of 30,000 in a battle which lasted only two days despite the valor displayed by the Iranians; see ibid., 334-38. See also ʿAlī-Akbar Bīna, *Tārīḵ-e sīāsī va dīplomasī-e Īrān,* vol. 1 (Tehran, 1954), for the text of these two treaties.

[6] For a discussion of the dual nature of modernity and its emancipatory as well as dominative aspects see, for example, Johan Fornas, *Cultural Theory and Late Modernity* (London, 1995).

the oppressive institutions wherein the concept of critique plays a central role. The same duality is expressed in the notion of law in early Iranian appropriation of modernity. According to the positivist interpretation, law is viewed primarily as order, regulation, and codification. In contrast, "positive law" manifests the universalizability of freedom and the rights and responsibilities of a generalized citizenship and the notion of government by consent and consensus, which ultimately posits the notion of legislation on the basis of popular sovereignty.[7] At the institutional level, the same dichotomy is displayed in the difference between the interest in merely an efficient bureaucracy, such as the creation of *majles tanẓīmāt* (organizational assembly), on the one hand, and the construction of a parliamentary constitution and representative assembly on the other.

Both of those tendencies had also appropriated the idea of the nation-state and nationalism from the modern West. But, while the positivist tendencies placed more emphasis on a notion of nationalism based on ethnic and historical identity (in Iran's case, the putative Aryan and pre-Islamic identity of the country), the universalizable approach leaned more towards a notion of nationalism based upon popular sovereignty within the confines of a nation-state. It is crucial to realize that both interpretations of modernity were expressed simultaneously in each of the discourses promulgated in the second part of the nineteenth century which are discussed here, while each also emphasized different aspects of each tendency to a different degree.

Before discussing the themes which emerged in the dual approach to modernity in late nineteenth-century Iran, it is necessary to consider briefly the conditions which lead to the dichotomy between "positivist subjectivity" and "universalizable subjectivity." As mentioned above, this was partly a reflection of the same dichotomy in the birthplace of modernity in Europe. However, what contributed to this dualistic appropriation of modernity in Iran was not only the impact of foreign imperialism, but also domestic despotism.[8] Obviously, the foreign imperialist encroachments toward Iran that often accompanied military intervention could not but result in an interest in a positivist appropriation of European subjectivity. Here, the inaction of the

---

[7] Here, "positive law" should not be confused with positivist interpretation of law, despite the common etymology, since they are used in an opposite sense in this context.

[8] For a discussion of the centrality of despotism in Iranian history, see Homa Katouzian, *The Political Economy of Modern Iran: Despotism and Pseudo-Modernism, 1926-1979* (New York, 1981).

domestic despotism and its inability to counter European hegemony, had two results. It partially reinforced the interest in positivist subjectivity, but it also partially gave rise to a consciousness about the nature of despotism in Iran and to seeking for ways to distribute the power invested and concentrated in despotism, which lead to an interest in universalizable subjectivity.

Malkom Khan: Positivist Law and Positive Law

The concept of *qānūn* or law emerged as a central theme in the socio-political discourse of the late nineteenth century among the leading advocates of reform in the Qajar Iran. Mīrzā Malkom Khan (1833-1908) was one of the earliest and most influential theorists who systematically addressed issues pertaining to modernity in Iran. He was born into an Armenian family in Isfahan. He was sent to France to study engineering on a state scholarship. It was there that he developed an interest in political philosophy and especially in Saint Simon's ideas about social engineering, as well as in August Comte's Religion of Humanity. Upon returning to Iran, he ostensibly converted to Islam, securing a teaching job for himself at the recently established modern polytechnic of Dār al-Fonūn. Soon thereafter he created a semi-secret association modeled on European Freemasonry, but unrelated to it, and engaged in a campaign to persuade the shah and the court elite to initiate modern reforms chiefly based on the Ottoman notion of organization, the Tanẓīmāt.[9] Initially, Nāṣer-al-Dīn Shah (r. 1848-96) received his proposal for reform positively, but soon became suspicious of Malkom's intentions and exiled him to Turkey. After that Malkom's life and career were characterized by sequences of patronage and disfavor by the shah for his ideas for reform; in the last decade of the nineteenth century, after he lost his ambassadorship to Britain, he became a radical critic of the political situation in Iran and published his famous and influential newspaper *Qānūn* in London.[10]

Malkom's discourse on modernity embodied the dual approach discussed above. On the one hand, he advocated the wholesale importation of European bureaucracy on the Ottoman model and, on

---

[9] Ervand Abrahamian, *Iran Between Two Revolutions* (Princeton, 1982), 65-66.

[10] For a detailed account of Malkom's career and life see Hamid Algar, *Mirza Malkum Khan: A Study in the History of Iranian Modernism* (Berkeley, 1973).

the other hand, he displayed some interest in at least rudimentary forms of democratic institutions and much more so in the ontological foundations of these institutions. In his positivist mood, he equated progress with the principles of order and organization. He wrote:

> If we want to find the path to progress through our own mental exercises we have to wait for three thousand years. The Europeans have discovered the road to progress and principles of organization just as they have discovered the principle of the telegraph during the past two or three thousand years and have developed certain formulas for these principles.[11]

He then went on to recommend the "installation" of "principles of organization" in Iran, just as easily as one could install the telegraph in Tehran without wasting time.[12] Malkom's obsession with the principle of organization is in turn reflective of his idea about the lack of a strong administrative system in Iran in the nineteenth century. He said, "In a nutshell, we do not have an 'executive apparatus' in Iran, and as long as we do not set up this principal apparatus, all our words and writings are entirely futile and a source of disgrace."[13] Malkom also seems to have developed a very strong impression of the efficiency of European bureaucracy, especially the state bureaucracy. The Europeans, in his view, had not only developed factories for the production of objects, they had also developed factories for the production of "humans." Just as in the first type of factory, in which raw materials entered one end and finished products emerged from the other, so there were human factories where ignorant children were poured into one end and from the other end came engineers and perfect thinkers. In a similar vein, Malkom extended his factory analogy to explain the working of the European legal system and modern banking in terms of "production" of justice and money.[14] However, the most impressive of these second types of "factory" for Malkom Khan was the "state apparatus." He wrote:

> In Europe, among these human factories, they have one factory which is located at the center of the government and animates

---

[11] Mīrzā Malkom Khan, "Ketābča-ye ḡaybī," in *Majmūʿa-ye āṯār-e Malkom Khan*, ed. Moḥammad-Moḥīṭ Ṭabāṭabāʾī, (Tehran, 1327 Š./1948) 13.

[12] Mīrzā Malkom Khan, "Ketābča-ye ḡaybī," *Majmūʿa-ye āṯār*, 13.

[13] Mīrzā Malkom Khan, "Dastgāh dīvān," in *Majmūʿa-ye āṯār*, 148.

[14] Mīrzā Malkom Khan, "Ketābča-ye ḡaybī," *Majmūʿa-ye āṯār,* 11-12.

> all other factories. This great apparatus is called the apparatus of bureaucracy. Anyone who is interested in knowing what miracles human reason is capable of [producing] should investigate this apparatus of bureaucracy. The organization, welfare, prosperity, and the greatness and the entire progress of Europe depends on the proper organization of this apparatus.[15]

Malkom also expressed the urgent need for reform in the Iranian military as he referred to the Iranian defeat at the hands of Russia in 1813 and 1828.[16] However, he pointed out that success in military reform was contingent upon the state apparatus becoming organized.[17] Malkom's interest in "organization" (*naẓm*), which bordered on an obsession, was typical of his age and very prevalent in the region.[18] Yet, this obsession stemmed from the reality of the imperialist onslaught facing Iran and the entire region. He shrewdly observed that the government of Iran in facing the encroachment of European hegemony was not any different from the Ottoman government and that the surge in the power of Europe had made the survival of "barbarian governments" impossible. From now on, all governments on the earth must be organized like European governments or they would be conquered and subjugated by them.[19]

Malkom concluded that the precondition for acquiring Western bureaucratic organization rested on modern sciences and technology. He thought the misfortune of the previous rulers of Iran was due to their ignorance of the new sciences and technologies. He pointed out that the reason for the success of Japan had been the sympathetic attitudes of its statesmen to modern science, even though they did not have formal training in the sciences. He then concluded that while in the time of the ancient Persian kings "the organization of affairs rested on 'natural reason,' the contemporary organization of all European governments rests entirely on science."[20]

---

[15] Mīrzā Malkom Khan, "Ketābča-ye ğaybī," *Majmūʿa-ye āsār*, 11.

[16] Mīrzā Malkom Khan, "Dastgāh dīvān," *Majmūʿa-ye āsār*, 89.

[17] Mīrzā Malkom Khan, "Dastgāh dīvān," *Majmūʿa-ye āsār*, 90.

[18] The concept of *tanẓīmāt* first emerged in the Ottoman Empire, as the reforms initiated there were designated by this term. It is derived from an Arabic root, *naẓẓama*, meaning to put in order.

[19] Mīrzā Malkom Khan, "Dastgāh dīvān," *Majmūʿa-ye āsār*, 95.

[20] Fereydūn Ādamīyat, *Fekr-e āzadī* (Tehran, 1961), 117.

Malkom Khan's later discourse in the 1880s and 1890s specifically focused on the role of law in response to Nāṣer-al-Dīn Shah's intransigent despotism and his inability to counter Western hegemony.[21] In keeping with the positivist aspect of his views as manifested in his emphasis on order and organization, Malkom presented a very instrumental view of the role of law as a means to counter hegemonic force against foreign domination of Iran. In an article in his newspaper *Qānūn*, he discussed the Russians' utilization of bureaucratic institutionalization of power to their advantage without limiting the power of the emperor as a model for the Iranian state. He argued that:

> The maximum power imaginable is concentrated in the hands of the Russian emperor. But despite such a dominating power, he is not able to mete out punishment on anyone without the order of the [judicial] bureaucracy. No one has placed any limitations on the emperor's power. The emperor himself, owing to his education and enlightened knowledge, willingly has made the enactment of laws and observations thereof the basis of his splendor. The emperor has made himself, more than anyone else, obedient to the law since obeying the law has given him dominance over twenty "lawless" kings.[22]

The above passage might be interpreted as a ruse by Malkom to encourage the shah to give up some of his power, but it is also a strong move towards the establishment of modern bureaucracy in the state apparatus in Iran. This seems to be one of the earliest theoretical attempts to replace the autocratic rule of despotism with bureaucratic rule.[23] To institutionalize his ideas regarding this conception of law, Malkom proposed the creation of an "Organizational Assembly" (Majles Tanẓīmāt). But he was careful to point out that this type of assembly had nothing to do with a parliamentary system and a representative assembly, about which the court ministers attempted to create confusion to discourage the shah from instituting such reforms.

---

[21] Malkom Khan's motivations for his critique of Nāṣer-al-Dīn Shah's despotism were not entirely altruistic. His personal vexation with the shah for dismissing him as his ambassador to Britain after the lottery fiasco was equally strong. See Algar, *Mirza Malkum Khan*.

[22] Mīrzā Malkom Khan, *Qānūn*, 20 April 1890.

[23] As it transpired in the twentieth century with the advent of the Pahlavi dynasty (1925-79), despotism and bureaucratic rationality were combined to institutionalize the state power in the hands of Pahlavi monarchs.

Malkom charged this Organizational Assembly with the task of creating laws for the country.

It is instructive to examine briefly Malkom's understanding of this type of law. In his monograph *Daftar qānūn* (Book of Law), he wrote, "Every injunction which is issued from the legal apparatus (*dastgāh qānūn*) in accordance with a 'determined agreement' is called law, and it is necessary for this law to be definitively issued by the legal apparatus."[24] What is of crucial significance in this passage is the phrase "determined agreement" (*qarār moʿayyan*) because while the agreement stems from the non-representative assembly of the Majles Tanẓīmāt, it nevertheless contains the seminal concept of contract and therefore the potentiality of a conception of law based on consensus. This latter view is further developed and reflected in Malkom's later discourse. For example, in a letter written in 1903 to Mīrzā Naṣr-Allāh Khan Mošīr-al-Dawla, Malkom argued:

> World history in the course of five thousand years has proved that the "essence" of human reason does not manifest itself except through the interplay of discourse and consensus of opinion. According to an eternal principle, justice, security, progress and prosperity and the entire benefits of life have never appeared in any part of the world except through the practice of consultation.[25]

Such a view is in turn contingent upon a conception of basic rights of the individual which Malkom expressed in an essay entitled "Ṣerāṭ-e Mostaqīm" (The Straight Path) in 1881. In this essay, Malkom posited four basic principles for human rights as security, freedom (*ek̲tīār* or *āzādī*), equality and achieved status. He divided security into the security of the person and that of property. He also elaborated on the concept of freedom by distinguishing such categories as the freedom of the body, speech, pen, thought, business (*kasb*), and association.[26]

It is important to note that underlying Malkom's conceptualization of freedom there is an ontological foundation of human subjectivity. He wrote,

> The nobility of our creation lies in [God's] having created us as subjects (*fāʿel-e mok̲tār*) and because of this nobility [He] has

---

[24] Mīrzā Malkom Khan, "Daftar-e qānūn," in *Majmūʿa-ye ās̱ār*, 138.
[25] Ādamīyat, *Fekr āzādī*, 121.
[26] Ādamīyat, *Fekr āzādī*, 214.

made us agents who through our reason and effort [*ejtehād*] are owners and protectors of our "rights of humanness"[i.e., human rights].[27]

He then theorized about the "alienation" of this subjectivity and its restoration:

Our great sin and [the cause of] our misfortune is that we have totally lost this nobility and this sacred agency, and for centuries we have begged others for our rights instead of seeking them in ourselves.[28]

The term Malkom Khan used to popularize his concept of subjectivity was *ādamīyat*. Rooted in the Semitic languages, the term *ādam*, meaning human being, was used by Malkom Khan as a familiar term in Islamic culture to disseminate his understanding of subjectivity. He contended that according to all religions and moral philosophies God had created us as *ādam* and, as a proof of our being *ādam*, He had made every individual human being the inheritor of "grand gifts" which may collectively be called the "rights of being *ādam*."[29] One of the most important aspects of Malkom's discourse on being *ādam* was its implications for a new approach to conceptualization of the idea of justice. For centuries in the Middle East, the idea of justice was contingent upon the advice to political rulers to restrain their oppression of their subjects. Malkom attempted to revamp the concept of justice by broaching the idea that to achieve justice it was incumbent upon the oppressed not to tolerate oppressors and to overthrow them.[30]

Concurrent with the publication of the newspaper *Qānūn* in the 1890s, Malkom was also responsible for the foundation of the League of Humanity (Jamᶜ-e Ādamīyat), an organization devoted to the

---

[27] Mīrzā Malkom Khan, "Nadā-ye ᶜadālat," in *Majmūᶜa-ye āṯār*, 215.

[28] Mīrzā Malkom Khan, "Nadā-ye ᶜadālat," *Majmūᶜa-ye āṯār*, 215.

[29] Mīrzā Malkom Khan, "Nadā-ye ᶜadālat," *Majmūᶜa-ye āṯār*, 214. Writing in a mostly religious milieu, Malkom here expressed the concept of subjectivity as "mediated subjectivity." Some Islamic approaches to subjectivity have been couched in terms of mediated subjectivity, following the precedent set in this period. For an elaboration on the concept of mediated subjectivity, see Farzin Vahdat, "Metaphysical Foundations of Islamic Revolutionary Discourse in Iran: Vacillations on Human Subjectivity," *Critique* 14(1999): 49-73.

[30] Ādamīyat, *Fekr āzādī*, 213.

propagation of his views, especially those pertaining to raising consciousness about the rights of citizens. While in exile, Malkom's influence was mostly intellectual and the organization was run by his sympathizers in Tehran and other cities.[31] There seems to be little doubt that Malkom's ideas about *ādamīyat*, or being a human, as he understood the notion of subjectivity, as well as the League of Humanity, were both much influenced by August Comte's notion of the Religion of Humanity.[32] Yet despite this strong positivist influence, the League was a crucial institution in the propagation of the idea of the rights of the individual citizen during the Constitutional Revolution of 1905-9. As a matter of fact, this characteristic of the League further corroborates the thesis regarding the dual nature of approaches of the Iranian theorists discussed here toward modernity. In a similar vein, the positivist aspect of Malkom's ontology was manifested in his very mechanical approach towards the raising of consciousness about human rights since, as noted earlier, he proposed to "produce" such humans by establishing "human-making factories" (*kārḵāna-ye ādam-sāzī*).

Malkom's discourse was also concerned with questions pertaining to the social universal and issues regarding the rights of the public. Very often he invoked familiar Islamic concepts and practices to explain his new ideas. This practice had the effect of being able to reach as many Iranians as possible rather than just a small elite. Similarly, even though his conceptualization of law was marred by strong positivist elements, nevertheless it was law with universal application. As he put it, "the law, all over the nation of Iran and regarding every individual Iranian subject, is equal."[33] Another aspect of universality which Malkom addressed was achieved status instead of ascribed status, which he recommended especially as the sole criteria for recruitment in government services and the military.[34]

In Malkom's discourse, there were no attempts to distinguish between the two aspects of modernity designated here as positivist and universalizable subjectivity. In fact, his discourse is mostly a mixed bag of the two, while as time passed he moved closer toward a conception of universalizable subjectivity. This mixture of the two aspects is best captured in his concise formulation of what he thought the law ought to be. He wrote: "The law should reflect the emperor's

---

[31] See Ādamīyat, *Fekr āzādī*, 213, for a detailed account of the League of Humanity and its members.

[32] Ādamīyat, *Fekr āzādī*, 200.

[33] Mīrzā Malkom Khan, "Ketābča-ye ḡaybī," *Majmūʿa-ye āṯār,* 26.

[34] Malkom Khan, *Dastgāh dīvān*, 75.

will and guarantee the public interest."[35] While this statement indicated a step toward the limitation of the arbitrary will of the shah and the achievement of popular sovereignty, the ambiguity contained within it reflects a very similar ambiguity regarding the responsibilities of the shah and popular sovereignty that formed the cornerstone of the Iranian constitution of 1906.

While Malkom Khan's discourse focused primarily on the questions pertaining to the political and legal spheres, the epistemological questions as well as ideas about national identity were prominent in the works of Kermānī, another influential thinker of the nineteenth century in the Iranian sphere of influence.[36]

Kermānī: Epistemological Concerns and National Identity

Despite his unsystematic method, Mīrzā Āqā Khan Kermānī may be considered one of the earliest thinkers in Iran who paid serious attention to philosophical questions and epistemological issues of modernity. In his discourse, a mixture of positivist and potentially emancipatory types of subjectivity may again be observed. The first modern western philosophical book translated into Persian was Descartes' *Discourse on Reason*, which was published in 1860.[37] But Kermānī seems to have been the first person in Iran to attempt to ground Iranian thought in modern western philosophical tenets. He also seems to be one of the earliest theorists of modern nationalism in Iran who tried to create a pre-Islamic national identity for Iran.

Abu'l-Ḥosayn Khan, later to be known as Mīrzā Āqā Khan Kermānī, was born in 1853 in a small village near the town of Kermān in central Iran. His diverse family background seems to have had a direct impact on his education. On both his mother's and father's sides, his immediate

---

[35] Mīrzā Malkom Khan, "Ketābča-ye ḡaybī," *Majmūʿa-ye āṯār,* 25.

[36] Malkom Khan was not the only person at the time to focus on political-legal questions and conceptualizations of law. The treaties of another contemporary thinker, Mīrzā Yūsof Khan Mostašār-al-Dawla, entitled *Yak kalema*, referred to the law as the key in opening Iran's door to modernity and was also influential. The arguments advanced in this book are in close parallel to those of Malkom Khan, but in general have more religious overtones. Of much interest is Mostašār-al-Dawla's invocation of a verse from the Koran (17:70) to construct a "mediated subjectivity," where humans are depicted as God's vicegerent on earth. See Mīrzā Yūsof Khan Mostašār-al-Dawla, *Yak kalema* (Tehran, 1985), 55.

[37] Fereydūn Ādamīyat, *Andīšahā-ye Mīrzā Āqā Khan Kermānī* (Tehran, 1978), 73.

ancestors were prominent members of Sufi orders. His mother's grandfather was a prominent Zoroastrian leader who later in his life had converted to Islam. Kermānī's line of descent also included famous physicians, prominent judges, and long established aristocrats, and one of his unorthodox grandfathers had been murdered in accordance with a *fatwa* issued by an orthodox mullah.[38] As Mangol Bayat has observed, such a diverse background must have had a deep influence on Kermānī's philosophical and political views.[39]

Kermānī received a traditional Iranian education, including study of Persian literature, Arabic, Islamic history and "schools of thought," Islamic jurisprudence and Hadith, mathematics, logic, philosophy and mysticism, and traditional medicine. Among his teachers in philosophy and "sciences" (*ṭabīʿīyāt*) was the renowned Iranian philosopher Ḥājjī Sabzevārī. Later, Kermānī learned French and some English as well as pre-Islamic languages of Iran.[40] When he was about thirty years of age, as a result of a fierce disagreement with the governor of Kermān, he secretly fled his home town and gained asylum in Istanbul to escape extradition attempts by Kermān's governor. In Istanbul, Kermānī became more familiar with new ideas and philosophies as he associated with different intellectual and political circles in the Ottoman capital. During this period he and his close lifetime associate, Sheikh Aḥmad Rūḥī, married the two daughters of Ṣobḥ-e Azal.[41] Kermānī's life ended tragically when he and Rūḥī were extradited to Iran for allegedly plotting the assassination of Nāṣer-al-Dīn Shah in 1896 and were put to death in the same year.

Kermānī considered a seminal status for philosophy as a "sublime and universal science." Philosophy to him was "to know the truth of objects and beings according to the original and natural order." He further believed that the purpose of philosophy was the "elimination of chaos [stemming from] the darkness of ignorance and achievement of rational order and entrance into the light of truth."[42] He also thought

---

38 Ādamīyat, *Andīšahā-ye Mīrzā Āqā Khan Kermānī*, 14.

39 Mangol Bayat, "Mirza Aqa Khan Kirmani: A Nineteenth Century Persian Nationalist," *Middle Eastern Studies* 10/1, 1974, 30.

40 Ādamīyat, *Andīšahā-ye Mīrzā Āqā Khan Kermānī*, 14.

41 After the bloody repression of the Babi movement in Iran in the mid-nineteenth century, the movement was split into two. One was led by Ṣobḥ-e Azal, who remained closer to the doctrines of the Babi movement, and the other was led by Azal's half-brother, Bahāʾ-Allāh who founded the Bahai religion as a new dispensation.

42 Ādamīyat, *Andīšahā-ye Mīrzā Āqā Khan Kermānī*, 76. Even though Kermānī was a prolific writer, and twenty books and treatises were attributed

of this "noble science" as the primal cause of the "movement of thought" and "transformation of nations from barbarous primitiveness to the worlds of civilization and urbanity." Without philosophy, he contended, no real result from any other science could be obtained.[43] Kermānī's assessment of classical Greek philosophy, however, reveals some interesting points about his own discourse. Kermānī fancied himself as an arch-materialist and as such praised Socrates for "bringing down philosophy from the sky to the earth," but since Socrates' philosophical approach posited the subject as the center of the enterprise of knowledge instead of giving priority to matter, Kermānī was more interested in the Greek "materialist" philosophers such as Pythagoras, Democritus, and Heraclitus.[44]

Despite such a preference, Kermānī, in his own positivist fashion, acknowledged the centrality of human subjectivity in relation to matter. This "bipedal animal," he argued, like all beings, follows the laws of matter, but since in his relations with matter and nature he intervenes in them, he deviates from the laws of nature. This fact, he thought, was observable as a result of human "interpolation" (*taṣarrof*) into nature. Through experience, he claimed, we realize that social institutions which are created by human reason, more often than not, are incompatible with the laws of nature.[45] Yet Kermānī nonetheless reduced the human body to chemical compounds and considered the workings of human mind to be a physical function of the central nervous system. There are "nerves," he claimed, in the human brain which are most of the time in a state of motion, and "thought and reflection appear as a result of their movement." [46]

In accordance with his materialist formulation of subjectivity, Kermānī accounted for the perennial nature of despotism in Iran in geographic terms, and yet considered the freedom of the individual and thought as essential.[47] In a treatise entitled *En šāʾ Allāh mā šāʾ Allāh*, Kermānī criticized Iranians for abandoning human volition and resorting to metaphysical explanation for

---

to him, very few of his works have been published and of these many are not available. As a secondary source, Ādamīyat, *Andīšahā-ye Mīrzā Āqā Khan Kermānī*, seems to be a thorough representation of his works. It has been used here as a major, but not the only, source for this section.

[43] Ādamīyat, *Andīšahā-ye Mīrzā Āqā Khan Kermānī*, 76.

[44] Ādamīyat, *Andīšahā-ye Mīrzā Āqā Khan Kermānī*, 77.

[45] Ādamīyat, *Andīšahā-ye Mīrzā Āqā Khan Kermānī*, 99.

[46] Ādamīyat, *Andīšahā-ye Mīrzā Āqā Khan Kermānī*, 99.

[47] Ādamīyat, *Andīšahā-ye Mīrzā Āqā Khan Kermānī*, 173.

events and the power of providence. Muslims, he thought, instead of acting on the world, want to influence the course of events by uttering phrases such as *en šāʾ Allāh* ("God willing"). The same fatalistic inaction, he argued, which sealed the fate of Byzantine Christians during the siege of Constantinople also caused the defeat of Iranians in their confrontations with the Afghan invaders who put an end to the Safavid Empire in the early eighteenth century.[48] Indeed, the supreme God has designated a means for achieving every goal and has left the welfare of humankind to the personal efforts of individuals.[49] In a book called *Reżvān* (Paradise), following the tradition in Persian literature of a debate with a hypothetical opponent, Kermānī contrasted human volition and freedom and the idea of providence. He admonished his hypothetical opponent by claiming that:

> The human essence is always open to progress and unlimited perfection, so that the pure God [*Haq*] has esteemed and privileged it, but its progress or decline is entirely dependent on the will of the self [*nafs*] and his effort.[50]

In his book *Āʾīna-ye sekandarī* (Alexandrian Mirror), Kermānī condemned submission to the terrestrial powers also. He wrote:

> Deterministically, Iranians attribute the adversity or prosperity in the world to the will of the shahs and do not consider themselves as having any role in the changes of the realm. They do not fancy themselves as the origin of any influence in the world.

Then in a footnote he added that the reason why the Iranians have not progressed in any field is the false attitude, which derives from powerlessness or laziness, whereby Iranians do not consider themselves participants in the rights of the nation.[51]

Despite this element in Kermānī's view on human subjectivity, his theory of nationalism was based on a collectivist interpretation of subjectivity. The foil against which he attempted to create a collective nationalist subject were the Arabs and Islam. The Iranians, he maintained, never accepted Arab and Islamic rulers willingly, and all

---

48 Ādamīyat, *Andīšahā-ye Mīrzā Āqā Khan Kermānī*, 200-202.

49 Ādamīyat, *Andīšahā-ye Mīrzā Āqā Khan Kermānī*, 201.

50 Ādamīyat, *Andīšahā-ye Mīrzā Āqā Khan Kermānī*, 200.

51 Mīrzā Āqā Khan Kermānī, *Āʾīna-ye sekandarī*, (n. p., 1906), 47.

of the rulers of Iran ruled by bloodshed and oppression. According to this analysis, the politics of oppression is both corrupt and corrupting. It has corrupted the Iranians because people living under oppression and terror will lose their courage and virtue, and lethal diseases such as fear, cowardice, deception, hypocrisy, and sycophancy befall them. Thus, in Kermānī's view, Arab and Islamic domination of Iran robbed Iranians of their "ethos of superiority, magnanimity, and nobility."[52]

Kermānī's portrayal of Arabs is characterized by chauvinist and racist epithets and a pseudo-scientific approach. He used the adjectives "ignorant, savage, lizard-eaters; bloodthirsty, barefoot, camel-riders; desert-dwelling nomads" to describe the Arabs, whom he regarded as the cause of Iran's misery ever since their conquest of the country in the seventh century.[53] In conformity with his positivistic side, he applied nineteenth-century racist theories of phrenology to distinguish the Arabs and Jews as Semites from the Iranians as Aryans by their presumed respective physical features.[54] Kermānī's solution to this national "alienation" of collective subjectivity at the hands of the Arabs and Islam was a return to the pre-Islamic religion of Iran, Zoroastrianism, and the putative glories of Iran's pre-Islamic dynasties.[55]

As mentioned above, Kermānī's views on the mode of modernization in Iran were very much influenced by his positivist epistemology. He was aware of the positivist school of thought among the European "isms," and mentioned it by name.[56] The appropriation of natural science methods and paradigms and their application to social and political discourse, which was very prevalent in the West at that time, also influenced Kermānī's writing and thought. Thus, at the foundation of his epistemology, he believed that not only does the

---

[52] Ādamīyat, *Andīšahā-ye Mīrzā Āqā Khan Kermānī*, 202.

[53] Bayat, "Mirza Aqa Khan Kirmani," 45-47.

[54] Bayat, "Mirza Aqa Khan Kirmani," 45-47.

[55] Bayat, "Mirza Aqa Khan Kirmani," 48. As historical events showed in the twentieth century, after the triumph of positivist modernity in Iran with the advent of the Pahlavi dynasty, Iranian nationalism drew heavily on the themes of pre-Islamic civilization discussed here by Kermānī. Yet it is important to note that his reconstruction of ancient Iran as a source of cultural identity was not unidimensional. While he praised the state religion Zoroastrianism of ancient Iran and the principle of the shah's rights and people's duty to obey him as one of the pillars of Iran's prosperity, he also paid much attention to Mazdak, the radical prophet of Iran in the late fifth century, for his egalitarian and republican ideas.

[56] Ādamīyat, *Andīšahā-ye Mīrzā Āqā Khan Kermānī*, 78.

process of thinking stem from the physical activity of the central nervous system, but also both internal perception and external phenomena are determined by mechanical principles. As he put it, "geometric equation and arithmetic operations [have become] the guide and the measure of subjective and objective states."[57]

The simultaneous presence of positivist and potentially emancipatory elements in Kermānī's discourse, on the other hand, are evident in his abstractions on the ontology of movement. He posited that human material existence had originally been unified with the material existence of vegetables and animals, but they became separated later. The essence of animal and human existence, he thought, lies in perception and movement. But this movement, in his view, was constituted of wheels and mechanical instruments and means of electrical motion.[58] Thus, in contrast to the static view of traditional ontology, Kermānī's ontological view of movement portends a dynamic perception of human existence. Drawing on the seventeenth-century Iranian philosopher Mollā Ṣadrā, Kermānī presented a view of change in terms of "transformation of essence" (*ḥarekat jawharī*).[59] But at the same time, Kermānī exposed this very dynamism to the danger of degradation by subjecting it to scientific positivism as well as Social Darwinist determinism.[60] Much in agreement with this positivist aspect of his ontology, Kermānī leaned toward a lopsided emphasis on a "developmentalist" attitude in his approach to modernization and a reduction of human subjectivity to Faustian dimensions of mere economic development. For example, he considered a society civilized only if "it can provide its necessities for life and the means for its livelihood.... Ultimately, the more perfect a civilization, the more developed its means of livelihood would be."[61] Similarly, he articulated an interestingly futuristic and Faustian view of human intervention in nature as human agency. According to him, the "ignorant lowly primitive" human has now reached a stage where

> he has made visible the stars ... created artificial moonlight and inexhaustible rays [of light] ... made ice from fire and from ice [made] electricity ... and soon will have the audacity to intervene in the planets and contrive suns and stars from electricity and

---

[57] Ādamīyat, *Andīšahā-ye Mīrzā Āqā Khan Kermānī*, 100.
[58] Ādamīyat, *Andīšahā-ye Mīrzā Āqā Khan Kermānī*, 89.
[59] Ādamīyat, *Andīšahā-ye Mīrzā Āqā Khan Kermānī*, 96.
[60] Ādamīyat, *Andīšahā-ye Mīrzā Āqā Khan Kermānī*, 96-97.
[61] Ādamīyat, *Andīšahā-ye Mīrzā Āqā Khan Kermānī*, 106.

> preserve planets from being destroyed; and start consorting and fraternizing with their inhabitants; and achieve an eternal life...and sit on the throne of happiness.[62]

Despite Kermānī's strong positivist sides, his discourse also reveals a well developed critical streak. In the less abstract parts of his discourse, he focused on the state, religion, and philosophy (*ḥekmat*). What is central to the state, he thought, is force and intimidation (*tarsāndan*). Religion, on the other hand, is primarily concerned with dogma (*bāvarandan*) and belief. Among these, only philosophy is concerned with understanding (*fahmandan*) through reasoning (*estedlāl*) and better argument.[63] Accordingly, he pursued an independent and critical attitude towards categories of knowledge. He wrote:

> I am proud that after hearing scattered discourses and consorting with different peoples and reading many books and works of many persons, without interrogation and close examination I did not merely imitate [them].... I walked with my own feet and observed with my own eyes....[64]

He then paid homage to the Mutazalites, the early Islamic critical philosophers, for their application of the principle of doubt to every belief and for seeking reason and "incisive argumentation."[65]

From this approach to critical attitude, Kermānī extrapolated to forge a conception of positive law. If humans, he argued, are capable of managing a thousand affairs of their daily life, due to their independent consciousness, and can invent a thousand types of sciences, techniques, and industries, then surely they "would not be helpless [in creating] laws and practical ethics."[66] As we saw before, Kermānī must have been in favor of a universalization of the process of lawmaking since he thought the people must be "participants in the rights of the nation." In his famous treatise *Haftād o do mellat* (Seventy-Two Peoples) Kermānī criticized all religions and sects known to him for their particularity and marginalization of the non-faithful and the heterodox, while he reserved his severest condemnation for those societies

---

[62] Ādamīyat, *Andīšahā-ye Mīrzā Āqā Khan Kermānī*, 92.
[63] Ādamīyat, *Andīšahā-ye Mīrzā Āqā Khan Kermānī*, 111-12.
[64] Ādamīyat, *Andīšahā-ye Mīrzā Āqā Khan Kermānī*, 80.
[65] Ādamīyat, *Andīšahā-ye Mīrzā Āqā Khan Kermānī*, 81.
[66] Ādamīyat, *Andīšahā-ye Mīrzā Āqā Khan Kermānī*, 120.

operating on the basis of a caste system. Significantly, he concluded this essay by reflecting on the comments of an Indian pariah praising the universality of the modern legal system as practiced in Britain.[67]

In general, Kermānī's discourse was quite complicated and contained the two moments of modernity discussed throughout this article. Ironically, this duality in the discourse of Kermānī is symbolically captured in his praise for human volition, a volition which he viewed embodied in the person of Napoleon.[68] Even though most of his works were not published during his lifetime, his influence on the intellectual process and the consequent political events in Iran was very important.

While the core of Kermānī's work consisted of foundational issues of ontological and epistemological significance as well as the question of national identity, the domain of culture was the central focus of Āk̲ūndzāda.

Āk̲ūndzāda: Culture and Cultural Change

In many respects the work and lifetime occupations of Āk̲ūndzāda closely paralleled the themes which preoccupied Kermānī. However, perhaps because of the different cultural milieus within which each worked, their thematic emphasis were also different. Just like Kermānī, Āk̲ūndzāda was writing from outside of the Iranian borders, in the Caucasus, which, during his adolescence, had been annexed by Russia in the treaty of 1828. As a result of the subsequent uprisings and their suppression, the Caucasus witnessed the creation of a fertile intellectual atmosphere where Russian exiles were very active in forging a revolutionary discourse and emphasizing cultural themes in its development.

Mīrzā Fatḥ-ʿAlī Āk̲ūndzāda (1812-78) was born in the village of Nukheh near the town of Shaki in the southern part of the Caucasus. When he was very young, Āk̲ūndzāda's mother separated from his father, and his education came under the supervision of his mother's uncle, who was a man of letters. When he was nineteen years old, he started studying Islamic jurisprudence and logic (*feqh* and *osūl*) with

---

[67] Mīrzā Āqā Khan Kermānī, *Haftād o do mellat* (Tehran, 1983), 118-21. This should not be interpreted as Kermānī's insensitivity to problems of imperialism and colonization. He had many harsh words for Western colonization and exploitation of the East. Indeed, one can observe in his discourse the embryonic stages of discontent towards modernity as a response to colonization. See Ādamīyat, *Andīšahā-ye Mīrzā Āqā Khan Kermānī*, 288-89.

[68] Ādamīyat, *Andīšahā-ye Mīrzā Āqā Khan Kermānī*, 294-95.

a mullah of heterodox leanings who dissuaded him from pursuing a career as a cleric.[69] Later he attended a Russian school for one year (1833). A year later, he was employed as a translator in Tiflis, where he became familiar with diverse and avant-garde intellectual circles and was integrated into the rich cultural milieu of that city. Then he became familiar with some of the most prominent contemporary Russian thinkers such as Gogol and Pushkin.[70] He was also exposed to the ideas of the French Enlightenment, albeit indirectly and through Russian translations.[71] Āḵūndzāda's intellectual work may be divided into three relatively distinct periods. At first, he wrote plays and a novel, all promoting a spirit of social critique. Then he switched his attention to the question of alphabet reform as a means of a radical cultural change to be achieved through mass education. When discouraged by the idea of alphabet reform as a means of achieving cultural change, he turned his efforts to a campaign for religious reform to create a mass scale change in the culture. It was during this period when he wrote his controversial book *Maktūbāt-e Kamāl-al-Dawla* (The Letters of Kamāl-al-Dawla) and tried to publish it, without any success, until his death.[72]

Āḵūndzāda in his early phase thought that the time for classical Persian literary style, represented in the famous *Golestān* by Saʿdī and *Zayn al-majāles* had lapsed and now the most effective means of cultural change was drama and novel which he considered to be part of drama.[73] He also advocated the use of satire as a means of critical social analysis in preference to the traditional style of heavy emphasis on exhortation and pontification. In a later phase of the development of his thought on this issue he wrote:

> *Kritika* [critique] is not written without fault finding, scolding, and without satire and mocking. *The Letters of Kamāl-al-Dawla*

---

[69] Fereydūn Ādamīyat, *Andīšahā-ye Mīrzā Fatḥ-ʿAlī Āḵūndzāda* (Tehran, 1970), 143.

[70] Ādamīyat, *Andīšahā-ye Mīrzā Fatḥ-ʿAlī Āḵūndzāda,* 19.

[71] Maryam Sanjabi, "Reading the Enlightenment: Akhundzada and His Voltaire," *Iranian Studies* 28/1-2(1995):39.

[72] For a full biographical account of Āḵūndzāda's life and intellectual development see Ādamīyat, *Andīšahā-ye Mīrzā Fatḥ-ʿAlī Āḵūndzāda* and his own autobiography in Mīrzā Fatḥ-ʿAlī Āḵūndzāda, *Maqālāt*, ed. Bāqer Moʾmenī (Tehran, 1972). The *Maktūbāt-e Kamāl-al-Dawla* has only been published outside Iran, under the title *Maktūbāt*, by Iranian expatriates after the Islamic Revolution of 1979 (n.p., n.d.).

[73] Adamiyat, *Andīšahā-ye Mīrzā Fatḥ-ʿAlī Āḵūndzāda*, 54.

> is *kritika* and not preachment and exhortation. A truth written in the style of preachment, exhortation and [couched in] patronizing and paternalistic [terms] would never have any effect on human nature which is used to malefaction. Human nature always loathes reading and hearing preachings and sermons but is eager to read *kritika*.[74]

This new approach to literature by Āḵūndzāda reveals two important elements of his work and thought. First, that he was aware of the enormous potential of literature for any notion of cultural change. Second and more important, however, was his realization that authoritarianism contained in the old style of exhortation and sermonizing was anti-democratic and therefore his choice of satire represented a more democratic means of achieving his cultural goals.

This emphasis on culture, it seems, derived from a turning point in the appropriation of modernity by Iranian intellectuals of the late nineteenth century. Reflecting a sense of disappointment with the stress on the adoption of technical aspects of the modern West epitomized in the process of *tanẓīmāt*, Āḵūndzāda came to believe that the failure of Islamic nations in their efforts to modernize was due to their privileging of technical and pragmatic elements of European progress over theoretical aspects of progress.[75] Āḵūndzāda stated that "people must be prepared for the acceptance of European thoughts. European thoughts [implanted in the minds of the people of Iran] must be prior to trade with Europe and its products."[76]

In order to achieve such "preparation" and cultural transformation, Āḵūndzāda focused on two closely related issues. He proposed the ideas of the alphabet and later script reforms as a means of rapid increase in mass literacy. Reasoning that the Arabic-Persian script, because of its connected letters, has hampered the spread of literacy among Islamic peoples, he first proposed the modification of the Arabic-Persian writing system and later advocated the adoption of a modified form of Latin script.[77] He also raised the related issue of universal education for all as the most important means of modernization of Islamic countries. Keenly aware of the importance

---

[74] Mīrzā Fatḥ-ʿAlī Āḵūndzāda, *Alefbā-ye jadīd va maktūbāt*, ed. Ḥamīd Moḥammadzāda (Tabrīz, 1357 Š./1978), 206.

[75] Āḵūndzāda, *Alefbā-ye jadīd*, 289.

[76] Ādamīyat, *Andīšahā-ye Mīrzā Fatḥ-ʿAlī Āḵūndzāda*, 165.

[77] For a full discussion of Āḵūndzāda's proposals for reform of the alphabet and script see Āḵūndzāda, *Alefbā-ye jadīd*.

of the universality of modern education, Āḵūndzāda criticized the confinement of literacy to urbanites while excluding those in the countryside. Just as it was the case in Prussia and America, he proclaimed, all men and women should receive education so that the public can benefit.[78] There is little doubt that these ideas contained kernels of emancipatory value in the Middle Eastern and Iranian context of the period. However, in conjunction with this possibility of liberation, Āḵūndzāda, also introduced an element of "force" along the concept of education which has been adopted by the Iranian educational system and has vitiated its universal emancipatory potential. The compulsory education he was proposing would be the result of the decree from a great reformer, as he mentioned Peter the Great or Frederick the Great as examples, rather than the consensual will of the population. He wrote:

> According to the law of Frederick the Great, the king, who is the defender of the country and protector of the nation, has the same authority over any child born to any of his subjects, as the father has over the child. Therefore, if the king forces this child to learn reading and writing for his/her own good from age nine to age fifteen, this type of force cannot be called oppression, but indicates affection and love, which, as the saying has it, is called "coercive benevolence" (*tawfīq-e ejbārī*).[79]

On the other hand, one of the central concepts that Āḵūndzāda developed was the notion of critique, or as he called it *kritika*. Accordingly, he considered freedom of thought the *sine quo non* for the achievement of *kritika*, as he believed that, eventually and gradually, "as a result of the interplay of discourses and of different ideas, truth would come into focus." Similarly, as long as human societies do not offer

> freedom of thought to their individual members and force them to be content with what their forefathers and religious founders have established ... without using their reason in the affairs of the community ... these individuals would resemble the horses in a mill, rotating around a pre-determined circle everyday....[80]

Āḵūndzāda's notion of freedom is constructed on the basis of a deeper and more radical notion of human subjectivity and agency,

---

[78] Ādamīyat, *Andīšahā-ye Mīrzā Fatḥ-ʿAlī Āḵūndzāda*, 81.
[79] Āḵūndzāda, *Alefbā-ye jadīd*, 158.
[80] Ādamīyat, *Andīšahā-ye Mīrzā Fatḥ-ʿAlī Āḵūndzāda*, 142.

which he, more than any other theorist among his peers and ever since, articulated in terms of a confrontational relation between the human subject and the monotheistic deity. He irreverently questioned what he perceived to be a master/slave relationship between the human and the deity in monotheism as antithetical to any notion of justice and equality and considered the concepts of hell and heaven as a reflection of oppression and wrath and therefore not befitting human nature.[81] He also accused the creator of never acknowledging the power of human understanding since "we are his slaves."[82] The celestial and the terrestrial authoritarianism of despots, according to Āk̲ūndzāda, has resulted in an abject and sycophantic attitude among the people of the East towards authority.[83] Āk̲ūndzāda then turned his critique back to humans by depicting the idea of a monotheistic God as a projection of their own passions and abominations, desires and quest for status and prestige, and their own vengefulness.[84] For these reasons, he advocated human reason over revelation and thus, in his estimation, reversed the process by which the guardians of religion have retarded and "imprisoned" reason for a few thousand years.[85]

What Āk̲ūndzāda proposed as the content of this human reason, however, was nothing but a positivist view of modern science. Reflecting this positivist attitude, he repined that our God, instead of informing us of America, the steam engine, or electrical power, tells us about Belqīs, the city of Sheba, and the story of Solomon and the Hoopoe (*hūdhūd*).[86] This type of lamentation served as an excuse to call for a transition from a religious and metaphysical world view to one based on natural sciences. In the same book, *The Letters of Kamāl-al-Dawla*, addressing an imaginary prince named Jalāl-al-Dawla who received his correspondences, Āk̲ūndzāda wrote,

> As long as you and your co-religionists are not informed of the science of nature and astronomy, and as long as your knowledge of supernatural events and miracles among you is not [based on] scientific principles, you and they will always believe in

[81] Āk̲ūndzāda, *Maktūbāt*, 183.
[82] Āk̲ūndzāda, *Maktūbāt*, 88.
[83] Āk̲ūndzāda, *Maktūbāt*, 52-3.
[84] Āk̲ūndzāda, *Maktūbāt*, 108.
[85] Āk̲ūndzāda, *Maktūbāt*, 94.
[86] Āk̲ūndzāda, *Maktūbāt*, 88.

> supernatural events, miracles, magic, talisman, fairies, jinnis, saints, peris, and such delusions and will remain ignorant forever.[87]

What is of most importance is that Āḵūndzāda suggested that natural sciences should become the guide and criteria for questions pertaining to the practical/ethical sphere. He argued that there are three spheres in every religion. They consist of beliefs, devotions, and the practical/ethical sphere, and the latter is the main purpose of all religions and the first two are secondary.[88] So far we have needed the first two spheres to attain the practical/ethical sphere, but if we find a means to achieve our practical goals without subservience and enslavement, then we do not need the beliefs and devotions.[89] Then he concluded that this means is provided by the modern European sciences which have obviated the need for the spheres of devotion and belief.[90]

In order to illustrate his ideas, Āḵūndzāda utilized a short period of Ismaili history as a point of reference.[91] He narrated the account of Ḥasan b. Moḥammad, known as ʿAlā Ẕekrehe al-Salām, who as the leader of a heterodox Ismaili sect in the late twelfth century declared the Šarīʿa (Divine Law) annulled, decreed the unveiling of women, and banned polygamy.[92] All these measures, taken by Ḥasan b. Moḥammad, constituted for Āḵūndzāda the essential foundation of what he called "Islamic Protestantism," by which he meant a religion in which "God's rights (*ḥoqūq Allāh*) and worshiper's duties (*takālīf ʿebād Allāh*) are annulled and only human rights remain."[93]

What lies at the core of Āḵūndzāda's thought can be found in his ontological views, which he grounded in a pantheistic approach. First, he rejected the notion of a transcendent creator and a creation fixed in a master/slave relationship. "The universe," he wrote, "is but one complete force, one complete being." He then advanced another

---

[87] Āḵūndzāda, *Maktūbāt*, p, 94.

[88] Āḵūndzāda, *Maktūbāt*, 220-21.

[89] Āḵūndzāda, *Maktūbāt*, 222.

[90] Āḵūndzāda, *Maktūbāt*, 222.

[91] The Ismailis were a sect within the "extreme" Shiites founded in late eighth century. They were known for their heterodox views and practices. See, for example, Farhad Daftary, *The Assassin Legends: Myths of the Ismailis* (New York, 1995), and Bernard Lewis, *The Assassins: A Radical Sect in Islam* (repr. London, 1985).

[92] Āḵūndzāda, *Maktūbāt*, 134-37.

[93] Āḵūndzāda, *Maktūbāt*, 32.

pantheistic notion which posits all parts of the being, whether the emanating or the emanated, the particular and the universal, as equal. He wrote: "the 'origin' and the 'end' are the same; neither the 'origin' nor the 'end' have priority over one another."[94] Therefore, all "particles" of this unified "being" are equal and none has any authority over the other, and no miracles willed by any of these particles can be performed. This is so because, Āḵūndzāda argued, what governs the relations between these particles of being is an eternal and omnipotent law which determines all the events in this world.[95] Based on this reasoning, Āḵūndzāda denied the possibility of free will since even emanation is not by free will, because any notion of free will would negate the possibility of equality between the universal being and the particular:

> In reality, the universal and the particle is but one being which is manifested *belā eḵtīār* ("without willing") in infinite multiplicity and in different forms only in accordance to the said *principle* and under *its own laws and conditions*.[96]

Then, in a footnote, he further explained that necessity (*jabr*) is the lack of will on the part of the universal (*vojūd koll*) in its emanation, and if someone interprets necessity in any other way, he or she has not understood.[97]

Interestingly, Hegel used a similar concept of pantheism to arrive at subjectivity and freedom. Here Āḵūndzāda utilized the same idea only to arrive at the necessity and determinism of the laws and principles, of which the scientific laws constituted the concrete form. Therefore, it is no accident that Āḵūndzāda in the same section where he discussed these rather abstract issues, alluded to the physical laws governing the events in the universe. For example, he considered the sun and the moon as "particles" of the universe which as such are subject to the "eternal law" which determines the state of all other "particles."[98]

As I have tried to show in this section, Āḵūndzāda's allusion to the possibility of subjectivity on the part of the particular on the one hand, and negating this very possibility by positing a natural science

---

[94] Āḵūndzāda, *Maktūbāt*, 95-96.
[95] Āḵūndzāda, *Maktūbāt*, 96-97.
[96] Āḵūndzāda, *Maktūbāt*, 102-3; emphasis added.
[97] Āḵūndzāda, *Maktūbāt*, 103.
[98] Āḵūndzāda, *Maktūbāt*, 97.

determinism, on the other hand, constitutes a duality in the ontological core of his discourse which found its way in very concrete forms into different aspects of his thought. This duality in fact closely corresponds to the duality between positivist subjectivity and universalizable subjectivity, as discussed above, and exhibits the same tension between the two. Perhaps the most sinister manifestation of Āḵūndzāda's positivism was what may be called "enlightenment from above." As Maryam Sanjabi has argued, this approach to modernity ended up calling for an enlightened despot such as a Peter the Great or Frederick II to put the house of Iran in order and bring modernity to it.[99] As Iranian history later clearly reveals, this role was fulfilled by the Pahlavi monarchs, but at the expense of the eclipse of the emancipatory moment of modernity. Perhaps the most ironic aspect of the unintended consequence of Āḵūndzāda's discourse was that in attempting to create a notion of human subjectivity through his radical views on Islam, he alienated his potential audiences, the majority of whom had strong attachments to religion. He seems to have been aware of such a consequence, but rejected the pleas for toning down his rhetoric because, as he put it, his work would be as ineffective as those of Rūmī, Šabestārī, Jāmī, and other Sufi thinkers before him.[100] In a similar vein, Āḵūndzāda's views on Iranian nationalism portended the dwarfing of freedom and democracy since they were not primarily based on a notion of citizenship rights, as they defined Iranian nationality in contradistinction to the "otherness" of the Arabs.

Thus, again in the case of Āḵūndzāda, we come across a mixture of potentially emancipatory ideas and at the same time their very negation side by side. This duality is expressed in his call for a constitution, a liberal universal education, and emancipation of women along with his practical/ethical positivism, racist nationalism, and the idea of enlightenment from above by a Great Man.

Ṭālebof: A Discourse of Conflict and Reconciliation

Compared to his colleagues and their themes on modernity as discussed thus far, Ṭālebof offers more developed notions of universalizable subjectivity, although as we will see, he too exhibits strong strains of positivism now and then. This tendency in Ṭālebof is also accompanied by an inclination to acknowledge and an attempt to reconcile some of the contradictions emerging in the process of Iran's early encounter with modernity. Writing in the late nineteenth and

---

[99] See Sanjabi, "Reading the Enlightenment."

[100] Āḵūndzāda, *Maktūbāt*, 184.

early twentieth centuries, compared to his somewhat earlier colleagues, he was perhaps more exposed to these contradictions and therefore more aware of the complexities involved in the process of the encounter with modernity.

ʿAbd-al-Raḥīm Ṭālebof (1832-1910) was born into a middle class family of artisans in Tabrīz. His father and grandfather were both carpenters.[101] This background and his later successful business enterprise in the Caucasus may also be related to his more complicated and less dogmatic views on modernity in Iran. At age sixteen, he left Iran for Tiflis and studied in modern schools of the Caucasus and later settled in Tamar Khan Shureh in Daghestan. A total of eleven books are attributed to him.[102] Apparently he wrote all of them after age fifty-five.[103] Ṭālebof's writing had a direct impact on the Constitutional Revolution (1905-9) in Iran, and he was elected to the first parliament (Majles) convened in 1906 as a deputy for his birthplace of Tabrīz, but for reasons that are not entirely clear he did not attend the parliament.

One of the central concepts in Ṭālebof's discourse also revolved around the notion of critique. He began his famous three volume work, *Ketāb-e Aḥmad* (The Book of Ahmad), with the statement that our humanity started the day we started to question and seek the nature of things.[104] He also attributed the very possibility of progress in a nation to the practice of *krītīka* (critique) "in the practical-discursive sphere of natural interests."[105]

It is not difficult to see that Ṭālebof's notion of critique is predicated upon his concept of freedom as a basic category in human affairs. He considered freedom as an end in itself,

> *Āzādī* [freedom], unlike our other discourses or practices, is not a "means" to produce an end, as for example walking is to travel, as

---

[101] Fereydūn Ādamīyat, *Andīšahā-ye Ṭālebof Tabrīzī* (Tehran, 1984), 1.

[102] Īraj Afšār, *ʿAbd-al-Raḥīm Ṭālebof Tabrīzī: āzādī va sīāsat* (Tehran, 1978), 19-20.

[103] Ādamīyat, *Andīšahā-ye Ṭālebof Tabrīzī*, 3.

[104] ʿAbd-al-Raḥīm Ṭālebof, *Safīna-ye ṭālebī, yā Ketāb-e Aḥmad* (2 vols., Istanbul, 1893-94), 1:2. *Ketāb-e Aḥmad* was first published in two volumes in 1893 and 1894 in Istanbul. Both volumes contain discussions in simple language on the science and technology known to him. In the style of the book, he was very much influenced by Rousseau's *Émile*. He later added a third volume with the subtitle *Masāʾel al-ḥayāt* (Tiflis, 1906), where he paid more attention to ethical and philosophical issues.

[105] ʿAbd-al-Raḥīm Ṭālebof, *Masālek al-moḥsenīn* (Tehran, 1968), 100.

> reading is to learning, as eating is to gain bodily strength.... Therefore we realize that everything we see is a means to an end except freedom [which exists] only for freedom ... hence we call it an abstract term.[106]

But this "abstraction" in Ṭālebof's discourse finds a concrete determination as right. "Right is born with the human," he wrote in his *Masāʾel al-ḥayāt* (The Questions of Life), "from the day of birth to the day of death."[107] At this point in his discourse Ṭālebof was faced with the question of grounding his concept of freedom and right. For this purpose he suggested a term in Persian which seems to be very close to the concept of subjectivity.[108] He advanced the Persian term "*manī*" to convey such a meaning. This term derives from the Persian term "*man*" meaning "I" and *manī* is the noun form. *Manī* may be translated as "Ipseism" or "Egoism," which have similar connotations. Traditionally *manī* or its Arabic equivalent *anānīya* have had a similar negative connotation as the term egoism does in English. But here Ṭālebof uses the concept of *manī* in a positive sense:

> In order to produce Right, we have one source and one origin ... which is constituted of my *manī*, your *manī* and his/her *manī*. The origin [lies] in our language by means of which we express the right.[109]

Ṭālebof's discussion of right and freedom was not confined to the individual level as he extrapolated from the individual to the universal of collectivity. The cornerstone of his extrapolation lies in what he called the "collision" of the right of the Self with the right of the Other.[110] Without such a collision of rights, he argued, and hence creation of universal rights, mutual happiness is not possible.[111] After

---

106 Ṭālebof, *Masāʾel al-ḥayāt*, 95-96.

107 Ṭālebof, *Masāʾel al-ḥayāt*, 73.

108 He also grounded his conceptualization of freedom in terms of a natural right in his essay "Īżāḥat dar ḵoṣūṣ-e āzādī": "whether in Arabic *ḥorrīyat*, in Persian *āzādī*, or in Turkish *özgürlük*, it may be defined as natural freedom [by] which all men by nature and birth are free in all acts and words and except for their commander, that is their will, there are no impediments in their deeds and words. God has not created any force external to man to impede him; and no one may dispose of our freedom, let alone give it or take it away from us." Quoted in Afšār, *Ṭālebof Tabrīzī*, 88.

109 Ṭālebof, *Masāʾel al-ḥayāt*, 74.

110 Ṭālebof, *Masāʾel al-ḥayāt*, 73-74.

111 Ṭālebof, *Masāʾel al-ḥayāt*, 74-75.

right is transmitted from particular to universal, it creates a *manī* for the collectively. This view of the individual and collective subjectivity led Ṭālebof to define the concept of law (*qānūn*), which as we saw earlier was defined often as a mere codification of despotic rule or bureaucratization of despotism, in terms of the rights of the individual as well as those of the collectivity. He wrote:

> *Qānūn* means the systematic articulation of specific principles of civil and political rights and restrictions pertaining to the individual and the collectivity, through which every person would be secure in property and life and equitably responsible for wrong acts.[112]

It is crucial to note that Ṭālebof made a distinction between a conception of law as organized (*montaẓam*) despotism and one derived from popular sovereignty, as he mentioned Tsarist Russia as an example of the former.[113]

In a similar way, Ṭālebof's approach regarding the question of nation and nationalism was enlightened and conducive to universal emancipation as it was not marred by chauvinism. He defined freedom as a "common spiritual capital ... which individual Iranians have gradually accumulated and deposited in a vault called the nation."[114] Ṭālebof extended his extrapolation to include not only intra-national relations but also the international rights. The same *manī* or selfhood which exists in an intra-national collectivity should also apply to the international community.[115] For this purpose, he suggested the creation of a league of nations to resolve the disputes of international conflicts.[116] Later, in *Masāʾel al-ḥayāt*, Ṭālebof expressed hopes for the creation of a socialistic federation of nations where all the inhabitants of the earth would be treated as the members of a family.[117]

Ṭālebof's theorizing on the concept of freedom was not confined to mere abstractions. He divided the domain of freedom into three principle spheres of life, opinion, and speech. From these he also derived secondary freedoms such as freedom of election, freedom of press, and freedom of assembly, which in turn lead to some tertiary freedoms.[118] Interestingly, he used the metaphor of monetary assets to

---

[112] Ṭālebof, *Masālek al-moḥsenīn*, 94.
[113] Ādamīyat, *Andīšahā-ye Ṭālebof Tabrīzī*, 39.
[114] Afšār, *Ṭālebof Tabrīzī*, 89.
[115] Ṭālebof, *Masāʾel al-ḥayāt*, 75-76.
[116] Ṭālebof, *Ketāb-e Ahmad*, 1:144.
[117] Ṭālebof, *Masāʾel al-ḥayāt*, 91.
[118] Ṭālebof, *Masāʾel al-ḥayāt*, 97.

describe the "possession" of opinions, according to which every person has a legitimate right to protect and should not be forced into an unequal "exchange" or to give these possessions away.[119]

As mentioned earlier, Ṭālebof acknowledged and discussed some of the conflicts engendered by the process of modernity and its impact on a country like Iran. The conflict between the individual and collectivity constituted for him a typical case in point. When the individual's right "collides" with that of society, even though the individuals' right is essential and immune from annulments, it could be suspended. "Alternatively," he wrote, "from the combination of two rights a third right may be created."[120] He gave the example of eminent domain as a legitimate case when the right of the individual may be suspended when in conflict with that of the collectivity.[121] However, Ṭālebof did attempt to preserve both the right of the individual and collectivity simultaneously by differentiating not the principles of the two rights but their extents: "Individual rights and collective or national rights are divided into two; symmetrical in principle but different in the extent."[122] He then proposed a legal system based on popular sovereignty and majority vote to create a balance between these two rights.[123]

Another area of conflict which Ṭālebof attempted to reconcile was that between the notion of popular sovereignty and its corollary positive law on the one hand and the divine law on the other. He never explicitly addressed the issue in terms of a conflict between the two spheres. Nevertheless, his extensive use of interpretation of religious beliefs is indicative of an implicit acknowledgment of conflict between the two spheres and hence the attempt at reconciliation. While he thought of the law as deriving from popular sovereignty, he wrote of the Šarīʿa as the "foundation" of the law in Iran and described the law as the consummation and enforcement of the Divine Law.[124] Earlier, in the second volume of *Ketāb-e Aḥmad*, he had explicitly stated that "if we enact laws for ourselves, its basis would be the pure Šarīʿa and the sacred explicit texts (*noṣūṣ*) of the Koran."[125] What makes such a reconciliation in his discussion possible is the equation of people's

[119] Ṭālebof, *Masāʾel al-ḥayāt*, 97-98.
[120] Ṭālebof, *Masāʾel al-ḥayāt*, 79.
[121] Ṭālebof, *Masāʾel al-ḥayāt*, 77.
[122] Ṭālebof, *Masāʾel al-ḥayāt*, p 80.
[123] Ṭālebof, *Masāʾel al-ḥayāt*, 84.
[124] Ṭālebof, *Masāʾel al-ḥayāt*, 84
[125] Ṭālebof, *Ketāb-e Aḥmad*, 2:11.

will with the will of God. "Hence, the law," he wrote in *Masāʾel al-ḥayāt*, "which is enacted for the reform of public character by the votes of the majority, will have the effect of celestial words, since the voice of the people is the voice of God."[126]

At the core of Ṭālebof's theories lies a theo-ontological view which represents the conflict between orthodox monotheism and heterodox pantheism. In *Masālek al-moḥsenīn,* which is an imaginary travelogue, Ṭālebof presented a narrative of genesis in which the universe is accounted for in terms of creation and emanation simultaneously. Using the first person pronoun as the voice of the creator, he stated,

> In the center of My eternal and protected Divinity, [I] created a nebulous moving light, which because of extreme heat under my command, at times separated a part of itself and projected it into space, the same part then became mobile also and assumed a spherical shape until the space was filled with moving spheres.... From the movement of the spirit of spirits [I] created light and heat and assigned them to educate the beings ... [I] assigned the earth, one of the small planets of the visible sun, as the habitat of man....[127]

At the same time, however, he spoke of the universe and beings in terms of pantheistic emanations, in contrast to the "creationist" tone of the above passage,

> particles of beings testify to the Unity of God (*waḥdat Allāh*), since beings are constituted of particles and every particle according to its capacity is both the one and carrier of unity.[128]

Arguably, those theorists whose ontological views were grounded in a pantheistic metaphysics were more likely to arrive at a theory of human subjectivity and its universalizability, which may eventually have crystallized in a notion of generalized citizenship and popular sovereignty. Here, by presenting both a pantheistic and monotheistic ontology, Ṭālebof seems to be attempting to bridge the gap between the two approaches which ultimately surfaces in the conflictual and simultaneously reconciliatory relations between positive law grounded

---

[126] Ṭālebof, *Masāʾel al-ḥayāt*, 137.

[127] Ṭālebof, *Masālek al-moḥsenīn*, 131-32.

[128] Ṭālebof, *Masālek al-moḥsenīn*, 130.

in popular sovereignty and the Divine Law. But here he is faced with the problem of where to locate human subjectivity vis-a-vis the Divine subjectivity. In order to solve this problem, Ṭālebof ingeniously invoked a theme from the Koran, according to which the human is given the mantle of God's vicegerency on earth as a limited subject.[129]

Ṭālebof discussed this conflict between positive law and Divine law in a very concrete fashion in a section of *Masālek al-moḥsenīn*. In an imaginary debate between him and an orthodox mullah, the mullah raises the questions of redundancy of positive law, given the elaborate injunctions of the Divine Law.[130] Ṭālebof retorts that "these [religious] injunctions were the very best and the most proper of all laws of civilizations and religions of the world a thousand years ago. But they have no [application] to a hundred years ago, let alone to our age." Then Ṭālebof admonished his opponent to "leave undistributed those injunctions of the Koran which were enacted for a specific time and are inapplicable now and instead enact new and applicable laws."[131] Again here, he grounded his attempt at reconciliation in terms of a philosophical view parallel to his dichotomy between emanation and "creationism" which viewed all the universe as "incidental" (*ḥādeṣ*) and therefore subject to change except the Necessary Being, and its word the Koran, which is exempt from any change. From this he arrived at the incongruent conclusion that those injunctions of the Koran belonging to the "incidental" sphere are subject to change while the Koran itself is not subject to change.

Ṭālebof was one of the first theorists who became aware of the potential conflict between modernity and national identity. He chastised the "westernized" (*mofarang*) Iranians who apishly imitated Western dress and languages.[132] In a famous passage he admonished the Iranians to preserve their Iranian identity and not to be deceived by the glitter of the West. The purpose of learning from foreigners, according to him, was,

> to become familiar with the management of the [affairs of] the country; to realize the [meaning of] love for the country; to worship the king; to respect your tradition and not accept anything from any country except science, industry and beneficial

---

[129] Ṭālebof, *Masālek al-moḥsenīn*, 144-45. As we saw before, ever since Malkom and Ṭālebof, this view of the human as God's viceroy has been utilized by religious theorists facing the same dilemma. See the Koran 2:30 (*al-Baqara)* and also 17:70 (*al-Esrāʾ*).

[130] Ṭālebof, *Masālek al-moḥsenīn*, 94.

[131] Ṭālebof, *Masālek al-moḥsenīn*, 95.

[132] Ṭālebof, *Ketāb-e Aḥmad*, 2:22-23.

> information. Do not imitate; be always and everywhere an Iranian and realize that the East is different from the West—the sun rises in one and sets in the other. This simple reason is enough to distinguish us from them.[133]

Ṭālebof seems to have been also quite conscious about the discontents of modernity. He warned about the false utopia promised by the concept of *civilisation* (used in French transliteration) which after one became familiar with its agents, one could smell its "diabolic miasma" and see through its monstrous lack of consciousness and empathy. He also saw the manifestation of selfishness in the mass poverty, homelessness, and prostitution found in European cities of his time.[134] Yet, despite these criticisms, Ṭālebof was aware that he could not reject modernity. In *Masāʾel al-ḥayāt,* the third volume of the *Ketāb-e Aḥmad*, he set up a debate between his fictitious son Aḥmad, who has now grown up and is well versed in modern sciences and philosophy, and another certain fictitious character named Āḡā ʿAbd-Allāh. Āḡā ʿAbd-Allāh argues against the process of modernity in Iran, based on an the observation that all the progress in the West is tantamount to the conquest of the markets and territories in other parts of the world through military might, resulting in tremendous carnage, bloodshed, and colonial domination and rivalry unprecedented in human history.[135] Aḥmad, Ṭālebof's fictitious son, rebuts these objections by saying that the struggle among humans is "natural," since the substance we are made of is comprised of two elements of "protecting the interests of the self" and "rejection of the other's interests."[136] Near the end of the debate Aḥmad concludes that "preservation of the self" and "the right of existence" is naturally given, and to make his point he mentions the struggle between Abel and Cain. Reminiscent of a Hegelian master/slave struggle, Aḥmad then tries to explain the wars of the nineteenth century as an outcome of this process of preservation of self-interests which would eventually result in the creation of nations with a sense of rights in the international arena.[137] Thus by analyzing the struggle for domination inherent in subjectivity, Ṭālebof arrives at the creation of rights, which he then extrapolates to nations and the gradual emergence of international rights.

---

[133] Ṭālebof, *Masālek al-moḥsenīn*, 194.
[134] Ṭālebof, *Masālek al-moḥsenīn*, 93.
[135] Ṭālebof, *Masāʾel al-ḥayāt*, 50-55.
[136] Ṭālebof, *Masāʾel al-ḥayāt*, 56-57.
[137] Ṭālebof, *Masāʾel al-ḥayāt*, 64-68.

Ṭālebof's considerable theoretical sophistication regarding the concept of rights led him to become conscious of the limited nature of citizenship if it is confined merely to the legal and political spheres. For this reason he advanced the idea of impossibility of the creation of a citizenry without the distribution of land among the peasants, for the first time, it seems, in modern Iranian history. This recognition was significant because it represents the beginning of the felt need for the expansion and deepening of the concept of universalizable subjectivity as citizenship.

What enriched Ṭālebof's approach was the dialectical nature of his discourse manifested in some paradoxes with which he seems to have been happy to live. These paradoxes are exhibited in an essay, for example, where he expressed a strong belief in modern sciences while simultaneously upholding the possibility of the "violation" of principles of physics by an Indian yogi.[138] In a similar vein, he considered freedom and necessity, human volition and destiny (*taqdīr*), to belong to the same mixed bag of life.[139]

All in all, compared to other theorists examined here, Ṭālebof's discourse seems to be the most intricate and conducive to universalizable subjectivity. Yet, even his discourse is not completely free from elements of positivist subjectivity. Even though his main view of law was that of positive law grounded in popular sovereignty, at times he expressed views of law very much consonant with a positivistic approach to law which considered the law as mere codification of arbitrary rules.[140] He was, at times, also a strong proponent of "enlightenment from above," as he elaborated on the Japanese model of "modernity" to be implemented in Iran.[141] Thus, the duality discussed at the beginning of this article can also be perceived here, albeit to a lesser degree.

Ṭālebof's discourse was particularly important because it raised the question of subjectivity and the struggle against imperialism as the Eastern nations developed a consciousness of their subjugated status and the need for them to attempt to close ranks to fight against

---

[138] See Ṭālebof, *Masālek al-moḥsenīn*, 220-21 for his advocating of science and 228-29 for his admiration for the Indian yogi.

[139] Ṭālebof, *Masālek al-moḥsenīn*, 65 and 150.

[140] Ṭālebof, *Ketāb-e Aḥmad*, 2:80-81.

[141] It is noteworthy, that among all the written constitutions available, Ṭālebof chose to translate and append to the end of his book the Japanese constitution, according to which the emperor was assigned the role of the enlightened despot. See Ṭālebof, *Masāʾel al-ḥayāt*, 137-51.

domination and gain their rights.[142] But, as I will discuss in the next section, this important theme was most elaborately developed by Jamāl-al-Dīn Afġānī as the champion of the anti-imperialist struggle.

Sayyid Jamāl-al-Dīn Afġānī: Anti-Imperialism and Subjectivity

Sayyid Jamāl-al-Dīn Asadābādī, known as Afġānī, was a major political thinker and activist whose personal legend and discourse have had a lasting influence on the nativist anti-imperialist struggle, not only in Iran, but more importantly across all Islamic countries and communities. As we saw before, a large part of the discourse on, and praxis of, modern subjectivity in Iran was a reaction to Western imperialism. This reactive subjectivity was in turn strongly represented by the discourse on positivist sciences, rationalized order, bureaucracy, and chauvinist nationalism. All these moments of reactive subjectivity to imperialism derived their origins in the West itself. Afġānī's discourse sought these as well as critical and emancipatory dimensions of subjectivity, but he recast them into an Islamic mold, as the most effective means of fighting imperialism. As will be examined subsequently, in the course of such a remolding, Afġānī's discourse had to succumb to a series of contradictions with crucial consequences for the emancipatory dimension of subjectivity.[143]

As Nikki Keddie has observed, what underlies Afġānī's discourse is a strong assumption that the modern world necessitates a view of human agency which is expressed in "activism, the freer use of human reason, and political and military strength."[144] It is interesting that in Afġānī's case the critical component in his approach to modernity was weightier than the positivist component which makes sense in the view of his commitment to the unorthodox "Islamic" philosophy. "If someone looks deeply into the question," he wrote, "he will see that science rules the world. There was, is and will be no rule in the world but science."[145] However, a few pages later he qualified this by saying that:

---

[142] Ṭālebof, *Masāʾel al-ḥayāt*, 89-90.

[143] Because of the relative familiarity of Afġānī, no biographical sketch is provided here. For a detailed biography of Afġānī, see Nikki Keddie, *Sayyid Jamal ad-Din "al-Afghani": A Political Biography.* (Los Angeles, 1972) and idem, *An Islamic Response to Imperialism: Political and Religious Writings of Sayyid Jamal ad-Din "al-Afghani"* (Los Angeles, 1968).

[144] Keddie, *Islamic Response to Imperialism*, 3.

[145] Sayyid Jamāl-al-Dīn Afġānī, "Lecture on Teaching and Learning," tr. in Keddie, *Islamic Response to Imperialism*, 52.

> A science is needed to be the comprehensive soul for all the sciences, so that it can preserve their existence, apply each of them in its proper place, and become the cause of progress of each one of those sciences. The science that has the position of a comprehensive soul and the rank of a preserving force is the science of *falsafa* or philosophy, because its subject is universal. It is philosophy that shows man human prerequisites. It shows the sciences what is necessary. It employs each of the sciences in its proper place. If a community did not have philosophy, and all the individuals of that community were learned in the sciences with particular subjects, those sciences could not last in that community for a century ... that community without the spirit of philosophy could not deduce conclusions from these sciences. The Ottoman government and the Khedive of Egypt have opened up schools for the teaching of the new sciences for a period of sixty years, and until now they have not received any benefits from those sciences.[146]

What is of crucial importance is that Afḡānī grounded his conceptualization of philosophy in the idea of reasoning and critical argumentation as he argued that "the father and mother of knowledge (*ʿelm*) is reasoning (*borhān*), and reasoning is neither Aristotle nor Galileo. The truth is where there is reasoning."[147] In another essay entitled "Favāʾed falsafa" (The Benefits of Philosophy), Afḡānī took his argument one step further by contending that philosophy was even prior to revelation, and the latter is but a preparatory stage for the achievement of philosophy. In other words, Afḡānī argued that revelation was a base which would lead the way to a subjectivist epistemology based on philosophy. He first argued in favor of the centrality of critical faculties in humans:

> Philosophy is the escape from the narrowness of animal sense impression into the wide area of human perception. It is the removal of darkness of bestial illusions with the light of natural intelligence; the transformation of blindness and lack of insight into clear-sightedness and insight.[148]

---

[146] In Keddie, *Islamic Response to Imperialism*, 104.

[147] In Keddie, *Islamic Response to Imperialism*, 107. Translation slightly modified.

[148] Sayyid Jamāl-al-Dīn Afḡānī, "The Benefits of Philosophy," tr. in Keddie, *Islamic Response to Imperialism*, 110.

Then he discussed the role of Islam and the Koran in preparing the pre-Islamic "savage" Arabs to embrace the philosophical traditions developed by more civilized nations:

> In sum, in that Precious Book [the Koran] with solid verse, He planted the roots of philosophical sciences into purified souls, and opened the road for man to become man. When the Arab people came to believe in that Precious Book they were transferred from the sphere of ignorance to knowledge, from blindness to vision, from savagery to civilization, and from nomadism to settlement. They understood their needs for intellectual and spiritual accomplishment and for gaining a living.[149]

These ideas later developed, Afgānī argued, and Arabs realized that they could not progress further without the help of other nations:

> Therefore, notwithstanding the glory, splendor, and greatness of Islam and Muslims, in order to exact and elevate knowledge, they [the Arabs] lowered their heads and showed humility before the lowest of their subjects, who were Christians, Jews, and Magians [Persians] until with their help, they translated the philosophical sciences from Persian, Syriac, and Greek into Arabic. Hence it became clear that their Precious Book was the first teacher of philosophy to the Muslims.[150]

In the same essay, Afgānī presented a view of human action which may seem very much to correspond to a Faustian view of subjectivity. He recognized the necessity satisfying human material needs through agriculture and animal husbandry, procurement of water, construction of shelter, and preservation of health achieved through sciences and technology.[151] Yet, he considered critical philosophy to be the foundation of these sciences and technologies. As he wrote, "It [philosophy] is the foremost cause of the production of knowledge, the creation of sciences, the invention of industries and the initiation of crafts."[152] Furthermore, Afgānī argued that the satisfaction of

---

[149] In Keddie, *Islamic Response to Imperialism*, 114. Emphasis added.

[150] In Keddie, *Islamic Response to Imperialism*, 114.

[151] In Keddie, *Islamic Response to Imperialism*, 110. See also Sayyid Jamāl-al-Dīn Afgānī, *Ārā' va moʿtaqedāt-e Sayyed Jamāl-al-Dīn Afgānī*, ed. Mortażā Modaressī (Tehran: Eqbal, 1958), 118.

[152] Afgānī, *Ārā'*, 118.

material needs is just a prerequisite towards enabling us to pay attention to our souls.[153] Afḡānī's most explicit statement of his critical thinking was articulated in an article published on 18 May 1883 in *Journal des Débats* in response to Ernest Renan's uncritical attack on Islam as being inherently against modern civilization. In this article, Afḡānī demonstrated the baselessness of Renan's racist attitudes toward Arabs and yet praised the superiority of critical thought, i.e. scientific and philosophical thought over revelation.[154]

The aspects of Afḡānī's discourse discussed above constitute the part of his writings that targeted what he perceived to be the enlightened Muslim elite as his audience, and they were written in a highly abstruse and philosophical language. As I mentioned before, he also developed a parallel discourse which appealed more to the "masses"; a discourse which was motivated by his anti-imperialist goals, and which was in sharp contrast to his first critical discourse.

Afḡānī's "second discourse" is most sharply expressed in a famous essay entitled "The Truth about the Neyčerī Sect and Explanation of the Neyčerīs," written in 1881, even before he wrote the essays belonging to his critical discourse discussed above. In this essay, Afḡānī depicted a picture of an anti-imperialist collective subject, possessing political and military power incarnated in an Islamic nation which could stand up to Western hegemony.[155] He identified the concept of "social solidarity" as the linchpin of this collective subject, which the West, he believed, through its "agents" such as Sir Sayyid Aḥmad Khan was bent on subverting. Apparently drawing on Ebn Ḵaldūn's parallel concept of *ʿaṣabīya* (solidarity), Afḡānī's concept of social solidarity explained the longevity of civilizations and nations in terms of sets of beliefs which bonded the members of a society together and protected that society from external invasion and internal disintegration.

The Neyčerīs or "materialists" (as Afḡānī in his "second discourse" lumped together the unorthodox and critical thinkers, the socialists,

---

[153] Afḡānī, *Ārāʾ*, 111.

[154] Sayyid Jamāl-al-Dīn Afḡānī, "Answer of Jamal ad-Din to Renan, *Journal des Débats*, May 18, 1883," in Keddie, *Islamic Response to Imperialism*, 81-87. Interestingly enough, this essay has never been translated into Persian, thus veiling the heterodox and anti-religious aspect of Afḡānī's thoughts from his Muslim audiences.

[155] The "Neyčerīs" were the followers of Sir Sayyid Aḥmad Khan (1817-97), and the term *neyčerī* was derived from the English word nature, which Afḡānī used as a generic term representing unorthodox views and atheism. See Keddie, *Islamic Response to Imperialism*, for more details.

communists, and nihilists) were in his view determined to destroy the social solidarity of nations, Islamic or otherwise, throughout history.[156] What made social solidarity possible, in his analysis, was religious faith and specifically faith in a Transcendent Deity who would in the next world mete out reward and punishment as recompense to individual believers for their deeds while living on earth.[157] Afḡānī elaborated about components of religious faith which undergird the social order and social solidarity in society. These which he termed as "Religion's Three Beliefs," consisted of: (1) the belief that "there is a terrestrial angel [human], and that he is the noblest of creatures; (2) the certainty that one's community "is the noblest one, and that all outside . . . [one's] community are in error and deviation"; and (3) the belief that " man has come into the world in order to acquire accomplishments worthy of transferring him to a world more excellent, higher, vaster, and more perfect than this narrow and dark world."[158] As to the first and second components of the religious faith necessary for social solidarity and social order, Afḡānī reasoned that they were necessary for a sense of collective subjectivity *vis-a-vis* nature and other social collectivities.[159] It was the third belief, however, which was, as Afḡānī put it

> the best impulse towards civilization, whose foundations are true knowledge and refined morals. It is the best requisite for the *stability of the social order*, which is founded on each individual's knowledge of his proper rights, and his following the straight path of justice.... It is the best basis for the peace and calm of the classes of humanity, because peace is the fruit of love and justice and love and justice result from admirable qualities and habits. It is the only belief that restrains man from all evils, saves him from vales of adversity and misfortune, and seats him in the virtuous city on the throne of happiness.[160]

In contrast to this collectivist notion of agency, Afḡānī argued, the most effective means by which the Neyčerīs and unorthodox attempted

---

[156] Sayyid Jamāl-al-Dīn Afḡānī, "The Truth about the Neicheri Sect and an Explanation of the Neicheris," in Keddie, *Islamic Response to Imperialism*, 140.

[157] In Keddie, *Islamic Response to Imperialism*, 167.

[158] In Keddie, *Islamic Response to Imperialism*, 141.

[159] In Keddie, *Islamic Response to Imperialism*, 142.

[160] In Keddie, *Islamic Response to Imperialism*, 144.

to undermine social solidarity was by the introduction of individual subjectivity rendered by Afḡānī as "egoism" which denies the beliefs in reward and punishment in the afterlife:

> And since, because of these corrupt opinions, each of them [people corrupted by disbelief] believed that there is no life but this one, the quality of *égoïsme* [in French transliteration] overcame them. The quality of *égoïsme* consists of self-love to the point that if a personal profit requires a man having that quality to let the whole world be harmed, he would not renounce that profit but would consent to the harm of everyone in the world.[161]

However, to draw the conclusion that Afḡānī's discourse was against human subjectivity as such is inaccurate. What he and some other religious theorists in the second half of the twentieth century who have utilized religion in their socio-political analyses have conceptualized about human subjectivity can be best described as "mediated subjectivity." By "mediated subjectivity" is meant the notion of human subjectivity projected onto the attributes of monotheistic deity—attributes such as omnipotence, omniscience, and volitism, which are then partially re-appropriated by humans. In this scheme, human subjectivity is contingent on God's subjectivity. Thus, while human subjectivity is not denied, it is never independent of the Divine's and in this sense it is "mediated." In the Islamic discourse, this concept is usually expressed in the notion of the human as God's vicegerent, which in Arabic is rendered as *ḵalīfat Allāh* (God's Caliph or Successor). Although Afḡānī did not explicitly discuss the concept of *ḵalīfat Allāh* in his discourse, the ontological underpinning of it is nevertheless very much informed by this concept.

The subjectivity that is attributed to God and that which is attributed to the human converge in Afḡānī's thought in an article entitled, "Qażā va qadar" (roughly meaning "Destiny and Providence"). In that article, Afḡānī contrasted the concept of providence to that of necessity (*jabr*) by stating that while providence sets the general principles of phenomena, human volition also has an important role in the determination of events.[162] The belief in providence, Afḡānī stated, if not mistaken for the concept of necessity (*jabr*) would result in the "creation of courage and initiative, bravery and chivalry and encourages

---

[161] In Keddie, *Islamic Response to Imperialism*, 151.

[162] Sayyid Jamāl-al-Dīn Afḡānī, *Eslām va ʿelm: be-żamīma-ye resāla qażā va qadar,* ed. and tr. Hādī Ḵosrowšāhī (Tabrīz, 1348 Š./1969), 144-47.

man to engage in daring acts which the faint-hearted would fear."[163] A person who thus believes in God's destiny as well as humans' free will and ability to fulfill that destiny, he argued, would "never fear death in the defense of the people's and nation's rights and superiority. Nor would such a person be intimidated by death in rising up to fulfill what God has assigned to him."[164] Afḡānī concluded that this belief in providence, accompanied by the rejection of "necessity," caused the success of early Muslims and their domination and superiority over other nations and has to be emulated by the Muslims again.[165]

As Nikki Keddie has observed, Afḡānī, in the tradition of many Muslim classical philosophers, believed in the impossibility of freedom for the "masses," and this very condition, as articulated in his "second discourse," stands in sharp contrast to the promise of modernity as universal subjectivity. Yet, what the second discourse of Afḡānī accomplished was to point out the need for an indigenous form of subjectivity raised in native cultural soil to make resistance to Western hegemony possible.

Conclusion

The dual character of the intellectual appropriation of modernity in the second half of the nineteenth century in Iran is very much reflected in social movements such as the constitutional movement at the turn of the century and the institutions that were created as a result of the Constitutional Revolution of 1905-9. Thus, in the early twentieth century one witnessed the curbing of the despotic power of the Qajar shah, the creation of a representative assembly, the beginning of reform in the judiciary, and the establishment of political parties and civic associations, as well as a relatively free press, to promote the rights of citizenship as the embodiment of universalizable moment of subjectivity. On the other hand, one also witnessed a strong emphasis on economic and military development and expansion of bureaucratic control, as well as the emergence of a chauvinist nationalism, all underpinned by the positivist aspect of modernity and a nineteenth-century spirit of instrumental rationality and scientific worldview. However, very soon after the dust had settled in the aftermath of the Constitutional Revolution, the stage was set for the gradual de-emphasis of the emancipatory aspect of modernity and the build-up of positivist modernity. This process was undoubtedly pushed forward

[163] Afḡānī, *Eslām va ʿelm*, 142-43.

[164] Afḡānī, *Eslām va ʿelm*, 143.

[165] Afḡānī, *Eslām va ʿelm*, 144-47.

by the national and international conditions which accompanied the devastation of the First World War.

The socio-political conditions of Iran in the period between the establishment of the constitutional parliamentary system in 1909 and the advent of Reżā Shah after World War I, may be best described as chaos and disintegration caused by the civil war of 1906-9, foreign intervention and military occupation, extreme political factionalism and conflict, feuds among tribes and their domination of politics, and later the emergence of potentially separatist movements rooted in the assertion of newly discovered ethnic rights. Technological deficiency and lack of economic development, as compared to Europe and America in the twentieth century and as seen by Iranian intelligentsia, also contributed to the moving away from Iran's initial dualistic encounter with modernity and toward the holistic embracing of positivist modernity.

These disintegrating and chaotic forces created a milieu in which the preliminary stages for the eclipse of the emancipatory moments of modernity and overarching triumph of positivist modernity were set. Thus, at this stage Iran's dualist encounter with modernity in which universalizable subjectivity and positivist subjectivity existed side by side, gave way to a situation where positivist subjectivity became the dominant force in culture, society and the state, and resulted in the arrest of development of civil society. This process was set into motion by the intellectuals of the post-Constitutional Revolution who suitably paved the way for and sanctioned the advent of the Pahlavi regime and its agenda of a lopsided and heavy-handed positivist modernization for Iran, which became the dominant mode of modernity there ever since. There are two consequences and responses to this mode of modernity. As an alternative to this positivistic form of modernity, in Iran as in many other countries, there emerged a Marxist collective notion of subjectivity which collapsed the subject into the social universal to create a historical agent of history writ large, thereby negating the very freedom that subjectivity entails. Secondly, the Islamist movement in Iran has exhibited an intense ambivalence toward subjectivity and the individual as its ultimate beneficiary, resulting in a schizophrenic attitude toward the social and political corollaries of the notion of universalizable subjectivity, that is notions and institutional basis of general citizenship. Having said all this, the ideas related to the emancipatory aspect of modernity have survived the eclipse, and there are indications of their thematization in the contemporary post-revolutionary conditions in Iran.

Part Three
Travel and Society

Persian Travelogues: A Description and Bibliography

Iraj Afshar

The writing of travelogues in Persian (*safar-nāma*s) has a history too extensive to cover in a short article. Many books and treatises have been written even on subjects such as the etiquette of traveling. These writings are evidence of the antiquity of such literature in Persian. In many of the texts on Sufi beliefs and books on politics and ethics (the "Mirrors for Princes" genre), travel and its etiquette have been mentioned. Even quite recently, an anonymous author has written a book entitled *Maʿšūq al-safarāt dar ādāb-e safar*.

Pre-Qajar Travelogues

The first valuable travelogue in Persian was written by the renowned philosopher and poet Nāṣer Ḵosrow (d. 481/1088-89), who commenced writing in 437/1046 when he set out on his long and interesting journey [to Egypt]. About 130 years after him, the great poet Ḵāqānī (d. 595/ 1199) composed the *Toḥfat al-ʿErāqayn*.[1] This famous *maṯnavī* poem contained a description of the "Two Iraqs" (ʿErāq-e ʿArab and ʿErāq-e ʿAjam, "Arab Iraq" and "Persian Iraq") and the circumstances of his pilgrimage to Mecca (*ḥajj*). His enchanting ode (*qaṣīda*) about the palace of Tāq-e Kesrā at Madāʾen (Ctesiphon) near Baghdad might be considered a part of his travelogue. Another poet who wrote a travelogue, about a century later, was Nezārī Qohestānī, an Ismaʿili Shiʿite.[2] This poet's journey lasted for two years (678-79/1279-81) and

[1] [Aḥmad Monzavī, *Fehrest-e nosḵahā-ye ḵaṭṭī-e fārsī*, vol. 6 (Tehran, 1353 Š./ 1974), 2996-97, nos. 41493-513. Bibliographical references added to this article are marked in brackets–Ed.]

[2] [Ḥakīm Saʿd-al-Dīn Nezārī Qohestānī; see J. T. P. de Bruijn, "Nizārī Ḳuhistānī," *The Encyclopaedia of Islam: New Edition* (Leiden, 1960-), 8:83.]

his travelogue consisted of sound information about his itinerary from Qohestān to Isfahan and thence to Azerbaijan and Arrān.

The Indian mystic Jalāl-al-Dīn Moḥammad Moltānī (707-85/1307-84) authored a book entitled *Safar-nāma-ye makdūm-e jahānīān*. It was permeated by aspects of mysticism and naturally contained stories of miracles and bizarre things; nonetheless, it provided information about the places visited by this mystic. He describes himself in this book as *jahāngašt*, one who has traveled about the world.

Another early travelogue which is worth mentioning is the *Ḥejāzīya* written by Abu'l-Šarāf Moḥammad b. Ḥosayn b. ʿAlī Ḥosaynī Yazdī.[3] This travelogue described the author's journey to the Ḥejāz and pilgrimage to Mecca in 757/1356, during the reign of Sultan Ovays Jalāyer. The author discussed numerous historical events as well as the difficulties of his journey.

Yet another important travelogue was that of Ḡīās-al-Dīn Naqqāš Samarqandī. He was a member of a delegation which went to China in 825/1421-22 at the command of the Timurid ruler Šāhrok. Upon returning from China, he wrote a report about the journey which is thought to be the oldest Persian source of information about China. The text of this work has been preserved in two sources, the *Zobdat al-tavārīk* by Ḥāfeẓ Abrū and the *Matlaʿ-e saʿdayn va majmaʿ-e baḥrayn* by ʿAbd-al-Razzāq Samarqandī.

Also dating from the ninth/fifteenth century is the poem *Chahār takt* by Mīr Sayyed Ḥosayn Abīvardī,[4] a writer who befriended and corresponded with the much more famous poet Jāmī. This travelogue deals primarily with the conditions of the four great Muslim metropolitan centers of that era—Istanbul, Cairo, Tabriz, and Herat. Of course in describing his journey he also mentioned cities such as Akseka (in Georgia), Aleppo, Jerusalem, Medina, and Mecca.

The *Fotūḥ al-ḥaramayn* was a travelogue in verse composed by the poet Moḥī-al-Dīn Lārī in 911/1505-6 about the holy shrines of Mecca and Medina.[5] In this same century, ʿAlī-Akbar Ketāʾī, who was apparently a native of Transoxiana who had gone to China on a business trip, wrote an important report about his journey to China and the customs and traditions of its people which became famous under the title *Ketāy-nāma*.[6]

---

[3] [Aḥmad Monzavī, *Fehrestvāra-ye ketābhā-ye fārsī*, 3 vols. (Tehran, 1374 Š./1995), 3:75.]

[4] [Or *Čār takt*; Monzavī, *Fehrest*, 2753.]

[5] [Monzavī, *Fehrest*, 4046, no. 41809; also known as *Asrār al-ḥajj*.]

[6] [Monzavī, *Fehrest*, 4000, no. 41537; ed. Īraj Afšar (Tehran, 1979); ed. Fuat Sezgin (Frankfurt, 1994). It was written for the Ottoman Sultan Selim I.]

This valuable treatise, which was written in 922/1516, was the second Persian travelogue to deal with China. Fortunately, Orientalists have studied it for a long time; it has been translated into Turkish, Chinese, and French, and it is also to be published in Japanese.

We have knowledge of only a few travelogues from the Safavid period. Perhaps the oldest of them is the *Nūr al-mašreqayn* by ʿAbd-Allāh Beheštī Haravī.[7] It was written in the style of the *Toḥfat al-ʿErāqayn* and dedicated to Shah ʿAbbās (d. 1038/1629). It deals with the cities of Qom, Mašhad, and Sabzavār as well as the author's journey to India. During the same period, Maḥmūd b. Amīr Valī Balḵī wrote the book *Baḥr al-asrār fī manāqeb al-aḵyār* about his visit to Ceylon and India.[8]

As both these books suggest, travel to India was common and in vogue during the Safavid period. Many poets, physicians, and men of letters traveled to this region and often used their impressions and observations in their writings. A short travelogue in prose and verse by Sāʿī Šarvānī depicts this general enthusiasm about traveling to India. In this travelogue, Sāʿī said that he went from Ganja (now Kirovabad) to Tabrīz and then to Isfahan. While in Isfahan, he learned that an ambassadorial mission was returning to India so he took the opportunity to travel with them (1050-58/1640-48).

Also worth mentioning is a travelogue by Ṣafī b. Valī Qazvīnī which provides details about his journey to Mecca. It was written in 1087/1676-77.[9]

One of the most important travelogues known to us from the Safavid period is the *Safīna-ye solaymānī* by Moḥammad-Rabīʿ b. Moḥammad-Ebrāhīm.[10] This travelogue is the description of his journey during the years 1092 to 1094 (1681-83) as an ambassador to Siam. The *Safīna-ye solaymānī* is a treasure of first-hand and newly acquired information about a land which European travelers and explorers had not yet visited frequently. It also contains sound information about China and Japan. Therefore, it is a significant general source for the study of those regions.

---

[7] [Monzavī, *Fehrest*, 4054, no. 41866; ed. N. Māyel Haravī (Mašhad, 1998).]

[8] [Part. ed. Riyaz al-Islam (Karachi, 1980); H. M. Said and M. A. Zahid Khan (Karachi, 1984).]

[9] [*Anīs al-ḥojāj*, see Monzavī, *Fehrestvāra*, 1:64; Charles Rieu, *Catalogue of the Persian Manuscripts in the British Museum,* 3 vols. (London, 1876-95), 3:980 (MS Or. 1686). The author made the pilgrimage with the permission of Awrangzīb's daughter Zīb-al-Nesāʾ.]

[10] [Monzavī, *Fehrest*, 4038, no. 41760; tr. John O'Kane as *The Ship of Sulaiman* (New York, 1972).]

It should not be forgotten that in many of the historical and literary, even the poetical, travelogues useful information may be found here and there; for example, in Masʿūd Saʿd Salmān's mention of his travels and imprisonment in India and in his praise of Lahore, or the *qaṣīda* composed by Anvārī in praise of Baghdad. Such valuable and informative writings include Zayn-al-Dīn Vāsefī Haravī (b. 890/1485) in *Badāyeʿ al-vaqāyeʿ*;[11] Fażl-Allāh b. Rūzbehān K̲anjar in *Mehmān-nāma-ye Bok̲ārā*[12] (written in 915/1509-10); Moḥammad-Ḥazin Lāhijī (d. 1127/1715) in *Savāna-ye aḥvāl*; Kᵛāja ʿAbd-al-Karīm Kašmīrī in *Bayān-e vaqīʿ*;[13] and Moḥammad-Kāẓem Marvī in the book *ʿĀlam-ārā-ye nāderī* (written in 1157-66/1744-53).[14] The two latter writers both describe the battles and travels of Nāder Shah, whom ʿAbd-al-Karīm accompanied for some time.

Travelogue Writing in the Twelfth and Thirteenth Centuries A.H.

The traditional period of travelogue writing may be said to have extended to the beginning of the Qajar period. Travelogues written from the twelfth/eighteenth century onwards may be studied in detail so that the subject of this article may become clearer. These works will be surveyed for the period up to the commencement of the Constitutional Revolution.

It should be noted that during this period it was not only Iranians who wrote their travelogues in the Persian language, as Persian writing was still in vogue in India, and the inhabitants of Transoxiana and the Caucasus also wrote books in Persian. Since the travelogues by authors from those regions are in Persian, bibliographical research such as this should include notice of them, particularly so that their observations and opinions about the countries visited can be used to construct a comparative perspective on the writing of Iranian authors.

It should also be mentioned that some of the travelogues written in India were prepared at the orders or encouragement of British officials in that country. Works commissioned by Lockhart, Moorcraft, Leach, and Elphinstone are catalogued in C. A. Storey's *Persian Literature*.[15]

---

[11] [Monzavī, *Fehrestvāra*, 1:65-66; ed. A. Baldruf (Moscow, 1961).]

[12] [Ed. A. K. Arends (Moscow, 1976).]

[13] [Ed. K. B. Nasim as *Bayan-i-Waqi: A Biography of Nadir Shah Afshar and the Travels of the Author* (Lahore, 1970).]

[14] [Ed. Moḥammad-Amīn Rīāhī (Tehran, 1364 Š./1985).]

[15] [For examples, see Charles A. Storey, *Persian Literature: A Bio-bibliographical Survey*, 2 vols., (Leiden, 1927-), 2/1:145-59; similar works were commissioned by Russian authorities as well.]

During this period, a series of books on the geography of various cities were also written. Although these books are not exactly travelogues, they were often the product of travels by their authors and are worth considering. They include the booklets issued under the title of *Šarḥ-e manāzel* or the books written under the title of *Raport* ("Report"). A glance at the geography section of the catalogue of Persian manuscripts by Aḥmad Monzavī is sufficient to illustrate the great number of these works.[16]

If one wishes to know how many travelogues were written during this period, the number five hundred may be suggested on the basis of consultation of sources such as Storey, Monzavī, Ḵānbābā Mošār, a dissertation by Moḥammad Asadīān, and some forty years of personal observations and notes. The importance of travelogues does not lie only in their geographical, civil, and ethnological qualities or the mention of historical events and personal biographies. Many of the travelogues have been the means of transferring new scientific and cultural and even political meanings, as exemplified in the *Toḥfat al-ʿālam* by ʿAbd-al-Laṭīf Šūštarī, the *Ḥayrat-nāma-ye šoʿarā*, the *Safar-nāma* of Ḥājjī Sayyāḥ Mahallātī, and the *Safar-nāma* of Ḥājjī Pīrzāda Nāʾīnī. To some extent, the royal travelogues by Nāṣer-al-Dīn Shah also served this purpose.

Moreover, travelogues were one of the practical means for the arrival and dissemination of foreign words in Persian and the development of Persian literary style. The Persian-speaking traveler, upon reaching a new land, had to learn the words related to daily life and the civil and social customs there; he often recorded them in the course of explaining matters pertaining to that place. Thus Hindi and English words appear in travelogues about India; Russian words in travelogues about Russia; or English, French, and occasionally German words in travelogues about Europe. Many Turkish words also entered Persian thanks to travelers who wrote about the Ottoman Empire. The literary taste, geographical insight, and historical interests of the travelogue authors further influenced their writing. The travelogue writer who was a poet, or who remembered couplets, decorated his own writing with such verse in order to promote that particular style.

Before turning to the question of bibliography, it must be remembered that a clear line of demarcation cannot be drawn between memoirs and travelogues. Each travelogue contains some element of the memoir, and many memoirs include records of travel. Many of the important memoirs by Iranian dignitaries have this quality and deal

---

[16] [E.g., Monzavī, *Fehrest*, 4001, no. 41543; 4043, no. 41785.]

with matters regarding travel: Examples include the memoirs of ʿAbbās Mīrzā Molkārā, Moḥammad-Ḥasan Khan Eʿtemād-al-Salṭana, Mīrzā Ṭāher Bašīr-al-Molk Šaybānī, Qahramān Mīrzā Āʾīn-al-Salṭana, Moḥammad-ʿAlī Khan Moṣaddeq-al-Dawla Ḡaffārī, Ḥosaynqolī Khan Neẓām-al-Salṭana Māfī Qarāgozlū, Mahdī Khan Momtaḥen-al-Dawla Šaqqāqī, ʿAbd-Allah Mostawfī, and Mahdīqolī Khan Hedāyat—all of which have the same importance for historians and scholars which independent travelogues would have. This brief study of travelogues does not provide sufficient space to study these and similar writings in detail, but this notice should serve to draw the attention of interested readers to recognize and investigate such memoirs.

For purposes of this research, an analytical table of all the important travelogues, some 234 in number, written during the years 1100-1324/1688-1906 has been prepared. Of these, about two hundred were composed after the year 1200/1785-86, so it is clear that that century was a period when travelogue writing in Persian was in vogue. The most important categories and representative examples of this literature are discussed in the remainder of this bibliographical essay.

Geographical Classification

The objective here is to know the regions which were most commonly visited during the nineteenth century. Since the authors were all Muslims, it is not surprising that the most common type of travelogue dealt with the pilgrimage to Mecca (*ḥajj*). The hajj was a religious duty and the desire of every Muslim who could afford it, although in those days the journey was very difficult and required a good deal of time. Generally big caravans used to set out for Mecca and the Ḥejāz every year. Pilgrimage to other sacred places such as the shrines of Karbalāʾ and Najaf, made before the hajj or after it, was quite common, and Shiʿites from various cities in India and Iran used to visited these places and have left travelogues about them.

Generally, travelers from northern regions of Iran traveled to Istanbul via Russia and from there proceeded via Syria and Egypt or Karbalāʾ and Najaf to Mecca. Probably they used the routes via Baghdad and Kermān for the return. But travelers from the southern parts of Iran adopted the route via the Persian Gulf and Indian Ocean, generally using Būšehr as a port. Travelers enjoyed Istanbul more than other cities on their route, and they stayed there because it was so pleasant. Most travelogue writers did not neglect visiting such recreational and pleasure-seeking places. Of course, Beirut and Cairo were also objects of attention and praise.

A good example of the pilgrimage to Mecca which has presented various details and aspects of such travel is the travelogue of Mīrzā

Moḥammad-Ḥosayn Farahānī, which has fortunately been translated into English and is available for readers.[17] The travelogues of Farhād Mīrzā Moʿtamed-al-Dawla (a prince and government notable),[18] ʿAbd-al-ʿAlī Adīb-al-Molk (secretary and writer),[19] Maʿṣūm-ʿAlīšāh Nāyeb-al-Ṣadr (dervish and Sufi),[20] ʿAlī Khan Amīn-al-Dawla (enlightened government official and reformer),[21] Solṭān-Moḥammad Sayf-al-Dawla (son of Fatḥ-ʿAlī Shah),[22] and others also deal with the pilgrimage.

India was also a destination for many travelers, both for trade and tourism. The first such Iranian travelogue of the period under consideration was *Toḥfat al-ʿālam* written by ʿAbd-al-Laṭīf Šūštarī,[23] who was a learned man and a student of theology who stayed for a long time in India. In addition to geographical, cultural, and anthropological observations, the book he wrote about India also contained information about Europe which he had heard at second-hand. He also recorded the behavior of Englishmen he had seen in India. Before him Mollā Fīroz Zardoštī and Mīrzā Mahdī Ḵorāsānī, the envoy of Šāhroḵ Mīrzā Afšār, also wrote travelogues about their travel to India, but no doubt *Toḥfat-al-ʿālam* is more important than these travelogues. In addition to it, *Merāt al-aḥvāl* (or *Jahān-nāma*) by Aḥmad Behbahānī should be mentioned; it exists in numerous manuscripts.[24] At the beginning of the next century, Veqār-al-Malek ʿAlī Tabrīzī wrote a book entitled *Jām-e Jam-e Hendūstān* which is the result of the author's journey to India and his observations.[25] This book deserves a new edition owing to its contents, arrangement, and reliability. Another important Iranian travelogue about India is one

---

[17] [Ed. Ḥāfeẓ Farmānfarmāʾīān (Tehran, 1964); tr. Hafez Farmayan and Elton L. Daniel as *A Shiʿite Pilgrimage to Mecca* (Austin, Texas, 1990).]

[18] [*Safar-nāma-ye Farhād Mīrzā*, ed. Ḡolām-Reżā Ṭabāṭabāʾī (Tehran, 1366 Š./1987); ed. Esmāʿīl Navvāb Ṣafā (Tehran, 1366 Š./1987).]

[19] [*Safar-nāma-ye Adīb-al-Molk ba ʿatabāt*, ed. Masʿūd Golzarī (Tehran, 1364 Š./1985).]

[20] [*Toḥfat al-ḥaramayn va saʿādat al-dārayn* (Bombay, 1306/1889; new ed., Tehran, 1362 Š./1983).]

[21] [*Safar-nāma-ye Amīn-al-Dawla*, ed. Eslām Kāẓemīya (Tehran, 1354 Š./ 1975).]

[22] [*Safar-nāma-ye Sayf-al-Dawla maʿrūf ba Safar-nāma-ye Makka*, ed. ʿAlī-Akbar Ḵodāparast (Tehran, 1364 Š./1985).]

[23] [Monzavī, *Fehrest*, 2994-95, nos. 41477-92; ed. Ṣamad Movaḥḥed (Tehran, 1363 Š./1984).]

[24] [Monzavī, *Fehrest*, 4049-50, nos. 41833-41.]

[25] [Tabriz, 1316/1899.]

written by an official in Bombay, Mīrzā Fażl-Allāh Ḥoseynī Šīrāzī.[26] It is the result of his visits to various cities in connection with his survey of the condition of Iranians in India. In addition, the book *Safarnāma-ye Solṭān-al-Vāʿeẓīn ba Hend*, also known as *Toḥfat al-ḵāqānīya*, discusses the condition of India in the thirteenth/nineteenth century.[27]

It is also proper to remember the travelogues of Persian-speaking Indians who traveled to Iran, Transoxiana, or cities in the Ottoman Empire. One of these books is *Vaqāyeʿ-ye manāzel-e Rūm* by Ḵᵛāja ʿAbd-al-Qāder who traveled from India to the ports of the Persian Gulf.[28] From there, he reached Istanbul via Basra in the year 1199. The other significant book is *Aḥvāl-e safar-e Bokārā* written by Mīr ʿEzzat-Allāh, the envoy of W. Moorcraft to Kāšḡār, Ḵoqand, Bokhara, and Kabul. Ḥājjī ʿAlī Mīrzā Dehlavī travelled extensively in Fārs and left a useful travelogue under the title *Zobdat al-aḵbār fī savānat al-asfār* as his memorial.[29]

Iranians generally travelled to cities like Bokhara, Samarqand, and Ḵoqand by choice, but most of the people who reached Khiva and Ḵᵛārazm were government officials from Iran such as Reżāqolī Khan Hedāyat, known as Lāla Bāšī, who was a poet and writer and who went to Kᵛārazm as an ambassador.[30] The report of Esmāʿīl Khan Mīrpanja was the result of his long years of imprisonment in Kᵛārazm after being captured by Turkomans. Qahramān Mīrzā Āʾīn-al-Salṭana (Nāṣer-al-Dīn Shah's nephew) wrote a travelogue on Transoxiana which was the result of his interest in touring and excursions.[31]

Most of the traveler authors who went to Russia, Europe, and Istanbul via the Caucasus wrote descriptions of Baku, Ganja, Tiflis, Erevan, and other cities; that is why the number of travelogues about Caucasia, which was the gateway to Russia and Europe, was substantial.

The first travelogue about Europe, as various sources indicate, was by one of the Persian writers from India—that is, the *Šegarf-nāma-ye velāyat* written by Mīrzā Eʿteṣām-al-Dīn b. Tāj-al-Din Tājpūrī, who

---

[26] [*Sīāḥat-nāma-ye Hindūstān*; Monzavī, *Fehrestvāra*, 1:139-40.]

[27] [Monzavī, *Fehrestvāra*, 1:69.]

[28] [Ed. Mohibbul Hasan (London, 1969).]

[29] [Monzavī, *Fehrest*, 4008-9, nos. 41590-91.]

[30] [*Safarat-nāma-ye Ḵᵛārazm*, ed. ʿAlī Ḥosūrī (Tehran, 1977); ed and tr. Charles Schefer, *Relation de l'ambassade au Kharezm de Riza Quoly Khan...*, 2 vols. (Paris, 1876-79; repr. Amsterdam, 1975).]

[31] [Probably the *Rūz-nāma-ye safar-e Ḵᵛārazm*; see Monzavī, *Fehrest*, 4005, no. 41568.]

went to England in 1199/1784-85.[32] He described the natural, civil, and recreational sights as well as the foods of that country in his book. This travelogue was interesting to read even for Englishmen because the Persian-speaking Eastern writer discussed customs and traditions which looked strange to him while being simultaneously charmed and attracted by the comforts and pleasures of British life. He found the beauty, coquetteishness, and charming appearance of the women particularly novel. Eʿteṣām-al-Dīn was a mediocre poet but, having been schooled in the culture of poetic taste according to Perso-Indian norms, composed a *qaṣīda* (ode) or *qetʿa* (distich) in praise of each of the British nobles with whom he became acquainted and the distinguished ladies and spouses among the aristocrats and dignitaries. They are quite interesting to read. These qualities became the reason for the fame of his travelogue among British people, especially those in India. A selection of this travelogue has been translated into English.[33]

After Eʿteṣām-al-Dīn, Abū Ṭāleb Eṣfahānī, whose ancestors had gone to India, wrote an outstanding, readable, and informative travelogue about the condition of European countries and nations which will always hold the foremost position among such accounts. The name of this travelogue is *Masīr-e ṭālebī fī belād-e Afranj*, and it has been translated into English, French, and German.[34]

The first Iranian travel book on Europe was the *Ḥayrat-nāma-ye safar*, which was the report of the journey of the political mission of Mīrzā Abu'l-Ḥasan Khan Šīrāzī, better known as Īlčī.[35] He named his book *Ḥayrat-nāma*, "Book of Amazement," and its contents show that Īlčī was indeed amazed at seeing Europe and its civilizational progress. In this travelogue, too, the observations of the author about women and social conditions in England and European countries are

---

[32] [Monzavī, *Fehrest,* 4043, no. 41786.]

[33] [Tr. James Edward Alexander as Mirza Itesa Modeen, *Shigurf namah i Velaet: or, Excellent Intelligence concerning Europe* (London, 1827).]

[34] [Monzavī, *Fehrest,* 4052, nos. 41849-57; ed. Ḥosayn Ḵadīv-jam (Tehran, 1974); tr. Charles Stewart as *The Travels of Mirza Abu Taleb Khan in Asia, Africa, and Europe during the years 1799, 1800, 1801, 1802, and 1803,* 2 vols. (London, 1810 and reprints); tr. Charles Malo as *Voyages du prince persan mirza Aboul Taleb Khan...* (Paris, 1819).]

[35] [Monzavī, *Fehrest,* 3999-4000, nos. 41535-46; ed. Ḥasan Morselvand (Tehran, 1364 Š./1986); ed. and tr. Margaret Cloake as *A Persian at the Court of King George, 1809-10: The Journal of Mirza Abul Hassan Khan* (London, 1988).]

quite interesting to read. Five years later Mīrzā Abu'l-Ḥasan was sent to Russia and produced another travelogue about that journey entitled *Dalīl al-sofarā* (although it was actually written by his secretary).[36]

Three years later, Mīrzā Ṣāleḥ, who was from the same city as Mīrzā Abu'l-Ḥasan Khan [Shiraz], came to England to study the modern sciences. Mīrzā Ṣāleḥ's travelogue really belongs to a different type than those mentioned thus far. Since Mīrzā Ṣāleḥ stayed for a long time in England and was diligent in his studies, he was able to make a profound observation of European civilization and was able to introduce the culture and civilization of those lands in a more informed way.[37]

The travelogues written about Europe in the nineteenth century are numerous and include accounts by two Iranian kings, Nāṣer-al-Dīn Shah[38] and Moẓaffar-al-Dīn Shah.[39] Each of them went to Europe three times and wrote travelogues about each trip. Since the travels were royal ones, and the travelogues were published in their own lifetime, the works became famous. Nonetheless, none of these travelogues had the importance and credibility of those by Mīrzā Abu'l-Ḥasan Īlčī, Mīrzā Ṣāleḥ Šīrāzī, Reżāqolī Mīrzā (*Romūz al-sīāḥa*),[40] Ḥosayn Sarābī

---

[36] [*Dalīl al-sofarāʾ: Safar-nāma-ye Mīrzā Abu'l-Ḥasan K̲ān Šīrāzī (Īlčī) ba Rūsīya*, ed. Moḥammad Golbon (Tehran, 1357 Š./1978); the secretary was Mīrzā Moḥammad-Hādī ʿAlavī Šīrāzī. See the article by Anna Vanzan in this volume.]

[37] [*Safar-nāma-ye Mīrzā Ṣāleḥ Šīrāzī*, ed. Esmāʿīl Rāʾīn (Tehran, 1347 Š./1968); see Monzavī, *Fehrest*, 4035, nos. 41736-38.]

[38] [Nāṣer-al-Dīn Shah, *Vaqāyeʿ-e mosāferat va sīāḥat-e sahat-e Farangestān...*, ed. Mīrzā Moḥammad-ʿAlī Šīrāzī (Bombay, 1297/1880); *Vaqāyeʿ-e mosāfarat va sīāḥat-e dovvom-e farangestān...*, ed. Mīrzā Moḥammad Šīrāzī (Bombay, 1298/1881); *Rūznāma-ye k̲āterāt-e Nāṣer-al-Dīn Šāh dar safar-e sevvom-e Farangestān*, ed. Moḥammad-Esmāʿīl Reżvānī (Tehran, 1369 Š./1990); tr. J. W. Redhouse as *The Diary of H. M. the Shah of Persia During His Tour Through Europe in A. D. 1873* (London, 1874, repr. with new introduction by Carole Hillenbrand, Costa Mesa, Calif., 1995); tr. Albert Houtum Schindler and Baron Louis de Norman as *A Diary Kept by His Majesty the Shah of Persia During his Journey to Europe in 1878* (London, 1879); tr. Hans Leicht as *Ein Harem in Bismarcks Reich: Das ergötzliche Reisetagebuch des Nasreddin Schah* (Tübingen, 1975).]

[39] [*Safar-nāma-ye mobāraka-ye šāhanšāhī* (Bombay, 1903); ed. ʿAlī Dehbāšī as *Safar-nāma-ye mobāraka-ye Moẓaffar-al-Dīn Šāh ba Farang* (Tehran, 1361 Š./1982); *Dovvomīn safar-nāma-ye Moẓaffar-al-Dīn ba Farang*, ed. Fak̲r-al-Molk (Tehran, 1362 Š./1983).]

[40] [Monzavī, *Fehrest*, 4001-2, nos. 41545-48; tr. James Baillie Fraser as *Narrative of the Residence of the Persian Princes in London in 1835 and*

(*Makzan al-vaqāyeʿ*),[41] Ḥājjī Pīrzāda Nāʾīnī[42] and others. They were kings, and what they wrote was intended to be in keeping with royal dignity; still, some new and important material may be found among the references and allusions of the royal travelogues.

Naturally, the journeys of the kings inspired the princes and dignitaries of the country to want to travel too. But in those days European travel for Iranians was expensive and not everyone could go to those countries except for travelers like Ḥājjī Sayyāḥ Mahallātī[43] and Ḥājjī Pīrzāda Nāʾīnī, who were able to undertake such a long journey without any concern as dervishes and wanderers. Pleasure-seeking people like Dūst-ʿAlī Khan Moʿayyer-al-Mamālek naturally visited for a short time and came back after spending huge amounts of money but without any achievements.

Since Nāṣer-al-Dīn Shah has been mentioned, it should be said that he loved touring and excursions in general and was interested in reading travelogues by other writers. He was particularly fond of travelogues by foreigners who, as tourists or explorers, had traveled to distant countries and strange districts of the world, such as Stanley in Africa, or persons who had traversed the valleys of the Amazon, the deserts of Tibet and China, or the polar regions. The true testimony to this fact is the large number of travelogues which were caused to be translated from English, French, Russian, German and even Turkish at the orders of this king, and their manuscripts were present in his royal library. Naturally he, with such a spirit, had read the travelogues about individuals such as Farrok Khan Amīn-al-Dawla (in *Makzan al-vaqāyeʿ*) and Ḥosayn Khan Ājūdānbāšī (*Čahār faṣl*),[44] and he had to some extent become acquainted with Europe through the information written by his officials in their books.

Journeys to Europe, which had no rival from the point of view of industrial and scientific progress and political power, were of great

---

1836, with an Account of Their Journey from Persia and Subsequent Adventures, 2 vols. (London, 1838).]

[41] [Secretary to Farrok Khan Amīn-al-Molk/Dawla; see Monzavī, *Fehrest*, 4048-49; nos. 41824-32.]

[42] [*Safar-nāma-ye Ḥājjī Pīrzāda*, ed. Ḥ. Farmānfarmāʾīān, 2 vols. (Tehran, 1342-43 Š./1963-64).]

[43] [Moḥammad-ʿAlī Sayyāḥ Maḥallatī, *Safar-nāma-ye Ḥājj Sayyāḥ ba Farang*, ed. ʿAlī Dehbāšī (Tehran, 1363 Š./1984).]

[44] [By ʿAbd-al-Fattāḥ (or Mīr Fattāḥ) Garmrūdī, *Šarḥ-e maʾmūrīyat-e Ājūdānbāšī*, ed. Moḥammad Mošīrī (Tehran, 2536=1356 Š./1977; see Monzavī, *Fehrest*, 4035-37, nos. 41739-50. The delegation traveled to Europe in 1254-55/1838-39.]

interest to the notables of Iran, including courtiers, government officials, and traders. Of course the limited number of intellectuals had their own role in this regard, but these people preferred the gateways to Europe for visiting and acquiring news. Istanbul, Bombay, and Baku were their preferred sites.

The discarded politicians of Iran, such as Reżāqolī Mīrzā and his brother Najafqolī Mīrzā, the sons of Šojāʿ-al-Salṭana, wrote travelogues about Europe.[45] So, too, ʿAbbās Mīrzā Molkārā, the brother of Nāṣer-al-Dīn Shah, wrote the story of his exile to Baghdad.[46] Each of these works has remarks on political policies, the love of freedom, and the ruling principles of Europe (mostly England and France) in mind. The idea was that the governing system of Iran should also undergo change. Such thoughts are manifested in their travelogues. We see in the Baghdad memoirs by ʿAbbās Mīrzā that he used the word "constitutional" in its political sense for the first time in Persian (several years before the first whispers of constitutional government in Iran began).

Travelogue writing developed and expanded in the time of Nāṣer-al-Dīn Shah, and thereafter the writers used this literary style as a good means for expressing their patriotic and political views. Among them, Ṭāleb Tabrīzī wrote *Masālek al-moḥsenīn*,[47] and Zayn-al-ʿĀbedīn Marāgaʾī wrote the imaginary *Sīāḥat-nāma-ye Ebrāhīm Beyg* as a critical study of social and political topics.[48]

When Iranians referred to "Europe," they primarily intended the countries of Western Europe. This is why Russia is generally mentioned apart from Europe under its own name. The travelogues of people of traveled to Russia are also numerous, but the most important ones are those which were compiled and written in connection with political or plenipotentiary missions and the dispatch of delegations for congratulations or condolences. They are generally lengthy books such as the travelogues of Abu'l-Ḥasan Khan Īlčī Šīrāzī (1229/1813-14), Mīrzā Masʿūd accompanied by Ḵosrow Mīrzā and Moṣṭafā Bahā-al-Molk Afšār (1244/1828-29), Mīrzā Moḥammad-Ḥosayn Ṣadr (1268/1951-52), Ḥabīb-Allāh Sayf-al-Molk Afšār (1271/1854-55), and Moṣṭafāqolī Khan Mīrpanja (1300/1882-83).

---

[45] [See above, n. 40.]

[46] [*Šarḥ-e ḥāl-e ʿAbbās Mīrzā Molkārā*, ed. ʿAbd-al-Ḥosayn Navāʾī (Tehran, 1325 Š./1946).]

[47] [ʿAbd-al-Raḥīm b. Abī Ṭāleb Najjār Tabrīzī (Ṭālebof), *Masālek al-moḥsenīn* (Tehran, 1347 Š./1968).]

[48] [*Sīāḥat-nāma-ye Ebrāhīm Beyg*, ed. Moḥammad-ʿAlī Sepanlū (Tehran, 1364 Š./1985).]

Most of the travelogues about Europe include a chapter on the circumstances and conditions of France, but there is a unique monograph in Persian on this subject which was written in the early years of political relations with that country by an individual who was Iran's consular representative. It deserves a special mention. This work was a brief treatise on "the condition of France, its country, and its capital, which is the city of Farīz (Paris)." Its author was Dāwūd b. Zādor from the family of Šāh Načar Šāpūr. He was an Armenian who, in addition to this Persian monograph, wrote two books in French and published in Paris (1818) on the condition of Iran in that era. After that, he planned to write a monograph to introduce France to Iranians to be published in Iran and which, in his own words, would be "proper and worthy." With an introductory letter from a certain "Dūkṭūr Rūšlū" (Richelieu?) whom he described as the "*mīn īsṭr*" (minister), he visited the interesting and attractive sites and government offices, assisted by two interpreters. He collected information about them and presents it in his monograph, which is currently being edited for publication by the author of this article. He wrote this monograph in the year 1235/1819-20. It consists of information about such things as the system and regulations of the kingdom, gardens, sixty royal schools, conditions of houses, women, baths, three hundred "kitchens" (i. e. restaurants), 320 "caravanserais called *ḥawṭīl* [hotels], four hundred coffee houses, three buildings for children "whose fathers are not known," and a "training center for dogs."

Information recorded about England in the travelogues is more copious than that about other countries. This is not surprising, since England had always been an object of interest for Iranians because of the political influence of England dating from the time of Fatḥ ʿAlī Shah and the long standing rivalry between England and Russia over Iran.

Knowledge of America (*Yangī Donyā*) by Iranian dignitaries began in the time of Amīr Kabīr and expanded following the establishment of an American embassy in Iran and the steps taken by the Iranian government to establish an embassy in the United States. Journeys to America then became common. The first Iranian who wrote a travelogue about America was Mīrzā Moḥammad-ʿAlī Khan Moʿīn-al-Salṭana Raštī Eṣfahānī. He went there in 1309/1891-92 and after two years of travel wrote a travelogue and published it in Paris.[49] After him, we know Mīrzā Ebrāhīm Ṣaḥḥāfbāšī visited America,[50] and

---

[49] [*Safar-nāma-ye Šīkāgow* (Paris, 1318/1902-3; ed. Homāyūn Šahīdī, Tehran, 1363 Š./1984).]

[50] [*Safar-nāma-ye Ebrāhīm Ṣaḥḥāfbašī Tehrānī*, ed. Moḥammad Moširī (Tehran, 1357 Š./1978).]

Mok̲ber-al-Salṭana was able to see America in 1321/1903-4 when he went on a trip round the world with ʿAlī-Aṣḡar Khan Atābak.[51] It is claimed that Ḥājjī Sayyāḥ also went to America, but there is no trace of that in his travelogue.

Another major category of travelogues are those which were written about the provinces and cities of Iran itself. Perhaps the internal travelogues should be divided in two general groups. One group consists of the description of personal journeys; the other consists of those written by government dignitaries and resemble official reports. Contrary to the practice of our own time that government representatives report only about the mission on which they were sent, officials in the past paid attention to various geographical, historical, and social topics in their travelogues. Their writings are a basic and valuable source for historical and geographical studies.

Fortunately, travel reports about all the four quarters of Iran and most of its important cities are available. The dispatching of officials to far-off and remote cities during the fifty years of Nāṣer-al-Dīn's reign was absolutely fashionable; on the basis of available manuscripts it can be said that no less than seven travelogues about Baluchistan are extant, as are various reports and brief travelogues about the boundaries of Khorasan including Sarak̲s, Kalāt, and ʿAšqābād. These travelogues were either prepared by the officials sent out by the governors of Khorasan or by officials sent by the king from Tehran.

There are also numerous travelogues about the journey from Tehran to Khorasan because many of the persons who went on pilgrimage to Mašhad wrote such books. Nāṣer-al-Dīn himself made two trips to Khorasan and wrote a travelogue about each of them.[52] In addition, one of the courtiers who accompanied him on the journey, Mīrzā Qahramān Amīn-e Laškar, also wrote a travelogue whose contents can be compared with those of the shah's travelogues.[53] The travelogues about Khorasan generally consist of histories and observations of the cities of Semnān, Dāmḡān, and Šāhrūd and occasionally Bojnūrd and Qūčān (because the traveler varied the return to Tehran by taking the northerly route). Bojnūrd, adjacent to Russia, constituted a border region and had added importance because of the rebellions of the Turkomans along the frontier; governors of that area were always respected by the king. To show the importance of that place, it is

[51] [*Safar-nāma-ye Makka*, ed. Moḥammad Dabīr Sīāqī (Tehran, 1368 Š./1989).]

[52] [*Safar-nāma-ye K̲orāsān* (repr. Tehran, 1361 Š./1982); ʿAlīnaqī Ḥakīm-al-Mamālek, *Rūz-nāma-ye safar-e K̲orāsān* (Tehran, 1286/1869).]

[53] [Monzavī, *Fehrestvāra*, 1:89.]

enough to mention that its governor used to come to Tehran occasionally to inform the king about the condition of that region. Two travelogues about the area by Seham-al-Dawla Šādlū Īlkānī are extant.

There are also official reports and travelogues about Fārs, including three outstanding works of scholarship on the province written by powerful and learned authors. Since they wanted to write about the history and geography of the province, these three authors traveled extensively in the province, and the books are the result of those travels. These writers are Mīrzā Ḥasan Fasāʾī (author of the *Fārs-nāma-ye nāṣerī*);[54] Mīrzā Jaʿfar Ḵūrmūjī (author of *Āṯār-e jaʿfarī*);[55] and Forṣat-al-Dawla Šīrāzī (author of *Āṯār-e ʿAjam*). Forṣat-al-Dawla explicitly included a travelogue as part of the *Āṯār-e ʿAjam*, so that aspect of his book is the most vivid.[56]

Azerbaijan, being the seat of the crown prince, had special importance, and there were many travelogues about it. Because it was situated on the way to Caucasia, travelers to or from Europe by that route also described its cities. The Crown Prince Moẓaffar-al-Dīn was fond of hunting and excursions and wrote about his travels to Marāḡa, Ardabīl, and Moḡān.[57] Mīrzā Qahramān Amīn-e Laškar, who was in charge of financial affairs of Azarbaijan for some time, has given the accounts of his stay and travels in the province during the years 1300-1302/1882-85.[58] Probably the best travel report including social and historical information about Azarbaijan is ʿAbd-al-ʿAlī Adīb-al-Molk's travelogue entitled *Dāfeʿ al-ḡorūr.*[59]

The travelogues of ʿAbd-al-Ḡaffār Najm-al-Molk about Aḥvāz and Šūštar, including the prospects for building a dam on the Dez river, and travelogues related to Lorestān, Kurdistan, ʿErāq-e ʿAjam and the Jebāl areas are all good examples of these works appropriate for research in the field of conditions and circumstances of cities during the Qajar period.[60]

We know in particular that Eʿtemād-al-Salṭana, because he was planning to write the geographical encyclopedia known as *Merāt al-boldān*, used to send officials to cities or requested scholars and writers from those places to write treatises about their city and province. Fortunately a large part of this information has been preserved in eight manuscript volumes,

---

54 [Ed. Manṣūr Rastgār Fasāʾī (2 vols., Tehran, 1367 Š./1988); part. tr. by Heribert Busse as *History of Persia under Qajar Rule* (New York, 1972).]

55 [Tehran, 1286.]

56 [Lithograph (Bombay, 1312/1894); ed. ʿAlī Dehbāšī (Tehran, 1362 Š./1984).]

57 [*Rūz-nāmaye vaqāyeʿ-e safar-e Moḡān*; Monzavī, *Fehrest*, 4007, no. 41578.]

58 [Monzavī, *Fehrestvāra*, 1:89.]

59 [Ed. Īraj Afšār (Tehran, 1349 Š./1970).]

60 [*Safar-nāma-ye Ḵūzestān*, ed. Moḥammad Dabīr Sīāqī (Tehran, 1362 Š./1983).]

two of which are in the Malek National Library and the other six in the old Royal Library. Naturally, most of the details included in these booklets and treatises are the result of local travel by their authors.

Categories of Travelogue Writers

As noted earlier, among the kings of Iran, Nāṣer-al-Dīn Shah and Moẓaffar-al-Dīn Shah have written travelogues. There are seven of these by Nāser-al-Dīn—the two journeys to Khorasan, three to Europe, a trip to the Atābāt (Baghdad, Karbala, and Najaf), one to ʿErāq-e ʿAjam (the central part of Iran comprising Tehran, Isfahan, and Arāk), and a journey to Māzandarān as well as some short travelogues. Moẓaffar-al-Dīn wrote travelogues about his trips to Europe.

There are also many travelogues by Qajar princes such as Solṭān-Moḥammad Mīrzā Sayf-al-Dawla (putative son of Fatḥ-ʿAlī Shah),[61] Farhād Mīrzā Moʿtamad-al-Dawla,[62] ʿAbbās Mīrzā Molkārā,[63] K̠osrow Mīrzā,[64] Najafqolī Mīrzā and Reżāqolī Mīrzā (sons of Šojāʿ-al-Salṭana),[65] Ẓell-al-Solṭan,[66] Maḥmūd Mīrzā,[67] Moḥammad-Valī Mīrzā,[68] Sām Mīrzā,[69] Eʿtezād-al-Salṭana,[70] and others.

Military commanders and army officers also form a group who were commissioned for leading military expeditions or finding suitable roads for the advance of men and guns and as a result wrote travel reports stating the particulars about various forts and roads. Works by officials on the telegraph line and road construction are similar in nature.

There are many travelogues written by ambassadors, dignitaries of state, or rulers and governors, and the value and utility of their books and travel reports are unquestionable since they were obliged to provide realistic details for the information of the king. Even when they wrote the travelogues for their own personal satisfaction, the depth of their writing is greater than that of ordinary travelogues.

---

[61] [See above, n. 22.]

[62] [See above, n. 18.]

[63] [See above, n. 46.]

[64] [*Safar-nāma-ye K̠osrow Mīrzā ba Peṭorzbūrġ*; Monzavī, *Fehrestvāra*, 1:106.]

[65] [See above, n. 40.]

[66] [Presumably his memoirs, the *Sargoẕašt-e masʿūdī* (repr. Tehran, 1362 Š./1983).]

[67] [*Safar-nāma-ye K̠ūzestān*; see Monzavī, *Fehrestvāra*, 1:108.]

[68] [*Safar-nāma-ye Makka*; see Monzavī, *Fehrestvāra*, 1:125.]

[69] [*Safar-nāma-ye čaman-e solṭānīya*; see Monzavī, *Fehrestvāra*, 103.]

[70] [*Safar-nāma-ye Lārījān*; see Monzavī, *Fehrestvāra*, 1:119.]

There are also examples of travelogue written by men of letters, poets, mystics, and merchants. Most of the works by writers, poets, and mystics are adorned with poetry and historical and literary allusions. They often reflect a different taste and perspective from other travelogues. For example, one might mention the travelogue by Ḥājjī Pīrzāda Nāʾīnī which consists of numerous minute literary and historical points. It is the only travelogue where we find the personal and scholarly biography of someone like Edward Browne and his Persian teacher Moḥammad-Bāqer Bavānātī and can come to know about their mutual consultations and conversations.[71]

Women constitute another group of travelogue writers, although we know only of a few travelogues by them. It has been possible to identify three such works which were definitely written by women. The oldest of them [from the Safavid period] is the versified travelogue about Mecca written by the spouse of Mīrzā K̲alīl Raqamnevīs.[72] As the manuscript is dated 1104/1692-93, it must have been composed some time before that. It is composed of 1300 couplets. Another travelogue is about the ʿAtābāt and Mecca and was written by the daughter of Moʿtamad-al-Dawla and wife of Naṣīr-al-Dawla Šīrāzī about her journey in 1297/1879-80.[73] The other short travelogue is by K̲āvar Bībī Šādlū, the sister of Sehām-al-Dawla Šādlū Bojnūrdī, who traveled from Bojnūrd to Tehran around 1317/1899-1900.[74] The descriptions by this woman, who reflected the tribal spirit, about the houses and lives of Tehran's dignitaries is interesting to read and mirrors the state of Tehran in the past century.

Kinds and Themes of Travelogues

Finally, Persian travelogues may also be categorized according to a typology based on the primary purpose for the travel:

Pilgrimage: i.e., narratives consisting of information about the ʿAtabāt (the shrines of Karbalāʾ, Najaf, Samarrā, and Syria), Mecca and Medina, Qom, Mašhad, and other shrines in Iranian provinces such as the shrine of Šāh Čerāḡ in Shiraz and the threshold of Sahl b. ʿAlī near Solṭānābād of Arāk.

Tourism: i.e., narratives which mostly provide information about travels to Europe, India, the Caucasus, Russia, and Transoxiana.

---

[71] [See above, n. 42.]

[72] [Monzavī, *Fehrest*, 4033-34, no. 41725.]

[73] [Monzavī, *Fehrestvāra*, 1:125.]

[74] [*Safar-nāmahā-ye Sehām-al-Dawla Bojnūrdī*, ed. Qodrat-Allāh Rowšanī Zaʿfaranlū (Tehran, 1374 Š./1995).]

State Missions: i.e., the reports related to the military, foreign embassies, mapping, the telegraph, road construction, geographical studies, the census, and the quarantine.

Hunting and Recreation: i.e., descriptions of the conditions of mountains, valleys, and rivers and information on various kinds of hunting, such as the travelogues by Nāṣer-al-Dīn Shah, Āʾīn-al-Salṭana, Ẓell-al-Solṭan, Moʿayyer-al-Mamālek, etc.

Education: i.e., works written by students in Europe such as Mīrzā Ṣāleḥ Šīrāzī, Mīrzā Mahdī Khan, and Momtaḥen-al-Dawla Šaqāqī, or by scholars in the religious shrines of the ʿAtabāt such as Mīrzā Moḥammad-Ḥasan Najafī Qūčānī.

Captivity and Exile: i.e., works like the travelogues by the fugitives ʿAbbās Mīrzā Molkārā, Najafqoli Mīrzā and Reżāqolī Mīrzā, or the Esmāʿīl Mīrpanja who was held captive by the Turkomans.

Most of these travelogues have dealt with matters of nature and climate, distances between cities, descriptions of caravansaries, ways of living, prices of commodities, important buildings and constructions, classes of people, nobles, dignitaries, men of letters and scholars, customs and manners, hospitality, local products, histories of cities, and strange and wonderful things. Therefore if an interested student selects the classification of information given in Persian travelogues as the topic for a thesis and is able to separate the subjects and ascertain the routes of travel with the help of a computer, he will be able to provide a still more accurate and clearer identification of the contents of this matchless treasure than has been possible here.

Travelogues by Berezin: A Nineteenth-Century Russian Traveler to Iran

Elena Andreeva

> ...a traveller's chief aim should be to make men wiser and better, and to improve their minds by the bad, as well as good examples of what they deliver concerning foreign places.
>
> —Jonathan Swift

More than 150 Russian travelogues about Iran were published in the form of books and articles during the nineteenth and early twentieth centuries. These accounts and their authors have received surprisingly little attention from scholars.[1] However, the Russian travelogues of this period add a specific dimension to modern Iranian history and serve as a valuable source of information on Qajar Iran and its relationships with Russia and Britain. At the same time, Russian travelogues can be used as material for a study on Russian "Orientalism." This article is an attempt to combine both approaches: to introduce the vast body of Russian travelogues about nineteenth and early-twentieth century Iran and to introduce Russian "Orientalists" in terms of their similarities to and differences from their colleagues in western Europe. The life and works of Il'ia Berezin (1819-96), a famous Russian scholar who traveled to Iran in 1842, has been selected

[1] The following works deal with Russian travelogues on Iran in the nineteenth and early twentieth centuries: Boris Dantsig, *Russkie puteshestvenniki na Blizhnem Vostoke* (Moscow, 1973); idem, *Blizhniĭ Vostok v russkoĭ nauke i literature* (Moscow 1973); Firuz Kazemzadeh, "The Origin and Early Development of the Persian Cossack Brigade," in *The American Slavic and East European Review* 15(1956):351-63; Masʿūd Nūrbaḵš, *Bā karāvān-e tārīḵ* (Tehran, 1991); Saʿīd Rahbar, *Negāhī dīgar ba dīdārī kohan* (Stockholm, 1997).

as a representative example for this study.[2] Berezin's travelogues are among the most fascinating, comprehensive, and scholarly ones of their type. Berezin also belongs to the same group of people, that is, scholars and men of letters, who have been discussed by Edward Said in his study of Orientalism. To achieve the above-mentioned goals, Berezin's travel accounts must be analyzed in their historical context and in the context of the author's background.

Nineteenth-century Iran, which was ruled by the Qajar dynasty (1796-1925), was characterized by economic and military weakness and disunity. The Qajar rulers were not able to resist pressure from the European colonial empires, primarily Russia and Britain. The intrusion of Western powers became an additional factor in the stagnation of Iran in the nineteenth and early twentieth centuries. By that time, Russia, after a century of westernization, had developed a colonialist outlook on expansion to alien lands. Apart from Russia's drive to gain access to warm water ports, it was believed that colonies could make the empire rich and that the empire could in return bring the colonized people to civilization and Christianity, following the tantalizing example of British India.

After two unsuccessful wars with Russia, under the terms of the 1813 Treaty of Golestān and 1828 Treaty of Torkmānčāy, Iran lost most of its Caucasian possessions and surrendered other significant rights to Russia.[3] Russia's increasing presence in the Caucasus, along with its steady advance into Central Asia, alarmed Great Britain. The so called "Great Game" for domination over Asian politics began, with

---

[2] Publications on Berezin include N. A. Kuznetsova and B. M. Dantsig, "I. N. Berezin—Puteshestvennik po Zakavkaz'yu, Iranu i Blizhnemu Vostoku," *Kratkie Soobshcheniya Instituta Vostokovedeniya* 22(1956):92-100 (a brief survey of Berezin's travels in a number of Middle Eastern countries); Jean Calmard, "Berezin" in *Encyclopaedia Iranica* (London, etc., 1990), 4:163-64; and the several papers presented on the occasion of Berezin's centenary in 1919 which focus on specific areas of his scholarly activities: V. Barthold, "I. N. Berezin kak istorik," in *Zapiski kollegii vostokovedov* 2(1925):51-72; B. Vladimirtsov, "I. N. Berezin—Mongolist," *Zapiski kollegii vostokovedov* 2(1925):192-94; I. Krachkovskiĭ, "Melochi dlya kharakteristiki I. N. Berezina," *Zapiski Kollegii Vostokovedov* 2(1925):177-79; I. S. Oldenburg, "I. N. Berezin, kak puteshestvennik i issledovatel' iranskikh narechiĭ," *Zapiski kollegii vostokovedov* 2(1925):173-76; A. Samoĭlovich, "I. N. Berezin, kak turkolog," *Zapiski kollegii vostokovedov* 2(1925):161-72.

[3] Firuz Kazemzadeh, *Russia and Britain in Persia, 1864-1914: A Study in Imperialism* (New Haven, 1968), 5-6.

Russia and Britain as the main players throughout the century. Iran became one of "the pieces on a chessboard upon which is being played out a game for the domination of the world."[4] In the 1850s, a struggle over concessions and loans began. The Anglo-Russian Convention of 1907 settled British and Russian differences in Tibet and Afghanistan and divided Iran into spheres of interest: northern and central Iran with the cities of Tehran and Isfahan fell into the Russian sphere; the southeast went to the British sphere; and the area in between was made a neutral zone. Although the preamble to the Convention of 1907 mentioned the integrity and independence of Iran, the Iranian government was not even informed about the terms of the treaty.

The reflection of imperialism in modern Orientalism has been demonstrated by Edward Said, who defined Orientalism as a discourse of power and the domination of Europe over the Orient. He showed how scholars, writers, and travelers separated themselves from the Orient, which they treated as their "Other" in order to construct its representation in their writings. According to Said, the body of knowledge gathered by Orientalists was used by imperial governments in their colonial policy. Any Orientalist work, therefore, could serve imperial goals, regardless of whether or not the authors intended to work in the service of imperialism, or of the degree to which they were supporting their governments. The age-old tradition of travel literature was not an exception: it also became connected with the commercial, political, and scientific interests of the colonial empires.

The concept of Orientalism has been largely seen as the creation of western Europe. Surprisingly, Russian Orientalism has received no attention from scholars, with the exception of those few works that deal with lands colonized by the Russian Empire: the Caucasus, Central Asia, and the Crimea.[5] This article is therefore an exercise in research on Russian Orientalism in the Middle East, although it is limited to the analysis of a single Russian traveler and of a single Middle Eastern country.

The peculiarities of Russian Orientalism derive from the unique place which Russia occupies among European countries. By the late eighteenth and early nineteenth centuries, the geographical position

---

[4] George N. Curzon, *Persia and the Persian Question,* 2 vols. (London, 1892), 1:3-4.

[5] Susan Layton, *Russian Literature and Empire: Conquest of the Caucasus from Pushkin to Tolstoy* (Cambridge, U. K., 1994); Daniel R. Brower and Edward J. Lazzerini, eds., *Russia's Orient: Imperial Borderlands and Peoples, 1700-1917* (Bloomington, Ind., 1997).

and historical evolution of Russia resulted in a split of identity and national character between pro-Western and pro-Eastern concepts. According to the well-known words of Aleksandr Bestuzhev-Marlinskii, a nineteenth-century Russian writer, "a two-faced Janus, ancient Russia simultaneously looked toward Europe and Asia. Its way of life comprised a link between the settled activity of the West and the nomadic indolence of the Orient." The conquest of the Eastern territories, especially the Caucasus, together with the recurrent Russo-Turkish wars, stimulated an intellectual and political engagement with the persistent dilemma of Russian cultural identity. On the one hand, identifying the Caucasus and Asian territories as the Orient or as the "Other" allowed Russia to extend her Western model of superiority to the other eastern territories, such as Iran and the Ottoman Empire, and to intensify her sense of European-ness in economic, religious, cultural, and moral terms. Yet many Russian intellectuals, Romantics in particular, could not declare the Orient its "Other" because of Russia's Asian cultural and political roots, and because Asian peoples had comprised a part of the empire since the sixteenth century. In some sense, for Russians, the Orient was both Self and Other.

Accordingly, the feelings of Russian travelers to the Middle East were different from those of the French and British travelers researched by Edward Said. "The French pilgrim was imbued with a sense of acute loss in the Orient. He came there to a place in which France, unlike Britain, had no sovereign presence," while for the British, "the Orient was defined by material possession, by a material imagination, as it were."[6] For Russian travelers of this period, as we shall see in the travelogues by Berezin, the most important concept to be proven appears to have been that of Russia as a great and civilized empire, equal to the western European empires, especially to that of the British. Apparently many Russians abroad were trying to conceal any feelings of national inferiority engendered by the split in conceptions of the national identity and to compensate for such feelings by overemphasizing their European-ness and the perceived inferiority of the "Orientals."

The flourishing of "Oriental" Russian travelogues in the nineteenth and early twentieth centuries was directly inspired by the Western world's great interest in the Orient during this period. Russia joined the European *renaissance orientale* at the end of the eighteenth and beginning of the nineteenth centuries. Arabic and Persian literature in European translations

---

[6] Edward Said, *Orientalism* (New York, 1979), 169.

and European "Oriental" works had a great impact on the emergence and development of Russia's fascination with the Orient, of which the Romantic movement was an important element. This interest was intensified by the ongoing wars against the Ottoman Empire and the warfare in the Caucasus. In addition, engagement with the Middle East was stimulated by the development of Oriental Studies in Russia at the beginning of the nineteenth century. The teaching of Oriental disciplines, mainly languages, started in 1805 at Kazan University, in 1811 at Moscow University, and in 1819 at St. Petersburg University. In 1815, the famous Lazarev Institute of Oriental Languages was founded in Moscow. In 1818, the Asian Museum was created in St. Petersburg and was to accumulate a great collection of Oriental books, manuscripts, and art.

In the early nineteenth century, following the establishment of the Qajar dynasty and the increasing involvement of Iran in European politics, there was a significant rise in the number of Europeans who traveled to Iran and, accordingly, a new burst of travel accounts.[7] Numerous travelogues about Iran were produced in the nineteenth and early twentieth centuries by British[8] and Russian travelers, so that travel writing seems to be one more form of rivalry between Russia and Britain in Iran. For Russian travelers, Iran was attractive as a southern neighbor, almost an extension of the recently conquered Caucasus, an important target of the colonial Tsarist policy, and still an exotic or at least a little known place. Over 120 Russian travelers went to Iran in the nineteenth and early twentieth centuries and published accounts of their trips. A number of them, such as Berezin, published several works about Iran. Those Russians who went to Iran were military officers and diplomats, or scholars and scientists, sometimes those interested in trade, or those traveling for pleasure. The majority of Russian travelers on their way to Iran went through the Caucasus and Transcaucasia and spent most of their time in the northern part of Iran where the main cities of Tehran, Tabrīz, and Mašhad were located. This area was of special importance to Russia because of its

---

[7] Ann Lambton demonstrated the great increase in the presence of the foreigners in Iran in the second half of the nineteenth century by the following numbers: "In the middle of the nineteenth century, there were some 150 Europeans in Persia; by the 1890s there were some 800 and by 1900 about 1,000": A. K. S. Lambton, *Qajar Persia* (Austin, 1978), 207.

[8] "... in the nineteenth century the number of books of Persian travel written in English (including American), amounted to over one hundred": Michiel Henderikus Braaksma, *Travel and Literature: An Attempt at a Literary Appreciation of English Travel-Books about Persia from the Middle Ages to the Present Day* (Groningen, 1938), 71.

proximity to the new imperial territories in the Caucasus, Transcaucasia, and Central Asia, as well as for its proximity to the Caspian Sea, where Russia had ships. In reality, this region had become a Russian sphere of political and trade interests long before the Anglo-Russian Convention of 1907.

Il'ia Nikolaevich Berezin (1819-96), was one of the first *bona fide* Russian Orientalists to travel to several Middle Eastern countries, including Iran, and to publish accounts of his travels. The background of the traveler shapes his world outlook and political orientation; hence his particular selection of information and his perspective on Iran: "A travel book is a book about the writer's identity thrown into relief against the foreign landscape, or filtered through the foreign context."[9] Berezin's biography is that of a successful and famous scholar and an important participant in the cultural and educational activities of mid-nineteenth century Russia.[10] His father was a government official at a factory; his mother belonged to a family of gentry from the Ukraine. Berezin was born in the district of Perm in the Urals. He studied first at home with tutors from the Russian Orthodox clergy, then at a district school in Ekaterinburg, and later he was transferred to the gymnasium in Perm at public expense.[11] In 1837, he graduated from the Oriental Faculty of the University of Kazan, which in the first half of the nineteenth century was the major center of Oriental studies and languages in Russia. He studied with Mirza Kazembek (1802-70), the famous professor of Persian, Arabic, and Turkish philology. Berezin obtained a master's degree in Oriental Philology in 1841 and in the next year, together with another graduate student from the same faculty, Wilhelm Dittel (1816-48), was sent by the university on a scholarly trip to the Middle East including Transcaucasia, Iran, Mesopotamia, Syria, Egypt, Constantinople, and the Crimea. A detailed set of instructions for this three-year-long voyage was composed by Kazembek. It defined the places to visit, the time-table to follow, and the objects to study. The students' primary goal was the study of spoken "Muslim" languages and their dialects (Turkish, Persian and Arabic), as well as the literatures in these languages. They were also expected to study the life, customs, manners, religion, and culture of the Oriental peoples; to examine

[9] Joan Corwin, "Identity in the Victorian Travel Narrative" (Ph.D. diss., Indiana University, 1987), 5.

[10] On his biography, see Calmard in *Encyclopaedia Iranica*, 4:163-64; Kuznetsova and Dantsig, "I. N. Berezin"; Dantsig, *Vostok v russkoĭ nauke i literature*, 116, 201; S. Vengerov, *Kritiko-biograficheskiĭ slovar' russkikh pisateleĭ i uchenykh* (St. Petersburg, 1889-1904), 3:66-69.

[11] Vengerov, *Kritiko-biograficheskiĭ slovar'*, 67.

historical monuments; and to copy interesting inscriptions. Besides that, they were required to collect specimens of rare plants, seeds and insects, and to purchase coins and books for the university. With few exceptions, as in cases when he had to make changes due to the condition of his health or to the political situation in the area, Berezin followed Kazembek's instructions closely, as he stated in his report.[12]

Upon his return from the Middle East, Berezin was appointed a professor of Turkish at the University of Kazan, and then at the University of St. Petersburg, when the Oriental Faculty was moved there in 1855. Berezin had broad scholarly interests and was involved in the development of higher education and in the intellectual and cultural life of his times. In his autobiography, he mentions that his official appointments at different periods included those of Curator of Coins and Medals at the University of Kazan, Censor of Oriental Books printed in Kazan, and the editor of the Kazan *Provincial Bulletin.* In St. Petersburg, he was a member of a commission to foster writers and scholars, editor of the Oriental section of the *Encyclopedic Dictionary* (1861-63),[13] member of a commission to reform the university charter, and a Head Keeper of Oriental Coins at the university.[14] In the 1870s, Berezin undertook the editing of the *Russian Encyclopedic Dictionary* (1873-82), which was successfully completed and made its editor famous.[15] Berezin was a member of the Asiatic Societies in Paris and London and an active participant in the Russian Geographical Society (founded in 1854). His doctoral thesis, "An Outline of the Internal Structure of the Olus of Jowsi" (1863), was, according to Barthold, written in a rush and therefore contained some defects.[16] From the late 1870s, Berezin became less involved in the activities of learned circles, although he did participate in the Fourth Congress of Orientalists in Florence.[17]

Very little information is available about Berezin's teaching. We know that he taught courses on Ottoman history and literature. Barthold points out that Berezin, though a talented and well-educated scholar

---

[12] Berezin, "Izvlechenie iz godichnogo otcheta puteshestvuyushchego po Vostoku Magistra I. Berezina," in *Zhurnal Ministerstva Narodnogo prosveshcheniya (ZMNP)* 46/4(1845):23-50.

[13] This edition was never completed, according to Barthold, "I. N. Berezin kak istorik," 59.

[14] Vengerov, *Kritiko-biograficheskiĭ slovar'*, 68.

[15] Barthold, "I. N. Berezin kak istorik," 60.

[16] Barthold, "I. N. Berezin kak istorik," 67-69.

[17] Barthold, "I. N. Berezin kak istorik," 69-70.

and writer, did not appreciate teaching very much. Barthold quotes Berezin as saying that he was not interested in teaching "in an empty room in front of just two or three students."[18]

Berezin, who was an encyclopedic scholar, left an extensive body of academic and popular works. He published numerous articles and reviews in magazines and newspapers. A complete bibliography of his works has not yet been assembled, but it is known that during his years of teaching at the University of Kazan alone (1846-55) he published more than thirty works.[19] His scholarly and intellectual interests were remarkably broad: a philologist, involved in linguistic and historical research, he also worked in folklore and numismatics. An Iranist and Turkologist, he also studied Arabic and its dialects, Armenian dialects, and even tried to work with the Malaysian language and with cuneiform characters. Besides that, he became interested in Mongolian and Manchurian languages in connection with Turkic languages and Mongolian history.[20] In addition, he wrote poetry and fiction and was an expert in Romance literatures.[21] Berezin also drew skillfully. On the one hand, these accomplishments gave the charm of great erudition to all his works. On the other hand, however, they created an air of excessive self-confidence and often led him to superficial and rash conclusions and errors. Some surface judgments on Middle Eastern topics appear in his travel accounts, especially in the early articles.[22] To a great degree, these can be explained by the author's youth, his lack of experience, and the short period of time he spent in each country. At the same time, a certain diffuseness of his activities, combined with a keen sensibility to public success and popularity prevented him from completing many of his works, including his most significant one, the edition and translation of *The History of the Mongols* by Rašīd-al-Dīn. His *Library of Eastern Historians* and *Turkish Chrestomathy* were left unfinished as well, while, according to Oldenburg,[23] his *Persian Grammar* contained nothing new. Only a small part of his intended *Puteshestvie po Vostoku* (Travels in the Orient) was published. The complex approach to the Orient as an object of general, unspecialized study, together with the

---

[18] Barthold, "I. N. Berezin kak istorik," 70.

[19] Dantsig, *Blizhniĭ Vostok,* 116.

[20] Samoĭlovich, "I. N. Berezin, kak turkolog," 162.

[21] Krachkovskiĭ, "Melochi," 177-83.

[22] For example, his unscholarly and half-joking description of Sufism and the *lūṭīs* in "Izvlechenie iz godichnogo otcheta," 46-47.

[23] Oldenburg, "I. N. Berezin," 176.

underscoring of the past glory of the Orient contrasted with the worthlessness of its present, was typical of the Orientalists of his generation. Barthold commented that the changes that occurred in Russian Orientalism in the late nineteenth century did not influence Berezin, and he states that the virtue of Berezin's generation of Orientalists consisted more in formulating the problems rather than in finding the answers.[24]

Berezin spent three years traveling in the Middle East. He left Kazan in June 1842; went to Astrakhan; then by way of the Caspian Sea to Tarkhu; and from there to Derbent, Kuba, Baku, Sal'yany, Lenkoran, and Āstārā. Early in October, he crossed the Iranian border and arrived at Ardabīl. He fell ill there and was able to resume his journey only in mid-October. He reached Tabrīz and spent two months there. In order to see the Moḥarram processions in Tehran, he decided not to go to Rašt, as he had been instructed, but instead proceeded to Tehran via Zanjān and Qazvīn. He stayed in the Iranian capital for two months and then headed for Isfahan, passing through Qom and Kāšān. He was in Isfahan early in March and continued his travels after a month. He spent more than a week exploring Persepolis and in mid-April was in Shiraz. Two weeks later, he went through Kāzerūn where he stayed for three days, on the way to Būšehr. After a week, in June 1843, he left Iran by way of the Persian Gulf, taking a boat from Būšehr to Basra.[25] He devoted an article to the description of Karbalāʾ and Kāẓemayn, the Shiʿite holy places; to the Shiʿite pilgrimage; and to some other rituals.[26] While traveling in Mesopotamia and Syria, Berezin also visited Baghdad, Mosul, Diyarbakir, Aleppo, Antioch, Beirut, Jaffa, Jerusalem, and Damascus. In early February 1844, he went to Egypt, visited Alexandria, and spent two months in Cairo. He stayed in Constantinople for eleven months (July 1844 to June 1845) and traveled back to Russia via the Crimea.

Berezin spent three years in the Middle East (June 1842 to June 1845), including eight months in Iran from October 1842 to June 1843. During the whole period of his travels, Berezin kept a diary and made about three hundred detailed drawings of various sites and about forty diagrams.[27] Later he used his diaries in writing his travel accounts.

---

[24] Barthold, "I. N. Berezin kak istorik," 72.

[25] Berezin, "Izvlechenie iz godichnogo otcheta," 23-24; "Obzor trekhletnego puteshestviya po Vostoku Magistra Kazanskogo Universiteta I. Berezina," in *Zhurnal Ministerstva Narodnogo prosveshcheniya* 55/4(1847):2-5.

[26] Berezin, "Kerbelia," in *Magazin zemlevedeniya i puteshestviĭ* 5, Moscow, 1848; cited in Kuznetsova and Dantsig, 97-98.

[27] Berezin, "Obzor trekhletnego puteshestviya," 24.

Apparently, the area of studies and travel was mapped out too broadly for the three years allotted. Thus, his works on the dialectology of Persian, Arabic, and Turkish bear the shortcomings resulting from the insufficient time of his travels[28] and from "the lack of special linguistic training, which he could not receive at the University and which he did not acquire through studying of the works extant at that time."[29]

Berezin published a number of articles inspired by his travels; these reflected fragments of his impressions and some problems of the Orient.[30] According to his own statements,[31] he was planning to write a complete travelogue about his whole journey. This project, however, like many of his other projects, was never accomplished. It is impossible to guess now how long the whole travelogue would have been, but one of his reviewers predicted in 1850 that it could have reached ten volumes if written in the same manner as his *Puteshestvie po Dagestanu i Zakavkaz'yu*.[32] Only the first two volumes were written and published. The first volume of the planned *Puteshestvie po Vostoku* (Travel in the Orient) was titled *Puteshestvie po Dagestanu i Zakavkaz'yu* (Travel in Dagestan and Transcaucasia) and was out of print by 1849. Three years later, his *Puteshestvie po severnoĭ Persii* (Travel in northern Persia) was published. It covered only the description of the northern part of Iran and of Tehran. Some additional information about southern Iran was provided in the articles written by Berezin about Būšehr, the port on the Persian Gulf.[33] The travelogues by Berezin earned him great popularity, and they produced a number of reviews in the newspapers and magazines of the time.[34] *Puteshestvie po Dagestanu i Zakavkaz'yu* was republished in 1850. From his travelogues, a section on foreign trade in Tabriz has been translated

[28] Oldenburg, "I. N. Berezin," 175; Krachkovskiĭ, "Melochi," 177-79; Samoĭlovich, "I. N. Berezin, kak turkolog," 165-67.

[29] Samoĭlovich, "I. N. Berezin, kak turkolog," 165.

[30] See a partial bibliography in Vengerov, *Kritiko-biograficheskiĭ slovar'*, 68-69.

[31] For example, see Berezin, "Obzor trekhletnego puteshestviya," 24; idem, *Puteshestvie po severnoĭ Persii* (2nd ed., Kazan, 1852), 150, 250.

[32] P. Savel'ev, "*Puteshestvie po Dagestanu i Zakavkaz'yu* I. Berezina," in *Zhurnal Ministerstva Narodnogo prosveshcheniia* 65/6(1850):104.

[33] Berezin, "Inoĭ mir," in *Russkiĭ vestnik* 9(1857):201-23; idem, "Bender-Bushir i angliĭskaia èkspeditsiya na iuge Persii," in *Sankt-peterburgskie vedomosti* 19(1857).

[34] See a partial bibliography of reviews in Vengerov, *Kritiko-biograficheskiĭ slovar'*, 69. Some of these reviews will be discussed below.

into English by Charles Issawi,[35] and the section on Moḥarram processions in Tehran has been partly translated into French by Jean Calmard[36] and into English by Peter Chelkowski.[37]

The analysis presented here is based primarily on *Puteshestvie po severnoĭ Persii*,[38] with occasional use of Berezin's other travel accounts. *Puteshesivie* is a sizable volume of almost 350 pages, with bibliographical notes and supplements. The supplements include several inscriptions, with translations by Berezin; a table of the goods imported to Tabriz; a table of some meteorological observations carried out in Tabriz and Tehran; and an extract from the *Geography* by Ḥamd-Allāh Qazvīnī about the area of Ardabīl, again with translation by the author. The volume also contains endnotes, mostly citations from works of European scholars and travelers. The book opens with a portrait of Moḥammad Shah originally painted in watercolors by an anonymous court painter. Berezin tells about the artist, who was a "Seid" (sayyid), and about his works, together with a brief excursus about Persian painting; but he does not give the artist's name.[39] The book is embellished with several masterly drawings and maps made by the author himself. Berezin considered the maps of Tehran and "the ruins of Rey" among his best works.[40] Unfortunately, it does not contain a map of his itinerary. His other drawings included a plan and a view of Tabrīz, a diagram of Fatḥ-ʿAlī Shah's palace in Karaj, and a drawing of the main jewels from the shah's treasury. In addition, the account gives notes on the "weeping for Husayn's family": "la Husayn, va Husayn" [*sic*]. Oldenburg has correctly noted that the drawings, though less documentary than modern photos, gave to Berezin (and to his audience, it may be added) a first-hand sense of shapes and colors.[41] Berezin's gift of observing and catching every detail helped his readers to follow him and to imagine more vividly the scenes and views he was describing. Thorough, slow-paced, and almost non-selective depiction of every object and theme is a distinctive characteristic of all his travel accounts.

---

[35] Charles Issawi, *The Economic History of Iran:1800-1914* (Chicago, 1971), 105-8.

[36] See the references in Calmard, *Encyclopaedia Iranica*, 4:163-64.

[37] Peter Chelkowski, "Popular Arts: Patronage and Piety," in Layla S. Diba, ed., *Royal Persian Paintings: The Qajar Epoch* (London, 1998), 90-99.

[38] Hereafter referred to as *Puteshestvie.*

[39] *Puteshestvie*, 248-50.

[40] Berezin, "Obzor trekhletnego puteshestviya," 24.

[41] Oldenburg, "I. N. Berezin," 174.

Unlike the travelogues of the previous century, the nineteenth century accounts were not solely informative and scholarly, they also meant to entertain and carried a significant autobiographical element. All of Berezin's travelogues were addressing a broad, general audience; he was entertaining his readers while providing information and descriptions, combined with historical background, often with emotional commentary. As for the interdependence of "objective" observations and "subjective" reflections, there is a difference between *Puteshetvie po Dagestanu i Zakavkaz'yu*[42] and *Puteshestviee po severnoĭ Persii.* In *Puteshestvie*, Berezin's comments become less frequent and straightforward, less abrupt and emotional, more reserved; he tries to be "objective." Yet all these new developments probably did not mean that Berezin's views on the important issues, such as Russian imperial politics, Islam, and "the Orientals" underwent significant changes. He simply assumed some more moderate mode of expression. Therefore, in analyzing his beliefs in *Puteshestvie,* it is often useful to examine the similar problems as evidenced in his earlier travelogue.

The authority reflected in the accounts of Berezin had several sources. The most important was that, in his own eyes, he represented the Russian Empire and was unambiguously proud of it. On the opening pages of his *Puteshestvie po Dagestanu* he talks about "our rich Caucasian areas" and declares that "from the eastern shore of the Caspian Sea, Russia can stretch her hand out to Khiva and Bukhara, and, if desired, much further."[43] Commenting on the war which imperialist Russia was fighting in the Caucasus, Berezin exclaims with striking patriotic enthusiasm, "Our wise Government, motivated by truly philanthropic values, is showing the well-considered and voluntarily-chosen way towards the righteous goal!"[44] He claims that "these battles we fought against barbarian civilization; this war is taking place between darkness and light; this blood is shed against the fallacious teaching of a fanatic and for the tranquillity of the Motherland."[45] This praising of Tsarist colonial politics by Berezin is reminiscent of discourses by such apologists for British imperialism in the Orient, including Iran, as Henry Creswicke Rawlinson or George N. Curzon. Outright declaration of the civilizing mission of the Russian empire in the Orient is not to be found in Berezin's *Puteshestvie,* perhaps due in part to the difference in the political status of Iran, the

[42] Hereafter referred to as *Puteshestvie po Dagestanu.*

[43] Berezin, *Puteshestvie po Dagestanu* 1:14.

[44] Berezin, *Puteshestvie po Dagestanu* 1:92

[45] Berezin, *Puteshestvie po Dagestanu* 1:97.

Caucasus, and Transcaucasia in their relationships with Russia. However, the indirect affirmations of domination and power by the Russian Empire over the "inferior" Orient represented by Iran permeates most of his narrative. His travelogue carries clear dichotomies: primitiveness and civilization; bestiality and humanity; immaturity and maturity; emotion and reason; evil and good.[46] Barthold makes the following comment concerning Russian Orientalism in the second half of the nineteenth century: "The period in the history of Russian Orientalism when needs of scholarly Orientalism were totally sacrificed to the real or alleged interests of the national life, is closely connected with the name of Kazembek and his most talented students."[47]

Like most Russian university professors of that time, Berezin had liberal political views.[48] However, like many other Russian travelers abroad, he turned into an apologist for Russian imperial politics when he crossed the Russian borders or arrived in lands newly colonized by Russia. For him, the civilizing mission of the Empire in the Orient, including Iran, appeared more important than the struggle between Tsarism and democratic movements. All this supports the classic thesis about the interdependence of imperialism and nationalism: "In the nineteenth century, imperialism … names a historically crucial process by which an 'other' conceived as exotic is represented and subordinated for the purpose of strengthening the worldly place of a metropolitan nation-state."[49]

The attitude of Orientalist authority reflected in the travelogues derived from one more source: what Michel Foucault calls *emplacement,* in other words the institutional site "that provides the source, the point of application, and the instruments of verification for the Orientalist savant."[50] In the case of Berezin, it was the University of Kazan and the Russian Geographical Society which served as "producers of empowering affiliations" for the scholarly traveler. These affiliations in turn made the travelers "valuable information collectors in the service of the institutions of power and knowledge."[51]

---

[46] Dissanayake and Wickramagamage, *Self and Colonial Desire*, 16.

[47] Barthold, "Obzor deyatel'nosti fakul'teta 1855-1905," in *Materialy dlya istorii fakulteta vostochnykh iazykov* 4(1910):30, cited in Dantsig, *Blizhniĭ Vostok*, 113.

[48] Kuznetsova and Dantsig, "I. N. Berezin," 92.

[49] Jonathan Arac and Harrier Ritvo, eds., *Macropolitics of Nineteenth Century Literature: Nationalism, Exoticism, Imperialism* (Philadelphia, 1991), 3.

[50] Ali Behdad, *Belated Travelers: Orientalism in the Age of Colonial Dissolution* (Durham, N. C., 1994), 101.

[51] Behdad, *Belated Travelers*, 101.

Being Russian for Berezin is naturally equal to being European; the two adjectives used as synonyms in his travelogues. He often refers to himself as a European, rather than as a Russian.[52] At every moment of his trip, he remembers being a European, which seems to be very significant for his defining of self-identity in front of the Oriental "Other." He draws the border between "Us" (Europeans) and "Them" (Orientals): "In its customs the Orient is mainly the opposite side of Europe—almost everything that we consider white, Persians see as black and vice versa."[53] His many references to West European travelers such as Ouseley, Malcolm, Olearius, Frazier, Morier, Chardin, and others, as well as his epigraphs taken from their travelogues, at least partly seem to serve the same goal—to prove that he is one of them. Berezin also emphasizes the friendly relationship between Russians and other Europeans, in particularly the British, in the "hostile" atmosphere of Iran. On a personal level, this affinity becomes more important than the rivalry between the Russian and British Empires. For example, Berezin describes his visit to the British Residency in Būšehr with a lot of sympathy, if not admiration.[54] For Berezin and many other Russians in Iran during this period, the British embodied the true "Self" as opposed to the "Other."

Berezin was born and spent his early life in the semi-Asian regions of Perm and Kazan. As if rejecting the fact of Russia being a semi-Asian country, he became attracted to European culture and studied European languages. According to Samoĭlovich, Berezin published several works in French. French was the language spoken in his home in Tsarskoe Selo[55] (the country residence of the emperor and the upper echelon of the nobility close to St. Petersburg).[56] Berezin described his conversation with his British hosts at their Residency in Būšehr, when he referred to himself as "a native of Siberia." He commented on the reaction which his word caused, and which he had expected: "The British could hardly believe my words; perhaps they did not believe them at all, for the notion of Siberia which the residents of East-India had could not be flattering to my homeland."[57]

---

[52] See for example: Berezin, *Puteshestvie*, 38, 108, 136, 160, 285, 286; idem, "Inoĭ mir," 210, 219.

[53] Berezin, *Puteshestvie*, 275-76.

[54] Berezin, "Inoĭ mir," 226-29.

[55] It was not unusual for the aristocracy and well-educated people in Russia of that time to use French as their first language.

[56] Samoĭlovich, "I. N. Berezin, kak turkolog," 163.

[57] Samoĭlovich, "I. N. Berezin, kak turkolog," 228.

Berezin's preference for the West-oriented face of the Russian Janus made him support the social movement of the so-called "Westernizers." They emerged in Russia in the 1840s and were proponents of the western European way of development for Russia. Berezin used to write articles for their organs, such as *Otechestvennye zapiski, Sovremennik,* and *Russkiĭ vestnik.* In Russia the main opponents to the ideology of Occidentophilism were the so-called Slavophiles. They believed that the way for Russia was totally different from that of the Western Europe because it was based on Russia's originality. Berezin alludes to this dispute on the future of Russia in his essay "V Karavansarae" (In a Caravanseri). A conversation with an Iranian boasting of "Persian originality" reminded Berezin of "the stupid arguments of our Slavophiles."[58]

The nineteenth-century traveler's representation of the Orient required the traveler to develop a "discourse of discovery." The theme of obstacles and the hardships of travel becomes crucial because it turns the traveler into a hero who overcomes the "hostile" world and triumphantly brings back home strategic information or knowledge about the Orient.[59] Berezin complains about the innumerable obstacles and inconveniences of which he became a victim: he suffered from bad accommodations, dirt, dishonest Orientals, and so on. "It was not under my lucky star that I entered famous Iran,"[60] he declared at the beginning of his account. He also admits: "If I did not take upon myself the duty of a narrator about the Orient and its imaginary wonders, I would never agree to bore the readers with verbose descriptions of what is hardly worth a description."[61]

In European works about the Orient, one of the main logical operations upon which a representation of the Orient is based is "surveillance": the Orientals "are obligated to show themselves to view for the white men, but they themselves lack the privilege of the gaze," "gazed upon, they are denied the power of the gaze; spoken to, they are denied the power to speak freely."[62] Berezin describes with great excitement his observation of the "Mountaineers" in the Caucasus: "[How thrilling] it is to watch the Mountaineers, real, desperate

---

[58] I. Berezin, "V karavansarae," in *Russkii vestnik* 25(n.d.):708; cited in Samoĭlovich, "I. N. Berezin, kak turkolog," 163.

[59] Behdad, *Belated Travelers*, 103-4.

[60] Berezin, *Puteshestvie*, 5.

[61] Berezin, *Puteshestvie*, 35-36.

[62] David Spurr, *The Rhetoric of Empire: Colonial Discourse in Journalism, Travel Writing, and Imperial Administration* (Durham, N. C., 1993), 13.

Mountaineers, to watch them while being invisible to them!" His use of a telescope[63] is symbolic in this sense: he sees the subjects of his observations, but cannot himself be seen. The same trope of observation is used in the travelogue on Iran.[64] The traveler in Iran is as distant from his "objects" as was the traveler in the Caucasus and Transcaucasia.

Berezin's representation of Iran and its people is marked by the contemptuous attitude and the air of superiority of a representative of the civilized European world towards the backward and uncivilized Orient whose time of glory had passed. He is disappointed in the condition of every facet of the social, political, economic, and spiritual life of contemporary Iran. He consciously distances himself from the object of his study: for him the Orient is "the other world" (as he entitled his article about Bandar-e Būšehr). This feature of his work has been noted by both contemporaries of Berezin[65] and by later scholars. According to Samoĭlovich, Berezin belonged to the type of scholars who, while admitting that study of the Orient is important and interesting for the sake of scholarly disciplines or perhaps for the study of their own country and in its cause, dislike the Oriental countries and their peoples. According to Krachkovskiĭ, "Berezin was studying the Orient, but unlike some other scholars, was hardly able to feel the live Orient."[66] Krachkovskiĭ brings a striking proof of this thesis: the poems Berezin was composing in Tehran, in Basra, and on the Euphrates were not different in the style of the poems he wrote in Kazan and Perm.[67] These romantic poems picture the same characters, such as robbers and Cossacks, or talk about the same personal feelings: "The absence of local color is rather astounding."[68]

Sarcastic comments and notes ridiculing people and their habits are spread through the pages of the travelogues. For example, Berezin recorded his conversation with the officials in Ardabīl, and his translation of Persian traditional greetings and conventional phrases make them sound ridiculous and funny:

---

[63] Berezin, *Puteshestvie po Dagestanu* 1:57.

[64] For example, see Berezin, *Puteshestvie*, 47.

[65] See, for example, the reviews by Ushinskiĭ, "*Puteshestvie po severnoĭ Persii* Berezina," in *Sovremennik* 41(1853):84; "O. S." in *Biblioteka dlya chteniya* 119(1853):3-5.

[66] Krachkovskiĭ, "Melochi," 181.

[67] The only exception known is a romantic poem about the Euphrates: Krachkovskiĭ, "Melochi," 181.

[68] Krachkovskiĭ, "Melochi," 181.

> Then the real conversation began, in which praising of the Prince had the most important place, and praising of their city the least significant; at the same time, my guests were very skillfully making inquiries about the goals of my trip. When I explained them how far I was going, the whole company exclaimed unanimously: 'Adjaib-garaib' How amazing and astonishing! According to the rules of Persian courtesy, it meant approximately the following: 'Look how you, godless one, are making fools of us!'[69]

Before Berezin introduces the way Iranians build their houses, he notes in passing: "You need a house, my favorable reader ... I only pretend so because it could not occur to anyone to build his house in Persia... ."[70] Berezin was criticized by his reviewers for the tone of mockery and caricature he employed in his travelogues: "He decided to turn the assumed title of *a traveler in the Orient* into the role of an oriental Figaro, who laughs at the Orient with a sarcasm which has no place in any part of the world. It is very difficult to understand why the learned and honorable title of *the traveler to the Orient* ... seems so funny to him, an Orientalist."[71]

Berezin describes the wretchedness, poverty, and filth of most of the places he visited in Iran. However, what the author observes does not cause any feeling of compassion in him: the sufferings of "the Other" can not be considered suffering of human beings like "the Self," or the Orientalist. Readers are brought to the conclusion that Iranians do not deserve any sympathy because their miseries are engendered through their own faults: they are lazy, dishonest, greedy, cowardly, and ignorant. Some of the typical characteristics attributed to Iranians by Berezin are the following: "of all the Muslim nations, Persians can be considered the first among liars and braggarts"; "cowardice is characteristic of all the Persians"; "the morals of Persians are in a state of deep decay"; "donkeys are the most hardworking creatures out of all the inhabitants of the Orient"; "Persians are cruel to animals; bloody scenes generally do not impress them much"; "noble passions are rare among the Persians; selflessness is not to be found"; "the best scholars of Persia hardly could pass the test in all subjects

---

[69] Berezin, *Puteshestvie*, 12.

[70] Berezin, *Puteshestvie*, 36.

[71] "Kritika: *Puteshestvie po Dagestanu i Zakavkaz'yu* N. Berezina" in *Biblioteka dlya chteniya* 105(1851):2. See also similar critiques in P. Savel'ev, "*Puteshestvie po Dagestanu i Zakavkaz'yu* I. Berezina," 105.

for being one of our district school teachers."[72] On several occasions, Berezin in his books and articles calls Iranians *tuzemtsy* (aborigines or natives), which in Russian has a pejorative connotation meaning "uncivilized" or "barbarous." Many Iranian customs are presented as ridiculous because they differ from what the author is used to, or from what he considers "civilized" and therefore the correct way of doing things:

> Persian taste has an inclination for everything unnatural: for example, Persians dye their hair and the tails and legs of their horses; women put beauty-spots on their faces and get rid of the hair on certain parts of their bodies; while the highest artificiality is found in their speeches and books: here metaphors are piled on top of another."[73]

One of his reviewers reproached Berezin for ridiculing the poverty of a strange people, as well as for mocking their customs: "We ourselves do not like it when strangers jeer at our Motherland; therefore, it is natural to conclude that it is also bad of us to speak without respect of what is native to others."[74] Barthold, who wrote his article about Berezin in 1919, explained that the "unilateral notion of the fundamental difference between the psyches of the people of the East and of the people of the West" advocated by Berezin was common to most Russian Orientalists of that period.[75]

The few positive qualities noticed in Iranians by Berezin are described in an ironic or condescending manner. He allows that the Persians have certain natural gifts, such as intellectual abilities, but adds that "without a proper education and under the strong influence of religious fanaticism these abilities come to nothing."[76] He says that Persians are famous for their politeness and tact and immediately describes some "rules of etiquette" according to which "guests are treated differently not only according to the place they have in the conversation, but also according to the food they are served."[77] "One of their main gifts is wit," he says, and explains: "But here, too, we

---

[72] Berezin, *Puteshestvie*, 263, 264, 279, 121, 266, 267, 163.

[73] Berezin, *Puteshestvie*, 268.

[74] "Kritika: *Puteshestvie po Dagestanu I Zakavkaz'yu* N. Berezina" in *Biblioteka dlya chteniya* 105(1851):11.

[75] Barthold, "I. N. Berezin kak istorik," 55.

[76] Berezin, *Puteshestvie*, 265.

[77] Berezin, *Puteshestvie*, 265.

cannot ignore the bad side of Persian wit: most of it is spent on ribaldry."[78] All these negative comments inevitably bear wide generalizations about all Iranians or all "Orientals." He does not see the people he meets as individuals, but rather as representatives of a certain type or group; and first of all as "Orientals," whom he thinks he knows so well. Positive references about some persons are scanty and serve as exceptions only to support the general rules. For example he recalls with much gratitude his reception at the house of Mīr Kāẓem Khan in Sarāb in the absence of the master. The owner's wife, whom the travelers were not able to meet in person, was giving orders from her quarters. The comments make the readers think that to a great extent the travelers enjoyed their staying there because they were not bothered by their hosts: " ... this veiled courtesy employed to satisfy not only our needs, but our every whim, had its special charm. In spite of our insistence, none of the servants would accept the smallest reward. I always recalled with a special gratitude this peaceful corner, which made me forgive many shortcomings in the Persians!"[79] Berezin's articles about Bandar-e Būšehr ("Inoĭ Mir" [The Other World]) is different from his travel books and can be defined as an essay about several individual characters. Berezin describes in detail his conversations with some of his acquaintances and their personalities in comparison to each other. The main figures in the article are Mīrzā ʿAlī, a Persian and a Shiʿite; Berezin's servant Yūsof, an Armenian; the captain of the boat which was to deliver the author to Basra, a Sunni Arab; and Aretiun, an Armenian merchant. These people are described with a lot of sympathy and good humor, though the essay is not free from comments concerning Shiʿite and Sunni fanaticism and the "moral slums of the Muslim Orient."[80]

"Fanaticism" is the word used by Berezin in regard to Islam. For Berezin, as for the other Russian travelers of that period, the determining element of "the Otherness" of the Iranians was the religious one: Iran and its people were seen first and foremost as non-Christian, with their "backwardness" and "barbarism" as a sign and a natural consequence of their being Muslim. To a great extent, this view was shaped by imperial ideas and policies vis-a-vis the colonized peoples of the Caucasus and Central Asia—to become Russia's subjects, the non-Christians were to become Russians, with the conversion to Russian Orthodox Christianity as the main component

[78] Berezin, *Puteshestvie*, 267.

[79] Berezin, *Puteshestvie*, 31.

[80] Berezin, "Inoĭ mir," 219.

of this process.[81] Berezin talks about "Muslim fanaticism" as the determining feature of the Persian character; according to him, it is the only factor which has an actual influence on the lower classes in Iran.[82] He tells discrediting stories about dervishes, their fanaticism and greed.[83] He also tells of the "hatred or contempt" towards the "infidels," particularly among the lower classes and the clergy. He cites examples of this hostile attitude: children used to throw stones at him when he was walking in the streets of Iranian cities; sometimes adults also participated; a mulla refused to sell him some books because he was a non-Muslim.[84] "This religious fanaticism was the reason for the death of Griboedov, [who is] never to be forgotten," states Berezin. Briefly he mentions that it is "fanaticism" which is responsible for the women's covering their faces and their seclusion. Berezin accuses Iranians of one more sin—hypocrisy. He tells stories about mullas who break religious rules if they can benefit from doing so, and on several occasions tells about Muslims drinking heavily: "You should not think that Persians drink for pleasure; not at all: they drink in order to become drunk."[85] Berezin favors non-Muslim Persians. He tells about "Gebrs" (Zoroastrians), "these living ruins of the past," who are being oppressed by the Muslims, and who, though more hard-working than they, are never rich.[86] Of all the "Orientals" met by Berezin in Iran and described by him, the Armenian merchant, Aretiun, stands out as a person who was able to become a friend of the fractious traveler. "I have met very few people, especially in the Orient, who would win one's sympathy so quickly and strongly." But the reason for this sympathy seems to be that Aretiun spent most of his life in India among the British and "became a real European, with his noble views on life and social demands."[87]

The miserable condition of Iran in the modern age is contrasted by Berezin with the glorious past, including the Muslim past. Iran for Berezin is a country of splendid ruins: "Naturally, first, last, and always, the most remarkable thing in Persia is its ruins."[88] Inevitably,

---

[81] Michael Khodarovsky, "Ignoble Savages and Unfaithful Subjects: Constructing Non-Christian Identities in Early Modem Russia," in Brower and Lazzerini, *Russia's Orient*, 10.

[82] Berezin, *Puteshestvie*, 236.

[83] See for example, Berezin, *Puteshestvie*, 62; idem, "Inoĭ mir," 216.

[84] Berezin, *Puteshestvie*, 273-74.

[85] Berezin, *Puteshestvie*, 274, 275, 279.

[86] Berezin, *Puteshestvie*, 164-65.

[87] Berezin, "Inoĭ mir," 219.

[88] Berezin, *Puteshestvie*, 127.

descriptions of every architectural site (mosques and palaces) are accompanied by laments about "the bygone splendor."[89] Iranians, according to Berezin, are not worth their own past glory because they do not remember their own past and often assign construction of a mosque or a palace to the wrong period or to the wrong person.[90] Berezin was an admirer of Muslim architecture, in particular that of the Safavid period (1501-1736):

> The newest Persian architecture is a subject of high interest, which until the present has not attracted the attention it deserves. The beginning of this architecture dates back to the time of the introduction of Islam into Persia: at least I do not see anything similar in the remains of the Persepolis palace; the best epoch of this art in Persia is the period of the Safavids."[91]

Berezin's interest in the Islamic architecture of Iran is one of his valuable contributions to the field of Middle Eastern studies since he wrote about the monuments of this architecture with much enthusiasm and admiration at a time "of excessive passion for antiquity and in particular for excavations, which still held true for the twentieth century."[92]

Like his contemporaries and colleagues, Berezin did not believe in the progress of the "Orient," which was perceived as stagnant and backward when compared to the progressive and civilized West: "As for the question whether we can expect anything from Persia on its present course, the answer is almost certainly negative: insignificant improvements in some areas of administration and in people's morals are superseded by the huge misuses [of power]. On one side, there is corrupting Shiʿism; on the other, disorganized rule suppresses the development of national character; the one hope is in a benevolent Providence."[93] Barthold points out that Berezin denies possibilities of renewal for the East not only in regard to the Muslim Orient, but also in regard to China in his two articles on China and its relationship with Europe.[94]

---

[89] Berezin, *Puteshestvie*, 117.

[90] For example: Berezin, *Puteshestvie*, 131.

[91] Berezin, "Izvlechenie iz godichnogo otcheta," 44-45.

[92] Barthold, "I. N. Berezin kak istorik," 54.

[93] Berezin, *Puteshestvie*, 291.

[94] Barthold, "I. N. Berezin kak istorik," 57.

In the middle of the nineteenth century, the literary trend of Romanticism was yielding to Realism. Most of the Russian travelogues of this period, including those by Berezin, were "anti-Romantic"—they rejected Romanticism and often deliberately ridiculed it and its fascination with Oriental exoticism and sensuality. Berezin's travelogues belong to the literature of Realism, though they contain slight elements of Romanticism. Moreover, most of the Russian travelers in Iran were not looking for a "romantic" place to escape from the Western world, or from civilization and rationalism. They were in Iran on official or scholarly missions, and reported about their trips. The travelogues by Berezin are scholarly and rational. He knew the Russian literature of Romanticism of the first half of the century and was well aware of its popularity. He starts his *Puteshestvie po Dagestanu* with a paragraph that is meant to let his readers know what they should not expect to find in his accounts:

> The die is cast: the ship *Astrakhan* is weighing anchor, and I am leaving for a far and difficult way to the Orient, to the motherland of genuine and eternal truth and religious delusions, of practical admonitions of Sadi and fervent reverie of Hafez, to the country of sweet sherbets and mental drowsiness, of the roses that are fragrant for ever and beauty that fades so fast, of the most sophisticated compliments and the most intricate curses, mysterious delights and unexpected dagger-thrusts. I am going to the country where fate might throw into my hand the all-powerful Seal of Solomon, which all the genies obey implicitly, and I might come back to my motherland on the wings of the legendary Simorgh, having obtained mysterious power over unseen forces of nature![95]

Some romantic descriptions of nature in the Caucasus can be found in Berezin's *Puteshestvie po Dagestanu,* but they are absent from *Puteshestvie.* In his descriptions of Iran, Berezin mentions such anti-Romantic subjects as the absence of the "Oriental splendor," with decay, poverty, and dirt in its place; the "imaginary wonders" of the Orient, or even the "unpleasant, sour air" in an *anderūn*; after a detailed and down-to earth description of its furniture he explains: "Nothing else interesting is to be found in the *anderūn*s: in my opinion, playful imagination inhabits them in vain with all the delights of sweet

[95] Berezin, *Puteshestvie po Dagestanu* 1:1-2.

Oriental bliss."[96] At present, writes Berezin, "the wonders of the Orient lie only in contrasts with the common order of things."[97]

To a certain extent, the feeling of disappointment in the Orient expressed by Berezin was similar to the feelings of other "belated" travelers of the mid- and late nineteenth century. "Travelling in the Orient at a time when the European colonial power structure and the rise of tourism had transformed the exotic referent into the familiar sign of Western hegemony," these Orientalists experienced a sense of belatedness, of having missed the authentic experience once offered by a world that was already disappearing.[98] The same disappointment and small expectations from a journey to Iran is reflected in some of the reviews of the travelogues by Berezin. "He has been to where everybody goes, has seen the same things everybody sees, and says the same things everybody has said and heard a hundred times before his book appeared ... It is difficult to write anything new and worth of attention about northern Persia now," notes one of the reviewers.[99]

The range of the subjects treated by Berezin is amazingly wide. His *Puteshestvie po severnoĭ Persii* is an encyclopedia of information about northern Iran in the mid-nineteenth century. Berezin combined several goals in his narrative: he gave a detailed description of the route he followed and the cities he visited, as well as presenting extensive information concerning various aspects of life in Iran; its economics, architecture, politics, government, rulers, army, history, culture, customs, characteristics of different social groups of Iranians, foreigners in Iran, and so on. It is difficult to think of a topic which has not been reflected in this account. Berezin's descriptions are solid, leisurely, and rich in detail. It is unfortunate that the biased approach of European superiority left its mark on the narrative.

Berezin's accounts of Iranian cities he went through are excellent; they are vivid and scholarly at the same time. History, architecture, topography, climate, suburbs, trade, agriculture, administration, and the inhabitants are presented in a way that creates an individual personality for every city and little town on his way. Berezin paid much attention to Ardabīl and Tabrīz, and especially to Tehran. The author deals with numerous general topics, such as the Iranian house,[100]

---

[96] Berezin, *Puteshestvie*, 15, 35, 42.

[97] Berezin, *Puteshestvie*, 140.

[98] Behdad, *Belated Travelers*, 13.

[99] "O. S.", "Kritika: *Puteshestvie po severnoĭ Persii* N. Berezina," in *Bublioteka dlya chteniya* 119(1853):4-5.

[100] Berezin, *Puteshestvie,* 37-44.

its construction and structure; markets (*bāzārs*);[101] caravanserais;[102] and villages.[103] For example, he starts his account of an Iranian bazaar with a description of the construction of the shops:

> The shops are built out of brick, in one story, six and a half meters and more in height; usually they are divided by a cross partition into two parts, the front one, where the shop owner sits, and the back one, where he keeps his goods. The shop is elevated from the ground by about one meter and is locked from the side of the bazaar with wooden boards. The top of each shop is shaped like a small cupola; and between the shops on both sides of the bazaar—large square cupolas are built, so that if one looks at a Persian bazaar from an elevated spot, a long line of large cupolas is seen, with small cupolas at both ends, like small mushrooms around large ones. During the daytime, light comes from the small holes in the big cupolas, which in bad weather also let rain and snow in on the crowd; as well as heat and dust during the summer—not too much, though. In order to protect the goods from dust in summer, the ground in the bazaars is watered down.[104]

Then Berezin compares the Iranian market with a market in Moscow, saying that they are very similar, though there are some differences; such as the curvature of the lines in the Iranian markets and in the range of goods, which he describes. After that, Berezin proposes that his reader and he walk together in a Persian bazaar and, being invisible, observe the people there. A precise description follows of the shops, shopkeepers and their goods: fruit, shoes, meat, fabrics, carpentry, arms, food, and so on.[105]

Berezin had an interest in the foreign trade of Iran; he was concerned with Russian interests in the Caspian area and in northern Iran, as well as the rivalry between Russian and British trade. The range of the goods, their prices and quality, and the trade routes are treated in his *Puteshestvie po Dagestanu* and *Puteshestvie po severnoĭ Persii*.[106] Berezin sees the main problem of the weak development of Russian trade in Iran in the low quality of the Russian goods in comparison with

---

[101] Berezin, *Puteshestvie*, 45-49.

[102] Berezin, *Puteshestvie*, 50-52.

[103] Berezin, *Puteshestvie*, 106-8.

[104] Berezin, *Puteshestvie*, 45-46.

[105] Berezin, *Puteshestvie*, 47-49.

[106] Berezin, *Puteshestvie po Dagestanu* 1:11-16; *Puteshestvie*, 59-69.

those of the British: "For Russian trade to blossom in Asia, Russian industry has to achieve a level at least close to that of the West European. Who does not know that, to this day, products of Russian manufacture cannot compete with foreign ones, in particular the British."[107] In his travelogue on Iran he talks about the same problem of quality, which impedes the development of trade: "Obviously, Russian merchants have a great interest in the development of our trade with Persia; but until now not a single successful attempt has been made."[108] Berezin presents social and national types of the inhabitants of Iran: merchants, rulers, peasantry, Jews, Zoroastrians. Classes of people are described next to the types of land ownership and the system of taxation.[109] The trade tariffs are given in the same part of the text, along with the characteristics of Iranian merchants and trade.[110] An ethnographer would find much interesting material in these travelogues—information on national types and costumes, types of houses of rich and poor people, holidays, beliefs, and traditions.

About half of the travelogue on Iran is devoted to the city of Tehran. Chapters V to VIII not only talk about the city itself but its buildings, gardens, and history. In these chapters Berezin presented most of the information he had collected on the government and politics of Qajar Iran in the mid-nineteenth century. The court of Moḥammad Shah (r. 1834-48), the Iranian army, and the ministers and administration received the most careful treatment.

Chapter VIII is about the Moḥarram processions in Tehran. Berezin makes his readers familiar with the history of the Persian religious drama, the *taʿzīa*. He has also translated part of a play and included it in his narrative. The value of this part was already noticed by a reviewer in the mid-nineteenth century: "For the first time [performance of the famous Persian] religious drama has been presented in a detailed and fascinating manner in Mr. Berezin's book," says the author, who considers this chapter "the most important part of the book."[111] This favorable reaction did not prevent another reviewer, though, from expressing an opposite opinion about the presentation of *taʿzīa:* "There is nothing important or interesting in these mystery-plays."[112] The work

[107] Berezin, *Puteshestvie po Dagestanu* 1:14-15.

[108] Berezin, *Puteshestvie,* 67.

[109] Berezin, *Puteshestvie*, 233-35.

[110] Berezin, *Puteshestvie*, 62-64.

[111] O. S., "Kritika: *Puteshestvie po Severnoĭ Persii* I. Berezina," in *Biblioteka dlya chteniya* 119/5(1853):5.

[112] Ushinskiĭ, "*Puteshestvie po severnoĭ Persii* Berezina," 89.

of Berezin on *taʿzīa* has received due attention in the works of the modern scholars Jean Calmard[113] and Peter Chelkowski.[114]

The text of the account is very dense and incorporates a great number of Persian words and statistics. Berezin's masterly use of rich and scholarly language, his ample erudition, his generous talent for narrative together with the flavor of his humor make the book both entertaining and informative. Berezin uses the conversational style, talking directly to his readers, suggesting that they follow him or share his impressions. It is the personality of the narrator and the image of travel, of the road, that give complete unity to the varied matter of his account.

Conclusion

Russian travelogues of the nineteenth and early twentieth centuries in general and the travel accounts by Berezin in particular provide copious information for a historian or an ethnographer who deals with modern Iran. At the same time, the data supplied should be analyzed and utilized in the context of Russian Orientalism, with heed paid to its generic and peculiar features. Considering "Orientalism's discursive heterogeneity,"[115] we can conclude that it is striking to note the extent to which Berezin was a representative type.[116] His individual style correlated, partly consciously, partly unconsciously, with contemporary Russian national ideology and national tradition. He has been called by one modern scholar "the Orientalist (in every sense)."[117] It would probably be more accurate to define Berezin as "the *Russian* Orientalist in every sense."

---

[113] See Jean Calmard, "Le mécénat des representations de ta'ziyeh," in *Le Monde Iranien et L'Islam* 4(1976-77):133-62; idem, "La Patronage des Ta'ziyeh: Elements pour une étude globale," in Peter Chelkowski, ed., *Taziyeh: Ritual and Drama in Iran* (New York, 1979), 121-31.

[114] Peter Chelkowski, "Dramatic and Literary Aspects of Ta'ziyeh-Khani: Iranian Passion Plays," in *Review of National Literature* 2(1971):121-38; idem, "Ta'ziyeh: Indigenous Avant-Garde Theatre of Iran," in idem, ed., *Taziyeh*; idem, "Mourning Becomes Revolution," in *Asia* (May/June 1980):30-45; idem, "Popular Shi'i Mourning Rituals: From Maqatil Literature to Drama," in *Papers from the Imam Husayn Conference,* London, 6-9 July 1984.

[115] Behdad, *Belated Travelers*, 13.

[116] Said, *Orientalism*, 263.

[117] Susan Layton, "Nineteenth-Century Russian Mythologies of Caucasian Savagery," in Brower and Lazzerini, *Russia's Orient*, 88.

ʿAbd-Allāh Mostawfī in Russia, 1904-1909

James Clark

As Russia's economic, political, and eventually military penetration of Iran advanced over the nineteenth and early twentieth centuries, thus augmenting its importance in Iranian affairs, an increasing number of Iranians journeyed northwards in search of work or trade, in order to study, or in an official capacity.[1] One of the most important accounts by an Iranian describing his sojourn in Russia comes from the young Iranian diplomat ʿAbd-Allāh Mostawfī, whose recollection of the five years he spent there is to be found in his three-volume memoir *Šarḥ-e zendagānī-e man* (The Story of My Life).[2] His only work, it has become a classic and is one of the single richest sources for social and political history available for the Qajar and early Pahlavi periods. The section concerning his stint as an embassy official stationed in St. Petersburg is especially valuable, not only because of the description it gives of conditions existing in Russia at a time of political upheaval, but also by reason of the insights it offers into the status and behavior of the large number of Iranians who had found their way to Iran's northern neighbor around the turn of the century.

The descendent of prominent nineteenth-century accountants, Mostawfī had graduated in the fall of 1904 as a member of the first

---

[1] Two other notable Iranian travel accounts to Russia are Mīrzā Moḥammad-Hādī ʿAlavī Šīrāzi, *Dalīl al-sofarāʾ: Safarnāma-ye Mīrza Abu'l-Ḥasan Khan Īlčī ba Rūsīya*, ed. Moḥammad Golbon (Tehran, 1357 Š./1978) and Mīrzā Ṣāleḥ Šīrāzī, *Gozāreš-e safar*, ed. Homāyūn Šahīdī (Tehran, 1362 Š./1983).

[2] ʿAbd-Allāh Mostawfī, *Šarḥ-e zendagānī-e man yā tārīḵ-e ejtemāʿī va edārī-e dawra-ye qājārīya*, 3 vols. (Tehran, 1340 Š./1961). The work has recently been made available in a translation by Mostawfī's grand-daughter, Nayer Mostofi Glenn (*The Administrative and Social History of the Qajar Period [The Story of My Life]*, 3 vols. with continuous pagination, Costa Mesa, Calif., 1997).

class to finish the recently-established School of Political Science in Tehran—the only "institution of higher learning in Iran" at the time—where he had concentrated on the study of law. The following spring, he and his fellow graduates received their first assignments from the Iranian Foreign Ministry. To make use of their newly acquired knowledge, they were dispersed to various embassies and consulates abroad, with Mostawfī being assigned to the embassy in the Russian imperial capital of St. Petersburg. Departing from Tehran in late winter on what was his first trip abroad, he made the long trek across the Caspian Sea to Baku and thence by train to the city on the Baltic. For the next five and a half years, Mostawfī spent his time not only engaged in his new work, but also astututely observing the society, events, and personalities around him.

The neophyte Iranian diplomat arrived in the Russian capital just before spring in 1905 to behold an environment quite different from his native Iran. For him, St. Petersburg represented "a modern capital" with straight streets that intersected "at right angles" rather than the "narrow winding" ones with which he was so familiar in Iran. He was also impressed by the network of transportation consisting of a system of canals (*ābgīrhā*), stout bridges under which boats glided past, and broad streets bordered by wide sidewalks.[3] Despite the heavy rains and snow it received in winter, he found it to be "one of the cleanest cities in Europe," a cleanliness typical of all Russian cities.[4]

The very different nature of housing in St. Petersburg especially caught his attention. Most of the city's population lived in huge communal buildings that covered an entire block, all of which belonged to the wealthy. Whereas structures in Iran were usually only one story high and rarely exceeded two, those in St. Petersburg were typically four to five stories in height, with each story containing eight to twelve

---

[3] Mostawfī, *Šarḥ,* 2:96-97; tr., 408.

[4] Mostawfī, *Šarḥ*, 2:96-97, 98; tr., 408-9. Nāṣer-al-Dīn Shah, during his first trip to Europe in 1873, was similarly impressed by the orderliness and cleanliness of some places in Russia. For example, he wrote of the royal garden at Peterhof, "What is strange is that a garden this big was so clean that it did not have any leaves or rubbish. All of the trees are forest species, but they have been planted in order and in rows like streets." He made a similar observation concerning the garden at Tsarkoe Selo: Nāṣer-al-Dīn Shah Qājār, *Safarnāma-ye Nāṣer-al-Dīn Šāh* (Tehran, 1343 Š./1964), 38, 41. For an English translation of this travelogue, see *The Diary of H. M. the Shah of Persia During His Tour through Europe in A.D. 1873*, tr. J. W. Redhouse (London, 1874; repr. Costa Mesa, Calif., 1995).

apartments and each building having twenty to sixty families.[5] He noted that "hardly anyone in the city owned his own home," which meant that "a change of address every couple of years was an accepted fact." Differences in the cost of apartments within a building, depending on the particular location of each, resulted in a situation whereby "within the same building, one could find families of all levels of society, from noble to lower middle class, living together." This system of housing, and the "maintenance of the public area" that went with it, "was common all over Russia."[6]

Mostawfī soon developed an appreciation for St. Petersburg's distinctive climate, and he found May to be the most enjoyable month to be in the city because it offered a brief respite between the cold and snow of winter and the rains of summer. He remarks that

> It was well worth coming from so far away to breath the beautiful air here. It was sunlight for about fifteen hours on spring days; in summer, it lasted nineteen hours. During the month of April, the last cold spell of the long winter was ended. The last of the ice on the lakes of Lagoda and Onega would melt and flow into the Baltic Sea. Plants would grow, and trees sprout leaves. The weather was mild and dry. The humidity, snow, and rain of winter waned all about. The singing of the nightingale soothed the ear. The greenness of the natural and cultivated lawns was beautiful to view.[7]

The summer rains, often accompanied by thunderstorms, lasted up to three days at a time and frequently interrupted cherished summer outings. The subsequent dampness made the season indistinguishable from winter save for the absence of cold. "God forbid," he exclaimed, "that the cold and rain don't stop in May, because then it would be impossible for the people to enjoy themselves that year."[8]

The pleasures and modern aspects of St. Petersburg did not mean that it was immune from less welcome phenomena, however, one of which was the ravages of disease. Mostawfī says that a cholera epidemic reached the city in 1907 after first spreading through Iran, where it had broken out three years earlier, and then had moved on to Central Asia, the Caucasus, and finally Russia. At its height, seven

---

[5] Mostawfī, *Šarḥ*, 2:97.

[6] Mostawfī, *Šarḥ*, 2:97-98.

[7] Mostawfī, *Šarḥ*, 2:99-100; cf. tr. 410.

[8] Mostawfī, *Šarḥ*, 2:100; tr., 410.

hundred people a day were dying in the city, a number which Mostawfī considered "not serious" given its total population of one and a half million. He noticed that the waxing and waning of the disease took on a particular pattern in the city. On Sundays, after people left their homes, a "few victims" would appear, particularly among the "hard-drinking laborers." It would run its course through the following week and then begin anew after the next weekend. The number of victims correspondingly tended to rise on or after holidays. The epidemic continued to linger on, and he says there appeared "no way to rid the capital city ... of this disease." It was still present two years later when Mostawfī left St. Petersburg, claiming "eight to twenty casualties all the time."[9]

Language presented no problem to the young diplomat, for the Russian upper classes with whom the embassy personnel interacted the most spoke at least two foreign languages, and "especially French." This meant that learning Russian was not necessary even for socializing.[10] A notable example of this multi-lingual social elite was Czar Nicholas II, who spoke English, French, German, and Russian, and could adroitly switch from one to the other depending upon the circumstances. An ambassador leading a delegation to meet with him thus had the choice of using any one of those four languages in addressing the monarch, and "the Emperor happily obliged." Mīrzā Ḥasan Khan Mošīr-al-Molk, the Iranian ambassador, preferred to speak Russian with him since he had learned it during a previous stay in Russia and spoke it well. The other members, however, conversed with him in French.[11] Mostawfī was fluent in French, being a member of the Iranian elite and thus having received a western-style education while in Iran. In fact, he spoke the language so well that in Paris the executive secretary for the French president complemented him on his knowledge of the language and assumed that it was not his first visit to France.[12]

"As long as we spoke French," Mostawfī says, "the way to social life was open" in St. Petersburg.[13] The social season in St. Petersburg

---

[9] Mostawfī, *Šarḥ*, 2:256; tr. 518. The epidemic spread to Iran in 1322/1904-5 from India and Afghanistan; ibid, 87, tr. 381.

[10] Mostawfī, *Šarḥ*, 2:94; tr., 406.

[11] Mostawfī, *Šarḥ*, 2:123; tr., 427. Several new biographies of Nicholas II have appeared since the fall of the Soviet Union, the most noteworthy being Robert D. Warth, *Nicholas II: The Life and Reign of Russia's Last Monarch* (Westport, Conn., 1997).

[12] Mostawfī, *Šarḥ*, 2:225; tr., 496.

[13] Mostawfī, *Šarḥ*, 2:94; tr., 406.

began in mid-fall and attained its height around Christmas time and New Year.[14] He was entirely ignorant of European customs and traditions upon his arrival in the country, however. Not desiring to be caught unprepared, he spent that first summer familiarizing himself with the proper etiquette and preparing himself for entrance into the upper circles of Russian society wherein he spent much of his time thereafter and which he came to know so well.[15]

Though Mostawfī moved in the circles of Russian high society and strove assiduously to adapt himself to their manners and ways, he was critical of the ways of the Russian elite and their structured lives of ease achieved at the expense of the masses. For the Russian aristocracy, the year was divided into two parts. They "consumed so much gold and wine in winter and lived lives of such ease that in summer they had to go to the spas of Europe to give back what they ate in winter. They had to suffer for a while with enormous expenses until they prepared themselves for winter life and consuming the same gold and wine."[16] Mostawfī felt that the Russian aristocrats' "palaces ... in the city and even their properties in the country [*amlāk*] were so majestic and their lifestyle so expansive and elaborate that the English lords, the grafs, and the manners of the Germans and Austrians could not hold a candle to them." Their children were "educated in the best schools of St. Petersburg or Europe."[17] Mostawfī's landlord in St. Petersburg, an aristocrat and a magistrate, exemplified this type of individual. He had a son who possessed a general education and spoke fluent German and French, and his family's "financial power" was beyond calculation. They had built several structures containing sixty to seventy apartments (*ložmān*) for renting out and that employed a special taste.[18]

Possessing an abundance of time and money, the Russian upper classes spent much of their time in search of ways to spend them, which very often took the form of entertainment. The restaurants of the city were one of the prominent gathering places for this elite. The most elegant of these were the Cuba, Canton, Oder, and Ernest. The patrons of such establishments paid only for their elegance because "in St. Petersburg a restaurant's elegance was more desirable than its food." Indeed, "People didn't go to restaurants to eat, but most went

---

[14] Mostawfī, *Šarḥ*, 2:115; tr., 422.

[15] Mostawfī, *Šarḥ*, 2:114-15; tr. 422.

[16] Mostawfī, *Šarḥ*, 2:128.

[17] Mostawfī, *Šarḥ*, 2:128-29; tr., 431.

[18] Mostawfī, *Šarḥ*, 2:128; tr., 431.

to show off and occasionally to have fun." For this reason, such establishments were not interested in reducing the price of their food to increase the quantity they sold. They were primarily concerned with attending to "the outward appearance of the place" as "they knew there was no money to be derived from eating."[19]

Another popular destination for the wealthy of St. Petersburg society were some nearby islands whither they sallied "for fun and pleasure in full regalia" each summer afternoon, and where they would tour the park in carriages. On their way home, they would eat dinner at Ernest on the outskirts of St. Petersburg, which boasted a Rumanian orchestra that could even play Persian music. Members of the Russian middle class, on the other hand, dined at the Aquarium.[20] The latter boasted a garden that "did not have anything to show for its name but a glass pool [*ḥawż*] with a light in the middle of it and a few white fish." But with payment of an entrance fee, one could also take in outdoor shows or an indoor one that featured a "one-act variety show with music and dance." There was also a large restaurant with private rooms "where people stayed up until one or two having fun." "There were five or six of these summer gardens" in St. Petersburg, Mostawfī says, of which he considered the Aquarium the best and the Tovrid "not bad."[21]

Though on the one hand critical of the lifestyle of the Russian elite, on the other Mostawfī and his colleagues took full advantage of the upper classes' places of entertainment. One night they attended the Aquarium's theater; the variety show included a pretty Arab woman named Fāṭema and Mademoiselle Datelle, a French woman in her late thirties who although "not pretty" and lacking "a good voice" sang with spirit and liveliness "some of the funniest and sharpest French songs" with double entendres. Mostawfī was particularly impressed by one of her acts, in which she sang the "Presidential Salute" to the tune of the "Māšīš"—a popular dance at the time included in most shows—and acted it out without dancing, such that knowledge of French was unnecessary to grasp her point. The author considered her variety act that night to be better that anything he later saw when he actually went to Paris.[22]

Nāṣer-al-Dīn Shah had found the novel experience of watching a Russian ballet performance not only intriguing, but also difficult to

---

[19] Mostawfī, *Šarḥ*, 2:98; tr., 409. The Canton Restaurant even had "very large palm trees," which were understandably hard to maintain in the cold northern climate and later burned in a fire.

[20] Mostawfī, *Šarḥ*, 2:100; tr., 410-11.

[21] Mostawfī, *Šarḥ*, 2:99; tr., 410

[22] Mostawfī, *Šarḥ*, 2:144; tr. 442.

explain to an Iranian audience: It was "a performance [*bāzī*] and dance without speaking. In its course, they both dance and perform in various ways, which it is impossible to describe."[23] Mostawfī was no less amazed by this masterpiece of dancing for which the Russians are famous" and "how the ballerina made such fast pirouettes on pointed shoes." The performances were quite popular, and tickets to the ballet as well as the opera at the Marie Theater in St. Petersburg were "very difficult to obtain." In Mostawfī's opinion, the Vienna opera was superior to that of St. Petersburg, but the latter's "music was comparable to that in any European capital.[24]

Whereas restaurants offered a forum for social appearances by the Russian elite, families normally entertained guests at home, with the hostess showing "all her hospitality in serving guests the best, as Russian pride required" and the host doing similarly with drinks. Such parties occurred almost nightly in the city, with participants drinking and playing bridge and other card games until two or three o'clock in the morning. People attended such parties "one, two, three, up to every night a week," and these tended to shape the pattern of their lives. People who did so "never woke up before noon," after which they usually drank a cup of tea for breakfast and then ate lunch at one o'clock. Dinner was served at seven o'clock, with "supper or a late dinner" coming at one o'clock in the morning "in the case of large elaborate parties." The daily routine was quite different for the lower classes of Russian society, who had to be at work by eight o'clock in the morning and therefore normally ate a larger breakfast an hour earlier. They ate lunch and dinner at the same time as the upper classes, but retired earlier in the evening.[25]

It was customary for the foreign embassies in St. Petersburg to move to resorts outside the city in order to escape the heat of the summer months. Thus, in the middle of May 1905, the Iranian embassy moved to Tsarskoe Selo (Czar's Village) with a "makeshift office and the minimum necessities for living and working."[26] Nearby was the popular summer resort of Pavlovski, which accommodated visitors who stayed the day as well as ones who remained the entire season. Visitors who only came for the afternoon and evening would arrive around four o'clock by train and take advantage of the "public park and the entertainment area." A flower garden and large sitting room offered

[23] Nāṣer-al-Dīn, *Diary*, 24.

[24] Mostawfī, *Šarḥ*, 2:186; tr., 471.

[25] Mostawfī, *Šarḥ*, 2:99; tr., 410.

[26] Mostawfī, *Šarḥ*, 2:104, 105; tr., 414, 415.

"excellent music," with an orchestra on Sundays. A surrounding pine forest with grass and wild flowers provided "a very pleasant place" for them to stroll. A large crowd would gather by five o'clock when finding a seat in the "very large restaurant" of "at least two hundred tables" became difficult. Entertainment continued into the early morning on Saturdays and Sundays. To accommodate these visitors, weekend trains ran until midnight between May and September.[27]

The czar had a summer home in Tsarskoe Selo as well, but he rarely stayed there save for a "couple of times a year," preferring instead to stay at his "real summer residence" in Peterhoff.[28] Peterhoff was actually part of the Kronstadt military base, and the royal palace there overlooked a body of water and had "numerous lakes, lawns, game areas, and beautiful flower gardens." The gardens and lawns flanked a row of fountains that extended to the edge of the surrounding woods. This particular mix of art and nature, Mostawfī says, convinced "many people ... that the park at Peterhoff was superior to Versailles.[29]

Those who worked at the embassy were not the only Iranians to be found in St. Petersburg. Mostawfī says that the number of Iranian students studying at schools in Russia increased yearly around the turn of the century, as the sons of the upper classes went to study at institutions such as the Polytechnic in Moscow and the Cadet School, the law school, and Nicholas Military School in St. Petersburg.[30] There were also lower-class Iranians who found their way to St. Petersburg and whom Mostawfī condescendingly refers to as "runaways and misfits." Most of them came from the Iranian province of Azerbaijan and included Armenians, Assyrians, and inhabitants from the cities of Ardabīl and Haštrūd. These, after first obtaining a passport and entering Russian territory "under the pretext of starting a small business," stayed a while in the Caucasus, learned some Russian, and then traveled northwards. They begged for the most part, some using groups of five or six boys whose services they exploited in exchange for a place to sleep. Others performed shows on the streets using monkeys and musical instruments such as harmonicas. Some of these Iranians saved enough money to "buy a piece of land in their village" when they later returned to Iran. There was no fraternization between them and the

[27] Mostawfī, *Šarḥ*, 2:104-5; tr., 414-15.

[28] Mostawfī, *Šarḥ*, 2:105; tr., 415. For a history and description of the czar's estate at Tsarskoe Selo, see Robert K. Massie, *Nicholas and Alexandra* (New York, 1967), 117-28.

[29] Mostawfī, *Šarḥ*, 2:139; tr., 439.

[30] Mostawfī, *Šarḥ*, 2:85-86, 89, 934; tr., 400, 402-3, 405-6.

Iranians of higher social standing who worked at the embassy, unless it was to settle a dispute among them, such as one that might occur "over the loss of their monkey or the children."[31]

One of the most interesting of these Iranian expatriates in St. Petersburg was the merchant Mašhadī Ḥasan Eṣfahānī. This man's seeming inattention to his appearance contrasted sharply with the attitude of upper class Iranians. Mostawfī first met him one day at the embassy and noticed that he was dressed in "a second-hand wool serge jacket," black percaline pants, a hat of "imitation Persian lamb skin" that "had become slightly yellow," wool socks, and "shoes with the heels pressed down." Mostawfī encountered him again by chance on his trip to Paris, where Mašhadī Ḥasan had moved after making a large and unexpected profit selling his goods in Russia. Virtually nothing about him had changed. He bore exactly the same appearance as before, "the same beard, the same look ... except it was slightly more worn." Only his shoes and socks were different.[32]

While Mostawfī and many Iranians like him saw adaptation to the ways and manners of Russian society as only reasonable, there were others who harbored objections to some aspects thereof, especially concerning the relationship between the sexes. Mīrzā Maḥmūd Khan Ehtešām-al-Salṭana relates that when attending a musical and dance performance in St. Petersburg, his companion Mok̲ber-al-Salṭana abruptly rose from his seat and left the theater and then sent a note to Mīrzā Maḥmūd Khan telling him to join him immediately. Obviously angry, Mok̲ber al-Salṭana told him, "You are a Muslim and a religious man. Why do you allow these forbidden [*nâ maḥram*] women to dance in front of you?" Surprised that he would bring this matter up so late in their trip, Mīrzā Maḥmūd Khan responded, "We are staying in a European country, and it is now almost one month that we have been living among these 'forbidden women'." But Mīrzā Maḥmūd Khan says that Mok̲ber-al-Salṭana refused to heed his advice.[33]

Although Iranians were found as far way as the Russian capital, most who lived within the domain of the Russian empire resided much closer to Iran, in the Caucasus. Most of them were seasonal workers who came in search of employment from the nearby Iranian province of Azerbaijan, their migration facilitated by the common knowledge of Turkish and the lifting of a ban on travel abroad during the reign of

---

[31] Mostawfī, *Šarḥ*, 2:90; tr., 403.

[32] Mostawfī, *Šarḥ*, 2:233-35; tr., 501-3.

[33] Mīrzā Maḥmūd Khan Ehtešām-al-Salṭana, *K̲āṭerāt-e Ehtešām-al-Salṭana*, ed. Moḥammad-Mahdī Mūsavī (Tehran, 1366 Š./1987), 202-3.

Moẓaffar-al-Dīn Shah (1896-1907). They tended to work in the factories of the region, especially in the oilfields of Baku. After acquiring a temporary visa upon entering Russian territory in the spring, they worked until the fall, when they returned home. If they decided to stay for a longer period of time, they obtained a resident visa for either work or business.[34]

As a result of this migration to Russia, the selling of passports to Iranian citizens in Russia became an important source of income for the Iranian embassy and consulates in the country. Prior to the beginning of this phenomenon, travel between Iran and Russia had not been enough for the government seriously to consider income from selling passports, which "remained at the local consulates with a larger portion going to Caucasia." No way of accounting for the revenue gained from these sales existed prior to the establishment of a systematic method of accounting because passports were not stamped. Instead, the Iranians were sold a form, which may have been "printed locally in Tiflis." When the rate of immigration increased, the income from such sales expanded such that the bulk of a consulate's revenue came to depend on the number of passports it sold, with the embassy in St. Petersburg receiving "a fat share" of the revenue from the total. The Iranian government gradually brought this haphazard system under control by 1904. The issuance of passports was standardized, with a limit being placed on the profit a consulate could make from selling them. In addition, the passports were only printed in Tehran; a passport office was created within the Foreign Ministry; documents were regularly stamped and accounts kept; and specific rules and regulations were published. Revenue from this activity thereafter reached 300,000 to 400,000 tumans per year.[35]

Rather than spending the summer of 1905 at Pavlovski, the staff of the Iranian embassy instead went to the resort of Terioki on the Gulf of Finland, which possessed a "beautiful garden," restaurant, and

---

[34] Mostawfī notes that the only cost for the seasonal laborers was the fee for the visa, which was two tumans for a worker's passport and three for a businessman's. This loss of labor was strongly criticized by some, such as the expatriate publications in Calcutta and Egypt. The influential novel *Sīāḥat-nāma-ye Ebrāhīm Beyg* likewise attacked it. Mostawfī, however, saw this phenomenon as "a very natural and harmless thing to do"; Mostawfī, *Šarḥ*, 2:92; tr., 404. For Zayn-al-Dīn Marāḡaʾī's depiction of the plight of these Iranians living in the Caucasus, see his *Sīāḥat-nāma-ye Ebrāhīm Beyg*, ed. Moḥammad-ʿAlī Sepanlū (Tehran, 1364 Š./1985), 18-24.

[35] Mostawfī, *Šarḥ*, 2:93; tr., 405.

casino. Unlike Pavlovski, whose proximity to St. Petersburg allowed people to visit it for a day, Mostawfī says that the patrons of Terioki normally spent the entire summer there.[36] The many Russians who visited the town were furthermore drawn to it by certain commercial privileges their government alloted to the Finns. In order to protect its own industries in the effort to industrialize, the Russian government implemented high import tariffs on foreign goods. However, it exempted the Finns from the payment of customs duties. This meant that there were no customs until one neared St. Petersburg. This situation created the opportunity for smuggling from Finland as Russians bought items such as fabrics, china, crystal, and various other goods, all at half the Russian prices, and brought them home. Visitors to Terioki "who did not care about fashion or tailoring," says Mostawfī, "could provide themselves with a wardrobe costing half as much as one in St. Petersburg." Even the wives of Russian generals and ministers returned with bags bulging "from a day or two in the country.[37]

Mostawfī's visit to Terioki also introduced him to the uneasy relationship that existed between the Finns and their Russian overlords. Despite the "privileges" and "financial benefits" they received from the Russians, the Finns vigorously resisted Russification and constituted, in Mostawfī's view, "the Russians' enemy of enemies."[38] Though Russian was compulsory in Finnish schools, Mostawfī "never saw a Finnish patriot who spoke the language well," even after a century and a half of Russian rule. He says that Finnish carriage drivers at the station were reluctant to carry Russians. On one occasion a driver belatedly answered "in very poor Russian," hesitated, and feigned being already engaged, all despite the prospect of receiving a good fare. Such "ill-temper" on the Finns part "had become second nature to them because they hated the Russians." Their hatred was so intense that it sometimes went beyond mere attempts at avoidance and led to murder. Once the summer tourist season had come to an end, Mustowfi says, "a Finnish patriot with a knife would not hesitate to attack and finish off a Russian walking through the woods." Such enmity towards Russians, he says, tended to unite the Finns, even to the point that the

---

[36] Mostawfī, *Šarḥ*, 2:132; tr., 433.

[37] Mostawfī, *Šarḥ*, 2:132-33; tr., 434.

[38] Mostawfī, *Šarḥ*, 2:133; tr., 434. The policy of Russification in Finland was reversed in 1905 in reaction to the unrest that was sweeping the empire. See Hugh Seton-Watson, *The Decline of Imperial Russia, 1855-1914* (New York, 1952), 242-43.

perpetrator of such a crime would be acquitted because of a supposed "lack of evidence."[39] When drivers learned that Mostawfī was not Russian, however, they tended to shed their gloominess and compete for his business, even offering to convey him free of charge. When one carriage driver overheard Mostawfī and a companion speaking Persian and realized they were not Russians, he "softened immediately and was happy to take us home." Thereafter, Mostawfī used the ploy of speaking some Persian to let the driver know he was not a Russian.[40]

Mostawfī believed that the system of government and administration in Russia had changed little over the previous three hundred years, and at the beginning of the twentieth century remained essentially the same as that created by Peter the Great (1682-1725). The emperor appointed the cabinet ministers, a government council, and members of the senate. The government council initiated laws that the senate and emperor then approved. The laws were then "activated" by an ukaz or royal decree.[41]

Perhaps the most powerful persons in Russia, however, stood outside this official structure. They were the courtiers surrounding the czar, whose actions tended to disrupt the normal workings of the government apparatus, "especially during the reign of Nicholas II." Mostawfī did not believe the czar was at fault for this state of affairs, however. Personally, he was "kind and harmless." The fault instead lay with these "people around him" who "took advantage of him by manipulating public affairs."[42]

The courtiers of the Rusian royal court wielded their power in various ways. They had "a great influence" on how laws were executed in the country, even having the capability to create their own decrees to negate the ones the government enacted. They manipulated the system to their own ends. Prisons were originally built in Siberia "to develop" the vast region by eventually freeing the prisoners so that they could work and settle the land. The courtiers, however, used them "to satisfy their [own] greed." A case in point concerned a courtier who coveted the wealth and daughter of a certain merchant. After being denied these, he had the police "fix a dossier" on the man who was then sent to a Siberian prison. The courtiers likewise used their influence to exploit the government through its ministries. Such corruption was widespread, Mostawfī claims, with "everyone [having] a share in the operation," and

---

[39] Mostawfī, *Šarḥ*, 2:133; tr., 435.

[40] Mostawfī, *Šarḥ*, 2:133; tr., 435.

[41] Mostawfī, *Šarḥ*, 2:124; tr., 428.

[42] Mostawfī, *Šarḥ*, 2:124; tr., 428.

the laws of the empire offered no protection against it. "The unfortunate individual who became a target of one of these attacks," Mostawfī states, "was finished forever." Although officials were assigned to investigate the different branches of government, even they "feared the influence of the courtiers and did not dare report the truth." The courtiers could even influence the verdicts of courts and alter their verdicts.[43]

Russia seemed to be a land possessing tremendous potential, an observation that was mentioned by other Iranian travellers, such as Nāṣer-al-Dīn Shah. While traversing the Russian steppe by train from Tzaritsin to Moscow on his first visit to Europe in 1870, the shah remarked,

> No matter how much I looked at the expanse, everywhere I saw green fields, flowers, plants, horses, sheep, pigs, and such like. And every six miles a good, populated village could be seen. These lands are famous for being fertile. Every place we looked, there was either cultivated land or pasture. We passed one good bridge over a lot of water that entered the river Don. Many small bridges could be seen along the road. Every two or three miles they have built a sentry post and every few farsangs a station .... The construction of the stations is very good. There are always several steamers for transporting passengers and goods ready in very station."[44]

As Mostawfī and Mošīr-al-Molk crossed the Ukraine, they were amazed at its extent and productivity. Their train passed fields of wheat so extensive "that they could not be measured." The Iranian ambassador observed that they had "been travelling through wheat fields for the past forty-eight hours at the speed of fifty kilometers an hour" without them coming to an end.[45]

Unfortunately, such vast resources were squandered without the benefits reaching the general populace. In Mostawfī's view, conditions prevalent in the country caused "ignorance and poverty to prevail" across the vastness of Russia, though the country possessed "every means" by which to advance, in addition to having money loaned by the French.[46] The Ukraine by itself was "capable of producing enough

---

[43] Mostawfī, *Šarḥ*, 2:125 tr., 428-29.

[44] Nāṣer-al-Dīn Shah, *Diary*, 20-21.

[45] Mostawfī, *Šarḥ*, 2:184; tr., 469-70.

[46] The French loaned the Russians funds in order to support the struggling Russian government and maintain it in an alliance against Germany; Mostawfī, *Šarḥ*, 2:123-24.

bread for all of Europe," Mostawfī believed, and "yet its own peasants went hungry because the products were sold in markets all over Europe, especially Germany, at great profit for the landowner."[47]

"In the Russia of those days," Mostawfī points out, "there were two classes of people: the aristocracy and the poor," supplemented by a "very small" middle-class.[48] The nobility and large landowners dominated the army and the civil service. The structure was firmly set and mobility between the three classes was virtually impossible. "For any individual from any other class of society to break into the ranks of the upper class," he says, "required an extraordinary turn of events."[49]

The wealthy monopolized the country's resources to such an extent that the general populace was "totally cut off from the two sources of progress," education and the possibility of economic advancement. Both wealth and education were restricted to the "select few" of the upper class, resulting in both "poverty and illiteracy" being commonplace throughout the country.[50] Mostawfī blamed this on the exploitation he associated with capitalism.

> The principle of capitalism and ownership in order to use the public to the advantage of capital was intensely at work in this country. The subject [*raʿya*] had no share of the harvest. Whatever he brought in was confiscated by the office overseeing the property. Aside from the daily wage, the amount of which was determined by the whim of the owner, nothing derived from his own exertions ever reached him. This wage was so little, and the goods he had to buy form the boss's overseer so expensive, that it was never certain it would fill his stomach.[51]

An opportunity to improve the lot of the Russian peasants came in 1861 when Nicholas I freed the serfs, thereby allowing them to leave the land and move wherever they wanted. Doing so "could have raised them from poverty," Mostawfī calculated. But most of them failed to take advantage of the chance. Instead, they chose to remain where they were and thus continued "to live under the tyranny of overseers and masters." No sharecropping existed in Russia whereby the farmers

[47] Mostawfī, *Šarḥ*, 2:126; tr., 429.
[48] Mostawfī, *Šarḥ*, 2:128.
[49] Mostawfī, *Šarḥ*, 2:125.
[50] Mostawfī, *Šarḥ*, 2:125; tr., 429.
[51] Mostawfī, *Šarḥ*, 2:125; tr., 429.

could share in the fruits of their labor. All farm land belonged to a "few unmerciful landowners." With time, use for the "simple-minded peasants" diminished further with the introduction of machinery. Mechanization produced superfluous workers, which in turn increased the burden on landowners, who, "unable to buy modern machinery" were forced to first sell and then abandon their land. The workers in Russian factories were no better off in Mostawfī's opinion. Exploitation of the industrial laborers was "even easier, since no one but a wealthy landowner could own and operate a factory."[52]

Domination of the land and factories of Russia were not the only sources of the wealth of the upper class. They also owned most of the large tenement buildings in the cities, which gave them "another substantial source of income" in the form of the collection of rent from "tenants, who had to handout a portion of their earnings to them every month."[53]

Given the aristocracy's fast hold on the wealth of the country in both the cities and the countryside, business proved to be the "only decent occupation" available for the middle-class. The aristocrats considered engagement in commerce beneath their social standing and even shunned marrying into the middle-class no matter how wealthy a family was. Thus, "the majority of the merchants never [had] a chance to expand." Even if a member of the middle-class did become affluent, though, he faced the threat of "immediately [becoming] the target of exploitation, cruelty, tricks, and false dossiers fabricated by the aristocracy, officers in the army, and civil servants.[54]

Mostawfī's contacts with the lower classes in Russia were so few that his clearest impression of the status of the Russian peasant came from what Ḥasan Pīrnīa Mošīr-al-Dawla related to him concerning an encounter with a family living in a forest outside Moscow. They lacked any utensils of any kind, drank water with their hands, and shared the cabin with their animals. The child appeared "ragged" and "pale-looking" and an object "sitting in the corner" of the room "was only recognizable as a woman by her clothes." The three meter square cabin was "a dug-out half a meter deep in the damp ground" with "a mud wall one meter high" and a roof of "grass and debris collected in the woods." The man had never been outside the forest, and he and his wife made a living by trading mushrooms and herbs they picked for bread and other things at a local store. Totally ignorant of Iran, the

---

[52] Mostawfī, *Šarḥ*, 2:125; tr., 429.

[53] Mostawfī, *Šarḥ*, 2:125; tr., 429.

[54] Mostawfī, *Šarḥ*, 2:126-27; tr., 429-30.

man asked where it was, whether the sun and stars shone there, and if the people spoke Russian. When Pīrnīa explained these things to him the man exclaimed, "Oh! I did not know that God had such a large territory!"[55]

Mostawfī's residence in Russia coincided with the beginning of a very tumultuous period in the foreign and domestic affairs of the country that set the tenor for the next decade. Russia and Japan had already been at war for two months in the Far East when Mostawfī first arrived in St. Petersburg in March of 1904.[56] The war went badly for the Russians from the start, and by the summer of 1905 a feeling of melancholy was sweeping over the country. The tune of a "sad farewell song to [the] homeland" became popular and could be heard in restaurants and cafes. Posters of "families bidding farewell to their sons going to war" covered the walls of stores. The czar, who was officially in charge of directing Russia's war effort, "felt let down and sad" and "sat at home," avoiding the front "like a broken down soldier." He did not appear in public "except once in a while at Molet's barbershop." Meanwhile, Russian troops continued to retreat "a hundred kilometers at a time," even after Lieutenant-General Linievitch replaced Nicholas II in formulating Russian strategy.[57]

The czar's only son, Alexis, was born in the summer of 1904, a few days after the Russian fleet suffered another defeat at the Battle of the Yellow Sea. The people took this as an ill omen and said that the prince's birth had brought bad luck. They forecast the end of the Romanov dynasty by pointing out that "it was predicted that the present house of the czars started with the name Alexis and would end with Alexis." Mostawfī considered this only "wishful thinking spread around by the revolutionaries."[58]

Russia's poor performance in the war generated vehement discontent, and "rebellion and unrest" began to occur across Russia

---

[55] Mostawfī, *Šarḥ*, 2:127-28; tr., 431.

[56] For an account of the Russo-Japanese war, see Denis and Peggy Warner, *The Tide at Sunrise: A History of the Russo-Japanese War, 1904-5* (New York, 1974).

[57] Mostawfī, *Šarḥ*, 2:134-35; tr. 435.

[58] Mostawfī, *Šarḥ*, 2:105; tr., 415. Mostawfī says that Alexis was born the same day of the battle and that the battleship Tsarevich was sunk there, both of which are in error. The battle of the Yellow Sea took place on 10 August 1905, not on Alexis's birthday, which came two days later. The Tsarevich was badly damaged in the encounter and spent the rest of the war at Kiao-chou, but she was not sunk as Mostawfī asserts; see Warner, *Tide at Sunrise*, 324-33.

on a daily basis.[59] Weary of dictatorship, the people formed "secret committees" in St. Petersburg and elsewhere; bombs were hurled at governors and heads of police, even at the Grand Duke Serge.[60] The insurrection eventually forced the czar to allow a Duma or representative council to open in 1906. By that time, however, the distance separating the positions of the government and the people was enormous, and they "criticized each other heavily." This lack of mutual understanding as well as the "constant conflicts among the legislators" in the assembly compelled the government to close the body after a time.[61] Nevertheless, the prospect of greater public participation in the politics of the country produced a demand to learn what was happening. In 1907, Mostawfī observed youths at train stations announced that "freedom has been announced and the Duma is reopened." The dynamic political atmosphere fostered an "avid desire to read" among the people, who yearned to know what was happening. Passengers gave their newspapers to the youths, who easily found others who wantged to buy them.[62]

The zeal of the revolutionaries was so intense that they took aim at the center of the imperial system and made attempts were on the life of Nicholas II. Prior to 1905, the diplomatic community in St. Petersburg had often been invited to the court to attend formal functions. The emperor normally received the foreign diplomats at Tsarskoe Selo on the first day of the new year, which should have been a day of celebration. That year both the war and the "internal uprising" that had been building since 1904 led to the cancellation of all such functions. The baptism of the crown prince, however, which was to take place on 6 January 1906, was made an exception to this, and plans went ahead as scheduled. The ceremony took place in a gazebo beside the Neva river, where Alexis was to be baptized in the presence of church and government officials. When guns located across the river fired what was to be a salute, however, their shots

---

[59] For an account of the 1905 revolution, see Andrew M. Verner, *The Crisis of Russian Autocracy: Nicholas II and the 1905 Revolution* (Princeton, 1990).

[60] Mostawfī, *Šarḥ*, 2:88; tr., 402.

[61] Mostawfī, *Šarḥ*, 2:88; tr., 402. The first Russian Duma was in session from May until July 1906, when it was dissolved by the czar. See Verner, *Crisis of Russian Autocracy*, 330-33; Seton-Watson, *Decline of Imperial Russia*, 254-56.

[62] Mostawfī, *Šarḥ*, 2:183-84; tr., 469. This is a reference to the second Duma, which convened from February to June 1907. See Verner, *Crisis of Russian Autocracy*, 333-41; Seton-Watson, *Decline of Imperial Russia*, 257-60.

instead struck the gazebo, landing "near the crown prince and the people around him" and killing a policeman. Other shells penetrated the window and floor of the reception area where Mostawfī was, but they harmed no one and caused little damage.[63]

This incident was "considered one of the worst incidents to befall the Russian Empire" at the time.[64] Attributed to revolutionaries, it resulted in the cancellation of the czar's audience with all of the "special guests" except for the ambassadors of the foreign embassies in St. Petersburg.[65] The czar and his family did not stay at the Winter Palace following the event. Neither did the baptism of Alexis take place. Thereafter, the czar stayed at Peterhof in the summer and Tsarskoe Selo in the winter where security was "extreme." The "identity of each guard was well investigated and only the most loyal ones guarded the royal family at both palaces.[66] The incident was neither discussed at social gatherings nor reported by the newspapers, "though everyone in St. Petersburg knew about it." The public was, however, informed of it later "in a subtle way" with the explanation that it was caused by the mistaken use of live ammunition. Despite a denial that any wrongdoing was involved in the incident, numerous officers, soldiers, and civilians were nevertheless executed for it.[67]

Following one year and seven months of war, the disastrous conflict with Japan finally came to an end in August 1905.[68] A humiliated Russia resented her losses. For example, although the Japanese annexed Korea after the war, the Russian government continued to subsidize the Korean embassy in St. Petersburg "just to show its disapproval."[69] Iranians, on the other hand, celebrated the ignominious Russian defeat at the hands of a lesser power. This sentiment caused resentment among the Russians. In response, Mīrzā Reżā Khan Dāneš Arfaʿ-al-Dawla convinced the Iranian government to send him to Russia both to appease Iran's northern neighbor and to offer congratulations on the birth of

---

[63] Mostawfī, *Šarḥ*, 2:120; tr., 425.

[64] Mostawfī, *Šarḥ*, 2:121; tr., 426.

[65] Mostawfī, *Šarḥ*, 2:120; tr., 425.

[66] Mostawfī, *Šarḥ*, 2:122; tr., 427.

[67] Mostawfī, *Šarḥ*, 2:121; tr., 426.

[68] Mostawfī, *Šarḥ*, 2:88; tr., 401. The United States mediated between the two sides, at the request of the Russians. After a period of negotiation, the peace treaty was submitted on 16 August and the cease-fire signed on 18 August, the day before Moẓaffar-al-Dīn Shah arrived in St. Petersburg (Mostawfī, *Šarḥ*, 2:135; tr., 436).

[69] Mostawfī, *Šarḥ*, 2:123; tr., 427.

the crown prince. Mostawfī says his real reason in going was to visit friends there. In any case, the mission was not a success, as Iranian court officials did not comprehend the purpose for the trip and it failed to have any discernable effect on the Russian attitude. It was therefore "dealt with in silence" as the ambassador "presented his dry, insincere letter, donned his gift, received a few medals, and left."[70]

Despite the turmoil that was occurring in Iran during the same period with the beginning of the Constitutional Revolution (1905-11), Mostawfī reckoned the political situation in Russia at the time to be "much worse." The closing of the parliament followed that of the Duma and "secret organizations were formed in every neighborhood and city carrying strange mottos totally against the government." Incidents occurred on a daily basis. With the aim of appeasing the populace, "the government was forced to give back some of the previous freedoms" it had taken away, such as freedom of the press. Taking advantage of this, the leftist or "Red" newspapers went to extremes, publishing articles in opposition to the government on a daily basis.[71]

From afar, Mostawfī followed the events back in Iran as the Constitutional Revolution began in 1905 (inspired in part by the uprising in Russia early in the year), a constitution and parliament were granted in 1906, and the conflict between the constitutionalists and the royalist supporters of Moḥammad-ʿAlī Shah intensified over the next two years. Mostawfī's sympathies clearly lay with the former faction in this struggle, in spite of the fact that he was ostensibly a representative of the government of Iran no matter which was in power. Taking advantage of the liberty he had to publish in the Russian press, he made a decision "to promote freedom" actively in Iran. After establishing acquaintances with correspondents of two of the best known publications in St. Petersburg, *Retch* (Speech) and *Ruskoe Slove* (The Talk of Russia), he translated articles from newspapers in Iran and gave them to be published in the Russian publications, which then "elaborated the issues" and assailed what they considered "the true elements behind the events in Iran." Considering himself an informed "Iranian patriot," Mostawfī defended what the Russian leftists wrote, thereby emboldening them to follow his "instructions wholeheartedly." He took such actions as signs that "democracy was in progress" in Russia. He furthermore believed that his propagation of news about

70 Mostawfī, *Šarḥ*, 2:106-7; tr., 416.

71 Mostawfī, *Šarḥ*, 2:270; tr., 530.

happenings in Iran affected Russian behavior by preventing them from committing acts similar to those that had occurred in Iran, such as the shelling of their own parliament.[72]

Mostawfī saw another "opportunity to promote democracy in Iran" when a liberal correspondent from the International Geographical Society interviewed him about conditions in Iran. Among the questions he was asked was one about the possibility of land reform by the constitutionalists. Mostawfī answered that this was unnecessary "because the farmer in Iran is not a wage earner like in Europe," and he went on to explain how the system worked. The article appeared without naming Mostawfī as its source and with the answers related verbatim. The correspondent even suggested that Europe adopt the Iranian agricultural system "to avoid the problems of land distribution and lazy farmers."[73] Though there were many things that Mostawfī believed Iran should adopt from Europe, this was one area in which he believed Iran was superior.

In the summer of 1909, the constitutionalists in Iran, having rallied against the royalists, began a steady advance on Tehran. Russians, both in the government and the general populace, watched closely as the government of Moḥammad-ʿAlī Shah crumbled. Both leftists and rightist Russian newspapers were quite accurate in their reporting of the events, Mostawfī states, although they presented contrasting points of view. The pro-government newspaper *Novoe Vremia* relayed the reports of Yatochetski in Tehran and advocated that the Russian army extend its involvement in Iran and occupy Tehran in order to avert carnage. The leftist publications *Retch* and *Ruskoe Slove*, on the other hand, staunchly opposed Russian intervention in Iranian affairs and used information that Mostawfī anonymously provided about the situation in Iran to attack *Novoe Vremia*.[74] These Russian newspapers were one source from which the the staff at the Iranian embassy in St. Petersburg obtained their information about events back home. The other was the Russian Foreign Ministry, to which Mofak̲k̲am-al-Dawla went every day to get the latest news, even though the reports inevitably reflected the Russian view of events.[75]

---

[72] Mostawfī, *Šarḥ*, 2:270-71; tr., 530. The Majles (Iranian Parliament) was shelled on 23 June 1908 by forces loyal to Moḥammad ʿAlī Shah. The Russian-led Cossack Brigade was at the forefront of the attack. See Edward G. Browne, *The Persian Revolution of 1905-1909* (repr. London, 1966), 207-8.

[73] Mostawfī, *Šarḥ*, 2:268-69; tr., 529-30.

[74] Mostawfī, *Šarḥ*, 2:281; tr., 538.

[75] Mostawfī, *Šarḥ*, 2:281, 284-85; tr., 538, 541-42.

Late in the spring of 1907, Mostawfī returned to Russia following two months leave in Iran. He accompanied Mošīr-al-Molk as part of a special delegation sent to the capitals of Europe to announce Moḥammad-ʿAlī Shah's ascension to the Iranian throne.[76] Mostawfī says that the members of the mission were essentially guests of the Russians, beginning in Rasht, whence the consul was kept informed of the group's progress from Tehran by telephone. The imperial vessel *Empress Alexandra*—"specially brought for them from Ḥajjī Tarḵān [Astrakhan]" to replace temporarily the usual mail ship—was waiting for them at the port of Anzalī and conveyed them across the Caspian to Baku.[77] On the train from Baku, city officials greeted them in formal dress at each station along the way.[78] Mostawfī did not attribute these gestures entirely to Russian respect for the Iranian dignitaries. "[A] Russian officer," he observed, "especially away from the capital, will exercise his utmost effort to earn a decoration from whomever it may be." Harboring the hope of gaining such rewards, "as soon as he is permitted, he goes all out to welcome and show his national hospitality to official visitors."[79] The mission was again entertained with "elaborate ceremonies" involving two honor guards before they crossed out of Russia and into Germany.[80] All in all, Mostawfī dismissed such gestures as no more than a demonstration of the dominance Russia could wield over "a weaker nation" like Iran.[81]

On the other hand, Mostawfī says that in the course of the five and a half years he spent in Russia, he never experienced anything but kindness from Russians, who even competed to help him. "The Russian people as individuals are very kind and hospitable people," he says, "especially to strangers in town." The only exception to this he encountered were the droshky drivers, who, recognizing him as a foreigner because of his accent, tried to charge him a higher fare.[82]

Such displays of "respect and welcome" from so many Russians amazed Mostawfī. He simply could not comprehend "how a

---

[76] Moḥammad ʿAlī Shah was crowned on 19 January 1907, eleven days after Moẓaffar-al-Dīn Shah had died following a long illness. See Browne, *Persian Revolution*, 133.

[77] Mostawfī, *Šarḥ*, 2:178; tr., 465-6.

[78] Mostawfī, *Šarḥ*, 2:182-83; tr., 468.

[79] Mostawfī, *Šarḥ*, 2:183; tr., 469.

[80] Mostawfī, *Šarḥ*, 2:187; tr., 472.

[81] Mostawfī, *Šarḥ*, 2:179; tr., 466.

[82] Mostawfī, *Šarḥ*, 2:101; tr., 411.

government composed of such individuals and groups could be so cruel. How could good individuals form such an ugly nation collectively?" he asked.[83]

When Mostawfī returned to St. Petersburg again from Vienna on the return leg of a trip to Europe, he happened to share a sleeping berth on the train with Alexander Baturin, an employee of the Russian Bank in Tehran who was returning from leave. The Russian was unreserved in his criticism of officialdom in native land and warned Mostawfī about the behavior of its customs officials in particular. Earlier on Mostawfī's trip to Europe, French and Belgian officials had merely inquired of Mostawfī whether he had anything to declare.[84] The experience at the Russian border was starkly different. Officials quickly collected all the "passports and every piece of hand luggage" from the passengers without leaving "as much as a piece of paper." Batourine explained that they gathered the passports because

> They are afraid that someone might enter Russia without a proper investigation of his identity, because they are scared to death of the Russian revolutionaries who are abroad. It is as if there were no revolutionaries at all inside Russia. This kind of behavior increased the number of revolutionaries in the country by a thousand a day. Aren't these revolutionaries abroad Russians too?[85]

The Russian then described how after the officials had haphazardly searched through all of the luggage confiscating banned material and taxing the remainder, the passenger would have to spend an hour rearranging the mess. "God forbid," he warned, "if something is found among the things that attracts the suspicion of this illiterate official." In that case, the "unlucky passenger" would have to be interrogated, and his case could possibly "end in arrest, a court hearing, and a lot of problems." Although the "idiots" thought revolutionaries could be kept outside the country, it was futile, Batourine said, the effort was futile given the conditions inside Russia, which worsened by the day.[86]

The customs inspection proceeded just as Baturin had described. However, Mostawfī's diplomatic passport, which lacked any specific information about him, confused the border official. After several

---

[83] Mostawfī, *Šarḥ*, 2:183; tr., 469.
[84] Mostawfī, *Šarḥ*, 2:189; tr., 473.
[85] Mostawfī, *Šarḥ*, 2:245; tr., 509.
[86] Mostawfī, *Šarḥ*, 2:245-46; tr., 509-10.

readings of a letter of introduction which Mostawfī gave him to clarify the matter, a second and then a third official came to discuss it, until the first man finally allowed him to take his bags without a search and "with a great deal of regret." Baturin returned two hours later to their compartment complaining loudly of paying customs duties that even exceeded the original price of the items, a thorough search of his bags, and the confiscation of his newspaper because "it is forbidden to bring in printed material."[87]

Shortly after Mostawfī's return to St. Petersburg, Mošīr-al-Dawla, the father of Mošīr-al-Molk, died, and the ambassador was quickly recalled to Iran.[88] At the time, an Iranian ambassadors had to provide furnishings for his embassy himself. As a consequence, the Iranian embassy was "almost stripped" of all its furnishings because most of them belonged to him. His things were either shipped to Iran or sold. The only means of transportation left behind was a "rusted troika." Deprived of proper facilities for entertaining guests at the embassy, Mostawfī and the others had to take them to restaurants instead.[89] The embassy "was sitting in oblivion, cut off from the rest of the world in a corner of Basinia Street" for lack of facilities. It just hoisted the flag on holidays and "for all practical purposes did not exist, inside or outside."[90]

The 1907 Convention between Russia and Britain establishing their respective spheres of influence in Iran, which was announced soon after Mošīr-al-Molk's return to Iran, contributed further to the decline in importance of the embassy in St. Petersburg.[91] Following the agreement, which ended the "Great Game" rivalry between the two powers in Iran, Mostawfī noted that the Russians refused to "observe formalities" any longer with the Iranian government. Another factor was Russian "grievance" toward the constitutionalists, who were in

---

87 Mostawfī, *Šarḥ*, 2:244-46; tr., 508-9.

88 Mošīr-al-Molk then assumed his father's title and became the minister of foreign affairs in the cabinet of Nāṣer-al-Molk. Within a few days, he was informed of the Convention between Russia and Britain concerning the division of Iran. In letters to the embassies of both countries in Tehran, he wrote "that Iran is an independent country and this agreement would not make any difference to the [Iranian] government's decision" (Mostawfī, *Šarḥ*, 2:248; tr., 511).

89 Mostawfī, *Šarḥ*, 2:252-53; tr., 515.

90 Mostawfī, *Šarḥ*, 2:253; tr., 516.

91 For the text of the agreement, see J. C. Hurewitz, ed., *The Middle East and North Africa in World Politics: A Documentary Record,* 2 vols. (2nd ed., New Haven, 1975), 1:538-41.

power at that time. The penetration of constitutionalist sentiments into the Caucasus and eventually into Russia itself was inevitable, according to Mostawfī, and the Russians blamed the entire issue on the Iranian government and retaliated.[92] Mostawfī considered this lack of respect for Iran to be typical of Russian attitudes toward non-Europeans. "The system in Russia was one of rudeness," he states. The Russians's "only kindness to a weaker nation" like Iran "was to send a stupid minister to a state dinner who had yet to learn the name of the shah of Iran!" More capable men, on the other hand, were dispatched to European capitals such as London.[93]

After more than a year without an ambassador, the Iranian embassy's appearance and functioning were once more restored when the new ambassador, Mīrzā Esḥāq Khan Mofak̲k̲am-al-Dawla, arrived in the fall of 1908. His furnishings were brought from Vienna, and he set up residence in Tsarskoe Selo, where he lived with his wife, and commuted daily to St. Petersburg. A working relationship eventually emerged whereby the ambassador assumed responsibility for the affairs of the embassy, while Mostawfī and rest of the other staff attended to problems that arose between Iranian citizens and the Russian police.[94]

Mostawfī's five and a half year sojourn in Russia came to an abrupt end about two months after the restoration of the constitutional government in Iran, in July 1909, when a telegram arrived stating that "your presence in Tehran is of more value than in St. Petersburg" and

[92] Mostawfī, *Šarḥ*, 2:254; tr., 517. The government of Moḥammad-ʿAlī Shah, hoping to thwart a rescue of the Constitutionalists besieged in Tabrīz, instructed the embassy in St. Petersburg to try and dissuade the Russians from sending their army to the city. Mostawfī spoke with Clem at the Russian Foreign Ministry, but failed to reverse the Russian (and British) decision to intervene (Mostawfī, *Šarḥ*, 2:277-79; tr., 535-36).

[93] Mostawfī, *Šarḥ*, 2:255; tr., 518. The reference is to a formal dinner held at the Iranian embassy to honor Mošīr-al-Molk during his visit in 1907. To represent it, the Russian government sent the Minister of Finance, Kakovosoff, who was commonly referred to as *batyushka* [father] and was obviously "careless" and "had no knowledge of protocol." He mistakenly gave a toast to "ʿAlī Moḥammad ʿAlī Shah." Mostawfī says that he was known for his "bad speeches," and that two months before he had made the "drastic mistake" of saying to the parliament when it was still open, "Thank God we do not have a parliament," instead of, "Our government is not parliamentarian," whereupon the "deputies demanded an explanation." The Russian newspapers had a field day with the faux pax (Mostawfī, *Šarḥ*, 2:185-86; tr., 471).

[94] Mostawfī, *Šarḥ*, 2:265-66; tr., 526-28.

that he was to return immediately. Mostawfī quickly assembled his belongings and two days later boarded the train to Baku.[95] Indicative of where Russian sympathies lay in the struggle between the constitutionalist and royalist factions in Iran, Mostawfī says that he was treated very well by officials on the train, apparently because they mistakenly believed that he was a member of the entourage of the deposed Moḥammad-ʿAlī Shah, whose year-long attempt to suppress the constitutionalists (the period known as the "Lesser Oppression") had ended in failure and who had arrived in the Caucasus to take up his abode in exile the day before.[96]

Mostawfī's memoirs thus provide many useful insights about the man and his times. The period of his residence in St. Petersburg was a tumultuous one for both Russians and Iranians. Their respective countries were experiencing the birth pangs of political and social transformation as democratic sentiments and ideals took root and challenged the autocratic systems that had theretofore existed in them. Mostawfī bears witness to how the Russian state sought to limit its own internal forces pressing for a representative government, while simultaneously involving itself ever more deeply in Iranian affairs and seeking to stifle democratic forces there just as it opposed them at home. The Iran to which Mostawfī finally returned had undergone many vicissitudes, and it was not long before the Russians and the British brought political and military pressure to bear in order to force the closing of the parliament and an end to Iran's Constitutional Revolution in 1911. Unlike Japan, which had assiduously adopted western technology and beaten Russia at its own game so to speak, Iran remained a weak and overwhelmingly traditional society at the beginning of the twentieth century. This only began to change significantly in the 1920's, when its political turmoil finally came to an end and a strong central government was established. With the experience that began with his stay in Russia, Mostawfī would continue to play an important role in the affairs of that period as well.

---

[95] Mostawfī, *Šarḥ*, 2:292; tr., 547.

[96] Mostawfī, *Šarḥ*, 2:292; tr., 547.

The Hajj and Qajar Travel Literature

Elton L. Daniel

With the rise of the Safavids, the conversion of Iran to Eṯnā-aš'arī Shi'ism, and the outbreak of Safavid-Ottoman hostilities, numerous forces tended to shift the focus of religious pilgrimages (*zīārāt*) by Iranian Muslims to Shi'ite shrines in or near Iranian territory, such as the tomb of Emām Reżā at Mašhad, numerous local tomb-shrines (*emāmzādas*), and the 'Atabāt in Iraq (Najaf, Karbalā', Kāẓemayn, Sāmarrā). The obligatory ritual pilgrimage to Mecca (*ḥajj*; hereafter anglicized as hajj), however, remained a potent factor in Iranian religious life, and the history of this institution in Qajar Iran provides a revealing indicator of the dramatic technological, social, economic, political, and cultural changes taking place during that period. A systematic history of the hajj in Qajar Iran remains to be written, and is well beyond the scope of this article, but there is every reason to believe that such a history would prove of great interest in many respects.

For virtually all of the Qajar period, the Ottoman Empire was custodian of the holy places in Arabia, a duty it took quite seriously. The Ottoman government was always concerned with the conduct of the hajj and at times was almost obsessed with regulating and observing the affairs of the pilgrims in great detail. Its archives related to diplomatic, economic, and internal affairs thus contain many documents related to the pilgrimage, but it remains unclear how significant they might be in the case of Qajar Iran.[1] In the nineteenth

---

[1] A recent example of the importance of the Ottoman material for Iranian studies in general is Bruce Masters, "The Treaties of Erzerum (1823 and 1848) and the Changing Status of Iranians in the Ottoman Empire," *Iranian Studies* 24(1991):3-15. For general studies on the hajj and its historical importance, see Naimur Rahman Farooqi, *Mughal-Ottoman Relations: A Study of Political and Dipomatic Relations between Mughal India and the Ottoman Empire, 1556-1748* (Delhi, 1989); Suraiya Faroqhi, *Herrscher uber Mekka: die*

century, the Ottomans periodically published statistical yearbooks for its various provinces, and some of these *Sāl-nāma*s for the Ḥejāz yield interesting information about such things as the numbers of pilgrims during those years but little else of specific value for the study of pilgrims from Qajar Iran.[2] There were also many general descriptions of the pilgrimage written during the nineteenth and early twentieth centuries, notably two books, both entitled *Merʾāt al-ḥaramayn* and written by officials with responsibilities for the conduct of the hajj, Eyüp Sabri (Ayyūb Ṣabrī) Pasha (1886) and Ebrāhīm Refʿat Pasha (1925), as well as works such as Moḥammad Labīb Baṭānūnī's *al-Reḥla al-ḥejāzīya* (1911).[3] None of these display any particular interest in Iranian pilgrims, and they are of very limited value for the present purpose. An otherwise interesting and useful work by an Iranian consular official in Jedda is likewise more interested in the general features of the hajj than its particular significance for Qajar pilgrims.[4] It may be that there are some pertinent documentary records available in Iran, but these, like the Ottoman records, have not been systematically investigated, and given the relative paucity of archival material on Qajar Iran in general it is doubtful that they would be of great use.

Geschichte der Pilgerfahrt (Munich, 1990); Idem, *Pilgrims and Sultans: The Hajj under the Ottomans, 1517-1683* (London and New York, 1994); Alan Rush, ed., *Records of the Hajj: A Documentary History of the Pilgrimage to Mecca* (Slough, U.K., 1993); Ian Netton, ed., *Golden Roads: Migration, Pilgrimage and Travel in Mediaeval and Modern Islam* (Richmond, U.K., 1993); Jacob M. Landau, *The Hejaz Railway and the Muslim Pilgrimage: A Case of Ottoman Political Propaganda* (Detroit, 1971); Karl Barbir, *Ottoman Rule in Damascus, 1708-1758* (Princeton, 1980); Michael Wolfe, ed., *One Thousand Roads to Mecca: Ten Centuries of Travelers Writing About the Muslim Pilgrimage* (New York, 1997); M. N. Pearson, *Pious Passengers: The Hajj in Earlier Times* (London, 1994); Abd-al-Majid Turki, *Récits de pelerinage á la Mekke: Étude analytique* (Paris, 1979); F. E. Peters, *The Hajj: The Muslim Pilgrimage to Mecca and the Holy Places* (Princeton, 1994); Michael Pearson, *Pilgrimage to Mecca: The Indian Experience, 1600-1800* (Princeton, 1996).

[2] E.g., the *Sāl-nāma-ye dawlat-e ʿālī-e ʿOṣmānīya* (Istanbul, 1302-3/1885-86); *Ḥejāz velāyatī sāl-nāmasī* (Mecca, 1303/1886).

[3] Ayyūb Ṣabrī Pasha, *Merʾāt al-ḥaramayn* (Constantinople, 1301-6/1883-1888); Ebrāhīm Refʿat Pasha, *Merʾāt al-ḥaramayn* (Cairo, 1344/1925); Moḥammad Labīb Baṭānūnī, *al-Reḥla al-ḥejāzīya* (Cairo, 1329/1911).

[4] Hoseyn Kazem Zadeh, *Relation d'un pèlerinage à la Mecque en 1910-1911* (Paris, 1912).

There is, however, one type of source material directly relevant to the study of the hajj in the Qajar period which is both extremely informative and relatively easy to access: the travel books written during the Qajar period by various pilgrims about their journeys to Mecca. These *safarnāmas*, which record the experiences and observations of the authors as they performed this important religious obligation, yield much fascinating data about the development of the practice of hajj and its historical significance in modern Iran. Before describing these and suggesting a few points that can be derived from them, it may be helpful to make some general comments regarding the nature and use of these sources.

Travel literature is common to any number of cultures and chronological periods, and scholars in many fields have begun to draw attention to its value for historical research.[5] During the age of imperialism, for example, European audiences had an apparently insatiable appetite for travel books, especially those dealing with the interior exploration of Africa and Asia as opposed to the accounts of maritime voyages which had been popular in earlier periods.[6] It has been noted in studies by several recent scholars how closely this literature meshed with the policies of imperialism, first of all by contributing to a sense of how greatly Europe or the West was differentiated from the "rest of the world" and secondly by depicting non-European areas in ways which tended to justify European hegemony, colonization, or exploitation.[7] Anyone familiar with the study of the Middle

---

[5] For theoretical discussion, see in particular Mary Louise Pratt, *Imperial Eyes: Travel Writing and Transculturation* (London, 1992) and Stephen Clark, ed., *Travel Writing and Empire* (London, 1999). The variety of work being done in this field is exemplified in such titles as B. J. Terwiel, *Through Travellers' Eyes: An Approach to Early Nineteenth Century Thai History* (Bangkok, 1989); John Ashmead, *The Idea of Japan, 1853-1895: Japan as Described by American and Other Travellers from the West* (New York, 1987); Charles Batten, *Pleasurable Instruction: Form and Convention in Eighteenth-Century Travel Literature* (Berkeley, 1978); Reinhold Schiffer, *Turkey Romanticized: Images of the Turks in Early Nineteenth Century English Travel Literature* (Bochum, 1982); Dorothy Hammond, *The Africa that Never Was* (London, 1970); Indira Ghose, *Women Travellers in Colonial India* (Delhi, 1998).

[6] On this concept, with specific reference to how it affected travel accounts of Iran, see the valuable pioneering study by Michiel Braaksma, *Travel and Literature: An Attempt at a Literary Appreciation of English Travel-Books about Persia* (Groningen, 1938); see also Pratt, *Imperial Eyes*, 9.

[7] Braaksma, *Travel and Literature*, 7-8 was very prescient in nothing the dual role of travel literature in both reinforcing the traveler's sense of a separate national identity ("Is not the Englishman abroad frequently much more 'English' than he

East in the modern period will of course know of many examples of this type of literature, ranging from the indefatigable Charles Doughty to the quaint Ella Sykes.[8]

However, it was not just in nineteenth-century Europe that travel literature became increasingly popular; it was in many ways a universal phenomenon. Certainly, the literary genre know as the *safar-nāma* (travel book) blossomed in great profusion during the Qajar period and in ways which raise some intriguing points of comparison with the contemporary explosion of travel literature in Europe. In his catalog of Persian manuscripts, which is representative but far from complete, Aḥmad Monzavī lists some 270 examples of works categorized as *safar-nāmas*.[9] Of them, only 41 are non-Qajar (half a dozen pre-Qajar—Timurid, Safavid, and the classic work of Nāṣer-e Ḵosrow—and the rest books written by Indians in Persian.) Of the Qajar works, there are 75 accounts of travel primarily or wholly within Iran, 64 in the Middle East (20 on the pilgrimage to Mecca, 10 to the ʿAtābāt, 34 to India, Central Asia, etc.), 64 translations of travel books written in European languages, and 26 accounts of travel by Persians to Europe.

---

would ever dream of being in England?") and awareness of the "other" ("the consciousness of belonging to and representing another civilization as well as another race, in short a different 'world'"); see also Pratt, *Imperial Eyes*. The question of the extent to which Qajar travel literature played a similar role in shaping as well as expressing a sense of Iranian national identity is well worth more extensive investigation.

[8] Charles M. Doughty, *Travels in Arabia Deserta,* 2 vols. (Cambridge, 1888); Ella C. Sykes, *Through Persia on a Side-Saddle* (London, 1898, 2nd ed., 1901). For general inventories of the genre and studies of travel literature, see Moḥammad-Ḥasan Ganjī, *Fehrest-e maqālāt-e jog̱rāfya'ī* (Tehran, 1341 Š./1962); Moḥammad-Taqī Pūraḥmad Jaktājī, *Fehrest-e tawṣīf-ī-e safar-nāmahā-ye engelīsī-e mawjūd dar Ketab-ḵana-ye mellī-e Īrān* (Tehran, 2535=1355 Š./1976); Idem, *Fehrest-e tawṣīf-ī-e safar-nāmahā-ye farānsavī-e mawjūd dar Ketab-ḵana-ye melli-e Īrān* (Tehran, 2535=1355 Š./1976); Makoto Hachioshi, *Ketāb-šenāsī dar zamīna-ye tārīḵ: jog̱rāfīyā va qawm-negārī-e maḥallī-e Īrān az šorūʿ-e čap-e sangī tā sāl-e 1373* (Tokyo, 1997); Moḥammad-Ṣadīq Homāyūnfard, *Fehrest-e tawṣīf-ī-e safar-nāmahā wa ketābhā-ye tārīḵī-e rūsī mawjūd dar Ketāb-ḵāna-ye mellī-e Īrān* (Tehran, 1362 Š./1983); Abu'l-Qāsem Ṣaḥāb, *Farhang-e ḵavar-šenāsīān: šarḥ-e ḥāl va ḵadamat-e dānešmandān-e Īrān-šenās va mostašreqīn* (Tehran, 2536=1356 Š./1977).

[9] Aḥmad Monzavī, *Fehrest-e nosḵahā-ye ḵaṭṭi-e fārsī,* vol. 6 (Tehran, 1353 Š./1974), 3991-4057; idem, *Fehrestvāra-ye ketābhā-ye fārsī,* 3 vols. (Tehran, 1374 Š./1996), 1:61-158. The article by Iraj Afshar in this volume further refines this inventory.

The number and distribution of these texts suggests the diverse range of cultural interests they may have served.

To date, the most attention has been given, rightly enough, to accounts by Qajar travelers of trips to Europe in works such as those by Nāṣer-al-Dīn Shah, Ḥājjī Sayyāḥ,[10] Ḥājjī Pīrzāda, and others. These are certainly interesting and important as Iranian examples of a phenomenon which has been called "transculturation," that is, the process by which peoples on the periphery of the world-system interact with the metropolitan centers of power and "determine to varying extents what they absorb into their own culture, and what they use it for."[11] However, it must be observed in light of the preceding data that these works constitute barely ten percent of the dramatically increased volume of travel literature during the Qajar period and thus should not be taken as the definitive indicator of its significance.

From the distribution of the titles, it is clear that most of the travel books did not deal with journeys to distant and exotic realms. They rather consisted of narratives about trips within Iran itself or to the Muslim lands adjacent to Iran—India, Central Asia, and the Ottoman Empire.[12] Numerous examples of these books are still in manuscript, unpublished, unstudied, and largely forgotten. Yet, like the travel books to Europe, these, too, have potentially a great deal to teach us about the process of change and transformation which occurred as the modern nation-state of Iran was being born, as well as the refinement of a distinctly Iranian identity. In particular, they speak to the Qajar discovery of Iran as a national entity and the question of its sense of place in its region and beyond that in the larger Islamic and non-Islamic world. It is with this

---

[10] Moḥammad-ʿAlī Sayyāḥ, *Safar-nāma-ye Ḥājj Sayyāḥ ba Farang*, ed. ʿAlī Dehbāšī (Tehran, 1363 Š./1984); tr. Mehrbanoo Deyhim as *An Iranian in Nineteenth Century Europe: The Travel Diaries of Haj Sayyah, 1859-1877* (Bethesda, Md., 1998).

[11] Pratt, *Imperial Eyes*, 6-7.

[12] Significantly, this applies even in the case of two shahs well known for their interest in trips abroad, Nāṣer-al-Dīn Shah and Moẓaffar-al-Dīn Shah. Neither made the pilgrimage, but Nāṣer-al-Dīn's visit to the Shiʿite shrines in Iraq produced works similar to a *ḥajj-nāma*, the *Safar-nāma-ye Karbalā* and *Safar-nāma-ye ʿAtabāt*; there are also accounts of his trips to Khorasan, Māzandarān, Qomm, and Europe. Many of Moẓaffar-al-Dīn's travelogues dealt with areas in and around Azerbaijan during his tenure as crown prince as well as his trip to Europe: They include *Safar-nāma-ye Marāḡa*, *Safar-nāma-ye K̲ōy*, *Rūz-nāma-e vaqāyeʿ-e safar-e Moḡān*, *Safar-nāma-ye Qarāča Dāḡ*, *Safar-nāma-ye Tehrān*, and *Safar-nāma-ye Farangestān*; see Monzavī, *Fehrestvāra*, 1:96, 101, 108, 115-16, 122, 124.

consideration in mind that attention may be drawn to the various accounts we have of Iranian pilgrimages to Mecca during the Qajar period.

The main examples of Persian pilgrimage literature from the Qajar period are summarized in the following preliminary inventory of authors and titles:[13]

1. Moḥammad-Walī Mīrzā Qājār Davallū, *Safar-nāma-ye Makka* (ca. 1206/1792).[14]

2. Mīrzā Jalāyer, *Safar-nāma-ye manẓūm* (ca. 1250/1833-34?).[15]

3. Ḥājj Mīrzā ʿAlī Khān Eʿtemād al-Salṭanah, *Safar-nāma-ye Makka* (1263/1847).[16]

4. Mīrzā Moḥammad-ʿAlī Farāhānī Ḥosaynī, *Safar-nāma-ye Makka* (1263-64/1848).[17]

5. Solṭān-Moḥammad Sayf-al-Dawla, *Safar-nāma-ye Makka* (1279/1864).[18]

---

[13] This inventory is based on material drawn from Monzavī and Storey, where full details may be found. Note that it does not attempt to include works by Indian authors writing in Persian (such as Ḵayrat ʿAlī). A few titles which are mentioned in various bibliographical sources but are apparently no longer extant or are of questionable content have also been omitted. Not all of these titles have been available for this study, as they are still in manuscript and were inaccessible to the author.

[14] MS Tehran, Sepahsālār Library, 2:2807 (Monzavī, *Fehrest*, 4032, no. 41715). The author was the son of Khan Moḥammad Khan and one of the leading generals in the service of Āḡa Moḥammad Shah; he died ca. 1213/1799.

[15] MS Tehran, Mellī Library, 837. This rhymed travelogue, one of the traditional genres for descriptions of the pilgrimage, is dedicated to Moḥammad Shah; little is known about the author. He made the pilgrimage overland via the ʿAtabāt.

[16] MS Mašhad, Āstān-e Qods, Rażawī 53. The author was the father of a great Qajar dignitary and intellectual, Moḥammad-Ḥasan Khan Eʿtemād-al-Salṭana (Sanīʿ-al-Dawla), and wrote this account of his pilgrimage at his son's request.

[17] MS Tehran, Majles Library, 2310. The author was the senior Malek-al-Kottāb, father of Moḥammad-Ḥosayn Farāhānī, who also wrote a pilgrimage narrative. This Farāhāni made the hajj overland via Baghdad and Damascus.

[18] Solṭān-Moḥammad Sayf-al-Dawla, *Safar-nāma-ye Makka*, ed. ʿAlī-Akbar Ḵodāparast (Tehran, 1364 Š./1985). Sayf-al-Dawla was a Qajar aristocrat who was reputed to be the 38th son of Fatḥ-ʿAlī Shah. In addition to being the oldest of the Qajar hajj travelogues for which we now have an edited version, his work is noteworthy for the extent to which it reflects the personality of the author, who seems to have been of an exceptionally sour disposition if not an outright misanthrope.

6. Anonymous, *Safar-nāma-ye Makka* (1288/1872).[19]

7. Farhād Mīrzā Moʿtamed-al-Dawla, *Hedāyat al-sabīl wa kefāyat al-dalīl* (1292/1875).[20]

8. Anonymous, *Safar-nāma-ye Makka* (1296/1879).[21]

9. Solṭān-Morād Mīrzā Ḥosām-al-Salṭanah, *Dalīl al-anām fī sabīl zīārat Bayt-Allāh al-ḥaram* (1297/1880).[22]

10. Moḥammad-Ebrahīm Moštarī Ḵorāsānī Ḥosām-al-Šoʿarā, *Safar-nāma-ye manẓūm* (ca. 1300/1883?).[23]

11. Moḥammad-Ḥosayn Farāhānī, *Safar-nāma-ye Makka* (1302/1885-86).[24]

12. Ḥājjī Pīrzāda, *Safar-nāma* (1303/1886).[25]

---

[19] MS Tehran, Mellī, 776. The author is unidentified but was one of courtiers of Nāṣer-al-Dīn Shah. He went on the pilgrimage via the "Mountain [or Desert] Route," leaving Najaf on 7 Ẕu'l-Qaʿda 1288/18 January 1872. Although it is potentially quite interesting because of the unusual route followed, the text is still unpublished; see Monzavī, 4033, no. 41716.

[20] Farhād Mīrzā Moʿtamad-al-Dawla, *Hedāyat al-sabīl* (Shiraz, 1294/1877); ed. Esmāʿīl Navvāb Ṣafā as *Safar-nāma-ye Farhād Mīrzā* (Tehran, 1366 Š./1987). The author was a celebrated Qajar dignitary, a son of ʿAbbās Mīrzā and uncle of Nāṣer-al-Dīn Shah, well known for his sophisticated literary tastes and abilities as well as his ultra-conservative politics. His travelogue clearly served as a model for some of those by his contemporaries, such as Farāhānī, who copied from it extensively.

[21] MS Tehran, Mellī 865. This narrative was by an unknown official at the court of Nāṣer-al-Dīn Shah. He made the pilgrimage via Baghdad, Hormuz, Jabal ʿĀmel, and Najaf, leaving Tehran on 2 Šaʿbān 1296/21 July 1879 and returning in Jomādā II 1297/May 1880.

[22] MS Tehran, Malek, 1376; Majles 441. The author was the thirteenth son of ʿAbbās Mīrzā and received his *laqab* in 1264 following military successes in Khorasan and Herat on behalf of Moḥammad Shah. He continued to be a powerful, if controversial, political power in Khorasan and was buried in Mašhad. Of all the unpublished *safar-nāma*s, his is certainly of exceptional interest since it is known from other sources that his visit to Mecca was connected with reforms to improve conditions for Iranian pilgrims. See Monzavī, *Fehrest*, 4000, nos. 41540, 41541.

[23] Ḥosām-al-Šoʿarā, *Safar-nāma* (Tehran, 1300/1883). See Monzavī, *Fehrest*, 4024, nos. 41731-33.

[24] Mīrzā Moḥammad-Hosayn Farāhānī (Golbon), *Safar-nāma*, ed. Ḥāfeẓ Farmānfarmāʾīān (Tehran, 1342 Š./1964); tr. Hafez Farmayan and Elton L. Daniel as *A Shiʿite Pilgrimage to Mecca 1885-1886* (Austin, Tex., 1990).

[25] Ḥājjī Moḥammad-ʿAlī Pīrzāda, *Safar-nāma*, ed. Ḥāfeẓ Farmānfarmāʾīān, 2 vols. (Tehran, 1342-43 Š./1963-65). This work should perhaps not be classed

13. Moḥammad Maʿṣūm ʿAlīshāh Nāyeb-al-Ṣadr Šīrāzī, *Toḥfat al-ḥaramayn* (1306/1889).[26]

14. Moḥammad-Ḥosayn Hamadānī, *Safar-nāma-ye Makka* (1307/1890).[27]

15. Anonymous, *Safar-nāma-ye Makka* (1309/1892).[28]

16. Mīrzā ʿAlī Khān Amīn-al-Dawla, *Safar-nāma-ye Makka* (1316/1898).[29]

17. Mahdīqolī Hedāyat Mok̲ber-al-Salṭanah, *Safar-nāma-ye tašarrof ba Makka* (1320/1903).[30]

---

with the other hajj travelogues, as it is primarily an account of the author's trip to Europe, the Ottoman Empire, and Egypt. However, it is of interest for the present purpose because it does contain an extensive section on the organization of the pilgrimage that the author observed during his visit to Damascus.

[26] Nāyeb-al-Ṣadr Šīrāzī, *Toḥfat al-ḥaramayn* (Bombay, 1306/1889); also ed. as *Safar-nāma-ye Nāyeb-al-Ṣadr Šīrāzī dar zīārat-e Makka* (Tehran, 1362 Š./1983).

[27] MS Hamadan; see Monzavī, *Fehrest*, 4030, no. 41708. This little known manuscript is an account of the pilgrimage by the author and his brother, which began on 27 Ramażān 1307/16 May 1890.

[28] MS Tehran, Adabiyyāt 393. It describes a pilgrimage by an anonymous courtier via Karbalā which commenced on 25 Šaʿbān 1309/24 March 1892 and ended on 9 Ṣafar/31 August. The text remains unedited; see Monzavī, *Fehrest*, 4032, no. 41718.

[29] Amīn-al-Dawla, *Safar-nāma-ye Makka*, ed. ʿAlī Amīnī as *Safar-nāma-ye Amīn-al-Dawla* (Tehran, 1354 Š./1975). The author was of course one of the most famous Qajar statesmen (1844-1904) and a protégé of ʿAbd-al-Ḥosayn Mīrzā Farmānfarmā. He requested permission to perform the pilgrimage after he was replaced as prime minister in 1898. He made the journey accompanied by his brother Majd-ol-Molk, his son Moʿīn-ol-Molk, and a retinue consisting of secretary, servants, cook, etc. He followed a fairly typical maritime route, which included a detour to Damascus via Beirut in order to visit the shrine-tomb of Zaynab Ṣoḡrā. He was in ill health during the trip and until his death at Lašta-nešā, a preoccupation reflected in his *safar-nāma* (which reads more like a personal diary than a travelogue).

[30] When the prime minister Amīn al-Solṭān Atābak fell from office in 1903, he requested permission to go on the pilgrimage and did so via the highly unusual method of travelling eastwards around the world to reach Mecca. The journey was described (although not until some forty years later) by his distinguished protégé Mahdīqolī Hedāyat Mok̲ber-al-Salṭana in the *Safar-nāma-ye tašarrof*, ed. Moḥammad Dabīr Sīāqī as *Safar-nāma-ye Makka* (Tehran, 1368 Š./1989).

18. Dāwūd b. ʿAlīnaqī Ḥosaynī, *Safar-nāma-ye Makka* (ca. 1324/ 1907).[31]

In terms of the authorship of these works, it must be admitted the *safar-nāma*s are not exactly representative of Qajar society as a whole or the actual constituency of the pilgrimage. A rather high proportion of them were written by government officials and surprisingly few by members of the ulema or by ordinary people.[32] Obviously, non-officials most certainly did go on the pilgrimage and in large numbers: Hoseyn Kazem Zadeh, for example, notes the case of a rich landlord from Isfahan who was accompanied on the pilgrimage by 150 of his tenants.[33] Dignitaries made up only a handful of the more than three thousand Iranian pilgrims in 1885.[34] The fact that most hajj narratives were written by bureaucrats and aristocrats need not be attributed to any special degree of piety among this class, nor was it entirely due to their advantages in terms of affluence and literacy. It may be partly explained by the fact that works by such authors were more likely to survive in public collections. It is also clear that some authors were deliberately encouraged to perform the pilgrimage as a means of familiarizing them with developments in neighboring countries. Such high-ranking bureaucrats and dignitaries were obliged to obtain a kind of official leave from service to perform the pilgrimage and were expected in return to prepare an official report on their experience, which would then be submitted to the shah (and were indeed read by him, as attested by notes in the manuscripts, before being deposited in an archive). In other cases, the authors performed the pilgrimage either when they were out of favor for some reason or near the end of their lives, and their motives for memorializing the trip are less obvious.

---

[31] MS Mašhad, Āstān-e qods, Rażavī 249. This work may be more in the nature of a pilgrimage guide than a pilgrimage travelogue; see Monzavī, *Fehrest*, 4030, no. 41709.

[32] Works by such authors may very well have been written and could still exist in private or religious libraries; the famous bibliography by Āqā Bozorg Ṭehranī, *al-Ẕarīʿa elā taṣānīf al-šīʿa* (Najaf and Tehran, 1355-/1936-) mentions several such titles, including Ebrāhīm b. Darvīsh Moḥammad Kāzerūnī, *Safar-nāma-ye ḥajj al-bayt*; Mīrzā Moḥammad-Ḥosayn Marʿašī Šahrastānī, *Safar-nāma-ye Ḥejāz*; Shaykh Mīrzā ʿAlī Ṣadr-al-Ḏākerīn Ṭehrānī, *Safar-nāma-ye Makka*; and Ḥosayn Ḏu'l-Qadr Šojāʿī, *Safar-nāma-ye ḥajj va rāh-nāmā-ye Ḥejāz*.

[33] Kazem Zadeh, *Relation*, 3-4.

[34] Farāhānī, *Safar-nāma*, 206, tr. 191-92 names three religious scholars, four bureaucrats, and two wives of dignitaries among the more than three thousand pilgrims.

In terms of content, this type of writing experienced an evolution of sorts during the Qajar period. Many of the accounts are like traditional guidebooks for pilgrims, with the narrator relegated to the background. Moḥammad-Ḥosayn Farāhānī, for example, deals mostly with information about travel arrangements, currencies, costs, sights, dealing with passport and customs officials, etc. Others, usually later ones, resemble personal diaries concentrating on the author's individual experiences and sentiments: for example, that of Amīn-al-Dawla is full of reports about getting up, drinking tea, eating, conversing with friends, the state of his health, etc. The contrast with earlier Qajar travelogues is rather like the difference between a Baedaker and a Robert Byron, and this may represent an important step in the development of the genre in that regard.[35]

The *safar-nāma*s also varied greatly in what they had to say about the hajj itself—that is the religious rituals involved or the visits to sacred sites in Mecca and Madina. In some, such as Sayf-al-Dawla or Amīn-al-Dawla, the pilgrimage itself is barely mentioned and one gets the impression that it was more the excuse than the purpose for the travel.[36] Others, such as Farāhānī, do discuss the ritual at some length. Such accounts are of most interest insofar as they provide a Shiʿite light on the rituals involved, since most other accounts, including those of the surreptitious European visitors like Burckhardt and Burton, are generally written from a Sunni perspective.[37] The Persian travelogues also naturally pay more attention to sites of special significance for Shiʿites or Persians such as the Baqīʿ Cemetery in Medina and the tomb of Aḥmad Aḥsāʾī than would their Sunni or European counterparts.[38] In terms of the basic pilgrimage rites and visits to sacred sites, however, the accounts are remarkably uniform not only among the Persian *safar-nāma*s but between them and the accounts by non-Persians. The similarity, for example, in the reports of places visited and scenes observed as given by Farahānī and those provided by

---

35 On this point, see the article by William L. Hanaway, "Persian Travel Narratives: Notes toward the Definition of a Nineteenth Century Genre," in this volume.

36 Solṭān-Moḥammad Sayf-al-Dawla, *Safar-nāma-ye Makka*, ed. ʿAlī-Akbar K̲odāparast (Tehran, 1364 Š./1985); Mīrzā ʿAlī Khan Amīn-al-Dawla, *Safar-nāma*, ed. ʿAlī Amīnī (Tehran, 1354 Š./1975).

37 J. L. Burckhardt, *Travels in Arabia* (London, 1829); Richard F. Burton, *Personal Narrative of a Pilgrimage to al-Madinah and Meccah*, 2 vols. (London, 1893).

38 Note the lengthy account of the Baqīʿ in Farāhānī, *Safar-nāma*, 281-88, tr. 267-74 as well as his report on the tomb of Aḥsāʾī, 284-86, tr. 270-71.

Richard Burton or Christian Snouck Hurgronje is quite striking.[39] This can presumably be explained by the fact that all pilgrims were firmly in the hands of the professional *moṭawwef*s and guides while they were in the Hejaz, and they were given an itinerary as fixed and conventional as that of any modern tour company.

Two other points about the Qajar *ḥajj-nāma*s deserve attention for their broader historical significance. First, it can be seen that the number of pilgrimage accounts increases dramatically in the last quarter of the nineteenth century. This quite clearly corresponds to a general increase in pilgrimage traffic during that period. In earlier periods, it seems only a few hundred Iranians were able to make the pilgrimage, but by the beginning of the twentieth century this had risen to 8,000 or more. In 1885, when Farāhānī made the pilgrimage, more than 3,000 Iranians went on the hajj, of whom 700 were *ḥajja-forūšī*s, *ʿakkām*, dervishes, etc.[40] Similar trends can be detected in general reports about the number of pilgrims in Qajar times.[41]

How might this phenomenon be explained? Although greater prosperity or increased piety may have played a part, there are really two major factors, one geopolitical and the other technological. The first relates to increased security for Iranian pilgrims due to improved relations with the Ottoman Empire. and the latter to the improved systems of transport, especially railways and steamships, introduced by European entrepreneurs.

From the sixteenth to the eighteenth century, the difficulties for Iranian pilgrims were not created by European powers (as the Portuguese domination in the Indian ocean caused difficulties for Mughal pilgrims), but by the hostility between Safavid Iran and the Ottoman Empire. Those two states were frequently at war with each other during that time, and the religious dimension of the struggle exacerbated Sunni-Shiʿi relations dramatically. When the Ottoman Empire was at war with Iran, Persian subjects were absolutely

---

[39] Farāhānī, *Safar-nāma*, 216-57, tr. 203-44; cf. Burton, *Personal Narrative*, 2:139 ff.; C. Snouck Hurgronje, *Mekka* (The Hague, 1888-89; tr. J. Monohan as *Mekka in the Latter Part of the Nineteenth Century*, London, 1931).

[40] Farāhānī, *Safar-nāma*, 205, tr. 191. A *ḥājjī-forūšī* performed the pilgrimage on behalf of another individual for a fee; the *ʿakkām* were caravan attendants who handled the baggage and other matters for the pilgrims. As regular visitors to Mecca, they represented a different category from the ordinary pilgrim who probably made the journey only once in a lifetime.

[41] See T. Hughes, *A Dictionary of Islam* (London, 1885), 159; Kazem Zadeh, *Relation*, 59; David Long, *The Hajj Today* (New York, 1979), 125-29.

prohibited from making the pilgrimage; in times of peace, any Persian or Shiʿite was still regarded as suspect and vulnerable to persecution or even execution. Only a small number of Iranians were allowed to enter Ottoman territory for the pilgrimage, and then only for a brief amount of time and subject to all sorts of regulations and restrictions, such as not being allowed to enter Baghdad while en route. There were unsuccessful efforts to prohibit Iranian pilgrims from visiting the ʿAtabāt, and at least in theory they were restricted to a stay of no more than ten days there. A *farmān* of 1564 further required that all Iranian pilgrims had to travel to Mecca via one of the official caravans via Damascus, Cairo, or Yemen. This meant they had to pay special fees to the Ottoman government and were barred from using the more convenient caravan route from Basra. Even then they were not necessarily safe. In 1568, the Ottomans reportedly murdered the Safavid vizier Maʿṣūm Beg, who was on pilgrimage, and blamed it on the Bedouin.[42] In 1580, a number of Iranian pilgrims were accused of being Safavid agents sent to spread propaganda among the pilgrims, arrested, and executed. Against this background, popular religious sentiments were so inflamed that Iranians or Shiʿites were sometimes prevented by mobs from entering Mecca, as happened in 1625 and 1634,[43] or not allowed to participate in the *voqūf* at ʿArafāt (without which, of course, a pilgrimage is ritually invalid). In Medina, they were generally forbidden to enter the Prophet's mosque and tomb, the accusation being that Shiʿite pilgrims would take the opportunity to desecrate the graves of Abū Bakr and ʿOmar. They typically had to lodge with the Naḵāwela, a poor and rather oppressed Shi'ite community forced to live outside the city walls of Medina.[44] While on the pilgrimage, Shi'ites were thus obliged to use prudent dissimulation (*taqīya*) to disguise their identity but still ran the risk of being harassed.

This unfortunate situation began to change after the fall of the Safavids and the failure of the last Persian siege of Mosul. In 1743, Nāder Shah began negotiating a treaty with the Ottomans which somewhat liberalized the pilgrimage arrangements, authorized the itineraries to be followed, and recognized the right of Iranians to have

---

[42] Eskandar Beg Monšī, *Tārīḵ-e ʿālamārā-ye ʿabbāsī*, tr. R. M. Savory as *History of Shah ʿAbbas the Great,* 2 vols. (Boulder, Colo., 1978), 1:253.

[43] Burckhardt, *Travels,* 251.

[44] On this community, see Burton, *Personal Narrative*, 2:1-3; M. S. Makki, *Medina Saudi Arabia* (Avesbury, 1982), 118-20; E. Rutter, *The Holy Cities of Arabia* (London, 1928), 245-46.

their own pilgrimage leader (*amīr al-ḥajj*).[45] However, conditions were still not very conducive to the pilgrimage since throughout the late eighteenth and early nineteenth centuries Ottoman control over the Ḥejāz was tenuous at best. One of the most potent threats continued to come from the militant Wahhābī sect in conjunction with the Saʿūdī tribe, based in Najd. The Wahhābīs not only threatened pilgrimage caravans in general and temporarily seized control of Mecca, they were also fanatically anti-Shiʿite and had made the ʿAtābāt a target of their raids.[46] Few Iranians would have wanted to travel across the interior of Arabia as long as the Wahhābī menace was there.

Later in the nineteenth century, Ottoman authority over its provinces was restored and relations between the Ottoman Empire and Iran moved from tolerance to friendship. Both states had common problems, which provided them with an incentive to co-operate, and the reformist elites in Iran looked to the Ottoman Tanẓīmāt as a model for their own reconstruction of Iranian society. The one event which both consolidated and best symbolized the new Turko-Persian relationship was Nāser-al-Dīn Shah's official state visit to the ʿAtabāt in 1287/1870.[47] This trip was encouraged by a group of the Iranian reformers, some of whom had served in diplomatic postings to the Ottoman empire, as a way of introducing the shah to Midḥat Pasha, one of the most progressive Ottoman reformers, who was governor of Iraq at that time; letting him see at first hand the material advantages of the changes introduced by the Tanẓīmāt; and laying the groundwork for the shah's first trip to Europe. In addition to this political dimension, the discussions between the shah and Midḥat Pasha led to accords which included measures that significantly improved conditions for Iranian pilgrims (both to the ʿAtabāt and Mecca) and provided better security against attacks on travelers.[48] Shortly after this the Iranian Prime Minister Mīrzā Ḥosayn Khan Mošīr-al-Dawla Sepahsālār (1871-73)

---

[45] The arrangements are discussed at some length in Robert W. Olson, *The Siege of Mosul and Ottoman-Persian Relations 1718-1743* (Bloomington, Ind., 1975), 100-106.

[46] The horrors of the Wahhābī sack of Karbalāʾ in 1801 have been described in J. B. Kelly, *Britain and the Persian Gulf* (Oxford, 1968), 100.

[47] This formed the subject of a *safar-nāma* by the shah himself; ed. Īraj Afšār as *Safar-nāma-ye ʿAtabāt* (Tehran, 1363 Š./1984).

[48] See Ali Haydar Midhat Bey, *The Life of Midhat Pasha* (London, 1903), 52-55; Maḥmūd Farhād-Moʿtamed, *Tārīḵ-e rawābeṭ sīāsī-e Īran wa Os̱mānī* (Tehran, 1327 Š./1948), 32-33; ʿAbd-al-ʿAzīz Nawwār, *Taʾrīḵ al-ʿErāq al-ḥadīs̱* (Baghdad, 1968), 435-39; Hamid Algar, *Mīrzā Malkum Khān* (Berkeley,

performed the pilgrimage himself and, during the course of his visit, regulated conditions for pilgrims in Medina as described by Farāhānī:

> I heard that previously people used to annoy and pick quarrels with Iranian and Shi'ite pilgrims in the Prophet's Mosque in order to extort money. The late [Grand Vizier] Mīrzā Ḥosayn Khan Mošīr-al-Dawla Sepahsālār, during his visit to Mecca, ordered Sayyed Moṣṭafā [the chief guide responsible for Iranian pilgrims] to be bastinadoed. He then decreed that each Iranian pilgrim pay one Levant dollar (about 6,000 Iranian dinars) [as a fee to visit the shrine] and after that the servitors are not to molest the Iranian pilgrims in any way....[49]

Probably as a follow-up to this, Ḥosām-al-Salṭana, during his visit to Mecca in 1880, took a number of steps to prevent exploitation or harassment of Shiʿite pilgrims, among other things by applying the bastinado to some of the camel-drivers and guides who had been fleecing Persian pilgrims.[50]

An additional political factor which apparently worked to the advantage of Iranian pilgrims was the friction developing in the late nineteenth century between the Ottomans and the sharifs of Mecca. Several of the travel accounts note how prominent Iranian visitors received invitations to meet Sharif ʿAwn-al-Rafīq or Sharif Ḥosayn, who showed their concern for the well-being of the Iranian pilgrims.[51] There was thus very little incentive for either Ottomans or local Arab officials to make trouble for the Iranians whose favor they were courting.

Another major stimulus to hajj travel in the Qajar period was what might well be described as a transport revolution. For much of the nineteenth century, Qajar pilgrims, like all others, had little choice

---

1973), 107 ff. Persian sources such as Ḥasan-e Fasāʾī, *Fārs-nāma-ye nāṣerī*, tr. Heribert Busse as *History of Persian under Qājār Rule* (New York, 1972), 368-72 generally discuss little beyond the religious aspects of the trip, but cf. Mīrzā ʿAlī-Khan Amīn-al-Dawla, *Ḵāṭerāt-e sīāsī*, ed. Ḥāfeẓ Farmānfarmāʾīān (Tehran, 1341 Š./1962), 33.

[49] Farāhānī, *Safar-nāma*, 280-81, tr. 266.

[50] Farāhānī, *Safar-nāma*, 209, tr. 95. These reforms may well be described in the unedited manuscript of a travelogue by Ḥosām-al-Salṭana, but it was not available for consultation here.

[51] Farāhānī, *Safar-nāma*, 244, tr. 231; Amīn-al-Dawla, *Safar-nāma*, 205 also mentions an interview with Sharif ʿAwn.

but to use the traditional means of transport to the Ḥejāz. One of these would be along the "official" route with the Ottoman caravan. Iranian pilgrims would join the Syrian caravan in Damascus, which would then proceed with an armed guard to Mecca. The great advantage of this arrangement as opposed to private caravans was thus the relative safety it offered: there was a very real threat of attack from the Banū Ḥarb bedouin along other routes if they were not paid enough protection money.[52] On the other hand, the Ottoman caravan was slow and incurred some extra expense because of the special fees and tolls that pilgrims were obliged to pay. Alternatively, Iranian pilgrims might be able to join the "Mountain [or Desert] Caravan" which linked Iraq and the Ḥejāz via the Jabal Šammār. This was technically illegal, but the Rašīdī amirs of Ḥāʾel were very interested in promoting it since it was a primary source of their revenue. It was also attractive to Iranian pilgrims since they could join it after visiting the ʿAtabāt. In addition, it was cheaper and sometimes safer than the Syrian caravan.[53] The impression one gets from the travel accounts is that for a while the Ottomans had been tolerating the use of this route, which would of course have reduced their income from the pilgrims, in order to promote the Rašīdīs and give them an additional incentive to oppose the Saʿūdīs/Wahhābīs. After the Ottoman-Iranian rapprochement, however, both governments took steps to close this route altogether. Thus, Farāhānī noted in 1885 that some Iranians who tried to disguise themselves and take this route back to Iran were caught, brought back in a humiliating way, imprisoned, and fined (with the proceeds going to the Iranian consul).[54]

In practical terms, this meant that a trip from Iran to the Ḥejāz and back by overland caravan could easily take a year or more. Pilgrims from northern Iran would typically have to make their way to Baghdad, then skirt the Syrian Desert by going up the Euphrates and crossing to Aleppo, and finally travel down to Damascus where they could join the Ottoman caravan to Medina and Mecca. Those in southern Iran might be able to cross the Persian Gulf and then try to make their way across the interior of Arabia. For all these travelers, however, using these routes was clearly dangerous, time-consuming, and expensive. In 1856, for example, the Amir Mohannā of Borayda annihilated an

---

[52] Farāhānī, *Safar-nāma*, 257, 260-61, tr. 245, 248-49 reported that in the year he made the pilgrimage (1885), there were threats to the pilgrims who took alternative routes and a group of from the Balkans were robbed and about a dozen killed.

[53] Farāhānī, *Safar-nāma*, 258-59, tr. 246-47.

[54] Farāhānī, *Safar-nāma*, 259, tr. 247.

Iranian pilgrimage caravan; in 1866, he held hostage a caravan carrying the wife of Āṣaf-al-Dawla.[55] In 1263/1847, Mīrzā Moḥammad-ʿAlī Farāhānī left Baghdad on 18 Šaʿbān/18 July going via Mosul, Diyarbakr, Aleppo, and Damascus (in order to avoid the hazards of traversing the desert) and did not arrive home in Tabrīz until 26 Jomādā I 1264/30 April 1848.[56] Similarly, in 1863, Sayf-al-Dawla spent almost four months by caravan just to get from Mecca to Beirut and then a month to go from Aleppo to Diyarbakr, two weeks from there to Mosul, and another three weeks to float by *kalak* down the river to Baghdad.[57]

Gradually, a number of changes in transportation were introduced, both by local and by European authorities, which intentionally or unintentionally tended to alter the possible routes by which Iranian pilgrims might reach the Ḥejāz and return. In Iran itself, these included the construction of some new roads and the establishment of carriage service, post horses, and hostels (*mehmān-ḵānas*), notably along the route from Tehran to the port of Anzalī. Though these improvements did not necessarily speed the trip, they made it safer and more comfortable and reliable. More important, easier access to Anzalī facilitated links with modern rail and sea transport. The Russians, for example, provided regular steamer services across the Caspian Sea from Anzalī to Baku. They also had adopted a deliberate policy of constructing railroads as a means of unifying their empire, and one of the most important of these was the Transcaucasian Railroad built from Poti to Tiflis between 1867 and 1872 and extended to Baku after the Russo-Turkish war of 1878. The effect of this innovation may be judged from the fact that when Edward B. Eastwick, the British chargé d'affairs in Iran, was traveling to Tehran in 1860, without benefit of railroad or Caspian steamer, it took him over two weeks just to go from Poti to Tiflis and almost three months to reach Tehran (but he did spend a lot of time hunting boar with Russian

---

[55] See Adolphe D'Avril, *L'Arabie contemporaine avec la description du pèlerinage de la Mecque* (Paris, 1868), 174-75; W. G. Palgrave, *Personal Narrative of a Year's Journey through Central and Eastern Arabia* (7th ed., London, 1875), 160 ff.

[56] Details of his *Safar-nāma-ye Makka* may be found in Monzavī, *Fehrest*, 4031, no. 41713.

[57] Sayf-al-Dawla, *Safar-nāma*, 124-251. He departed Mecca on 1 Moḥarram 1280/17 June 1863, Damascus on 14 Jomādā I/27 October (after a visit to Beirut), Diyarbakr on 15 Jomādā II/26 November, and Mosul on 29 Jomādā II/10 December.

aristocrats on the way).[58] It likewise took Sayf-al-Dawla about three months to go from Tehran to Poti in 1863.[59] By 1875, when the railroad was partially completed, Farhād Mīrzā Moʿtamad-al-Dawla could make the trip in half that time,[60] and in 1885, after it was finished, it took Farāhānī only two weeks to go from Tehran to Batum.[61] At the same time Russian, British, and French shipping companies had introduced steamer services in the Black Sea to compete with the very successful line operated by the Austrian Lloyd Company from Batum to Istanbul. These could, of course, then be used to connect with other steamer services in the Mediterranean. The opening of the Suez Canal thus made it quite feasible to travel by sea the entire way from Batum to Jedda and radically altered the logistics of hajj travel. Similar changes in travel logistics took place as a result of the development of maritime routes in the Persian Gulf and the opening of the Ḥejāz Railroad.[62]

The implications of these developments for travel in general, and the pilgrimage traffic in particular, were dramatic. They are well

---

[58] Edward B. Eastwick, *Journal of a Diplomate's Three Years' Residence in Persia* (London, 1864), 52-220. He arrived in Poti on 6 August and reached Tiflis on 23 August, after a rigorous trip by river barge, horseback, and on foot; after recuperating and socializing until 19 September, he went overland to Tehran via Tabriz, arriving on 23 October.

[59] He is not as precise as other authors about the dates of his itinerary, but does say he left Tehran on 4 Šaʿbān 1279/24 January 1863 (Sayf-al-Dawla, *Safar-nāma*, 1) and left Tiflis on 20 Šawwāl/9 April (79).

[60] In accordance with a prognostication (*fāl*), he departed Tehran on 7 Šaʿbān 1292/7 September 1875 and was in Poti on 6 Šawwāl/6 November, after having lingered in Tiflis for over a week. It had also taken him until 16 Ramażān/16 October to arrive in Baku, so most of his time was still spent in making the arduous journey from Tehran to Enzeli. Farhād Mīrzā, *Safar-nāma*, ed. Ṣafā, 29-80.

[61] He left Tehran on 16 July 1885 and arrived in Batum around 2 August; Farāhānī, *Safar-nāma*, 2, 95; tr. 2, 91.

[62] There were other changes that affected the pilgrimage traffic but had less impact on Iranians. Aware of the profits that could be made by providing transport for Muslim pilgrims, for example, British, Dutch, and French companies began developing routes in the Persian Gulf, and Indian Ocean. These would have been of use primarily for pilgrims with easy access to Bushire or other ports in the south of Iran; there is not a great deal of information about this reflected in the hajj travelogues. Although too late and too short-lived to have much impact on the Qajar pilgrimages, the Ottoman Ḥejāz Railway was completed in 1908 and expedited travel between Syria and the Ḥejāz.

illustrated in the case of Moḥammad-Ḥosayn Farāhānī in 1885. As noted above, the laborious and circuitous route followed by his father had taken approximately ten months of hard traveling. He, however, was able to use rail and sea transport to cover the much greater distance from Tehran to Mecca and back via Istanbul in a little over six months (of which nearly two of were spent sightseeing and dawdling in Gīlān for the winter).[63] The full impact of the changes are even more evident in the journey of ʿAlī-Aṣḡar Khan Amīn al-Solṭān Atābak as recorded by Mok̲ber-al-Dawla. When he requested permission in 1903 to perform the pilgrimage, he found he had five months before the hajj season and decided to use the spare time to make a trip around the world, leaving Anzalī in September to go to Moscow, Port Arthur, Peking, Yokohama, Honolulu, San Francisco, New York, Paris, and Cairo and still reach Mecca in time for the pilgrimage in February 1904.[64] In other words, by 1903 it was possible to perform the pilgrimage and traverse the globe in half the time it used to take just to perform the pilgrimage.

In terms of speed and economy as well as security, there were thus many new options for potential pilgrims, against which it would be difficult for the traditional overland routes to compete. Even after the improvements introduced on the Tehran-Anzalī route, for example, it took Farāhānī sixty-six hours of laborious travel, including seven hours on foot, to make the trip and cost six to thirty tomans, depending on exactly how one traveled and excluding food and accommodation.[65] The comparable distance from Anzalī to Baku by sea took barely a day and cost as little as five roubles (about one and a half Iranian tomans).[66] Likewise, in 1885, a trip direct from Istanbul to Yanboʿ or Jedda via the Suez Canal took less than two weeks by steamer and cost as little as ten tomans.[67] A steamer trip from Yanboʿ to Beirut cost nine tomans and took eight days (including two held in quarantine).[68] Even a journey by boat all the way from Yanboʿ to Bushire or Baghdad took only about three weeks as opposed to months by land. But an overland trip by caravan from Medina to Damascus

---

[63] He left Tehran in Šawwāl 1302/July 1885 and returned in Rabīʿ II 1303/ January 1886: Farāhānī, *Safar-nāma*, 2, 350, tr. 2, 325.

[64] Mahdīqolī Hedāyat Mok̲ber-al-Salṭana, *Safar-nāma-ye Makka*, ed. Moḥammad Dabīr Sīāqī (Tehran, 1368 Š./1989), 1-5, 249, etc.

[65] Farāhānī, *Safar-nāma*, 2-49, tr. 2-46.

[66] Farāhānī, *Safar-nāma*, 56, tr. 54.

[67] Farāhānī, *Safar-nāma*, 186, tr. 173.

[68] Farāhānī, *Safar-nāma*, 300, tr. 286.

might involve two months of travel and "untold expense."[69] Similarly, the fastest traditional method of conveyance between Mecca and Medina/Yanboᶜ (the "Flying Caravan") took two or three weeks, exposed the traveler to attack by bedouin, and, with all the miscellaneous expenses involved, cost seventy-one Levant dollars (about eighty-five tomans).[70] It is thus hardly surprising that in 1885 most Iranian pilgrims, at least 2,200 out of 3,000, used the new maritime and rail routes rather than the overland caravans. Only about a hundred tried to come via the "Mountain Route" and eight hundred by the Syrian caravan (with fifty dying from the hardships encountered).[71] This dramatic shift could hardly fail to have consequences for Iranians' experience of the pilgrimage in terms of both the places they visited and the people they encountered, as well as the necessity of learning to deal with passports, visas, customs, quarantines, currency exchange, and unfamiliar technology.

Innovations in transport may have thus stimulated Qajar interest in the pilgrimage, but they also created some unusual problems, especially for the very pious pilgrims. Some, such as the question of where to put on the *eḥrām* garb required for the hajj, were solved fairly simply: do so when the steamer crossed the latitude of the traditional place for performing the ritual or, to be really meticulous, do it once on the boat and again at the frontier of the *ḥarām*.[72] Others required more fundamental changes in thinking. For example, Farāhānī was openly perplexed at one peculiar difficulty created by the new methods of travel. He noted that on the trains and steamers water was kept in barrels with a common cup, and non-Muslims were free to use them. The water therefore was technically polluted and ritually impure for use by Muslims. At the same time, given the crowding in the trains and stations, it was impossible to avoid physical contact with non-Muslims, and this contact was, according to traditional teaching, also a source of ritual pollution. The implication was thus that anyone who wanted to be strictly conscientious would have nothing to drink and be constantly in a state of ritual impurity.[73]

Against this religious difficulty had to be weighed the benefits of this mode of travel in terms of its economy, convenience, and

---

69 Farāhānī, *Safar-nāma*, 258, tr. 246.

70 Farāhānī, *Safar-nāma*, 261, tr. 249. He indicates an exchange rate of about twelve thousand Iranian *dīnār*s to the Levant dollar.

71 Farāhānī, *Safar-nāma*, 205, tr. 191, reports that 1,200 went by way of Persian Gulf ports and 1,000 via Istanbul.

72 Farāhānī, *Safar-nāma*, 210, tr. 196.

73 Farāhānī, *Safar-nāma*, 75-77, tr. 70-74.

efficiency. This represented a classic dilemma of the modern age, and in Farāhānī one can see how a process of rationalization was already at work to deal with it. According to him, there were twenty-five sound Hadiths that small quantities of water remained pure upon contact with something impure unless its color, smell, or taste changed, while twenty-six Hadiths said it was impure. There was thus disagreement on the issue, and, in any case, it was a matter of religious preference, not obligation.[74] It was much harder to get around the question of the impurity of non-Muslims, but even there Farāhānī notes that some of the ulema were beginning to teach that non-Muslims can be regarded as ritually pure, or at least non-polluting, so that one could associate with them when necessary, in which case, he says, "things will go easier on one in foreign countries."[75]

This brings us to one of the deeper issues involved in the transformation of the pilgrimage in the Qajar period. In earlier times, it would never have been necessary for pilgrims from Iran to cross non-Muslim territory when performing the hajj; indeed they would have continuously been in some of the most conservative and traditional areas of the Muslim world. With the new means of travel, the pilgrims passed through a number of different lands and encountered a variety of different people. How did they react to this experience of what we now recognize as the phenomenon of a shrinking world and the creation of the global village?

To a certain extent, Iranian pilgrims insulated themselves while traveling. From the *safar-nāma*s, we can see that they often went on the trip with a group of friends and companions, they tended to seek accommodations with expatriate Iranians or fellow Shi'ites in foreign cities, and they remained largely to themselves when visiting sacred sites or performing the hajj rituals. In that sense, they did not interact a great deal with either non-Muslims or other Muslims, but they certainly did observe them and record their impressions about them. It is difficult to know exactly what to make of these comments since they tend to be rather superficial and stereotyped. They are also highly dependent on the personality of the individual traveler. Sayf-al-Dawla, for example, had by far the most sour disposition of the travelers, and he does not seem to have enjoyed anyone or anything he encountered during his pilgrimage. According to him, the people in the Caucasus were bad-looking, frivolous, and licentious. In Istanbul, they were pleasure seeking and undisciplined. Egyptian men were too dark,

---

[74] Farāhānī, *Safar-nāma*, 75-77, tr. 70-74.

[75] Farāhānī, *Safar-nāma*, 77, tr. 74.

skinny, poorly dressed, and prone to eye-disease; the women were too pale, fat, lazy, and disrespectful. Syrians were handsome, clean, and well dressed but unfriendly and greedy. Arabs in the Hejaz were arrogant, hard-hearted, ill-behaved, sharp tongued, avaricious, and boring. He did allow that Iraqis were happy and friendly, and commented that a mosque in Šemak̲ī was *bad nīst* (not bad), which for him was a high compliment.[76] By contrast, the affable Mok̲ber-al-Dawla and Atābak seemed thoroughly to enjoy talking with fellow travelers, meeting new people, visiting different places, etc.[77]

In any case, it is clear from many of the pilgrimage accounts that Iranian travelers did not need to go to Europe to be exposed to Western innovations or to suffer from a definite case of culture shock. The journey through the Caucasus seems to have been a particularly unsettling experience. Baku had become an oil town, and the boom had in fact created something of a wild west atmosphere there, but the reports of the Iranian travelers are astonishing. Sayf-al-Dawla, for example, was chagrined to find Muslims and non-Muslims mixing freely together, the women unveiled, and the children lazy and disobedient. People were Muslims in name but not in practice; there were all sorts of bandits; and every kind of vice was rampant. He also claims that taverns and brothels were everywhere, but he does not reveal how he found out about the existence of these dens of iniquity.[78] Farāhānī, a fairly well-educated, mid-level government official employed in the Ministry of Foreign Affairs was also clearly uneasy about traveling in this area. He says that during his diplomatic mission in India he had met many Englishmen, and although they were deceitful, cunning, and not very friendly they did have a certain dignity and respect for propriety. He was thus unprepared for the Caucasus, where he says that the Russians were coarse, rude, wicked, and tyrannical. The Russian officials claimed that everything was orderly, but in fact it the country was so lawless that "no one is secure in life, property, or his own affairs. One cannot spend a tranquil night in one's own home. There are many criminals, and few nights go by when there are not robberies and two or three people are killed on the streets." The police simply ignored complaints about theft and murder. Moreover, he claims, women and boys engaged openly in prostitution; husbands lived in fear of their wives and children since if they got angry they could run away to a brothel and the husband could do

[76] Sayf-al-Dawla, *Safar-nāma*, 52, 58, 72, 119, 143, 165, 221.

[77] Mok̲ber-al-Dawla, *Safar-nāma*, passim.

[78] Sayf-al-Dawla, *Safar-nāma*, 52, 58.

nothing about it. The people were thoroughly sacrilegious; they lived on pork, and they "exceed all bounds in drinking wine so that usually they are so drunk they are senseless."[79]

Having already been unsettled by the experience in the Caucasus, many of the travelers were just as disturbed about what they found in the Ottoman Empire and Egypt. Farhād Mīrzā, otherwise a rather urbane and cultured man, was invited to a diplomatic ball and was shocked to see women, married and unmarried, immodestly dressed and even dancing with whomever they pleased.[80] Sayf-al-Dawla also complained that Istanbul was a center of debauchery, where people dressed in European style, no kind of vice was prohibited, and speakeasies and dives *(mey-ḵānā*s and *qahva-ḵāna*s) were ubiquitous.[81] Farahānī allowed that the Ottomans were quite civil, although the women were too domineering; he seemed more worried about what he saw as a kind of creeping republicanism and secularization of the law that might spread to Iran and undermine the monarchy and society.[82]

At the same time that some of these pilgrims professed to be shocked by the spread of republicanism and secular society to Muslim lands, the free intermixing of Muslims and non-Muslims, and assertive women on the loose, they also began to display greater interest in the common problems facing Muslim countries and to develop new perspectives on relations between Muslims. One of the best examples of this is again Farāhānī. He described and denounced the recent British occupation of Egypt. He was particularly interested in the activities of Moḥammad Aḥmad the Mahdī of the Sudan and says he was provided with a detailed history of the Mahdī compiled by Mīrzā Ḥabīb-Allāh Khan, the Iranian consul in Jedda.[83] He was able to observe first hand the actions and attitudes of Sunnī pilgrims and says that he had discussions with members of the ulema in the Ḥejāz. He pointed out to his readers that there was no longer any persecution of Shiʿites in the Ḥejāz, that Shiʿites could openly practice the rituals in accordance with the Jaʿfarī rite, and that the differences between the Jaʿfarī and the Malekī schools in such matters were insignificant anyway. As a result, he strongly advocated the abandonment of the practice of *taqīya* and the development of a closer and more open relationship with the other branches of Islam.[84] The extent to which such

---

[79] Farāhānī, *Safar-nāma*, 68-70, tr. 65-66.

[80] Farhād Mīrzā, *Hedāyat*, ed. Ṣafā, 98-99.

[81] Sayf-al-Dawla, *Safar-nāma*, 96-97.

[82] Farāhānī, *Safar-nāma*, 135-46, tr. 128-38.

[83] Farāhānī, *Safar-nāma*, 192-96, tr. 178-83.

[84] Farāhānī, *Safar-nāma*, 242-43, tr. 228-30.

discoveries by pilgrims may have contributed to the reception of the pan-Islamist ideas then being developed by Jamāl-al-Din Afḡānī and others remains an open but intriguing question.

In sum, it can be seen that these accounts serve as a revealing barometer indicating the deeper socio-cultural changes taking place during the Qajar period. They can thus be put to good use to reveal the impact such changes had on both individuals and the institutions of the time.

Nineteenth-Century Iranians in America

M. R. Ghanoonparvar

Compared to the number of Iranians who visited Europe in the nineteenth century and the availability of dozens of Iranian memoirs of travel to Europe, few Iranians traveled to America at the time, and there is a relative dearth of diaries recounting travel to the United States and Canada.[1] Long distances and sea travel to the New World were obviously prohibitive, even for those Iranians who were adventurous enough to venture into journeys abroad; therefore, they rarely included America in their itineraries. And, of course, this is understandable, since whereas by the late nineteenth century travel to Europe was becoming commonplace for Iranian dignitaries and sometimes members of affluent merchant-class families, who were becoming ever more exposed to the technological advancements in European countries, relatively little was known about America even to these groups.

In the 1830s, Iranian contact with Americans was limited to a handful of missionaries who had made an effort to establish a few schools and hospitals in northeast Iran, particularly in the town of Orūmīya (Urmia). Due to political considerations related to the rivalry between the Russians and the British in increasing their influence in Iran, and wishing to establish contact with a country other than these two contenders in the region, the Iranian government at the time was quite willing to grant permission to the American missionary groups for their activities among the Iranian Christians. At the same time, however, these Americans confronted resistance and opposition by the local people, particularly the Armenian community. Nevertheless, these early

[1] For a bibliographical overview of Iranian memoirs of travel to Europe and elsewhere, see Iraj Afshar, "Bibliographical Survey: Types and Categories of Persian Travelogues" in this volume.

contacts eventually led to the establishment of friendship, trade treaties, and later diplomatic relations between the two countries.[2]

The first American ambassador to Iran was S. G. W. Benjamin, who went to Iran in 1883 and eventually published a book in 1887 entitled *Persia and the Persians*. But it took several years, in fact after the tenure of Benjamin as ambassador to Iran had ended, before the first Iranian ambassador was sent to Washington. This first Iranian ambassador to Washington was Ḥājj Ḥosaynqolī Khan Moʿtamed-ol-Vezāra, who was appointed ambassador in 1888. Ḥosaynqolī Khan, who later received the title of Ṣadr-al-Salṭana, had served in the Iranian foreign ministry for some years and was promoted to deputy foreign minister and served for a few years as the Iranian consul general in India.[3]

Ḥosaynqolī Khan's term as the first ambassador to the United States was only for one year, and although he expressed his desire to extend his tenure and stay in the United States, many of his rivals and enemies spoke ill of him to the shah, which resulted in his return at the end of that year. He was, however, a prolific letter writer, and during his stay in the United States, he sent letters and reports regularly to the Iranian foreign ministry in which he provided information, sometimes in minute detail, about his activities and particularly about life in Washington.

In one of his first letters upon arriving in the United States from Europe, Ḥosaynqolī Khan made a comparison between Europe and the United States. He described London as a "large crowded kitchen with walls, doors, and buildings and black and constantly gloomy weather that makes the native inhabitant melancholy," and then he contrasted European cities with New York, writing:

> The difference that exists between the ruined, depopulated, and unpleasant cities in central Asia and the city of Paris—and once here was much worse than there—also certainly exists between Europe and America.[4]

---

[2] A brief account of the history of these missionary activities is found in Homāyūn Šahīdī's introductory essay, "Dībāča-ye ba ṣīvā-ye gozāreš," in his edition of Moʿīn-al-Salṭana's *Safar-nāma-ye Šīkāgow* (Chicago Travel Memoirs), discussed later in this article (see below n. 16).

[3] Some details of early Iranian-American diplomatic relations as well as the story of the first Iranian ambassador to the United States are also provided by Homāyūn Šahīdī in his introductory essay.

[4] Šahīdī, "Dībāča," 108.

Ḥosaynqolī Khan was quite aware that the officials in Iran were very interested in any kind of information he could provide them about life in the United States and, hence, he even described in some detail the building that he rented from a Mrs. Smith to house the first Iranian Embassy, along with a copy of the lease. Moreover, it appears from his letters that the Iranian government was eager to learn about the modern military and to acquire military equipment.[5] Hence, he included in his report the price of American military uniforms, which he acquired from the Department of Defense, as well as the price of artillery from U.S. factories.[6] Furthermore, he was also interested in learning about the American economy, particularly American manufactured goods, imports, and exports. Again, comparing the United States to Europe, he reported:

> Although the United States is superior to Europe in terms of industries and inventions, in regards to textiles of every kind, it is quite behind Europe and, like other countries in the world, needs European fabrics, and people's clothing, for both men and women, comes from foreign countries, especially England.[7]

He then commented that American factories were trying to remedy this situation, and the United States government had imposed heavy taxes on such imports. Nevertheless, he observed, "this problem is a great shortcoming for the government and people of the United States."[8]

In another letter, Ḥosaynqolī Khan praised the American people and noted that he had been assigned to serve in a country that was "closer than other places to civilization" and added:

> The people of this country ridicule Europeans and consider them foreigners. You can see what a difference there is. All the people

---

[5] These interests of the Iranian government were by no means unique with regards to the United States. Most official travelers to Europe earlier were asked to write similar reports about technological and particularly military progress in Europe, which were often presented in the form of *safar-nāma*s [travel diaries]. For a discussion of some of these travel diaries, see M. R. Ghanoonparvar, "Understanding the Unknown," in *In a Persian Mirror: Images of the West and Westerners in Iranian Fiction* (Austin, Tex., 1993), 11-39.

[6] See Šahīdī, "Dībāča," 116. This letter is dated 12 October 1888.

[7] Šahīdī, "Dībāča," 116.

[8] Šahīdī, "Dībāča," 117.

> of the United States are like Mr. Pratt,[9] and even better than him. In a country with a population of 100,000 Mr. Pratts, who could imagine anyone treating anyone else unjustly. All the people are alert, intelligent, learned, polite, and wealthy. Women in this country are no different from men in their training and work. All government dignitaries are wage earners and servants of the people, and if they commit a violation, the people dismiss them. There are even two black slaves among the congressmen.[10]

Quite impressed by America and Americans, Ḥosaynqolī Khan described the American people as hard working and freedom loving. Everyone, he said, is the owner of the country, and every individual "a powerful king." After describing some of the wonders of industry, such as railroads, bridges, and war ships, he then observed:

> The essence of the religion of the prophet [of Islam] is found in the United States. Most people do not drink and do not waste their time of worship idly. What these people want on the whole is general peace; nevertheless, they do not reduce their fighting power.[11]

Apparently worried about the closure of the Iranian Embassy by his own government, Ḥosaynqolī Khan begged the Iranian government not to give up its direct contact with Washington. What seems to have impressed him most was the system of government, and on the whole, the meaning of democracy as practiced in the United States. He scolded those Iranians who had visited Europe before him and said:

> Those who went to Europe neither understood the meaning of politics nor what is meant by liberty and freedom.... Freedom does not mean drinking alcohol and playing with prostitutes.... Here [in the United States] women are given special respect.[12]

He then continued, "What can protect us from the enemy is learning sciences and granting freedom, educating children, and having laws." Moreover, he added:

---

[9] Edward Spenser Pratt was the third American ambassador to Iran. He was in Tehran while Ḥosaynqolī Khan served as the Iranian ambassador to Washington.

[10] Šahīdī, "Dībāča," 120. This letter, which is dated 7 October 1888, is marked "confidential."

[11] Šahīdī, "Dībāča," 121.

[12] Šahīdī, "Dībāča," 123.

> It must also be understood that the law of the country and the government are separate. God's Book is, of course, sacred and is for religious matters .... Hence, we must have a law in our country, like the Ottomans, who have Islam and respect the Koran and also have a constitution .... For God's sake, while the leadership of Iran is in your competent hands, think of a solution in this matter and make your offspring prosper. I swear soon the whole Iranian nation will be annihilated and reduced by foreigners .... You must remind his majesty of these matters.[13]

In a later letter, however, speaking of the greed of the Europeans, who were never satisfied and wanted to capture the whole world, he spoke of the United States as a powerful country that was established by those who escaped Europe and eliminated the natives like eagles devour a carcass or like leprosy that spreads to everything it touches.[14]

Ḥosaynqolī Khan's travels abroad and particularly his year as the first Iranian ambassador in Washington provided him with insight which eventually led to a sense of pessimism. Some years later, at the age of forty-seven, on the back of a biography of one of his relatives, he wrote: "I foresee destruction and darkness for Iran. May God have mercy on everyone."[15]

Ḥosaynqolī Khan's observations about America were. of course, not presented in the form of a formal *safar-nāma*. Rather, as was mentioned earlier, his travel notes were in the form of comments and observations in a series of letters he sent to his superiors in Iran.

Another Iranian traveler who visited the United States a few years later was Ḥājj Mīrzā Moḥammad-ʿAlī Moʿīn-al-Salṭana. Unlike many early travelers who were sent on official visits of one kind or another, Moʿīn-al-Salṭana, who was from a well-known merchant family, journeyed to the United States with a sense of curiosity and exploration. Having already visited Europe on earlier journeys, he was less in awe of the places he visited and things he saw in Russia and Europe. His main purpose was to arrive in the United States in time for the 1893 Chicago World's Columbian Exposition and also to travel throughout the United States.

---

[13] Šahīdī, "Dībāča," 123-24. This letter is addressed to (ʿAlī Aṣḡar Khan) Amīn-al-Solṭān (1858-1907).

[14] Šahīdī, "Dībāča," 126. This is also a confidential letter, dated 12 October 1888.

[15] Šahīdī, "Dībāča," 129. This statement is preceded by a brief autobiographical note by Ḥosaynqolī Khan.

Moʿīn-al-Salṭana's reaction to America in the beginning and also throughout most of his travels to various American states and cities was at times extremely positive and at other times quite negative. Because of his earlier visits to the West, he displayed little amazement or shock, as did many earlier travelers to Europe. But, like Ḥosaynqolī Khan, Moʿīn-al-Salṭana's frame of reference and standard for comparison of social behavior and technical advancements was Europe.

Moʿīn-al-Salṭana had a very keen eye for details. When he described a bridge, the railroad system, or even an elevator he provided measurements, weights, colors, the material used, and even costs. His description of the city of New York is an example:

> New York summers are extremely hot, and its winters extremely cold. It has no moderate weather. Its buildings are seven to fifteen stories high and are all designed and built with large stones, wood, and steel most beautifully. The length of the city has five streets, each eight English miles long. The avenues [*ḵīābān*] are named by numbers, for instance, First Avenue and Second Avenue. The streets [*kūča*] are all located between the avenues and every street opens into an avenue .... The streets are also all numbered, as are the houses on these streets.[16]

The descriptions that Moʿīn-al-Salṭana provided are sometimes so detailed that they seem tedious to a reader today. He devoted dozens of pages to describing the hotel in which he stayed in Chicago, where he most carefully measured, counted, and evaluated everything he saw: "I walked on the side of the building that faces the sea. Its length is eighty-six steps and width more than forty-five steps. It has ten stories, with a hundred rooms on each floor."[17]

Later on, describing what seems to be one of the hotel lobbies, he wrote that "they have placed twenty-eight chairs and five sofas for people to sit." The ceiling of the lobby, according to him, had twelve sections, each with twelve electrical lights, while "sixty-three lights hung from the ceiling."[18]

Moʿīn-al-Salṭana's *Safar-nāma-ye Šīkāgow* (Chicago Travel Memoirs) sometimes reads as a manual of sorts, as if the author

---

[16] Mīrzā Moḥammad-ʿAlī Moʿīn-al-Salṭana, *Safar-nāma-ye Šīkāgow,* ed. Homāyūn Šahīdī (Tehran, 1363 Š./1984), 295.

[17] Moʿīn-al-Salṭana, *Safar-nāma-ye Šīkāgow*, 348.

[18] Moʿīn-al-Salṭana, *Safar-nāma-ye Šīkāgow*, 351.

intended to reproduce back in Iran some of what he saw. This persistent eye for detail, however, extended to all aspects of American life, including entertainment, business, government, and social behavior. Although in regards to government, he did not especially advocate Iran's emulation of the United States, unlike Ḥosaynqolī Khan, his careful attention to the American political system suggests an implicit advocacy of it for Iran.

In various cities, Moʿīn-al-Salṭana also commented on the behavior of American people, and while he often sang their praises for being a free people, he was also sometimes repelled by the "unrefined" behavior he witnessed. In Philadelphia, for instance, he found the children to be "extremely impolite and savage." In a park where a band was playing music, he stated: "I would not dare walk even two steps away from where the band is playing. People here are not rational and proper. Except for a few, the rest are savages. One's life is in danger if one decides to go to a quiet corner of the park." Later, he commented: "The people of this city want to imitate Europeans, but it is clear that they have no breeding at all."[19] On the other hand, in his visit to San Francisco, which he found a delightful city in every respect, he gave the people a backhanded compliment:

> People of this city are mature and experienced and are not comparable to other people in America. They are extremely willing to imitate Europeans and to behave like them. But they are not imitators of the usual customs and conventions of Europeans. Moreover, they are also somewhat conceited, which is probably due to their wealth and prosperity. As they remember their gold and silver mines and their new industries, they consider other people in the world inferior to themselves.[20]

The only section of San Francisco that Moʿīn-al-Salṭana found appalling, and which in many respects reminded him of Iran, was Chinatown, where he discovered people wasting time idly, living in filth, squalor, and poverty.

Moʿīn-al-Salṭana's summation of his American tour and evaluation of America and Americans came towards the end of his journey in Europe on his way back to Iran. In Paris, he wrote, "It is amazing, now that I have returned from America to Europe, that Paris and

---

[19] Moʿīn-al-Salṭana, *Safar-nāma-ye Šīkāgow*, 229, 299.

[20] Moʿīn-al-Salṭana, *Safar-nāma-ye Šīkāgow*, 443.

London and their buildings, monuments, and theaters do not seem as attractive and beautiful as they did before the journey."[21]

Both Ḥosaynqolī Khan and Moʿīn-al-Salṭana can be categorized among the majority of travelers to Europe in the nineteenth century who were either high-ranking government officials or belonged to affluent classes. One traveler who was an exception to this rule was Ebrāhīm Ṣaḥḥāfbāšī, who traveled to Europe and the United States in the last decade of the nineteenth century. Although his travel memoirs apply to this visit, he indicates that he had visited the West frequently, having gone to some places as much as twenty years earlier. Essentially a businessman, he had set out on this journey to sell some jewelry for someone he does not mention by name, and since his funds were limited, he was obliged to travel frugally and count every penny he spent.

After spending a short time in Europe, in cities like Paris and London, with which he seems quite familiar, he finally set out on a ship for America with a second-class ticket. Unlike Moʿīn-al-Salṭana's detailed descriptions of his travels, Ṣaḥḥāfbāšī's are always very brief, in an almost telegraphic style, with each entry only a paragraph or at most one page long. His comments are always thoughtful and to the point. For instance, he wrote about traveling across the Atlantic Ocean:

> Proper life is how these people live, most freely. One lady laughed loudly, others joined in with her. No one ventured to say, 'Woman (*żāʿefa*), why do you laugh so much?' In any case, this ship has traveled 117 miles in twenty-four hours. They have made it so easy to travel that any blind man can do it, provided he knows the language. They have published all sorts of booklets and arranged them there. Any person who wants to travel to any part of America, could take the booklet for that region and read it. They have the maps of that state and all that is necessary for a traveler, including prices and other details.[22]

One of his main complaints about the United States was the high prices. Nevertheless, he observed, "This is not an expensive country. The problem is our [Iranian] money ... which is worth one-fifth of the money of other places."[23]

---

[21] Moʿīn-al-Salṭana, *Safar-nāma-ye Šīkāgow*, 472-75.

[22] Ebrāhīm Ṣaḥḥāfbāšī, *Safar-nāma-ye Ebrāhīm Ṣaḥḥāfbāšī*, ed. Moḥammad Moširī (Tehran, 1357 Š./1979), 63.

[23] Ṣaḥḥāfbāšī, *Safar-nāma*, 67.

The orderliness of people and social services particularly impressed Ṣaḥḥāfbāšī. Commenting on the railroad system on his way to Niagara Falls, he said:

> Traveling on the railroad in America is quite different from other places. These people all seem to be geography experts. No one asks directions, everyone carries a small bag with a map and knows where he must change trains, how long the train stops, where he should get on, where he should get off.[24]

Ṣaḥḥāfbāšī envied the Americans for their honesty. Having left his umbrella in a train car overnight, he found it the next morning precisely where he had left it. He noted:

> Since last night at least five hundred people have gotten on and off the train in various stations and because they did not consider this umbrella their own, they did not take it.[25]

He compared the people of America with his compatriots and contrasted their efforts to build their society through hard work to that of Iranians who lived lazily, only thinking about themselves and without possessing social consciousness. Americans even tried to benefit and learn from their religious sermons, as opposed to Iranians, for whom religion contributed to their backwardness and superstitious beliefs. He likened America to paradise, where people either "constantly read or when they speak, they do so quietly [only loud enough] for the other person to hear them." He further lamented:

> Alas that we miserable people lack all these characteristics .... Since we can fill our stomachs with a piece of bread, what need is there to seek education and distinguish between the good and the bad? Most people still do not distinguish between honor and shame, so they make a living by begging and religious charity. Not everyone is as stupid as I to run from the East to the West and from the West to the East to make a living. Some say that I am lucky to travel and see the world, whereas [I say] lucky is the person who knows nothing and sees nothing, because he sleeps soundly and envies no one.[26]

---

[24] Ṣaḥḥāfbāšī, *Safar-nāma*, 70-71.

[25] Ṣaḥḥāfbāšī, *Safar-nāma,* 70-71.

[26] Ṣaḥḥāfbāšī, *Safar-nāma*, 75-76.

In some respects, Ṣaḥḥāfbāšī's assessment of the United States, and particularly the contrast he saw between a socially, economically, and politically progressive America and a stagnant and backward Iran at the time, resonates with the words and observations of both Ḥosaynqolī Khan Ṣadr-al-Salṭana and Mīrzā Moḥammad-ʿAlī Moʿīn-al-Salṭana. While the first Iranian ambassador to the United States was particularly explicit in his observations concerning the political advantage of America with its democratic system of government over Iran's corrupt government bureaucracy and crumbling government rule, Moʿīn-al-Salṭana's attention to social and technological progress in the United States implicitly asserted the same. All three of these travelers of course dreamed about and expressed the wish that their own ancient country should emulate and learn from the newly established country they visited. Nonetheless, these hopes and dreams seem to have been shattered for at least two of them. Ḥosaynqolī Khan, as quoted earlier, predicted "a dark future" for Iran. And Ṣaḥḥāfbāšī, one of the first modern entrepreneurs in Iran, who engaged in international trade, possibly established the first movie theater in Iran, and became involved in the constitutional movement, was finally disappointed in the political situation in Iran and gave up on his country altogether. According to his son, in return for building the first bath house without a hot water pool [*ḵazīna*] and bringing cinema to Iran, as well as for his democratic views, his property was confiscated, and he was sent into exile by the government and eventually left with his wife and children for Karbalāʾ and later India.[27]

One difference between these visitors to America and many of the Iranian travel-diary writers who visited Europe is that all three were experienced travelers and based much of their observations about the New World on their earlier encounters with the West in Europe. It is noteworthy, however, that they could all foresee the important role that America would play on the global level in the ensuing century.

[27] See Moširī's introduction to Ṣaḥḥāfbāšī, *Safar-nāma*, particularly pp. 16-17.

Persian Travel Narratives: Notes Toward the Definition of a Nineteenth-Century Genre

William L. Hanaway

Travel narratives did not form one of the traditional genres of Persian prose writing at the beginning of the nineteenth century. A few earlier travelers had written accounts of their journeys, probably the best known being Nāṣer Ḵosrow's *Safar-nāma* in Persian and Ebn Baṭṭūṭa's *Reḥla* in Arabic, but there were not enough of these to conceive of them as a group and define as a recognizable genre. Other travel accounts, some by women, existed in manuscript, particularly of pilgrimages and journeys to the holy places in Arabia or Iraq and even journeys to Europe, but these were not widely known. When changes in world conditions at the end of the eighteenth century led more nineteenth-century Persians to travel in Europe, quite a few of them wrote and published accounts of their journeys, and thus laid the ground for the creation of a new genre of Persian prose works.[1]

When we think of Western travel narratives, we have in mind mostly those written in the post-Enlightenment period. Modern interpreters of these narratives hold that voluntary travel (as opposed to the official travel engaged in by the nineteenth-century Persians) offered the individual an opportunity for expanded experience which could be interpreted and integrated into the traveler's sense of self. The result of this process could be a change in the understanding of one's self and the world, and it is in this sense that eighteenth- and nineteenth-century travel accounts by Westerners can be thought of as a sub-category of autobiography. The situation of the nineteenth-century Persian travelers is quite different and cannot properly be described using European travel

[1] For notes on earlier travel accounts, see Mohammad Tavakoli-Targhi, "Imaging Western Women: Occidentalism and Euro-eroticism," *Radical America* 24/3(1993):73-74.

accounts as models. Until the twentieth century, when Persian sensibility changed under the influence of European Romanticism, Persian travel accounts remained quite strictly dynamic and utilitarian. This is not to say, however, that there were not subtle differences among them, and it is to these differences as well as the overall similarities that may be used to suggest the general contours of their generic identity.

In our own post-Romantic times, we think of genres as having two main characteristics. First, they can be said to resemble contracts between writers and readers, contracts that impose obligations which if not fulfilled will blur or compromise the generic identity of the work. Second, genres can be likened to family resemblances among people. We all know families in which each individual has a distinct appearance, but if we see the family assembled, certain common features become easily discernable. Genres today are thought to be characterized by both inner and outer form, but not thought of as strictly-bounded, norm-governed, prescriptive categories as they were before the Enlightenment, and as they were in pre-twentieth-century Persia. This discussion of Persian travel narratives will be based on today's conception of genre, not on that of pre-modern Persia.[2] The evidence provided by the travel accounts themselves will be presented in two major categories: the formal qualities of the works, and the self-presentation of the authors. Eight major travel narratives will be examined,[3] plus one fictional travel account.[4] What, then, are the conventions or the salient generic markers of nineteenth-century

---

[2] For discussions of genre theory, see Alastair Fowler, *Kinds of Literature* (Oxford, 1982) and R. Wellek and A. Warren, *Theory of Literature* (New York, 1956 or later eds.). For the differences in Persian and Western literature among travelogues, memoirs, diaries, and autobiographies, see Aḥmad Ašraf, "Tārīḵ, ḵaṭera, afsāna," *Īrān-nāma/Iran Nameh* 14/4 (1996):525-38.

[3] In chronological order they are: Mīrzā Abū Ṭāleb Khan, *Masīr-e ṭālebī*, ed. Ḥosayn Ḵadīv-jam (Tehran, 1352 Š./1973); Abu'l-Ḥasan Khan Īlčī, *Ḥayrat-nāma*, ed. Ḥasan Morselvand (Tehran, 1364 Š./1985); Mīrzā Ṣāleḥ Šīrāzī, *Safar-nāma*, ed. Ḡolām-Ḥosayn Mīrzā Ṣāleḥ (Tehran, 1364 Š./1985); Reżāqolī Mīrzā, *Safar-nāma*, ed. Aṣḡar Farmānfarmā'ī Qājār (Tehran, 1346 Š./1967); ʿAbd-al-Fattāḥ Garmrūdī, *Šarḥ-e ma'mūriyat-e Ājūdānbāšī,* ed. Moḥammad Mošīrī (Tehran, 2536=1356 Š./1977); Farhād Mīrzā, *Safar-nāma*, ed. Ḡolām-Reżā Ṭabāṭabā'ī (Tehran, 1366 Š./1987); Ḥājjī Pīrzāda, *Safar-nāma*, ed. Ḥāfeẓ Farmānfarmā'īān (Tehran, 1342 Š./1963); and Mīrzā ʿAlī Khan Amīn-al-Dawla, *Safar-nāma*, ed. Eslām Kāẓemīya (Tehran, 1354 Š./1975).

[4] Ḥājjī Zayn-al-ʿĀbedīn Marāḡa'ī, *Sīāḥat-nāma-ye Ebrāhīm Beyg*, ed. Bāqer Mo'menī (Tehran, 2537=1537 Š./1978; vol. 1 only).

Persian travel narratives: What are their formal characteristics, and how do they fit into the Persian literary tradition?

The general form of all these works, beginning with Nāṣer Ḵosrow, is that of a journal. The entries are arranged chronologically from the beginning of the journey to the end, and they record the daily experience (with some gaps) of the traveler, sometimes with other information added that is not strictly related to what happened that day. There is ample evidence, both direct and indirect, that the travelers revised their notes on their day-to-day experiences at a later time, or after the journey, shaping them into the form that they desired for circulation or publication. For example, Abū Ṭāleb Khan says that after he returned from his journey he assembled his scattered notes and wrote them up as a book.[5] Mīrzā Ṣāleḥ Šīrāzī, after a very long history of Moscow, St. Petersburg, and Napoleon's invasion of Russia, says that when he reaches England he will try to get more information to add to this description.[6] The same author gives a lengthy and detailed description of England and London in which all the dates are given according to the Christian calendar, filling in a gap in his journal entries between 16 June and 20 September 1818.[7] He gives a similarly detailed history of the Ottoman Empire, with a mixture of Muslim and Christian dates.[8] The dates reflect, no doubt, the nature of his sources. Mīrzā ʿAbd-al-Fattāḥ Garmrūdī, in his account of Moḥammad-Ḥosayn Khan Ājūdānbāšī's travels, describes the Ottoman Empire, Greece, and Italy in a more or less standardized manner,[9] and in his account of their travels in Europe, the journey from Trieste to Vienna is summarized in an efficient way that could only be done after the fact.[10] A major item of evidence for the later revision of raw notes is the reconstructed conversations. All the travelers except Ḥājjī Pīrzāda reconstruct conversations, and Garmrūdī, the actual author of Ājūdānbāšī's travel account, reconstructs both his own and Ājūdānbāšī's conversations. Reconstructed conversations are an important element in the self-presentation of the author, and add an autobiographical note to these otherwise strictly chronological accounts.

Autobiography was not a literary form or cultural practice in pre-modern Persia, and self-revelation was certainly not the aim of the

---

[5] Abū Ṭāleb Khan, *Masīr*, 4-5.

[6] Mīrzā Ṣāleḥ, *Safar-nāma*, 140.

[7] Mīrzā Ṣāleḥ, *Safar-nāma*, 193-260 (England), and 260-319 (London).

[8] Mīrzā Ṣāleḥ, *Safar-nāma*, 375-407.

[9] Garmrūdī, *Šarḥ*, 253-93.

[10] Garmrūdī, *Šarḥ*, 301-6.

travelers in their accounts: The dynamic journal form works powerfully against this. Nevertheless, the nineteenth-century travelers could not help revealing something of themselves, both in the substance of their accounts and in the form. The object of an autobiographer is to take possession of his or her past as a whole and impose some order, and therefore meaning, on it. A strictly chronological journal form, with little reflection on the meaning of events for the life of the writer, makes temporal sequence rather than reflection into a major source of meaning because we tend to interpret temporal sequences as causal ones.[11]

The fact that a modern autobiographer looks back on his or her life from an advanced age, selects material from it, and imposes an order on it ("emplots" it in Hayden White's terms)[12] makes autobiography share some of the formal qualities of fiction. This suggests that when the Persian travelers attempt to reconstruct conversations that they had engaged in during their travels, they were unconsciously taking a modest step in the direction of autobiography. This is because a reconstructed conversation can reveal something of the personality of the speaker. Out of all the conversations that a traveler had during the course of his travels, only certain ones are selected for reporting in the travel account. These conversations are chosen with a definite purpose in mind, are reconstructed in carefully thought-out ways, and inserted in specific places, to produce the effect that the author desires. What seems to have been their attempt to give texture and verisimilitude to their accounts also adds an autobiographical note to the travel narratives. Īlčī, for example, delights in quoting witty remarks that he made to entertain English women,[13] and Garmrūdī, in presenting his superior's eloquent and pithy replies to questions, reconstructs only conversations that present Ājūdānbāšī in the best possible light and

---

[11] See John Sturrock, "The New Model Autobiographer," *New Literary History* 9/1(1977):51-63.

[12] See Hayden White, *Metahistory* (Baltimore, 1973), "Introduction," esp. 7-11.

[13] Īlčī, *Ḥayrat-nāma*, passim. The original manuscript by Abu'l-Ḥasan Īlčī has been lost but copies exist in the K̲odā Bakš Library in Patna, the British Library, and elsewhere. The editor of the Persian text worked from a copy of the original now held in the Senate Library in Tehran, consulting no others. In addition to normalizing the author's spellings, the editor bowdlerized the text; in more than twenty places he has indicated in footnotes that sections ranging from a few words to a whole page have been omitted so as not to offend public taste and values.

that show him doing his job efficiently. Ḥājjī Pīrzāda does not reconstruct conversations, and this, no doubt, has to do with his personality.

The question of reconstructed conversations is also significant from another point of view. Most of the conversations that we read in the travel accounts sound unnatural because they are couched in the literary language of reported speech rather than the more informal language of direct speech. An example of this sort would be Mīrzā Ṣāleḥ Šīrāzī's conversations early in his account when he is deciding whether or not to accept the government's offer to be sent to Europe to study. He replies to a question of Āqā Esmāʿīl Tājer Borūjerdī in these words:[14]

در اینکه امورات سر نوشت قضارا آنچه باید و شاید در عالم کون و فساد
قادر ازلی مقرر کرده است، حرفی نداری.

Soon after this he says:

افسوس است از تو، اولا در هر سرزمین ملاحظه اشجار و انهار و کوهسار
و چمن و صحرا و براری، بالاخره هر آنچه از مخلوقات منظور میاید،
دلالت بر این میکند که صانع ازلي یکی است و در هر جا صنعت او بدون
تفاوت، به کار رفته و فیضان فیض او در دور و نزدیک رسیده، قطع نظر
از آن، الطرق الی الله بعدد انفاس الخلایق، بجای خود است.

and continues thus for eight more lines.[15] Īlčī, always at pains to present himself as witty and cultivated, asks in these terms about the affliction of gout during a conversation at Lord Camden's:

سبب زیادتی این مرض چیست؟ که اکثر از پیر و جوان و مردان و زنان به
این بلا مبتلایند؟

being careful to express himself in rhymed and assonant prose.[16] In this case, it seems unlikely that he would have tried so hard to be

---

[14] I have inserted the following three examples in the Persian script in order to illustrate to specialists the literary style of the time and to emphasize stylistic features such as diction, parallel synonyms, rhyming sequences, assonance, and common rhetorical devices. Such features cannot be adequately rendered into English and consequently the intended effects would be entirely lost in translation.

[15] Mīrzā Ṣāleḥ, *Safar-nāma*, 43-44.

[16] Īlčī, *Ḥayrat-nāma*, 233.

elegant when he had to communicate through an interpreter at all times. The problem that these writers faced was that no language or set of conventions had yet been created to render direct speech in written form. Progress in this direction had been made much earlier by the popular storytellers who related tales such as *Samak-e ʿAyyār*. These stories were probably written down by the storyteller or at his dictation and would reflect many aspects of oral style. They were not, however, often read by the educated individuals of the class that traveled abroad and wrote accounts of their journeys, and even if they had been, they would not have been considered models for creating narratives that included conversations. In fact, the nineteenth-century Persian travelers had no way of knowing that one could reproduce direct speech in a literary text, and this technique was not developed until Moḥammad-ʿAlī Jamālzāda and, a decade later, Ṣādeq Hedāyat and Bozorg ʿAlavī laid the foundations of a language of prose fiction in Persian. In any case, the reconstructed conversations are a formal element common to almost all the travel accounts and can be thought of as a generic marker.

It can be said about travel accounts in general that some are dynamic narratives and some are static. The difference lies in the relative proportions of description and reflection that the authors present. A dynamic account would be a description of the journey, moving from day to day or event to event with little or no reflection on the meaning of the experiences to the author. A static account would consist of the traveler's reflections on his travels, on humankind, and on the ways of the world, focusing largely on these matters rather than on the day-to-day mechanics of travel. All the travel accounts under discussion are, to varying degrees, dynamic rather than static narratives.

One factor that seems connected with the dynamic or static quality of the narrative is whether or not the traveler reveals explicitly a reason for writing his account. Some of the Persian travelers say clearly why they are writing theirs. Abū Ṭāleb Khan tells us that he decided to write his travel account in order to reveal to Muslims the wonders of the seas and the amazing sights of foreign lands that might not have come to their attention, to give them pleasure in learning about new things, and to stimulate others to seek them out.[17] Farhād Mīrzā wrote his travel book to be a guide to others making the pilgrimage to Mecca and Medina.[18] Īlčī says that he decided to write about his experiences in the form of a journal (*rūz-nāmča*) so that it would be useful to others traveling these same ways later, and that because of the many wonders

---

[17] Abū Ṭāleb Khan, *Masīr*, 4.

[18] Farhād Mīrzā, *Safar-nāma*, 13.

and countless novelties described therein, he would call it *Ḥayrat-nāma*.[19] Others simply begin their accounts with their departure from home and end them with their return. While it would be difficult to prove conclusively, it seems that the authors who say why they are writing their accounts reveal a more conscious didactic purpose and include less reflection or comment on the experience of travel (and therefore their narratives are more dynamic) than those who simply present us with journals. Whether or not the authors state their reasons for writing, all these accounts have an implicit didactic purpose which is to be useful to others who would travel after them by giving as much information as possible about, first, the "mechanics" of travel (i.e., distances between points, the condition of the roads, types of conveyances available, the quality of the lodgings, official formalities required along the way, and the like) and, second, the amazing or disturbing sights witnessed by the traveler. These are admirable purposes and are still being fulfilled by travel books today, the first by travel guides and the second by travelers' accounts.

The information that the Persian travelers present ranges from the encyclopedic to the autobiographical. Common to all are notes on the towns through which they pass, the officials they meet, and the difficulties of the road. Most travelers mention repetitive daily actions such as getting up, washing, praying, and eating. The most encyclopedic narrative of all is probably that of Mīrzā Ṣāleḥ, who, as we have seen, provides the reader with long historical accounts of European countries, obviously taken from both Western and Muslim books. Farhād Mīrzā seeks to provide the reader with precise, guide-book-style information such as the direction of travel by the compass, distances between points, the owners of the land through which he traveled, the names of local officials, the tonnage of vessels on which he sailed, the builders of bridges over which he passed, other items of geographical interest, exact times departure and arrival, philological notes (including the pronunciation of words),[20] and much more. Some time after the first printing of his book, the author added two short addenda in order to clarify certain matters that he had discussed in his account of his pilgrimage.[21] At the other end of the scale, Ḥājjī Pīrzāda gives very little information beyond what he actually observed. Nevertheless, he is an excellent observer and seems to have quite a

---

[19] Īlčī, *Ḥayrat-nāma*, 47-48.

[20] See Farhād Mīrzā, *Safar-nāma*, 26 for his notes on what steam vessels are called in Russian and French.

[21] Farhād Mīrzā, *Safar-nāma*, 355-59.

different idea from the other travelers of how to make his book interesting and useful. Ḥājjī Pīrzāda describes what interests him rather than providing a measure of dry, practical information that he thinks will be useful to future readers. While traveling through Fārs in the Iranian section of his itinerary, he describes many aspects of the natural scene around him. Varieties of trees, flowers, and fruit are all of interest to him, and his descriptions of some of the great gardens of Shiraz are written with real feeling. He has an eye for the unusual and bizarre, such as a servant falling from a horse and breaking a leg, or a horse becoming stuck in the mud of a river bottom near Qom.[22] One thing that he cannot seem to let pass without comment is a good meal, and on many occasions he mentions, and sometimes describes, the food.[23] As with other elements of these travel narratives, the quantity and nature of the information that the traveler gives us depends, to some degree, on his personality.

Other forces work to determine the generic nature of these narratives as well, and a powerful one is the influence of the literary tradition. All of these travelers were of the educated elite and had been well schooled in the Persian literary tradition. It is not surprising that this tradition helped shape their style of presentation in more than one way. For example, Īlčī, after invoking the Prophet, begins with a conventional opening phrase characteristic of storytellers: "Let it not remain hidden from the travelers of the age and the experienced and worldly-wise that Abu'l-Ḥasan, insignificant and entirely deficient, by order of ...."[24] This beginning seems appropriate for a travel account entitled *Ḥayrat-nāma*, and suggests that Īlčī had a sense of literary history. It also suggests that if the veracity of his account is not authenticated by other means, Īlčī's own authority by virtue of his position will be sufficient for the purpose.

Īlčī has a good sense of style, but it escapes from his control at times and betrays that he was subject to that bane of all writers, inconsistency. A little later in his narrative, as he is detailing his reasons and purposes for writing his *Ḥayrat-nāma*, he warns the reader not to expect his text to be adorned with piquant, rhythmical phrases and colorful images because his purpose is to report events, not engage in

---

[22] Ḥājjī Pīrzāda, *Safar-nāma*, 5, 6.

[23] E.g., on p. 21 he says: "That evening Ostād Ḥosayn, the cook from Tehran, cooked a very good *polow*, which we ate."

[24] Īlčī, *Ḥayrat-nāma*, 47: "*bar sayyāḥān-e rūzegār va jahān dīdegān-e tajroba-kār pušīda namānad, ke ḥaqīr-e sarāpā taqṣīr Abu'l-Ḥasan ... be ... amr-e....*"

word-play and elegant writing. The very next sentence, however, in which he asks the reader to be gracious enough to correct his errors, is written in a high literary style characteristic of the prose of his time.[25] Īlčī lapses frequently into lyrical descriptions of sights that charm him, violating his promise not to give us rhythmical phrases and elegant writing.[26] What this stylistic inconsistency betrays is not so much a lack of skill as a writer (which is not the case), but a reliance on traditional models of narrative and description.

The linear narrative style of the Persian travel accounts, where one event is followed by the next from beginning to end, allows little opportunity for a more sophisticated treatment of narrated time. Temporal sequence is the organizing principle in these accounts. This is not unexpected since there are few models of narrative in classical Persian prose that handle time in a significantly different manner, and those examples that did exist were not part of the canon familiar to these travelers. This refers, again, to the storytellers' romances such as *Samak-e ʿAyyār*, *Fīrūzšāh-nāma*, and others of this genre. These narratives, while basically linear, include many instances of anachrony.[27] With two exceptions, which will be discussed below, the travel narratives display little anachrony beyond an occasional example of prolepsis.[28] As for how the travelers themselves think about handling narrated time, Mīrzā Abū Ṭāleb Khan says that he will record events that he witnessed "*tārīḵ-vār*,"[29] implying that he will present them in the chronological fashion of a book of history. The other travelers do not characterize their method of ordering and recording events, but by calling their books "*rūz-nāma*," "*rūz-nāmča*," or "*daftar*," they imply a narrative of events ordered by linear time.

The exceptions to this rule are the accounts of Abu'l-Ḥasan Khan Īlčī, and of Mīrzā Abū Ṭāleb Khan. At the beginning of the *Ḥayrat-nāma*, Īlčī gives the reader a detailed analysis of the contents of the book, breaking down the narrative by *bāb*, *faṣl*, and *ṭarīq*. The segment of the journey between Constantinople and London is divided into

---

[25] Īlčī, *Ḥayrat-nāma*, 48: "*Motavaqqeʿ az makārem-e ašfāq-e soḵan-sanjān-e ḵazīne-ye maʿālī, va ṣeyrafīyān-e ganj-e nokta-dānī, ān ast ke be moqtażā-ye bozorg-menašī sahv va ḵaṭā-rā be qalam-e eṣlāḥ, moṣleḥ bāšand.*"

[26] An example is the description of a garden on p. 55.

[27] "All forms of discordance between the two temporal orders of story and narrative": Gérard Genette, *Narrative Discourse: An Essay in Method* (Ithaca, 1980), 40.

[28] "Any narrative maneuver that consists of narrating or evoking in advance an event that will take place later." Genette, *Narrative Discourse,* 40.

[29] Abū Ṭāleb Khan, *Masīr*, 4.

two *voqūf*, detailing events on land and those at sea. In each case he summarizes what he will present in each subdivision.[30] In doing this, he is following the familiar model of historians and writers of didactic books such as *Sīar al-molūk* by Neẓām-al-Molk. Nāṣer Ḵosrow did not introduce his *Safar-nāma* with such a summary of what was to follow.

The example of *Masīr-e ṭālebī* is more complicated and more interesting because of the way in which Abū Ṭāleb Khan conceives of his work and the way in which he interacts with the literary tradition.[31] It seems plausible that Abū Ṭāleb Khan thought of his book as we would think of a book today, as an integrated whole, and that he modeled it on a Western travel narrative. It is not known which travel book he might have known, but his way of handling time, of using poetry, and of tying the text together with internal references in the form of prolepsis and analepsis[32] are considerably more sophisticated than any of the later travel narratives considered here. His use of formal devices to unify the text is suggestive of the practice of novelists, and brings to mind Hayden White's ideas on "emplotment" in historical narrative. Abū Ṭāleb Khan is very much the hero of his own narrative, more so, perhaps, than any of the other travel writers including Īlčī. If we can think of him as the hero of his own book, we can also think of his narrative as having a "plot": In other words, he presents his travel narrative more as a "story" than as a simple, chronologically-ordered sequence of events. The nineteenth-century travel narratives developed into a stable genre that changed little over time. It is noteworthy that one of the very earliest travel accounts should also show the greatest literary sophistication. Change came to these, as it did to other Persian literary genres, when the literary and intellectual context in which they were produced began to change profoundly in the twentieth century.

It is worth giving a brief account of what seem to be the most significant features of *Masīr-e ṭālebī* that set it apart from all the other travel accounts. In the beginning of the book, Abū Ṭāleb Khan gives a brief hint of the factors that led him to make his journey and write this account of it. This is followed by what he

---

[30] Īlčī, *Ḥayrat-nāma*, 48-50.

[31] For a discussion of Abū Ṭāleb's life and relations with the British, see Juan R. I. Cole, "Invisible Occidentalism: Eighteenth-Century Indo-Persian Constructions of the West," *Iranian Studies* 25(1992):3-16.

[32] "Any evocation after the fact of an event that took place earlier than the point in the story where we are at any given moment." Genette, *Narrative Discourse*, 40.

calls a "*ğazal*" (a short lyric poem) which gives, in fact, an itinerary of his travels and includes at the end, in addition to his pen name "Ṭāleb," phrases in French and English.[33] Then follow his reasons for writing the book (as noted above), and then thirteen lines from a thousand-line *masnavī* that he wrote describing London. This short section is inserted here to support his claim that his book will be worth reading even by those who are reluctant to read anything because of the difficulties of making a living, or because of laziness and indifference. This is followed by more biographical information, more lines from the *masnavī* on London, and a six-line *qeṭʿa* (another short poetic form) containing a chronogram giving his father's date of death.[34] In the space of five pages, Abū Ṭāleb Khan has employed a prolepsis by introducing a poem written to describe a place which he has not yet reached in his narrative of travel, employed an analepsis by mentioning at some length the death of his father, and used poetry not merely to embellish his prose narrative but actually to forward its progress. Another example of this use of poetry is where he quotes a *qeṭʿa* of thirty-eight lines (written later in London) describing the kindnesses of his hosts in Ireland, which he says better expresses his meaning than would prose, which would go on too long.[35] While the use of poetry in didactic prose narratives is a familiar strategy in premodern literature, it is quite rare that poetry is used to advance the progress of the narrative by providing information not contained in the surrounding prose. There are numerous instances of this unusual use of poetry throughout *Masīr-e ṭālebī*.

Abū Ṭāleb Khan varies his narrative with prolepses too. During his description of his stop in Cape Town, he says:

> Without a semblance of doubt, after seeing this city, the excellent qualities of the city and the greatness of the buildings of Calcutta, which is renowned in Hindustan, were completely obliterated from my mind. And this obliterating of the earlier by viewing the later continued throughout this trip until I entered London, for after reaching Ireland and seeing Cork, I could remember nothing of Cape Town. When I reached Dublin, the capital of Ireland, the splendor of Cork faded from my mind, and likewise for Dublin after I saw London.[36]

---

[33] Abū Ṭāleb Khan, *Masīr*, 3-4.

[34] Abū Ṭāleb Khan, *Masīr*, 6-7.

[35] Abū Ṭāleb Khan, *Masīr*, 94-96.

[36] Abū Ṭāleb Khan, *Masīr*, 33.

Again, while in Ireland, he quotes a *ḡazal* that he wrote later in London and sent back to one of his Irish hostesses.[37] Later, while in London, he says: "The rest of the events will be described in lines to follow. I will now tell you about ...."[38]

In addition to manipulating the narrated time, Abū Ṭāleb Khan uses other formal means to give variety to his book. For example, he often inserts amusing anecdotes which he calls *laṭīfa*, sometimes laughing at himself and sometimes reporting on events. Longer anecdotes called *ḥekāyat* appear at frequent intervals. He will often pause to praise people, or food, or public buildings that have impressed him, thus slowing the forward movement of the narrative and making known his personal feelings. For example, he quotes the first line of a *maṯnavī* that he wrote about a certain Miss Barol (?) while visiting Henley.[39] Finally, at the beginning of Book II, he gives a recapitulation of what has gone before and preview of what is to come.[40]

Abū Ṭāleb Khan interacts with his literary tradition in a familiar way by using a great deal of poetry in his narrative. Most of it he wrote himself, but he also quotes well-known classical poets. Some of this poetry, as noted above, furthers the narrative progress, and some plays its more usual role of confirming or embellishing his points. He also seems to have thought carefully about his audience and concluded, reasonably, that they would be Persian-readers of India. What suggests this is his description of the tile-work on the tombs and shrines in Kāẓemayn, which he visited on his return to India. In the shrine city, he sees such tile-work for the first time and says that it does not exist in India or Europe. He describes the inscriptions and forms done in tile with great enthusiasm, sights that probably would have been familiar to many Iranians.[41] In sum, Abū Ṭāleb Khan's travel narrative is distinct and unique among the texts under consideration here, and it suggests that the author had a Western model in mind when writing it.

While, as mentioned earlier, the Persian travel narratives cannot plausibly be thought of as a special case of autobiography, this is not to say that the authors reveal nothing of themselves in their books. The matter of their self-presentation, what we learn of the authors as persons, will form the last part of this chapter. With all the travelers (possibly excepting Abū Ṭāleb Khan), their sense of self seems to be

[37] Abū Ṭāleb Khan, *Masīr*, 71.

[38] Abū Ṭāleb Khan, *Masīr*, 108.

[39] Abū Ṭāleb Khan, *Masīr*, 142.

[40] Abū Ṭāleb Khan, *Masīr*, 181.

[41] Abū Ṭāleb Khan, *Masīr*, 400-401.

closely tied to their sense of place.[42] In all cases, the place is Iran. One could say, in Eric Leed's terms, that for the Persian travelers self and place are thoroughly integrated realities. All the travelers studied here (except for Abū Ṭāleb Khan, who traveled on his own, and Farhād Mīrzā, who did not leave the Islamic world) were abroad in foreign lands on official business or under official auspices. They were not, like the modern, voluntary traveler, leaving home purposely to explore the unknown (even if that means going only from America to England) and to define him- or herself with the experience of travel. In reading modern travel accounts, one has the impression that the traveler's sense of self and place are not closely integrated and that the traveler welcomes, even seeks out, the opportunity to change the sense of self or to redefine his identity along with experiencing a new place. This attitude toward the portrayal of experience is elucidated by a modern critic in a discussion of James Joyce:

> He [i.e., James Joyce] became ... increasingly conscious of the paradox at the heart of the mimetic enterprise—that since the objective world must be represented, as it is experienced, through the prism of some individual consciousness, the artist seeking fidelity to fact must represent both simultaneously, must turn inward as well as outward. The quest for objectivity becomes the study of subjectivity, or rather the study of how the two interact.[43]

Although the Persian travelers had actually to leave Iran, they tried their best not to be too far from it in other ways. Whenever they landed in a new city they sought out, or were met by, the leaders of the local Persian merchant community. If they had friends or acquaintances there, they also looked them up, and it was usually the local Iranians who showed the visitor around and from whom the visitor received not only practical help but an introduction to the foreign city itself. In this way their reactions to the unfamiliar were, to some extent, guided by the attitude of their hosts. Īlčī notes that it is the habit of foreigners to walk around (*sayr*) places (in order to see the sights), implying that it is not the habit of Persians to do that.[44] We rarely read of a Persian traveler in a foreign city "going sightseeing" on his own: They always

---

[42] See Eric Leed, *The Mind of the Traveler: From Gilgamesh to Global Tourism* (New York, 1991), 11, for a discussion of this point in a different context.

[43] John Gordon, *Finnegans Wake: A Plot Summary* (Dublin, 1986), 1-2.

[44] Īlčī, *Ḥayrat-nāma*, 51.

go out with companions and are usually guided by resident Persians who know the ropes. By avoiding, as much as possible, the need to cope personally and alone with the unknown, the traveler avoids a direct challenge to his identity, and his sense of self is not perceptibly altered as a result of travel but remains strongly rooted, as always, in his sense of place. While the modern Western traveler writes about the pleasures of travel itself, the Persian travelers experience the unknown in a more controlled manner.[45]

The two greatest challenges that the Persian travelers had to face, and those which uniformly inspired them to write eloquent descriptions in their narratives, were storms at sea and the conduct of European women. These seem to represent the extremes to which Persians could be physically and morally challenged. Regarding the difficulties of travel, Leed says: "The sufferings of travel constitute a simplification of life that enhances the objectivity of a world within which the traveler becomes aware of an irreducible subjectivity, a self," and these two great challenges clearly highlighted in the Persian travelers the effect that Leed describes.[46] Travel within the Middle East was probably more physically difficult than was travel in Europe: the Persians all praise the means and facilities available to the traveler in Europe. When the traveler left Islamic lands and ventured into the Christian lands of Europe, however, the real challenges began. The Persian travelers met the physical problems of European travel well, but beside certain specific problems of locale such as the food and barriers of language, the Christian lands presented a moral challenge that was more difficult to deal with. It is this moral challenge that forced the traveler either to reaffirm his identity and his self image or run serious risks to his reputation.[47]

Persians in the nineteenth century were, with few exceptions, not a seafaring people, yet every traveler had to take to the water for some

---

[45] By all accounts, there were few pleasures of travel in any case. Many of the narratives begin with a freshness and excitement as the party moves out of Tabrīz in springtime and passes through the lush countryside of Azerbaijan. This excitement soon fades, though, when the first rains begin and the road through the mountains becomes rough and difficult. While the modern traveler often seems to enjoy the difficulties of travel as a sort of test of will, and may interpret them as such, our Persian travelers put up with the hardships of the road as simply part of the process of reaching their destination.

[46] Leed, *Mind of the Traveler*, 10.

[47] And, one might add, risk having his travel account bowdlerized by later editors, as is the case with the unfortunate Īlčī.

part of his journey to Europe. In almost every case they experienced a bad storm during the voyage, became very seasick and terrified, were convinced that the ship would sink and they would all perish, and wrote about the experience with strong feeling.[48] Their unfamiliarity with the sea and ships quite naturally produced great fear and stress during a storm, and the experience of liminality that they all felt stretched their sense of physical self to its limits. Here, indeed, we see Leed's "irreducible subjectivity" most clearly.

The descriptions of European women, especially of how they dressed for parties and balls and how they interacted with men (including Persian men) are almost as eloquent as the descriptions of storms at sea. Almost, because the challenge in this case was moral: How should the traveler behave in the presence of women of high status and unchallengeable reputation who behave in ways that most Persian men profoundly disapproved of? Even more difficult was how to write about this. The written reactions to the moral challenge range from that of Īlčī, who seems to have thrown himself into English social life with gusto, to Farhād Mīrzā (who did not actually go to Europe but who saw all he needed to see of the public behavior of upper-class Egyptian women) and Ḥājjī Pīrzāda, who condemned women's behavior in thundering terms. To write about these women involved a risk to the traveler's identity and public image. In the case of a storm at sea, one could safely reveal one's deepest feelings of fear and discomfort in plain language. There were no narrative models to fall back on, and the travelers' words perforce reveal their inner feelings unmediated by the conventions of the literary tradition. In describing European women, there is always a tension between what most of the Persian men instinctively felt to be erotic and alluring, and how they could describe their reactions in writing without compromising their public image or violating taboos against mentioning certain subjects in writing.[49] Īlčī had the least difficulty: he readily took to English social life and wrote of how he enjoyed drinking wine, flirting with attractive women (whom he often compared with houris of paradise), and even tells us that he fell in love with one of them.[50] At the other end of the

---

[48] Particularly striking descriptions of storms at sea are given by Ḥājjī Pīrzāda, *Safar-nāma*, 172-74, and Amīn-al-Dawla, *Safar-nāma*, 85-89.

[49] For a discussion of such taboos, see Paul Sprachman, *Suppressed Persian: An Anthology of Forbidden Literature* (Costa Mesa, Calif., 1995).

[50] One must learn this from the English translation of his *Ḥayrat-nāma*, as it has been expunged from the Persian edition. At one point he says to Sir Gore Ouseley: "As God is my witness I wish the women of Iran could be

scale, Farhād Mīrzā severely condemns upper-class Egyptian women who go about the streets dressed like European women. In an exchange with his guide in Cairo, who reported that the offending women were the daughters of ʿAlī Pasha, son of Šarīf Pasha, Farhād Mīrzā says: "I scolded him severely saying that this behavior is completely at odds with Islam. Embarrassed, he replied, 'Our country is free.' I said, 'Who said that there is freedom in Islam? What freedom is it that I must brave the dangers of the seas to travel to Mecca? What freedom is it that one must fast for a month and pray five times [a day], and so on?'"[51] His observations on freedom are oddly echoed by Ḥājjī Pīrzāda when he comments negatively on the claims of freedom made by Parisians.

Ḥājjī Pīrzāda is an acute observer who is able to depict what he sees in an objective manner, in simple Persian. He observes life around him in Paris, describing the behavior and dress of women in great detail. He, like all the other travelers, is fascinated by low-cut ball gowns that expose a woman's neck, shoulders, chest, and arms. He also observes how women behave on the streets and in other public places. Nevertheless, he is very disturbed by all this, and every so often his moral outrage bursts through (or is inserted into) his objective account. An excellent example of this is when he condemns in the most eloquent terms what he (mis-)understands to be Parisian life.[52] "In all of Paris," he says, "religion and faith and piety and spirituality and sanctity and truth and humanity and dignity and reputation and manliness and masculinity and honor emphatically are not to be found."[53] He thunders on in this vein for some time and then returns to a pleasant description of the Bois de Boulogne.

Writing for a Persian audience, the Persian travelers present themselves as firmly rooted in their place, Iran. Īlčī either did not care what people thought or did not intend his travel account to be published. Abū Ṭāleb Khan also enjoyed Western social life but visited the major

---

more like the women of England. Iranian women are chaste because they are forced to be—they are shut away from men; but English women are chaste by choice." Abu'l-Ḥasan Khan Īlčī, *Ḥayrat-nāma*, ed. and tr. Margaret Cloake as *A Persian at the Court of King George* (London, 1988), 135. For allusions to his falling in love, see 100, 104, 158, 172. The translator worked from a manuscript copy of the text belonging to a direct descendant of Abu'l-Ḥasan Khan and another copy in private hands (pp. 9-10).

[51] Farhād Mīrzā, *Safar-nāma*, 111.

[52] Ḥājjī Pīrzāda, *Safar-nāma*, 247-49.

[53] Ḥājjī Pīrzāda, *Safar-nāma*, 286-87.

Shiʿite shrines on the way home and expressed his repentance in a *qaṣīda* for what he might have done in Europe.[54] The rest of the travelers firmly resist any assimilation to European ways, while at the same time admiring certain aspects of European material progress. The challenges of travel, both physical and moral, served to confirm their sense of self rather than alter it. Even the pleasure-loving Īlčī observes the implicit boundaries that Persians erect around themselves and resorts to traditional images and modes of description when discussing his feelings about English women. This distancing, so characteristic of *ġazal* poetry, depersonalizes the description of persons and emotions that, if stated in plain language (as are descriptions of storms at sea), could transgress the implicit boundaries and openly reveal an inner life that social convention requires remain private. One can turn a blind eye to certain kinds of behavior, but one cannot ignore the written expression of emotions or descriptions of experience that should not be depicted in plain language.

To conclude, there are thus many reasons for believing that nineteenth-century Persian travel narratives form a discrete genre that can be identified by elements of inner and outer form. The generic markers that apply are as follows: They are prose accounts written in the first person. The subject matter is the actual travel experiences of the author. The mode is narrative with a small mixture of the dramatic. They are organized in the form of a journal, i.e., the narrative content is subdivided by days where the date and often the day of the week are specified. They all have an explicitly didactic purpose. The content is presented in a dynamic manner, with little reflection or interpretation. They contain reconstructed conversations that add texture and interest to the prose and unconsciously reveal something of the attitudes and personality of the authors. Their literary style can be said to be educated but relatively simple, with occasional lapses into high style. They all contain poetry in varying amount, some by the author and some quoted from earlier classical poets. They all assert Persian cultural and religious values. They are all of an appropriate size, neither too short to convey the information intended nor so prolix as to be boring. The final point in favor of my claim for the existence of this genre is the fact that there has been at least one fictional imitation of it. The *Sīāḥat-nāma-ye Ebrāhīm Beyg* by Zayn-al-ʿĀbedīn Marāġaʾī includes almost all the generic markers noted above, but it is not the account of a real journey.

---

[54] Abū Ṭāleb Khan, *Masīr*, 419-20.

Most of these generic markers will be found in all of the travel accounts, but there might be no single one that would contain them all. At the present state of our knowledge, this genre appears to be limited to more or less the nineteenth and twentieth centuries. Generic boundaries are flexible, though, and as hitherto unpublished travel accounts appear in print we might see the time frame of the genre extend backwards or even forwards, although the latter seems less likely.

BIBLIOGRAPHY

Persian Sources

Abū Ṭāleb Khan, Mīrzā. *Masīr-e ṭālebī*. Edited by Ḥosayn Ḵadīv-jam. Tehran, 1352 Š./1973.

Amīn-al-Dawla, Mīrzā ʿAlī Khan. *Safar-nāma*. Edited by Eslām Kāẓemīya. Tehran, 1354 Š./1975.

Āryanpūr, ʿAbbās. *Az Ṣabā tā Nīmā*. 2 vols. Tehran, 1350 Š./1971.

Ašraf, Aḥmad. "Tārīḵ, ḵāṭera, afsāna." *Īrān-nāma* 14:4(1996):525-38.

Farhād Mīrzā. *Safar-nāma*. Edited by Ḡolām Reżā Ṭābāṭabāʾī. Tehran, 1366 Š./1987.

Garmrūdī, ʿAbd-al-Fattāḥ. *Šarḥ-e maʾmūriyat-e Ājūdānbāšī*. Edited by Moḥammad Moširī. Tehran, 2536=1356 Š./1977.

Ḥājjī Pīrzāda. *Safar-nāma*. Edited by Ḥāfeẓ Farmānfarmāʾīān. Vol. 1. Tehran, 1342 Š./1963.

Īlčī, Abū'l-Ḥasan Khan. *Ḥayrat-nāma*. Edited by Ḥasan Morselvand. Tehran, 1364 Š./1985.

—. *A Persian at the Court of King George, 1809-10*. Edited and translated by Margaret M. Cloake. London, 1988.

Marāḡaʾī, Zayn-al-ʿĀbedīn. *Sīāḥat-nāma-ye Ebrāhīm Beyg*. Edited by Bāqer Moʾmenī. Vol. 1. Tehran, 2537=1357 Š./1978.

Reżāqolī Mīrzā. *Safar-nāma*. Edited by Aṣḡar Farmānfarmāʾī Qājār. Tehran, 1346 Š./1967.

Sayyāḥ, Moḥammad ʿAlī. *Safar-nāma*. Edited by ʿAlī Dehbāšī. Tehran, 1363 Š./1984.

Šīrāzī, Mīrzā Ṣāleḥ. *Safar-nāma*. Edited by Esmāʿīl Rāʾīn. Tehran, 1347 Š./1968.

—. *Gozāreš-e safar*. Edited by Homāyūn Šahīdī. Tehran, 1362 Š./1983.

—. *Safar-nāma*. Edited by Ḡolām-Ḥosayn Mīrzā Ṣāleḥ. Tehran, 1364 Š./1985.

Yūsofī, Ḡolām-Ḥosayn. *Dīdār-ī bā ahl-e qalam*. Tehran, 1355 Š./1976.

Western Sources

Adams, Percy G. *Travel Literature and the Evolution of the Novel*. Lexington, Kentucky, 1983.

Batten, Charles L. *Pleasurable Instruction: Form and Convention in Eighteenth-Century Travel Literature*. Berkeley, Calif., 1978.

Braaksma, M. H. *Travel and Literature*. Groningen, 1938.

Brown, Sharon Rogers. *American Travel Narratives as a Literary Genre*. Lewiston, Maine, 1993.

Cole, Juan R. I. "Invisible Occidentalism: Eighteenth-Century Indo-Persian Constructions of the West." *Iranian Studies* 25(1992):3-16.

Eickelman, Dale F., and James Piscatori, eds. *Muslim Travelers*. Berkeley, Calif., 1990.

Fowler, Alastair. *Kinds of Literature: An Introduction to the Theory of Genres and Modes*. Oxford, 1982.

Genette, Gérard. *Narrative Discourse: An Essay in Method*. Translated by J. E. Lewin. Ithaca, N. Y., 1980.

Ghanoonparvar, M. R. *In a Persian Mirror*. Austin, Tex., 1993.

Gordon, John. *Finnegans Wake: A Plot Summary*. Dublin, 1986.

Gunn, Janet V. *Autobiography: Toward a Poetics of Experience*. Philadelphia, 1982.

Leed, Eric J. *The Mind of the Traveler: From Gilgamesh to Global Tourism*. New York, 1991.

Les Récits de voyage. Paris, 1986.

Pascal, Roy. *Design and Truth in Autobiography*. Cambridge, Mass., 1960.

Sprachman, Paul. *Suppressed Persian: An Anthology of Forbidden Literature*. Costa Mesa, Calif., 1995.

Sturrock, John. "The New Model Autobiographer." *New Literary History* 9(1977):51-63.

Tavakoli-Targhi, Mohammad. "Imaging Western Women: Occidentalism and Euro-eroticism." *Radical America* 24/3(1993): 73-87.

Wellek, René, and Austin Warren. *Theory of Literature*. 3rd edition. New York, 1956.

Ḥājj Moḥammad-Ḥasan Amīn-al-Żarb: Visionary, Entrepreneur, and Traveler

Shireen Mahdavi

The subject of this article is the travels undertaken by Ḥājj Moḥammad-Ḥasan Amīn-al-Żarb, the first major Iranian entrepreneur. These travels are of particular interest since they were carried out for business purposes, unlike those of other contemporary Iranian travelers to Europe who went for pleasure as tourists.

Ḥājj Moḥammad-Ḥasan Amīn-al-Żarb was a self-made man whose father, also a merchant, had suffered bankruptcy. He came to Tehran from Isfahan in the mid-nineteenth century with only a cloak (*ʿaba*) on his back and a hundred rials of money in his pocket.[1] By 1863, he had begun the most extensive commercial enterprise in Iran and subsequently became the richest and most influential merchant in the country. He had agents in all the main towns of Persia and Europe with correspondents in Asia and America. He provided important luxury items for Nāṣer-al-Dīn Shah, the royal family and the aristocracy, and carried out all foreigners' transactions within the country, especially those of the diplomatic community. Simultaneously he invested capital in industry, importing glass, china, silk reeling, and other factories from Europe. Moreover, he was engaged in agricultural and mining projects, having in addition constructed a railway line on the Caspian Sea. He was also appointed master of the mint, hence the title Amīn-al-Żarb, and for all intents and purposes was personal banker to the shah.[2]

---

[1] The *ʿaba* is a traditional Persian cloak. The rial is a unit of currency which in the Qajar period was the equivalent of the *qerān*, ten of which made up a toman, which in 1839 was worth ten shillings and in 1891 worth five shillings. See Charles Issawi, ed., *The Economic History of Iran 1800-1914* (Chicago, 1971), 348-56.

[2] For details of his life and further bibliographical references see Shireen Mahdavi, "Haj Muhammad Hosein Amin al-Zarb and His World: A Case Study

Amīn-al-Żarb traveled extensively during his life. His first journey was from Isfahan to Kermān, where he went as a youth looking for his father, who had gone to Kermān on business, leaving the family without news of him, only to discover that he was dead. His second journey was from Isfahan to Tehran where he went to make his fortune. During his early years in Tehran, when he was consolidating his business, he traveled internally regularly and most frequently to Tabrīz, which was the most important commercial city in Iran. However, he did not undertake a major journey until 1863.

The year 1863 must be considered a momentous year for Amīn-al-Żarb. It was the year in which his commercial success took off, the year when he undertook the holy pilgrimage to Mecca (*ḥajj*/hajj), the year in which he married, and the year in which he and his family moved to the large house in which his son was born and in which he lived to the end of his days. It was the year in which he was finally established.

There are no direct accounts of Amīn-al-Żarb's hajj journey, and the only material available in the family archives are references made by him after his return. However, his experience must have been similar to others who undertook the journey and left accounts.[3] When Amīn-al-Żarb embarked on his journey to perform the hajj in Mecca, it was the first time that he had stepped outside the boundaries of his own country. The journey was long and arduous but provided new experiences both in the countries crossed en route and the means of transportation. There were still no roads suitable for carriages in Persia at this time. So the sight of roads paved with stones on which carriages traveled, post houses where horses were changed and accommodations offered, and above all railways and railway stations were a total novelty. But according to later references, it was the power of the

---

of Social Mobility in Qajar Iran" (Ph.D. diss., University of London, 1996); idem, *For God, Mammon, and Country: A Nineteenth-Century Persian Merchant* (Boulder, Colo., 1999).

[3] A number of *safar-nāma*s describing contemporary accounts of the *ḥajj* journey; they include: Nāyeb-al-Ṣadr Šīrāzī, *Toḥfat al-ḥaramayn: Safar-nāma-ye Nāyeb-al-Ṣadr Šīrāzī dar zīārat-e Makka va sīāḥat-e Īrān va Hend* (Tehran, 1362 Š./1983); Ḥājj Mīrzā ʿAlī Khan Amīn-al-Dawla, *Safar-nāma-ye Amīn-al-Dawla*, ed. Eslām Kāẓemīya (Tehran, 1354 Š./1975); Mīrzā Moḥammad-Ḥosayn Farāhānī, *Safar-nāma*, ed. Ḥāfeẓ Farmānfarmāʾīān (Tehran, 1342 Š./1964), tr. by Hafez Farmayan and Elton L. Daniel as *A Shiʿite Pilgrimage to Mecca 1885-1886* (Austin, Tex., 1990); and Sayf-al-Dawla Solṭān-Moḥammad, *Safar-nāma-ye Makka*, ed. ʿAlī-Akbar Ḵodāparast (Tehran, 1364 Š./1985).

steam engine with which Amīn-al-Żarb became fascinated since he saw its various uses in Egypt and, according to the register of his letters for the year 1287/1870-71, time after time he mentioned the power of steam engines and ordered both a steam tractor and a steam pump.[4] On that subject, he writes to his brother Ḥājj Abu'l-Qāsem Malek-al-Tojjār in Istanbul:

> The other matter is that if it were possible for you to buy a steam machine (*vāpūr*) which plows the earth and send it to Iran, it would be a good thing. Even if one sells it at cost, it does not matter, as it will be of use to the Believers. People will see it and want it. The lives of thousands of animals will be saved.[5]

It must have also been as a result of the influence of his hajj trip that in 1287/1878-79 he wrote a letter to the shah proposing the formation of a national bank in which once again he refers to the power of steam:

> They [the Europeans] thought of building steamships. A few of them gathered together and built [them] and operated them. When they saw that there is profit in it, they built railways and telegraph lines. [Then] they turned to building factories for silk reeling, sugar making, crystal producing, brocade and felt making; to such an extent that finally they supplied all the needs of the people with steam factories.[6]

Amīn-al-Żarb's letter to the shah did not result in the formation of a national bank with the capital of which factories could be built. But

---

[4] See the Mahdavī Archives (Tehran), register of copies of letters for the year 1287/1870-71, from Ḥājj Moḥammad-Ḥasan in Tehran to his brother Ḥājj Abu'l-Qāsem in Istanbul. The author of this article is deeply grateful to Dr. Aṣğar Mahdavī for putting at her disposal material from the Mahdavī Archives. For a detailed description of the Mahdavī Archives see Aṣğar Mahdavī, "The Significance of Private Archives for the Study of the Economic and Social History of Iran in the Late Qajar Period," *Iranian Studies* 16(1983):243-78. The documents in this archive are not systematically classified for citation.

[5] Mahdavī Archives, register of letters, 5 Rajab 1287/1 October 1870. The letter uses the word *vāpūr*, which literally means a steamboat. The term "Believers" is a euphemism for Muslims.

[6] National Bank of Iran, *Tārīḵ-e sī sāla-ye Bank-e Mellī-ye Īrān* (Tehran, 1959), 65-74.

Amīn-al-Żarb's fascination with the steam engine was instrumental for his own entry into the industrial field. It started with the importation of machinery for a silk-reeling factory in 1302/1884 and continued in 1303/1885 by obtaining from the shah the concession for an iron smelting foundry accompanied by other mining concessions in Nāyej in Māzandarān. Documents show that at the time of obtaining the concession Amīn-al-Żarb was not aware of the ramifications of this project.[7] Nor did he envisage the manner in which it would capture his imagination to the extent of investing most of his personal capital in it. Shortly after obtaining the concession he employed foreign engineers to do an initial survey. At the same time, he asked his brother Ḥājj Moḥammad-Raḥīm in France to buy and send furnaces for smelting ore. He canceled the order as a result of the survey, when he discovered that the geographical situation of the mine was such that it would be impossible to either transport a factory there or the equipment for building it.[8] Amīn-al-Żarb's search for a means of transportation between the sea and the mine took him on an odyssey of travels through Russia ending in Belgium and France. It was thus through the idea of a railway that the idea of a European trip was born.

On his outward journey, Amīn-al-Żarb's first port of call outside Persia was Baku, where he went to buy a one horse railway but discovered that it had to be obtained in Tiflis. When in Tiflis, he found not only that it was not available there, but by this time he had changed his mind about the horse-drawn carriage and decided to install a proper steam railway from Maḥmūdābād to Āmol. To acquire that, he had to go to Moscow. The two nights that Amīn-al-Żarb was in Tiflis, he was invited to dinner on both nights by Mīrzā Reżā Khan Moʿīn-al-Vozarā, the Persian consul, who also personally took Amīn-al-Żarb on a tour of the city. Amīn-al-Żarb cannot praise him enough in his letter to ʿAlī-Aṣḡar Khan Amīn-al-Solṭān, the prime minister.[9] According to the same letter, on the way to Moscow, in the Caucasus, he also met two brothers from Kāšān: Mīrzā Moḥammad-ʿAlī and Mīrzā Moḥammad-Ḥosayn, who were engaged in road building and

[7] Christian Bromberger, "La Sericulture en Gilan dans la second moitié du XIXe siècle," in Y. Richard, ed., *Entre l'Iran et occident* (Paris, 1989), 84-85.

[8] Mahdavī Archives, letter from Amīn-al-Żarb to Nāṣer-al-Dīn Shah, 1308/1890-91.

[9] Mahdavī Archives, letter from Amīn-al-Żarb in Moscow to Amīn-al-Solṭān in Tehran, 21 Ramażān 1304/13 June 1887. For more on Mīrzā Reżā Khan Dāneš (Moʿīn-al-Vozarā), see Mahdī Bamdād, *Sharḥ-e ḥāl-e rejāl-e Īrān,* 6 vols. (Tehran, 1347 Š./1968-69), 1:507-12.

who upon hearing that Amīn-al-Żarb was staying at a hotel insisted that he should stay in their house. Amīn-al-Żarb was very impressed by the achievements of the two brothers in Russia and tried to persuade them to come to Iran and undertake road building there, but they refused on the grounds that "there is no *qānūn* in Iran and therefore security of investment is not guaranteed."[10] The interesting fact about this meeting is that Amīn-al-Żarb quotes their remarks verbatim, reminiscent of the reformist and progressive thoughts of Mīrzā Malkom Khan who stressed the need for *qānūn* (civil law) in his writings.[11]

Wherever Amīn-al-Żarb went, he had his eyes open for commerce, and Moscow was no exception. He wrote to his son and agents that export-import of cotton, wool, and other things was easy in Moscow, if one had the know-how of what to buy and how to send it. He described Moscow as a town full of money and pleasure-seeking people, where money was thrown around like dust.[12]

Russia, which in the second half of the nineteenth century was considered backward and despotic compared to other European countries, appeared to Amīn-al-Żarb as a paragon of the rule of law and order compared to the arbitrary nature of power and justice and the constant on-going extortion in Iran. He was amazed by the fact that men and women strolled freely in the streets and wrote:

> men and unveiled women pass by; no one dares say so and so went too fast or that he is a Muslim, a Russian, or a Jew. Everyone is educated and well versed in the etiquette of human behavior."[13]

He went on to describe the places and museums—not only the extraordinary objects which they contained but the fact that there were guides versed in various languages to explain everything. However, it was the sense of security of the people as a result of the rule of law which impressed him most:

---

[10] On the brothers, see Bamdād, *Rejāl*, 3:457.

[11] For more on Malkom Khan see Hamid Algar, *Mīrzā Malkum Khān: A Study in the History of Iranian Modernism* (Berkeley, 1973). Algar is not very sympathetic to Malkom Khan. For a more objective view, see Shaul Bakhash, *Iran: Monarchy, Bureaucracy and Reform under the Qajars 1858-1896* (London, 1978).

[12] Mahdavi Archives, letters from Moscow to Tehran between 14-29 Ramażān 1304/6-21 June 1887.

[13] Mahdavī Archives, letter from Amīn-al-Żarb in Moscow to Amīn-al-Solṭān in Tehran, 21 Ramażān 1304/13 June 1887.

> Military officers, soldiers, ministers or governors are not allowed to put one step beyond their limit .... If I wanted to describe the industry and administration of this country, even fifty pages would not be enough. Although they say that in this domain of Russia oppression, injustice, and tyranny reigns, its people are like animals, and true justice can [only] be found in the Land of the Franks [Europe] ... [in actuality] people know that they have possessions and own property. No one has the right to confiscate someone else's property or to covet someone else's possessions and lay hands upon it .... The legal system is such that it is not possible for anyone to even look at someone else's property or possessions. The verdict of each case is evident. There is no necessity for a second verdict. After the charge has been established, the penalty is clear. There are no go-betweens. No one can prevent it [the execution of the penalty], be he the brother of the emperor.[14]

It is a terrible indictment of the situation of Iran with its lack of security and arbitrary confiscation of property that Russia, infamous for its despotism and lack of democratic institutions, which eventually led to a revolution, should have appeared to be such a haven to Amīn-al-Żarb.

The quest for the railway took Amīn-al-Żarb from Moscow to Belgium and thence to Paris. His brother Ḥājj Moḥammad-Raḥīm met him in Belgium, and a number of trips were undertaken between Belgium and Paris regarding the railway. A discussion of that subject is not within the scope of this paper. Suffice it to say that Amīn-al-Żarb spent approximately three months in Paris and France awaiting the completion of the order for the railway.

During this time, aside from writing to his son and agents in Tehran, Amīn-al-Żarb wrote regularly and in detail to Amīn-al-Sulṭān, both regarding the progress of his activities and the state of affairs in Europe. All the letters from Europe were sent open to his *ḥojra* (business office) in Tehran, where his secretary would make copies of them and then they would be sealed and given to the addressee. As far as can be known, this was an unusual procedure for the time and indicates that Amīn-al-Żarb may have had his eye on posterity. In these letters he did not confine himself to any particular subject but felt that as a passionate patriot he should report all that touched and affected Iran, its government, and its people. He constantly compared the state of Europe with Iran and went into a deep gloom. He was truly awed by

---

[14] Mahdavī Archives, letter from Amīn-al-Żarb in Moscow to Amīn-al-Solṭān in Tehran, 21 Ramażān 1304/13 June 1887.

the level of industrialization and employment found in Europe. In a letter to Amīn-al-Solṭān, he wrote:

> In Europe, everyone [ranging] from children to men to women, and even animals and dogs, are busy co-operating with each other to construct boats, *chemin-de-fer* [railways], and factories. From [a depth of] six hundred *zarᶜ* [cubits], they extract coal. In Iran, everyone is unemployed, preoccupied with watching everyone else [to see] what they buy or eat.[15]

In another letter to Amīn-al-Solṭān two days later he said:

> From Berlin to the borders of Belgium, there are so many factories that it appears as though the whole terrain is covered by them, and they say this is nothing compared to Farangestān [possibly meaning the rest of Western Europe].[16] Yesterday, I went to the manufacturers of crystal and gunsmiths and returned stupified, struck dumb with astonishment. I [also] went to the manufacturers of *chemin-de-fer*. This one factory alone has eleven thousand people working in it. There is such organization that no one is able to turn his head even for one minute. People in Iran are without any occupation, dying from lack of food and clothing. The income from one factory in Belgium is more than the income from all of Iran's agriculture and industry.[17]

Aside from industry, employment, and commerce, he also took it upon himself to report to Amīn-al-Solṭān on the state of the various Persian missions and ministers abroad. In describing these missions he was primarily concerned with the manner in which they upheld the prestige of their country. The highest marks went to Mīrzā Reżā Khan Moʾayyed-al-Salṭana, the first Iranian diplomatic representative in Germany. Amīn-al-Żarb described his house, furniture and carriages as in the highest style of elegance, comparable to the other missions.

---

[15] Mahdavī Archives, letter from Ḥājj Mohammad-Ḥasan Amīn-al-Żarb in Brussels to Amīn-al-Solṭān in Tehran, 17 Šavvāl 1304/9 July 1887. The *zarᶜ* was the basic unit of measurement and in some instances was the equivalent of 1.2 meters and in others 1.04 meters.

[16] *Farang*, *Farangestān*, and *farangī* were terms used to refer to Europe and its peoples, originating in references to the lands of the Franks.

[17] Mahdavī Archives, letter from Ḥājj Mohammad-Ḥasan Amīn-al-Żarb in Brussels to Amīn-al-Solṭān in Tehran, 19 Šavvāl 1304/11 July 1887.

He was impressed that Mīrzā Reżā Khan was able to hold his own in Bismarck's Germany and had forged connections with those around Bismarck and the court, amongst whom he mentions in particular the heir to the throne. To further illustrate Mīrzā Reżā Khan's connections, Amīn-al-Żarb described a dinner party given at the embassy, to which he was invited. It is interesting that in giving the list of the guests he began with the ladies. It must have been the first dinner party in which he participated and at which unveiled ladies were present. Although it was probably a novel and unusual experience for him, in the letter he was more concerned with the importance of the ladies than the fact that they were mingling freely with men. He identified one of the ladies as being the wife of the minister of court and the other as his sister. At the end of the dinner party, the guests insisted on giving Amīn-al-Żarb a lift in their own carriage, which he interpreted as an additional sign of the importance with which Mīrzā Reżā was held by the community.[18] Another official whom he praised was Mīrzā Reżā Khan Dāneš Moᶜīn-al-Vozarā, the consul-general in Tiflis, as opposed to the envoy extraordinary to St. Petersburg, Sayyed Maḥmūd Khan ᶜAlā-al-Molk, whom Amīn-al-Żarb criticized sharply for his meanness, for his residence (which was a couple of pathetic rooms in an inferior quarter of the town), and the disgraceful appearance this created for the prestige of Iran.[19] All three people mentioned by Amīn-al-Żarb were important diplomats of the period and went on to represent Persia in different countries.

Paris, the jewel of European capitals, must have been the most unique experience for Amīn-al-Żarb. Although he had seen some unfamiliar sights in the Ottoman Empire during his hajj trip and in Moscow, Warsaw, Berlin, and Belgium on his way to Paris, nothing could have prepared him for the magnificent town planning and the beauty of the city. Amīn-al-Żarb saw the beauty of Paris and wept for the fate and condition of his country. It was not so much the life style of the French which interested him but the institutions which catered to that life style. He realized that the institutions were able to function due to the existence of democracy on the one hand and security of property on the other hand, which encouraged private enterprise.

---

[18] Mahdavī Archives, letter from Amīn-al-Żarb in Brussels to Amīn-al-Solṭān in Tehran, 19 Šavvāl 1304/11 July 1887. For more on Mīrzā Reżā, see Bamdād, *Rejāl*, 2:23-24.

[19] Mahdavī Archives, letter from Amīn-al-Żarb in Brussels to Amīn-al-Solṭān in Tehran, 19 Šavvāl 1304 /11 July 1887. On Sayyed Maḥmūd Khan, see Bamdād, *Rejāl*, 4:39-44.

Comparing the dynamic state of France with the static and stagnant state of Iran made him desperately unhappy. On 11 Ẕu'l-Qaʿda 1305/ 20 July 1887, he wrote to Amīn-al-Solṭān:

> I cry day and night in this Paris which is not a place for sadness [but pleasure], and instead of tears, blood pours out of my eyes .... I observe the condition of this country and review those of Iran and become demented.[20]

In another letter he described some of the things which amazed him:

> Pursuit of science has enabled them to function, and their knowledge stems from diligence. Their *majles* [parliament] of ministers and sages has ordained things in such a manner that no one is able to exercise a [personal] grudge, interfere, or practice nepotism. The vouchers of merchants, grocers, and shoemakers are executed without delay or procrastination [as well as] that of ministers and others. Everyone goes about his own business and knows his duty. No one is after stealing, cheating or malevolence .... One hundred and ten thousand public carriages [for hire] move through the streets and boulevards of this town, in addition to the private ones and the street railway [tramway]. Every hour, people and merchandise arrive and leave to and from London, America, Berlin, Russia, and Austria. Not a sound is heard from anyone, no one knows what came and what went. I don't know what rules and regulations have been established. All of Iran does not have the population of Paris, [where] everyone is patriotic, listens to the commands of the government, and is obedient. The reason why things are as they are [in Iran] is that every one is occupied with wresting [possessions] from each other. [If] people see anyone having good property or substantial capital, they want to take it away from him.[21]

He went on to describe the benefits of bank notes as opposed to coins for the general economy of the country and the manner in which all exchanges, credits and investments, both private and public, took

---

[20] Mahdavī Archives, letter from Amīn-al-Żarb in Paris to Amīn-al-Solṭān in Tehran, 11 Ẕu'l-Qaʿda 1305/20 July 1887.

[21] Mahdavī Archives, letter from Amīn-al-Żarb in Paris to Amīn-al-Solṭān in Tehran, probably written in July 1887. The above translation is from page nine of that letter, the rest of which unfortunately is lost.

place through the medium of notes honored by the government through a central bank. It must be remembered that long before his European trip, Amīn-al-Żarb had proposed in 1878 the formation of a central bank to the shah, as discussed earlier. However, it was more the order, the harmony, and the regular activity and occupation of the population which impressed him. He wrote:

> All the people in Europe seem to be cut from the same cloth and united, ranging from the poor to the rich, from animals to human beings, and even the dogs cooperate with each other. Everyone is busy and working, and everyone, at every hour of day and night, knows what his duty is and what he should do.[22]

Obviously, European society and institutions were not in the ideal state painted by Amīn-al-Żarb, but the positive picture which he drew of Europe served to illustrate negative aspects of Persian society and institutions. When he spoke about the unity of the European people, he had in mind the constant intrigue and scheming which went on in the Persian court and government. When he talked about the activity of the population in Europe, he had in mind the inertia and unemployment of the Persian population. When he commented on the security of property there, he had in mind the endless confiscation of property which took place in Qajar Iran under different pretexts, a fate which eventually befell him as well. He dared not criticize the shah or the prime minister or hold them responsible for the state of affairs; therefore, his remarks always began or ended with compliments to them: It was the anonymous legions who were responsible for the ills of the country and who did not fulfill their duty.

Amīn-al-Żarb tried to adapt himself to European ways by donning European attire, as Ḥājjī Pīrzāda reported:

> Ḥājj Moḥammad-Ḥasan has changed his clothes in Paris. He was wearing trousers, jacket, tie and hat, but he has not abandoned his prayers and religious duties. He probably eats the meat slaughtered in the European manner.[23]

However, Amīn-al-Żarb's letters show that although he was impressed by the economic and political development of Europe, he

---

[22] Ibid.

[23] Ḥājjī Pīrzāda, *Safar-nāma*, ed. Ḥāfeẓ Farmānfarmā'īān, 2 vols. (Tehran, 1981), 2:13. Muslims must eat *ḥalāl* meat, that is the meat of an animal which has been ritually slaughtered.

did not enjoy the lifestyle. Although he did eat the meat, he missed Persian food, as he indicated in jest in one of his letters, sending a message to one of his friends saying that he [the friend] should be there to eat beef and potatoes. As he was a very devoted family man, he also missed his family.

Amīn-al-Żarb spent some time in Paris waiting to hear from Amīn-al-Solṭān regarding arrangements for the custom clearance of the railway equipment through Russia. While waiting for Amīn-al–Solṭān's reply, he went to Lyon and from there to Gange, where his brother Ḥājj Moḥammad-Raḥīm was resident, representing Amīn-al-Żarb and running a silk refining factory.[24] Not only was Ḥājj Moḥammad Raḥīm a resident of Gange, but he had also acquired a French wife, the daughter of the Ducros, the family from whom the Rašt silk reeling factory was bought.

Amīn-al-Żarb and Ḥājj Moḥammad-Raḥīm returned to Paris together, where shortly after their return they received Amīn-al-Solṭān's telegram saying that he had arranged for custom clearance through Russia. Finally at the beginning of September, Amīn-al-Żarb left Paris for Liège accompanied by Ḥājj Moḥammad-Raḥīm. In Liège, he arranged for the railway equipment, parts for the iron smelting foundry, three pieces of machinery for cleaning raw cotton, and two cotton presses to be shipped, and, having said his farewells to Ḥājj Moḥammad-Raḥīm, he left for Iran on 26 Ẕu'l-Ḥejja/16 September via Bohemia, where he wished to order some crystal. On his return trip from Europe, Amīn-al-Żarb was accompanied by four people—two French engineers whom he had employed for the railway, Mīrzā Jaʿfar Khan Sayyāḥ, the brother of Ḥājjī Sayyāḥ, and Qarapotoff, a resident of Baku and the owner of a wagon manufacturing factory. Six days later, they were in Vienna; and twelve days after leaving Liège, they had arrived at the Russian border at the port of Odessa. From Odessa, Amīn-al-Żarb went to Moscow, where he spent twenty days. In a letter which he wrote upon his return to the Minister for Foreign Affairs, he was ecstatic about the courtesy and treatment he received in Russia.[25]

In Moscow, the local merchants and factory owners entertained Amīn-al-Żarb and took him sightseeing both in Moscow and to the parks and resorts outside the city. From Moscow, he went to Batum,

---

[24] Gange is in the departement of Herault in the Languedoc in the south of France. For more information on the city, its inhabitants, and economic activity see *Grand Dictionnaire Encyclopédique* (Paris, 1983), 5:4664.

[25] Mahdavī Archives, letter from Amīn-al-Żarb to the Minister for Foreign Affairs, 1 Jomādā I 1305/15 January 1888.

Tiflis, and Baku. He describes in detail how the head of customs at Batum, Baku, and everywhere else accorded him every civility and facilitated the passage of the goods he was carrying with him. In his letter, Amīn-al-Żarb explained the royal treatment that he received as a result of the good will of the Russian government towards that of Persia and asked the foreign minister to write a letter to the Russian embassy acknowledging this and thanking them. Although the customs facilities may have been due to Amīn-al-Solṭān's intervention, the behavior of the merchants and factory owners must have been more personal. As Amīn-al-Żarb was known as a prominent merchant, and they had heard about his purchase of the railway line and his interest in industrial development, they hoped that as a result of the relationship some future business association might transpire.

Approximately six months after his return to Iran, Amīn-al-Żarb discovered that he had to go to Europe again to obtain further parts and machinery for the railway. In January 1889, while in Mašhad, he wrote to Amīn-al-Solṭān asking him to obtain the shah's permission for another trip to Europe. On 11 Jomādā II 1306/12 February 1889, Amīn-al-Solṭān wrote back, having obtained the shah's permission for the trip and wishing Amīn-al-Żarb success in acquiring the machinery necessary for the railway and the road.[26] Amīn-al-Żarb stayed in Mašhad for approximately three weeks and then left for Ashkhabad (ʿEšqābād) accompanied by his brother Ḥājj Abu'l-Qāsem Malek-al-Tojjār, who had obtained a concession for the Mašhad-Ashkhabad road. The brothers parted in Ashkhabad when, on 10 Rajab 1306/12 March 1889, Malek-al-Tojjār left for Mašhad and Amīn-al-Żarb for Baku.

From Baku, Amīn-al-Żarb went to Yalta, where he met Āqā Zayn-al-ʿĀbedīn Marāgaʾī, the author of *Sīāḥat-nāma-ye Ebrāhīm Beyg*, whose father, although Iranian by origin, lived for fifty years in Egypt, was engaged in commerce, became a prominent merchant, and was a friend of Amīn-al-Żarb.[27] Although at this point the two men were on friendly terms, later on, probably at the end of the reign of Nāṣer-al-Dīn Shah, when the *Sīāḥat-nāma* was written, he was highly critical of Amīn-al-Żarb not only as a person, but of his character and activities.

---

[26] Mahdavī Archives, letter from Amīn-al-Solṭān in Tehran to Amīn-al-Żarb in Mašhad, 11 Jomādā II 1306/12 February 1889.

[27] Ḥājj Zayn-al-ʿĀbedīn Marāgaʾī, *Sīāḥat-nāma-ye Ebrāhīm Beyg* (Calcutta, 1910, repr. Tehran, 1958).

From Yalta, Amīn-al-Żarb went to Paris via Odessa, Vienna, and Liège. He arrived in Paris on 22 Šaʿbān 1306/23 April 1889. His brother Ḥājj Moḥammad-Raḥīm joined him there from Ganja. The two brothers left Paris for Berlin and then on to Kassel, where they awaited Nāṣer-al-Dīn Shah's arrival on his third European trip. On 14 Šavvāl/13 June, Eʿtemād-al-Salṭana reported having seen the brothers.[28] The royal party left Kassel for Amsterdam on 16 Šavvāl/15 June and stopped in Essen on the way to visit the Krupp factories. The brothers followed the same route, as once again Eʿtemād-al-Salṭana related from Amsterdam that Ḥājj Moḥammad-Raḥīm had given the shah a French newspaper containing material critical of the shah that he had to translate.[29]

From Amsterdam, the brothers parted company with the royal entourage, which left for Belgium and then on to England. Amīn-al-Żarb, accompanied by Ḥājj Moḥammad-Raḥīm, went back to Paris. He stayed in Paris for ten days and left for Italy on 19 Ẕu'l-Qaʿda/18 July to go on a second hajj. Ḥājj Moḥammad-Raḥīm not only stayed in Paris, but gave a lunch party for some members of the royal party when they arrived in Paris.[30]

Amīn-al-Żarb went straight to Mecca from Alexandria and returned from the hajj via Alexandria to Cairo on 4 Moḥarram/31 August.[31] From Cairo, he returned on 14 Muharram/10 September to Paris once again, via Gange, to expedite the dispatch of the equipment and machinery he had purchased. So within two months, he was in Paris again. He spent two weeks in Paris staying at the house of Ḥājj Mīrzā Eṣfahānī in Passage Mazagran. Ḥājj Mīrzā was a turquoise merchant, and their connection went back to Isfahan. From Paris, he started on his journey home, only stopping in Leipzig in Europe, where he was engaged in the fur trade. Once in Russia, he stopped in both Batum and Baku to make customs

---

[28] Eʿtemād al-Salṭana, *Rūz-nāma-ye ḵāṭerāt*, ed. Īraj Afšār (Tehran, 1356 Š./1977), 648.

[29] Eʿtemād al-Salṭana, *Rūz-nāma*, 649.

[30] Eʿtemād al-Salṭana, *Rūz-nāma*, 655.

[31] On his return from Mecca to Cairo, Amīn-al-Żarb was accompanied by Ḥājj ʿAbd-al-Ğaffār Tabrīzī, who was a resident of Egypt and who later went to Iran and worked for Amīn-al-Żarb. Ḥājj ʿAbd-al-Ğaffār's son Mīrzā ʿAbd-Allāh also worked for Amīn-al-Żarb, first on the railway in Maḥmūdābād and later as the agent of both Amīn-al-Żarbs in Moscow. In Cairo, Amīn-al-Żarb stayed with Ḥājj Moḥammad Javād Meškī, whose family is still well known in Cairo, but who came originally from Isfahan and was linked to Amīn-al-Żarb through Isfahani connections.

arrangements and was in Rašt on 2 Rabīʿ I/27 October after a journey which took seven months.

Few letters survive from Amīn-al-Żarb's second European trip and hajj, and those in existence in the family archive are all addressed to his cousin Moḥammad-Javād, his agent in Moscow, and were sent to Tehran after his death. The letters are mainly about commercial transactions and customs clearance of the machinery purchased in Europe. However, the letters from the first European trip contain enough material to reveal Amīn-al-Żarb's reaction to and opinion of the West, which can only be understood in the context of his position in, and the state of, Qajar society.

Amīn-al-Żarb's financial success and activities generated a great deal of jealousy and resentment in the court and amongst the courtiers. Consequently, Amīn-al-Żarb's obsession with the fact that in Europe everyone was only concerned with his own affairs, a theme which runs throughout his letters, becomes comprehensible only within the context of the Persian society of his time. He reiterates this point upon his return from his first trip in a letter that he wrote to Rokn-al-Dawla, governor of Khorasan:

> That which is the principal asset of the lifeblood and existence of these people is their unity. They are united in body and soul. They do not begrudge, resent, or envy the possessions of others. Every hour and every minute, their objective is to increase the importance and greatness of their country. If someone regards a child or a lamb critically, they all unite to rectify it. They covet neither vast possessions nor horses and carriages nor gardens, but [their primary] preoccupation is the education and training of their people.[32]

The state of European affairs was not as rosy as Amīn-al-Żarb painted it, but certainly the degree of intrigue which was current in Nāṣer-al-Dīn Shah's court did not exist in Europe.

---

[32] Mahdavī Archives, letter from Amīn-al-Żarb in Tehran to Moḥammad-Taqī Mīrzā Rokn-al-Dawla in Mašhad, 9 Rabīʿ II 1305/25 December 1887. Moḥammad-Taqī Mīrzā Rokn-al-Dawla was the fourth son of Moḥammad Shah and the younger brother of Nāṣer-al-Dīn Shah. He was the governor of various provinces, including Zanjān, for the second time in 1289/1872 and, beginning in 1293/1876, was four times the governor of Khorasan. He was probably the governor who appointed Ḥājj Abu'l-Qāsem, Amīn-al-Żarb's brother, the Malek-al-Tojjār of Mašhad. For more on him, see Bamdād, *Rejāl*, 3:312-19.

Ḥājj Moḥammad-Ḥasan Amīn-al-Żarb was both a financial genius and a visionary. He grasped the fast-changing economic conditions in Iran and the outside world and benefited from them. His travels abroad made a deep impression on him, as a result of which not only his commercial sphere expanded but his passion for innovation and industrialization intensified. Witnessing the progress and achievements of the countries through which he traveled made him aware of both the need and the opportunity to involve his country in the post-industrial revolution of Europe.

As his letters from Europe demonstrate, aside from industrial progress, he was most impressed with the legal institutions which encompassed all members of the society regardless of class and office. This was not only due to the fact that the rule of law and justice was of great concern to him, but also to the fact that due to the arbitrary practice of confiscation of property prevalent in Qajar Iran he himself constantly felt vulnerable. His feeling of vulnerability was not groundless, as eventually the fate he feared most befell him.[33]

Although he benefited from the trade with Europe and admired not only its technology but its political institutions, on a personal level he spoke disparagingly of Europeans and distrusted them in connection with any kind of transaction. Amīn-al-Żarb's familiarity with the western lifestyle, his admiration for western technological and political institutions, and the impressions that his European travels made on him did not affect his private life or beliefs. Although he moved easily between the two worlds, East and West, unlike some members of the aristocracy who adopted a western lifestyle, his own personal life was conducted according to traditional Persian and Islamic family values, and the structure of his household was based upon them.

He was so engrossed with European industrial progress that when he realized the government would not undertake any of the necessary projects, he took it upon himself to launch a few of them with his own capital. However, circumstances mitigated against him. He operated in an era of foreign concessions, British and Russian rivalries, and bewildered but well-meaning Qajar shahs who were no match for their European counterparts. A combination

---

[33] For more on Amīn-al-Żarb being fined and the confiscation of his property see Mahdīqolī Hedāyat, *K̲āṭerāt va k̲atarāt* (Tehran, 1965), and V. S. Kosogovskii, *Iz tegeranskogo dnevika*, tr. ʿAbbāsqolī Jalī as *K̲āterāt-e Kolonel Kosogofskī* (Tehran, 1965), 180-83.

of court intrigue and foreign intervention prevented many of his projects from reaching fruition.

As the economic history of Iran during this period has not been sufficiently studied, it is not easy to evaluate the place of Amīn-al-Żarb within the social and economic contexts of his time. However, it would appear that had the activities of Amīn-al-Żarb and other indigenous entrepreneurs like him been allowed to develop further, Iran would have had a firm foothold on the ladder towards earlier industrialization and modernization.

Japan as Seen by Qajar Travelers

Hashem Rajabzadeh

Prior to the twentieth century, Iranians had little knowledge about Japan. In *Montaẓam-e nāṣerī*, an official history of Qajar Iran compiled by Eʿtemād-al-Salṭana in 1880, we find only a brief description of Japan.[1] *Al-Maʾāṯer va'l-āṯār*, by the same author, has a passage on the first Japanese delegation, headed by Yoshida Masaharu, visiting the court of Nāṣer-al-Dīn Shah in 1880.[2] In a courtesy call by the envoy, Mīrzā Saʿīd Khan, Nāṣer-al-Dīn Shah's foreign minister, expressed thanks for the warm welcome shown, and the hospitality extended, to his master in Japan during the shah's tour of Europe.[3]

Japan at this time had emerged successfully from the modernization challenge, defeated China in the war of 1894-95, confronted European powers, signed an alliance with England (1902), and set out to avenge herself for Russia's seizure of Port Arthur. As J. W. Hall says concerning Japan's new image after its victory over China, "It is unavoidable fact that the 1894-95 war with China marked Japan's coming of age in the eyes of the world."[4] It is therefore no wonder that informed people and even commoners in Iran viewed Japan with respect and admiration.

Early in the twentieth century, the image of an awakened and modernized Japan was being employed by Iranian writers to promote the cause of constitutional government as a prerequisite for social and

---

[1] Moḥammad-Ḥasan Khan Eʿtemād-al-Salṭana, *Tārīḵ-e montaẓam-e nāṣerī*, vol. 1, ed. Īraj Afšār (Tehran, 1363 Š./1984), 564.

[2] Moḥammad-Ḥasan Khan Eʿtemād-al-Salṭana, *al-Maʾāṯer va'l-āṯār*, ed. Īraj Afšār as *Čehel sāl-e tārīḵ-e Īrān*, 3 vols. (Tehran, 1363 Š./1984), 1:331; cf. Eʿtemād-al-Salṭana, *Montaẓam*, 473-74.

[3] Yoshida Masaharu, *Perushiya-no-Tabi* (Tokyo, 1894), 132.

[4] John Whitney Hall, *Japan: From Prehistory to Modern Times* (Tokyo, 1971), 303.

economic modernization.[5] In those days, the intelligentsia tried to use the image of a victorious Japan to advantage in the minds of Iranians who longed for freedom and progress. ʿAbd-al-Raḥīm Ṭālebof, one of the pioneers of modernist thought, acknowledged Japan's victory of 1905 over Russia as a result of "science and freedom."[6] The *Sīāḥat-nāma-ye Ebrāhīm Beyk*, an imaginary travel memoir written toward the end of the nineteenth century, used the example of Japan to criticize the frivolous trips of Nāṣer-al-Dīn Shah to Europe, commenting:

> Many resolute kings have never toured (overseas) and have revived their nations by their enlightened mind and insight. The emperor of Japan, for example, elevated his nation and his government to everybody's surprise without leaving his home (country).[7]

The Meiji Restoration and its social reforms, followed by economic achievements and political changes introducing the Constitutional Government, awakened Iranians to a socially advanced Japan and provided them with a good example to follow in their search for freedom and justice.

The impression was so strong that Amīn-al-Solṭān (later known as Atābak-e Aʿẓam), the influential prime minister of two Qajar kings, left Iran for an adventurous visit to the Far East immediately after his discharge from office in September 1903. He was accompanied on this trip by a celebrated young scholar and statesman, Mahdīqolī Hedāyat Mok̲ber-al-Salṭana (later the prime minister from 1927 to 1933), whose account of the journey in his memoirs exemplifies the intelligentsia's interest in Japan and their aspirations for their own country. The party arrived in Japan in December 1903, a few weeks before the outbreak of the Russo-Japanese War, and experienced many exciting moments.

Qajar Travelers to Meiji Japan

During the Qajar period, only a few Iranians ventured to Japan, of whom two are known to have written their memoirs. By far the most

---

[5] Nāẓem-al-Eslām Kermānī, *Tārīk̲-e bīdārī-e Īrānīān* (Tehran, 1362 Š./ 1983), contains many such references.

[6] See Fereydūn Ādamīyat, *Andīšahā-ye Ṭālebof Tabrīzī* (Tehran, 1363 Š./ 1984), 48-49.

[7] Zayn-al-ʿĀbedīn Marāg̲aʾī, *Sīāḥat-nāma-ye Ebrāhīm Beyk*, ed. Bāqer Moʾmenī (Tehran, 1357 Š./1978), 146.

important of these memoirs is the one compiled by Mahdīqolī Hedāyat Mok̲ber-al-Salṭana, whose account of his twenty-five day visit to Japan is in itself a comprehensive introduction to the country.[8] The other is the account by Mīrzā Ebrāhīm Saḥḥāfbāšī, a businessman who frequented Japan and the Far East, bringing some new ideas as well as some precious articles to sell in Iran.[9]

Some sources also suggest there were visit(s) to Japan by Ḥājjī Mīrzā Moḥammad-ʿAlī Maḥallātī, known as Ḥājjī Sayyāḥ, who is said to have traveled to many countries in Europe, Asia, America, and Africa over the course of some twenty years starting about 1858.[10] Ḥājjī Sayyāḥ's diary of Europe, published in Iran a few years ago,[11] is well known, but the present writer could not trace his diaries, which reportedly contain accounts of his journey(s) to North America, Japan, and the Far East, nor could he find any clue to verify his possible visit(s) to Japan.

A narrative account of some historical incidents in Qajar Iran published recently mentions an envoy sent to Meiji Japan by Nāṣer-al-Dīn Shah a few years after the much regretted death of his distinguished chancellor Mīrzā Taqī Khan Amīr Kabīr.[12] The envoy, Solṭān-Ovays Mīrzā,[13] the elder son of Farhād Mīrzā Moʿtamed-al-Dawla, after completing his mission and in response to the shah's insistent demand, supposedly sent a report by wire of that visit to Japan.

---

[8] Mahdīqolī Hedāyat Mok̲ber-al-Salṭana, *Safar-nāma-ye tašarrof ba Makka-ye moʿaẓẓama az ṭarīq-e Čīn, Žapon, va Amrīkā* (Tehran, 1324 Š./1945).

[9] Ebrāhīm Ṣaḥḥāfbāšī, *Safar-nāma-ye Ebrāhīm Ṣaḥḥāfbāšī Tehrānī*, ed. Moḥammad Mošīrī (Tehran 1357 Š./1979).

[10] For example, see Mahdī Bāmdād, *Sharḥ-e ḥāl-e rejāl-e Īrān,* 6 vols. (Tehran, 1363 Š./1984), 3:424.

[11] Ḥājjī Sayyāḥ, *Safar-nāma-ye Ḥājjī Sayyāḥ ba Farang*, ed. ʿAlī Dehbāšī (Tehran, 1363 Š./1984); see also Abu'l-Ḥasan ʿAlavī, *Rejāl-e ʿaṣr-e mašrūṭīyat,* ed. Ḥabīb Yag̲māʾī, (Tehran, 1363 Š./1984), 63-64.

[12] ʿAlī Vot̲ūq, *Tafannon va tārīk̲: čāhār faṣl-e tārīk̲* (Tehran, 1361 Š./1982), 78.

[13] For a brief biography of him see Bāmdād, *Rejāl*, 2:74-75. The prince is reported to have been a travel enthusiast, frequenting places of historical importance and natural beauty. The author of the *Fārs-nāma-ye Nāṣerī*, himself a close aide and personal physician of the prince, makes many references to accompanying the prince in his visits to various parts of Iran; see Mīrzā Ḥasan Ḥosaynī Fasāʾī, *Fārs-nāma-ye nāṣerī*, ed. Manṣūr Rastgār Fasāʾī (Tehran, 1367 Š./1988), 26-28.

In the transmission, a phrase was somehow altered to become a joke for the Qajar courtiers, who thereby disregarded its informative content as well as the original purpose of the mission. The author, however, does not mention any source nor make reference to contemporary historical works to support his account of this embassy, and the story cannot be substantiated.

An Enlightened Traveler

Mahdīqolī Hedāyat came from a respected aristocratic family that produced many noted scholars, statesmen of repute, and gifted writers. Born in 1280/1863-64, he was sent at the age of fifteen to study in Germany, but he soon returned and continued his study of Persian literature and music in Iran. He began his career as a statesman and an educator at the age of thirty. During the second visit of Moẓaffar-al-Dīn Shah to Europe, Hedāyat was one of his entourage, and he later played an important role in the issuance of the Constitutional Decree of 1906 by the shah and the formation of the first national assembly in Iran. He held ministerial portfolios and posts of provincial governor during the last years of Qajar rule and early Pahlavi era, before serving as the prime minister under Reżā Shah for six years (1927-33).

His travel around the world (from Siberia, China, Japan, North America, and Europe to Arabia) was initiated by the dismissal of Mīrzā ʿAlī-Aṣḡar Khan Amīn-al-Solṭān, the Atābak-e Aʿẓam, from the premiership by Moẓaffar-al-Dīn Shah on 15 September 1903. When the shah subsequently granted Atābak permission to leave for a pilgrimage to Mecca, Hedāyat writes: "Atābak asked me to go with him to Mecca and was willing to have my companionship, to which I agreed ...."[14]

Hedāyat accompanied Atābak as an aide and interpreter. As his reason for joining Atābak on this trip, he writes: "Besides my eagerness to make a pilgrimage to Mecca, it also occurred to me that the trip might give me a chance to prepare Atābak's mind for future reforms."[15]

From Anzalī they took the Caspian sea route to Baku and then went overland to Moscow, where they boarded the Trans-Siberian train for the long and exhausting journey to Port Arthur. There they boarded a ship for Chefu (Yantai), a port on the eastern shores of China. From there, they took a train to Tianjin and Beijing, and then again to Shanghai, whence they set out on a sea trip to Nagasaki. They arrived in Japan on 9 December 1903, and they visited Kobe and Kyoto before

---

[14] Hedāyat, *Safar-nāma*, 3.

[15] Hedāyat, *Safar-nāma*, 3.

coming to Tokyo on 14 December. They stayed in the Japanese capital until 6 January. Their departure for America from Tokyo harbor coincided with the outbreak of the Russo-Japanese War.

Hedāyat stayed a total of twenty-five days in Japan, of which twenty-two days were spent in Tokyo, but his descriptions of Japan and his comments on Japanese people and their life attests to his deep insight, the way a gifted scholar might present his findings after many years of research and observations. A great part of Hedāyat's memoirs require annotation to be understood and appreciated by an ordinary reader. It should be noted, however, that Hedāyat compiled, edited, and summarized his memoirs at the age of eighty-six, around 1945, more than fifty years after his memorable visit to Japan.[16]

Hedāyat and his fellow travelers met Sir Ernest Satow, a noted Orientalist and the British Minister in Beijing. Hedāyat refers, among others, to Engelbert Kaempfer's travel memoirs and the marvelous work of Sir Rutherford Alcock.[17] He quotes more than once from Basil Hall Chamberlain and his informative book *Japanese Things*,[18] and he criticizes the French author Pierre Loti for being unfair to the Japanese in his book *Madame Chrysanthème*.[19]

In his diary he follows a unique and fascinating style of writing, and his phrases are rich in proverbs, humor, maxims, and quotations from Persian, Islamic, and European literature. He gives a rather accurate geographical introduction to contemporary Japan, considers the Japanese of Mongol origin,[20] and explains that the name of the country, Nippon, means the place where the sun rises.[21]

His impression of order and discipline is evident from the moment of his arrival in Japan:

> We entered the quarantine of Nagasaki...The inspecting doctor checked the logbook and sanitary documents of the ship. We travelers, men and women, all gathered in the dining room of the ship. The doctor stood at the top of stairs, called each passenger by name (and checked) until all were cleared. We moved to the

---

[16] Hedāyat, *Safar-nāma*, 130.

[17] Sir Rutherford Alcock, *The Capital of the Tycoon* (repr. New York, 1969; originally published in 1863).

[18] Basil Hall Chamberlain, *Japanese Things; Being Notes on Various Subjects Connected to Japan* (repr., Tokyo, 1971).

[19] Pierre Loti, *Madame Chrysanthème*, tr. Laura Ensor (repr. Tokyo, 1973).

[20] Hedāyat, *Safar-nāma*, 115.

[21] Hedāyat, *Safar-nāma*, 93.

> deck and the ship was permitted to leave. It was an amazing scene, after having seen the chaotic situation of China.[22]

He also recalls once and again that authorities in Japan were already informed and prepared to receive the dignitaries only briefly after they had notified the Japanese minister in Beijing of their schedule.

The rule and order in Japan were in sharp contrast with the evident chaos in Russia and China. Hedāyat writes, "The Chinese looked distressed and were disgraced. Here (in Japan), people are proud."[23]

The perceptiveness of the Japanese and their insight into the world situation were other qualities admired by Hedāyat. In an account of his sea journey from Port Arthur to Chefu, Hedāyat writes:

> On Monday, 23 October 1903, our ship left the strait. The port is the shape of two overlapping circles. Gun batteries on the top of the hills are visible. Seeing this, we wondered more about the Japanese, little knowing that Japan, though an Asian country, was not asleep like us and had taken European [advanced] precautions.[24]

Comparing the situation in China and in Japan, he writes: "The Japanese [faced with the European threat] soon realized that he who throws a clod deserves to be hit with a stone [i.e, they should give them tit for tat]; thus they built their strength and prepared for war."[25] Hedāyat was moved by the atmosphere in Japan. "Public opinion, a new (socio-political) term, is at its peak," he writes, and "there are exhausting preparations under way for the Russo-Japanese War."[26] He found the public in Japan to be quite enthusiastic about the war.

Hedāyat, who was in Japan for almost one month after 9 December 1903, writes on the developments preceding the war:

---

[22] Hedāyat, *Safar-nāma*, 92-93.

[23] Hedāyat, *Safar-nāma*, 92-93.

[24] Hedāyat, *Safar-nāma*, 24. On Japanese preparedness, Hedāyat, *Safar-nāma*, 108, writes again (early January 1904, while still in Tokyo): "The foreign minister came to our hotel [to visit us]. Conversation was mainly about the possibility of importing some mules that are not available in Japan. The preoccupation here is the war with Russia to avenge their capture of Port Arthur."

[25] Hedāyat, *Safar-nāma*, 89.

[26] Mahdīqolī Hedāyat Mok̲ber-al-Salṭana, *Goz̲āreš-e Īrān va mašrūṭīyat* (Tehran, 1363 Š./1984), 158.

> Mr. Taft, the American governor of the Philippines, arrived in Tokyo an his way to Washington to assume his new post as the secretary of defense. He arrived on 4 January and was received with much consideration. It was apparent that the final decision on war was to be made after consulting him. During his two-day stay, there was much talk about the war. On 5 January, the foreign minister visited Marquis Itō (and carried messages between him) and the emperor twice alternately. In the evening, the foreign minister gave a dinner party in Mr. Taft's honor inviting Atābak (and his party). It ended at nine o'clock. The American minister plenipotentiary told us: "It has been ordered that the members of the cabinet should stay until the matter of war is resolved." All the guests left the party. The decision to go to war was announced the next day.[27]

Judging from the disappointing ignorance shown by the authorities upon his party's arrival in Port Arthur (December 1903), Hedāyat saw confusion in Russia's public administration, and later on found it to be in sharp contrast with the fantastic discipline of the Japanese. Hedāyat, who traveled through Russia and Manchuria a few weeks before the outbreak of the war, witnessed the low morale of Russian military personnel.[28] On the other hand, the high morale of the Japanese and their enthusiasm for the war was apparent. Hedāyat writes:

> [In Tokyo] we visited a military school. A number of officers had gathered at a corner. One of them, wounded in the Sino-Japanese War, was limping along. We were looking around when a tumult was heard and the limping officer jumped so high that his stick hit the ceiling. We were told that they had received the newspaper confirming the news of war. I remembered the Russian officers who felt depressed about such news. There is a great difference between the two.[29]

In a reference to the preparedness of the Japanese for the war, Hedāyat recalls an interview given to a Japanese reporter in Chefu:

> He asked me various questions to find out what we knew about Russia's preparations in Manchuria. I told him that I did not

[27] Hedāyat, *Safar-nāma*, 113.

[28] Hedāyat, *Safar-nāma*, 20-23.

[29] Hedāyat, *Safar-nāma*, 103.

> inquire after such things. He insisted further, and it seemed that he would not give up until an answer was given, so I said that they (the Russians) should have 100,000 men there, and I, in turn, asked him how the Japanese could fight and win a war in such a remote land overseas? He told me that the Japanese had convincing information that Russians had no more than 40,000 men there and could not bring in many more quickly, their munitions were insufficient, Japan would certainly win a victory, and the Japanese were willing to go to war but the Russians were avoiding it.[30]

Hedāyat also refers to another incident:

> In a [lunch] party given for us [on 1 January 1904], the minstrels played and sang. In the song [a sweetheart] says [to her lover],
>
> *Tomorrow when the Russo-Japanese war breaks out,*
> *you'll go to the front to fight,*
> *and I shall follow you to dress your wounds.*
>
> Atābak was lamenting that Japan would be defeated and harmed. I told him that I did not think so, and asked him to remember the way we were treated in Port Arthur, the Japanese reporter who interviewed us in Chefu, the Russian officers' delight in hearing the news of the suspension of war. I told him to compare these with the way we were received in Japan, the officers' excitement at the military school, and the song of the new year day, and I concluded that these people wouldn't be defeated, nor would they act rashly.[31]

Among the leaders of Japanese modernization, Hedāyat most admires Itō Hirobumi (1841-1909), the most celebrated aide to Emperor Meiji, as the "founder of modern Japan"[32] and the one "whose right management and instruction initiated Japanese progress."[33] He also hails Saigō Takamori (1827-77),[34] the ill-fated leader of the Restoration,

---

[30] Hedāyat, *Safar-nāma*, 29.

[31] Hedāyat, *Safar-nāma*, 108-110.

[32] Hedāyat, *Safar-nāma*, 118.

[33] Hedāyat, *Safar-nāma*, 102.

[34] According to Edmond Papinot, *Historical and Geographical Dictionary of Japan* (Tokyo, 1972), 525-26, "Saigō Takamori played a brilliant part in the Restoration War. Some time after, the question of intervention in Korean affairs was raised. Takamori's views being opposed by most of the ministers,

as "the one equal to one thousand men."[35] (The Japanese call a distinguished brave man "the one equal to a hundred.")

Hedāyat quotes from Itō Hirobumi's interpretation of the process of Japanese modernization, writing:

> Marquis Itō has a seaside villa and comes to the city (Tokyo) once in a while.... We went there by train. After lunch we had the opportunity for a dialogue .... Atābak started the discourse, saying: "We know that Japan's advance was made possible by Your Excellency's wisdom and instruction." Itō answered that the Emperor should be praised for all these achievements. Then Atābak asked Itō how they had started, to which he answered: "Being faced, from the outset, with a need for experts, we sent talented young students to Europe and America to master various fields of science and technology, and, when this task was accomplished, we established all kinds of schools in Japan."[36]

Hedāyat takes Itō's remarks as added support for his own conviction of the decisive role of education in modernization.

On Japan's determination to win a victory, the most impressive account is given in Hedāyat's description of the audience given by Emperor Meiji to his party shortly before the war:

> An invitation had been made by the deputy foreign minister for 25 December [1903]; the gate of the Imperial Garden was open. The emperor was a handsome man and of a nice figure. His eyes were not noticeably slanted. A man of dark complexion, he looked attractive and resolved. We were told that the emperor, determined to avenge the seizure of Port Arthur by the Russians, had not left his palace for eight years and was preoccupied with preparations.[37]

On a call they paid to Count Katsura, the Japanese prime minister, on 19 December 1903, Hedāyat writes:

---

he retired to Kagoshima. On February 15, 1877, Takamori at the head of 15,000 men took possession of Kagoshima, then marching northward, he met the Kumamoto army, defeated it and laid siege to that city. The last battle took place on Shiro-yama, September 24th. Saigō fell, wounded, and one of his faithful retainers, Beppu Shinsuke, put an end to his life."

[35] Hedāyat, *Safar-nāma*, 118.

[36] Hedāyat, *Safar-nāma*, 101-2.

[37] Hedāyat, *Safar-nāma*, 100-101.

> Asked by Katsura what he had done during his office to improve the economy, Atābak said, "We had an agreement with Russia limiting customs tariffs to five percent, and customs was out of our jurisdiction. We recently succeeded in revising the agreement." The count said: "Faced with a similar problem, we adopted the European judiciary system, enacted (necessary) laws and strengthened our military forces. Europeans could have no objection. Moreover, considering our military build-up, they consented."[38]

Hedāyat commends the cordiality among the Japanese leaders exemplified in the manner of Itō Hirobumi who introduced a few of his ex-ministers as his close friends, compared to the begrudging sense of jealousy among the Iranian ministers.[39]

He concludes his memoirs of Japan by recalling an incident exemplifying Japanese sovereigns' care for their subjects:

> It is said that Emperor Daigo[40] was pursuing a humble life. On noticing smoke rising from the house of one of his subjects, he told his wife that they had become rich and prosperous. His wife asked how that could have happened when they were living in a ruined house and wearing shabby clothes. The emperor answered that a sovereign's prosperity is in the well-being of his subjects, and the smoke rising from peoples' homes (indicating their affluence) points to their sovereign's richness.[41]

What fascinated Hedāyat most were the Japanese themselves, "who have excelled themselves outwardly and inwardly while preserving their traditional values."[42]

---

[38] Hedāyat, *Safar-nāma*, 100.

[39] Hedāyat, *Safar-nāma*, 102.

[40] Papinot, *Dictionary of Japan*, 64 writes, "Daigo-tennō, the sixtieth Emperor of Japan (898-930), was Prince Atsuhito, the eldest son of Uda-tennō. He ascended the throne at the age of 13. Listening to the calumnies of the Fujiwara, Tokihira, Sadakuni, and of Minamoto-nō-Hikara, he exiled Sugawara Michizane to Dazaifu (901). During his reign, literature shone brightly: The works of Kino Tsurayuki, Miyoshi Kiyotsura, Fukane Sukebito, etc., are still classics. For that reason the Engi era (901-922) is known in history as a period of prosperity."

[41] Hedāyat, *Safar-nāma*, 140.

[42] Hedāyat, *Safar-nāma*, 119.

His references to the appearance of the Japanese are interesting and reflect the Iranian image of the Japanese at the turn of the century. Japanese order and discipline surprise him, especially "considering their [short] stature compared to Europeans."[43] Visiting a tea house in Kobe on the first day of his stay in Japan, he unexpectedly finds that "the servants are all women, and not bad-looking (and rather pleasant)."[44] He later adds, "Japanese young women are, after all, not ugly,"[45] and "When we first arrived in China and Japan, people looked strange to our eyes. After a few days when we became familiar, we even found many of them good-looking and handsome."[46] He quotes from the opening chapter of a book on Japanese history, "The Japanese are the diamond edition of humanity," adding that the phrase suggests both the short figure and the magnanimity of the people.[47]

In his final analysis, he excuses their physical shortcomings in favor of their overwhelming spiritual qualities:

> The Japanese have dark complexion, slanted eyes, black hair, swelling chest, long torso, short hands, and are thin-bearded and flat-nosed; in contrast, they are characterized by open-mindedness and insight, and they are highly industrious and very hard-working. They are endowed with bravery, pride, and a sense of honor. Since we see things as correct or distorted based on our judgment, it is right for the Japanese to regard the eyes of other people as slanted.[48]

Hedāyat praises the attitude of Shintoism, the Japanese religion, which places honor above life, and the sense of pride and fighting spirit of the Samurai.[49] He says, "Japanese religion is based on worshipping the sun, and this is very natural since all plants and living things owe their growth to the light and warmth of the sun."[50]

Of Buddhism, he says, "The word 'Buddha' means enlightened. There are no divinities in (pure) Buddhism. Regardless of

---

[43] Hedāyat, *Safar-nāma*, 93.

[44] Hedāyat, *Safar-nāma*, 95.

[45] Hedāyat, *Safar-nāma*, 109.

[46] Hedāyat, *Safar-nāma*, 136.

[47] Hedāyat, *Safar-nāma*, 137.

[48] Hedāyat, *Safar-nāma*, 136.

[49] Hedāyat, *Safar-nāma*, 124, 138.

[50] Hedāyat, *Safar-nāma*, 119.

embellishments, all religions lead to the same [right] way, provided that the followers don't deviate from the path."[51]

He also concludes that "Buddhism in principle surpasses Catholic [*sic*] teachings. Superstitious elements are what religions everywhere have been embellished with. One can not say that other (religious) teachings on man's life are any better than the Confucian ethics."[52] He quotes from Engelbert Kaempfer that the Japanese, in their religious faith, "are more pious and more careful in practice compared to Christians."[53]

Hedāyat praises the Japanese as a people characterized by their "cleanliness, magnanimity, modesty, friendliness, filial piety, respect for elders, sense of justice, appreciation of the beauty of nature, patriotism, and value of life."[54] He appreciates the craftsmanship of the Japanese: "What is more interesting to see in Japan is the people's craft."[55] In Japan, he finds that every place is neat and clean. "Japanese cleanliness and elegance increase their natural charm,"[56] and "cleanliness is one of the virtues of the Japanese."[57]

Hedāyat commends the Japanese for preserving simplicity in life and their traditional values, and regrets that Iranians have been attracted and deceived by the fallacious aspects of European civilization.[58] In admiration of the balance he finds in Japanese life, he starts with a description of the Emperor's palace: "The mikado's residence is indescribably simple."[59] He notes that "Japanese life is adorned with purity and simplicity, and based on establishing a family;"[60] "Nothing of European 'boulevard' [immoral] manners has affected Japan;"[61] and

---

[51] Hedāyat, *Safar-nāma*, 122-23.

[52] Hedāyat, *Safar-nāma*, 89.

[53] Hedāyat, *Safar-nāma*, 137.

[54] Hedāyat, *Safar-nāma*, 115.

[55] Hedāyat, *Safar-nāma*, 96. On Japanese diligence, Hedāyat adds, p. 97, "They make every effort to exploit their skills, and they give the utmost attention to commerce"; p. 125, "The Japanese have a talent to advise"; and, p. 99, "To one's astonishment, the craftsmanship of the Japanese converts worthless material to something useful."

[56] Hedāyat, *Safar-nāma*, 94.

[57] Hedāyat, *Safar-nāma*, 115.

[58] Hedāyat, *Safar-nāma*, 131.

[59] Hedāyat, *Safar-nāma*, 100.

[60] Hedāyat, *Safar-nāma*, 126.

[61] Hedāyat, *Safar-nāma*, 111.

"Divorce is a rare incident in Japan."[62] "Decent ladies were not only veiled but cared that their voice be not heard by strangers."[63]

On Japanese love for elegance and beauty, he says: "They are very fond of outings and garden viewing, have an special interest in plants and flowers; their social gatherings are pleasant."[64]

Of Japanese self respect, he writes: "No beggars were to be seen in Japan, contrary to China, where they swarm."[65] He recalls an incident:

> A woman was carrying a basket of apples [to sell]. Atābak gave her half a yen, and we went on. She ran after us, insisting that we take apples for the money. We realized that she did not accept money for nothing. We were obliged to return (to her basket) and take some apples.[66]

He also praises the absence of the annoying custom of giving and accepting tips in Japan, and refers to incidents when the officers in charge of escorting or entertaining them refused to accept the money given to them as a tip.[67]

He admires the merit of self-control in Japanese people, and quotes from the British ambassador in Tokyo: "The day when the treaty of war and peace [i.e., alliance] was signed between England and Japan, there were demonstrations in London while in Tokyo they showed indifference." He adds, "The self-control of the [Japanese] two thousand year old monarchy exceeded that of the [British?] seven hundred year old government."[68] He praises the Japanese as "the people who do everything with firmness and dignity"[69] and observes that "opium smoking is forbidden in Japan, where they consider it the Chinese disease."[70]

In Hedāyat's memoirs, we find amusing descriptions of Japanese things, such as the Japanese drink made of rice (*sake*), Japanese braziers, musical instruments, floor mats, adults' and children's games,

---

[62] Hedāyat, *Safar-nāma*, 128.

[63] Hedāyat, *Safar-nāma*, 130.

[64] Hedāyat, *Safar-nāma*, 125.

[65] Hedāyat, *Safar-nāma*, 97.

[66] Hedāyat, *Safar-nāma*, 97.

[67] Hedāyat, *Safar-nāma*, 99, 105, 114.

[68] Hedāyat, *Safar-nāma*, 110 and idem, *Ḵaṭerāt va ḵaṭarāt* (Tehran 1329 Š./1950), 412.

[69] Hedāyat, *Safar-nāma*, 103.

[70] Hedāyat, *Safar-nāma*, 131.

Japanese dishes and their decorative arrangements. "The Japanese garment is also a long robe [similar to] the *šāl* or Kurdish wear, but made of silk."[71]

He also makes an elaborate reference to the Japanese literary heritage and quotes examples of its verses and proverbs.[72] He finds Japanese *haiku*, short poems consisting of seventeen syllables, similar to the Avestan Gathas[73] and quotes verses from the *Manyōshū*, an old Japanese anthology. He states, however, that the Japanese owe the origin of their literature to the Chinese,[74] and he finds the Japanese pen more expressive in drawing than in writing.[75]

The habits and traditions of the Japanese, like their eating manners, women's hairstyle, wedding ceremonies, funerals, and entertainment fascinate Hedāyat. Similarly, he appreciates the beauty and elegance of Japanese music, quoting from Confucius: "The [cultural] advancement of a nation is shown by its perfection in music."[76] He gives a fascinating account of the Japanese custom of *tsukimi*, viewing the full moon on an autumn night.[77] Among other things, he describes a kind of polo, arranged in Tokyo to entertain them, and played with soft balls made of cloth, most probably a tradition from ancient Iran. This polo game is only played on rare ceremonial occasions in Japan today.

Facts on relations and exchanges between ancient Iran and Japan are hidden in the mist of history. Matsumoto Seicho, a contemporary Japanese writer, in his book titled *Hi-no-Kairo* (*The Sun Route*) suggests that during the sixth and seventh centuries a group of Iranians arrived in Japan and influenced its culture. Hayashi Ryōichi, another Japanese writer, in his valuable book, *Shiruko Rōdo* (*The Silk Road*) mentions members of Iranian nobility who, after the decline of the Sasanian Dynasty, headed for China and thence to Japan, bringing with them many cultural souvenirs.

In this regard, Hedāyat notes that exchanges presumably took place between Iran and Japan in ancient times. During the luncheon following the delegation's visit to a naval port, he says:

---

[71] Hedāyat, *Safar-nāma*, 110; for his other comments on Japanese culture, see pp. 109-110.

[72] Hedāyat, *Safar-nāma*, 105, 112, 132-34.

[73] Hedāyat, *Safar-nāma*, 134.

[74] Hedāyat, *Safar-nāma*, 132.

[75] Hedāyat, *Safar-nāma*, 136.

[76] Hedāyat, *Safar-nāma*, 83.

[77] Hedāyat, *Safar-nāma*, 120.

> One of the (Japanese) hosts said that their minister of culture found in a manuscript discovered inside a Buddha statue that following Alexander's invasion an Iranian prince came to Japan, and the line of Japanese emperors extends to him. Atābak answered: "We know this much, that members of the Iranian royal family [fled and] were dispersed in the confusion, but where they went we don't know."[78]

Hedāyat adds:

> In the migration of a Mongol [sic] tribe to Japan that took place around that time, some Iranian royal princes have probably accompanied them. The details of events, if accurately recorded, don't correspond but [the shape of] hats [seen in monuments], the sun on the flag, and the symbols and motifs of chrysanthemums abundant in and around Persepolis makes one think [of the possibility].[79]

He further observed that in Japan also, "a chrysanthemum with sixteen petals, seen everywhere, is the royal seal [and symbol]."[80]

Hedāyat is critical of "the unrestrained freedom in Europe that fascinates and misleads people,"[81] and he admires the Japanese for preserving their values and their lifestyle: "The first thing unprincipled people imitate is appearance. This is the appearance that changes the negligent people's minds."[82] The Japanese "respond to Europeans with European manners but are loyal to their tradition among themselves. The unrestrained [aspect of] the European way of life does not appeal to them. They could not be deceived by fashion."[83]

Hedāyat, who had stayed in Europe as a student, is critical about Western nations which, he believes, consider only their own interests, want to profit by any means, and maintain an aggressive attitude towards Asians. He finds the American way of life more disagreeable than the European one, comparing the Europeans, in their restless search for material gain and accumulating wealth, to ants, and the Americans to fast-moving ants.[84]

---

[78] Hedāyat, *Safar-nāma*, 102.
[79] Hedāyat, *Safar-nāma*, 102.
[80] Hedāyat, *Safar-nāma*, 97.
[81] Hedāyat, *Safar-nāma*, 124.
[82] Hedāyat, *Safar-nāma*, 124.
[83] Hedāyat, *Safar-nāma*, 119.
[84] Hedāyat, *Safar-nāma*, 149.

Hedāyat finds Japan a good example to support his long cherished idea of the superiority of the Orient over the West. On European ambitions he writes, "They take all efforts to benefit in any way possible and lay hands everywhere. If a nation opposes their advances, they reject it as uncivilized, whereas the Asians have taught manners to other nations."[85]

Among the Europeans active overseas, Hedāyat criticizes the Catholic missionaries most, blaming them for having caused the Boxer uprising of 1900 in China.[86]

He finds a healthier society in Japan, where "no daughters in families are left unmarried, while in Europe eighty percent of girls are vagrant" and "Europeans are surprised to see in the East that daughters are obedient to their parents. However, having been criticized so much, nowadays Japanese men let their wives go first in foreign receptions, lest to offend the educated women."[87]

Oriental teachings suit the Japanese mind and life best: "Bushido [the spirit of the Samurai] is based on five Confucian principles, namely: subordination of the ruled to the ruler, filial piety, obedience of wife to her husband, obedience of younger to the elder, and frankness among friends; Mencius [372-288 B.C.] added a touch of democracy that is the beginning of disobedience."[88] He concludes by adding that "a nation which considers justice the very foundation of the Samurai thinking, finds nothing new in democracy."[89]

Finally, he names Japan as an ideally modernized country, writing: "The most commendable thing about the Japanese is their insight, by which merit they have adopted [from the outside] only what is worthy and desirable, maintaining their originality, and not being deluded by outward appearances."[90] Observing the situation some years later, however, Hedāyat regrets that the Japanese had gone a little too far in adopting European social customs and finds it difficult to make excuses for it. He shows sympathy for the Chinese, whom he regards as being held back by their modesty, self-reliance, seclusion, and the lack of such decisive and just leaders as the Japanese had. He concludes that, to set the stage for progress, "a nation can not be political; politics, rather, should be national."[91]

---

[85] Hedāyat, *Safar-nāma*, 119.

[86] Hedāyat, *Safar-nāma*, 89.

[87] Hedāyat, *Safar-nāma*, 128.

[88] Hedāyat, *Safar-nāma*, 139.

[89] Hedāyat, *Safar-nāma*, 139.

[90] Hedāyat, *Safar-nāma*, 118-119.

[91] Hedāyat, *Safar-nāma*, 139.

Hedāyat is one of the few Iranian statesmen who had a first-hand and highly insightful experience of Japan. Hedāyat, an ardent admirer of Japan after his short visit to the country in the winter of 1903-4, was sad to find a completely different atmosphere upon his return to Iran.[92] As noted earlier, he maintained that his main purpose in accepting Atābak's offer to accompany him on his trip to the Far East was to influence Atābak's mind and help him to prepare to enforce progressive measures in Iran. He thought that Atābak had indeed been impressed by his experiences abroad and had come to realize the needs of Iran.[93] He writes that Atābak had been awakened by Itō Hirobumi's remarks, and he laments Atābak's assassination shortly after returning to Iran.[94]

Hedāyat finds Moẓaffar-al-Dīn Shah too reserved to take reform measures: "The shah was a democrat by nature. Once he summoned me to Faraḥābād [Palace]; I went. Nobody was present except Sayyed Baḥraynī [the shah's guru]. Yet, he came close to me and quietly asked whether Japan has a parliament. I answered that it did, and had for eight years now."[95]

Hedāyat recalls another instance when he spent a whole night at the bedside of the ailing king, speaking about Japan as he had been instructed. He comments, "The king was so reserved that whenever I started to talk about Japan's progress [in the presence of others] he would ask me to speak of Japanese plants instead,"[96] and "whenever I was given an audience, the shah would ask me about Japan, but wouldn't listen to political remarks. Once I started to discuss Marquis Itō and his reforms, he would interrupt me and ask me to talk about Japanese plants instead."[97]

Mīrzā Ebrāhīm in Japan

During the decade preceding Hedāyat's visit to Japan, a merchant, who introduces himself in his memoirs as Ebrāhīm Saḥḥāfbāšī Ṭehrānī, had made several business trips to Japan, one taking him around the world from Iran to Europe, North America, Japan, the Far East, and India. His interesting diary remains. According to this book, published in Iran in 1978, the author, commissioned to sell some jewels, started his trip on 13 May 1897 from the port city of Anzalī, south of the

---

92 Hedāyat, *Ḵaṭerāt*, 136-37.

93 Hedāyat, *Ḵaṭerāt*, 135.

94 Hedāyat, *Ḵaṭerāt*, 152-59.

95 Hedāyat, *Ḵaṭerāt*, 142.

96 Hedāyat, *Gozāreš*, 143.

97 Hedāyat, *Gozāreš*, 137.

Caspian Sea, for Petrovsk and then to Moscow, where he took a train for Berlin, arriving there on 23 May. He spent a few weeks in Berlin, Paris, and London before leaving for North America on 9 July 1897. He made a cross-continent trip by train from New York to Toronto and then set forth on a long sea journey from Victoria to Yokohama, where he arrived on 15 August 1897.[98] According to his journals, his stay in Japan lasted forty-eight days, until 2 October, when he got on board a French ship for Hong Kong, Bombay, and Karachi.[99] He concludes his journals with an account of his arriving in the port of Karachi and dates the completion as 27 January 1898 (4 Ramażān 1315).[100]

This Mīrzā Ebrāhīm Khan is certainly different from the famous individual who was one of the first students sent in 1859 by the Qajar court to France to study there. He is also not to be confused with yet another Ṣaḥḥāfbāšī whose first name was (Ḥājjī) Esmāʿīl and who is credited with bringing new ideas and innovations to Iran such as the cinema and the phonograph.[101] The jeweler Mīrzā Ebrāhīm, who has recorded one of his business trips round the world in his journals, was apparently a younger son of the French-educated Ṣaḥḥāfbāšī and a brother of Esmāʿīl. Unlike the other two, this Ṣaḥḥāfbāšī was not a well educated person, nor did he know English or French well enough to speak them easily.[102] He was commissioned by a jewelry owner to find customers for some items of jewelry.[103] He complained once and again about the hardship he experienced during the trip.[104]

Before his recorded trip around the world, during which he spent several weeks in Japan, Ṣaḥḥāfbāšī had frequented Japan and India for business, and he refers to his twenty-years experience in overseas trips.[105] In his memoirs, Mahdīqolī Hedāyat makes references to Ṣaḥḥāfbāšī's frequent visits to Japan:

> In Tokyo, Atābak once said, "No Iranian has made such a trip [to Japan]." I said, "[Some] one has made it." He asked, "Who?" and I answered: "Ṣaḥḥāfbāšī has frequently come to Japan,

---

[98] Ṣaḥḥāfbāšī, *Safar-nāma*, 85.

[99] Ṣaḥḥāfbāšī, *Safar-nāma*, 91.

[100] Ṣaḥḥāfbāšī, *Safar-nāma*, 99.

[101] See Hāšem Rajabzāda, "Žāpon dar chašm-e Ṣaḥḥāfbāšī," *Kelk* 28 (1371 Š./1992):95-100.

[102] Ṣaḥḥāfbāšī, *Safar-nāma*, 34. 46, 71, 84.

[103] Ṣaḥḥāfbāšī, *Safar-nāma*, 49.

[104] Ṣaḥḥāfbāšī, *Safar-nāma*, 48, 76.

[105] Ṣaḥḥāfbāšī, *Safar-nāma*, 3, 12, 90.

> through India or Siberia." But I felt that he did not like my answer, and he was right to feel so, since visits [by different people and in different circumstances] are not the same [in quality].[106]
>
> On each trip to Japan, Ṣaḥḥāfbāšī used to bring back samples of manufactured items, and therefore many households here possess some Japanese wares.[107]

Ṣaḥḥāfbāšī himself refers to his previous visits to the Far East and India.[108]

Ṣaḥḥāfbāšī's first impression of Japan makes us think that he considered this country a part of the industrially advanced world, as he recalls the exchange of signals between the ship he was aboard and the lighthouse in Yokohama on the night they approached the port: "When entering into Japan, the efficiency of telecommunication system is a sign of the modernization of the country."[109] However, his first observation was of Japanese women appearing "naked" in public, about which he is most critical:

> The Japanese have no modesty at all. Among other incidents, I witnessed a woman who [after taking a bath] came out of the water in the presence of a group of men and put her dress on. I also noticed a woman in a beauty parlor where a man was dressing her up. They don't feel shame at all.[110]

It is, however, interesting that in this land where "there is no veil" and "men and women take baths together," he also says "men are modest and never gawk [at the women]."[111]

Ṣaḥḥāfbāšī's account of quarrels and violence among the Japanese[112] is nothing more than a generalization of some isolated incidents he happened to hear about.

Of the cities visited in Japan, Ṣaḥḥāfbāšī names only Yokohama (his entry and exit port); Kobe, where he visited and was fascinated by a marine-life exhibition;[113] and Tokyo, where he apparently spent

---

[106] Hedāyat, *Safar-nāma*, 114.
[107] Hedāyat, *Safar-nāma*, 125.
[108] Ṣaḥḥāfbāšī, *Safar-nāma*, 12, 98.
[109] Ṣaḥḥāfbāšī, *Safar-nāma*, 85.
[110] Ṣaḥḥāfbāšī, *Safar-nāma*, 85.
[111] Ṣaḥḥāfbāšī, *Safar-nāma*, 91.
[112] Ṣaḥḥāfbāšī, *Safar-nāma*, 87.
[113] Ṣaḥḥāfbāšī, *Safar-nāma*, 89.

most of his several weeks in Japan. His visit to Japan coincided with seasonal typhoons, some of which he experienced.[114]

Ṣaḥḥāfbāšī arrived in Japan some two years after the country's occupation of most of the Korean Peninsula and the end of her war with China and the Triple Intervention thereafter.[115] Under the circumstances, Ṣaḥḥāfbāšī understandingly shows mixed feelings about the Japanese advance: "I observed the condition of the Chinese and found them to be very oppressed and felt sympathy for them, especially after hearing about the way they are ruled and the injustices incurred because of the Japanese army's occupation of Formosa."[116] In another reflection, he blames the Chinese rulers for the sufferings of the nation: "The Chinese are very oppressed, decent, and humble people. They are never wicked or insolent. Nothing has caused this lack of spirit but the injustice and oppression of Chinese rulers who humiliate their subjects. All kinds of wrong doings, ignorance, and injustice are prevalent among the Chinese leaders."[117]

He finds an opposite situation in Japan, where "the injustices to the Chinese in Formosa were committed by ordinary soldiers and some low-ranking junior officers, while the Japanese Court of Justice does not endorse such practices."[118] On the contrary, "commoners in China are honest by nature, and transactions here are generally done on word," and "unlike the Japanese who are fraudulent and dishonest, the Chinese don't use trickery and are very trustworthy."[119]

Ṣaḥḥāfbāšī admires the diligence of the Japanese, who "from their children of four or five years old to the aged people, men and women are all busy in learning or doing some job," and "although

---

[114] Ṣaḥḥāfbāšī, *Safar-nāma*, 88.

[115] Hall, *Japan*, 303, notes that the relatively easy victory Japan gained over China in their War of 1894-95 "caught the world by surprise and demonstrated to the western powers Japan's quick mastery of modern weapons and warfare. The war also proved that Japan was a power to contend with in the Far Eastern area. The possible threat which Japan posed to the Western powers gained quick recognition in the Triple Intervention of 1895. Alarmed by the prospect of Japan's further expansion into the mainland, Russia, Germany and France moved to block Japan's acquisition of the Liaotung Peninsula as part of the spoils from war with China."

[116] Ṣaḥḥāfbāšī, *Safar-nāma*, 93.

[117] Ṣaḥḥāfbāšī, *Safar-nāma*, 92-93.

[118] Ṣaḥḥāfbāšī, *Safar-nāma*, 92-93.

[119] Ṣaḥḥāfbāšī, *Safar-nāma*, 97-98.

they can make a living easily, they never sit idle. Beggars are few and seen very rarely."[120] "These people live very economically."[121]

The Japanese, who "generally have slanted eyes, hairless skin and hard chests, and are squat and white-skinned,"[122] make their buildings more resistant against earthquakes,[123] cover the floor of their homes with a straw mat, and sit on a small mattress.[124] "They usually have cooked rice served with salted fish and vegetables eaten with two pieces of wood."[125] He also describes the *jin-rikisha*: "Their common means of transportation is a two-wheeled coach [pulled by] a man running as fast as a horse."[126] He does not enjoy the music played on a Japanese lute (*shamisen*) which he thinks is not played correctly or well, and therefore sounds out of tune![127] In general, his introduction to Japanese food and drink, and the way they were served, lacks the sophistication, excitement, and admiration with which Hedāyat describes them.

In explaining what the Japanese wear, Ṣaḥḥāfbāšī describes the wide belt (*obi*) which fastens ladies' kimonos and the folded part in the back (*otāiko*) as merely decorative things.

Ṣaḥḥāfbāšī generalized many of the practices he heard about in Japan and found them to be somehow similar to those prevalent in Iran. For example, he noted that in some of their habits, such as sitting on the floor and taking their shoes off before entering into a room, the Japanese were also very similar to Iranians.[128] Men's kimonos to him looked similar to the Iranian type of loose cloak (the *ʿabā*).[129]

On the spiritual life of the people, he realizes that "the Japanese are ardent believers,"[130] and finds that their custom of keeping Buddhist and Shinto family shrines or altars (*butsudan* and *kamidana* respectively) at home comes from their belief in superstitions. "Many sick people go to and ask the monks to write amulets for them, instead of visiting a doctor."[131]

---

[120] Ṣaḥḥāfbāšī, *Safar-nāma*, 87.

[121] Ṣaḥḥāfbāšī, *Safar-nāma*, 91.

[122] Ṣaḥḥāfbāšī, *Safar-nāma*, 86.

[123] Ṣaḥḥāfbāšī, *Safar-nāma*, 88-89.

[124] Ṣaḥḥāfbāšī, *Safar-nāma*, 87.

[125] Ṣaḥḥāfbāšī, *Safar-nāma*, 87.

[126] Ṣaḥḥāfbāšī, *Safar-nāma*, 86.

[127] Ṣaḥḥāfbāšī, *Safar-nāma*, 87-88.

[128] Ṣaḥḥāfbāšī, *Safar-nāma*, 86.

[129] Ṣaḥḥāfbāšī, *Safar-nāma*, 86.

[130] Ṣaḥḥāfbāšī, *Safar-nāma*, 86.

[131] Ṣaḥḥāfbāšī, *Safar-nāma*, 90.

Japanese Travelers to Qajar Persia

A brief review of Japanese travelers' accounts of nineteenth century Persia can shed some light on the process of observation and interaction from the opposite side.

In 1880, a few years after the Restoration (1868) and in the thirteenth year of the reign of Emperor Meiji (1867-1912), Japan sent an official delegation to Persia. The move was apparently initiated by Japan and agreed upon when Enomoto Buyo, the Japanese envoy in St. Petersburg, had an audience with Nāṣer-al-Dīn Shah who was on his way back home after visiting Europe.

Yoshida Masaharu (1852-1921), who headed this delegation, was representative of the enlightened statesmen of the late Edo period (1603-1867) and early Meiji Era (1867-1912) who led Japan to modernization. A son of a high ranking samurai from Tosa, he studied law, established a newspaper siding with the constitutionalists, and at the age of twenty-nine headed the first Japanese delegation to Persia and the Ottoman Empire (1880-81).

In this delegation Yoshida was accompanied by Furukawa Senya, an officer of the Japanese general staff, Yokoyama Magoichiro of Okura Trading Company, and four other merchants. They started their trip on 5 April 1880, from Tokyo Bay on board a Japanese warship, the *Hiei*, which was leaving for the Indian Ocean for a port call. Separated from the other members in Hong Kong, Yoshida and Yokoyama arrived in Bushehr earlier and had enough time to venture on a difficult trip to the ruins of Babylon.

The delegation experienced a hard time during the forty-two days traveling from Bushehr to Tehran where they arrived on 10 September and stayed for 110 days before leaving for Anzalī and Baku in early January 1881.

Besides the report Yoshida and Furukawa submitted to the Ministry of Foreign Affairs and the General Staff of Army respectively, each has written an interesting and informative account of the trip. Furukawa's *Perushiya Kiko* ("Persian Memoir") was published in Tokyo in 1890, and Yoshida's *Perushiya-no-Tabi* ("A Journey to Persia"), in 191 pages, was published in Tokyo in 1894.[132]

In his account, Yoshida recalls how he managed to encourage members of the delegation, most of them merchants with no experience

---

[132] A brief introduction to Yoshida's *Persian Memoirs* was published by Hāšem Rajabzāda in *Īrān-šenāsī* 5(1993), and a complete annotated translation of the memoirs by this author was published by Āstān-e Qods Publishers (Mašhad, 1994).

of traveling in harsh climates and difficult conditions, to stand the hardship of the trip. He writes, "We Japanese are very sensitive people and conservative by nature. We have a strong sense of shame and pride, which I was using to persuade my inexperienced companions."[133]

Due to inadequate communications, and faced with the stiff rivalry between the British and the Russians over Iran, the Japanese delegation had to undergo many hardships and face disappointment during its short stay in Iran. *Habl al-matīn*, the famous Persian newspaper published in Calcutta, suggested in its issue of 5 August 1912 that the main obstacle in the way of the delegation's success was Russia, which was blocking closer ties between Iran and the Ottoman Empire and Japan.

The delegation, whose main objective was to establish trade with Iran, and especially to find a market for Japanese tea, is said not to have been successful. But the impression it made and information it gathered were certainly valuable in the process of policy making in those crucial years for Japan.

Yoshida's delegation was followed by other Japanese travelers visiting Iran at the turn of the century and on the eve of the Constitutional Revolution of 1906. The late Inoue Eiji, an enthusiast of Iranian studies who lived in Iran for many years, in his diaries, *Waga Kaisō-no-Iran* ("My Memories of Iran"), published in 1986, has a chapter on the relations between Iran and Japan in the Meiji Era in which he briefly introduces travelers from Meiji Japan to Qajar Persia.[134]

He makes reference, among others, to Inoue Masaji who, while in his twenties and during the years he was studying in Vienna and Berlin, ventured on a forty-five day journey to Central Asia and Persia in the summer of 1902. His *Memoirs of Central Asia*, an interesting account of his trip, was published the following year.[135]

According to Inoue Eiji, when Masaji arrived in Tehran, he was delighted to find names of some renowned Japanese travelers, like Fukushima, the great explorer of Central Asia, in the book of the hotel at which he was staying.

Yoshida's memoirs contain many interesting accounts of his observations in Persia. He tried to see people and places with open eyes and an inquiring mind. Upon his arrival in Tehran, Yoshida paid

---

[133] Yoshida, *Perushiya*, 124.

[134] Inoue Eiji, *Waga Kaisō-no-Iran*, ed. Inoue Masayuki (Tokyo, 1986), 280-95.

[135] Inoue Masaji, *Chuo Ajiya Ryōkoki* (Tokyo, 1903).

a courtesy call to Mīrzā Ḥosayn Khan Sepahsālār, foreign minister of Nāṣer-al-Dīn Shah, one day before his sudden discharge from office, which Yoshida regrets since he had found Sepahsālār a driving force behind reform measures.

Yoshida, who was given audience by Nāṣer-al-Dīn Shah twice, appreciated the shah's curiosity about rail transportation and the military build-up in Japan, but he found that only a few high ranking officials could communicate in English or French, and fewer still of them cared about the interest of their country. While he found most of the government officials greedy and corrupt, he admired the good nature, diligence, and purity of the soldiers and commoners.

The natural beauty of Iran, the magnificence of its historical monuments, and the elegance of Persian art and architecture fascinated Yoshida. His description of Persian things and people's lifestyle, traditions, and customs, some of which he finds similar to those in Japan, is interesting.

Yoshida concludes his memoir by expressing his concern about the future of Persia, caught as it was between two rival powers, the Dragon and the Tiger, namely Britain and Russia (which Persians were calling the Lion and the Bear respectively): "If Persia does not move fast and make an effort to seek a remedy for the situation, it will most probably sustain a loss in the rivalry of the powers in the Far East. It worries me that Persia might become involved in what I have always been anxious about."[136]

Conclusion

The two travelers, Hedāyat and Ṣaḥḥāfbāšī, who visited Japan in the closing years of the nineteenth century or soon afterwards and left records of their visits, did not have a similar background, social status, or point of view.

Hedāyat was a member of a noble and influential family and a well-educated man who, while adhering to the old values of his traditional society, cherished modernization and the new technology. As a representative of the intelligentsia, he stressed the need for a strong and just leadership capable of handling the public administration efficiently and of checking the influence of the foreign powers which were competing with each other to exploit and colonize Iran. Hedāyat admired the Japanese people for their simplicity in life, diligence, contentment, self-respect, awareness, firmness, and dignity. As he observed, the affairs of state in Japan were left to a small group of

[136] Yoshida, *Perushiya*, 190.

meritorious, capable statesmen who considered the interest of their nation first and foremost. Hedāyat did not have an absolute belief in western democracy in the form of elective government which was cherished by nationalist elements in Iran on the eve of the Constitutional Revolution in 1906. He saw in Japan a good example to support his idea that education is the foundation of any desirable change and that "a nation cannot be political; politics, rather, should be national."[137]

Ṣaḥḥāfbāšī frequented Japan a few years before Hedāyat's visit, and he criticized the Japanese people for their superstitious beliefs, their social manners, and their appearance—mainly because of his misunderstanding of and lack of taste for Japanese things. However, he was also moved by their diligence, eagerness for learning, self-consciousness, and the frugal way in which they lived. He noticed signs of technological achievement and modernization from the moment his ship approached Japanese shores.

In comparing the comments Ṣaḥḥāfbāšī makes regarding the situation vis-à-vis China and Japan with those of Hedāyat, it is noteworthy that both attribute the fate of these nations to the qualities of their respective leaders. National political rulers made Japan a progressive and advanced country, and they caused humiliation, defeat and suffering for the Chinese people. While Ṣaḥḥāfbāšī is not moved by Japan and its people as much as Hedāyat was, and he gives a far less enthusiastic account of the country, it is evident from both their memoirs that their visits to Japan had confirmed and strengthened their belief in the dominant role a capable and just leadership plays in advancing a nation. In that sense, they were both advocates of what in modern politics is termed "revolution from above."

---

[137] Hedāyat, *Safar-nāma*, 139.

Eroticizing Europe

Mohammad Tavakoli-Targhi

The European woman (*zan-e farangī*) was the locus of gaze and erotic fantasy for many eighteenth- and nineteenth-century Persian visitors to Europe, who were thus both voyagers and voyeurs and hence might be called "voyageurs." The travelers' recounting of their experience provided material for the formation of a discourse on the women of Europe. Given the political hegemony of Europe, woman's body served as an important marker of identity and difference and as a subject of cultural and political contention. The eroticized depiction of European women by Persian male travelers engendered a desire for that "heaven on earth" and its uninhibited and fairy-like residents, who displayed their beauty and mingled with men. The attraction of Europe and European women figured into political struggles and contributed to the formation of new political discourses and identities. These discourses resulted in the valorization of the veil (*ḥejāb*) as an imaginary signifier of the self and the Other. For Iranian modernists, viewing European women as educated and cultured, the veil became a symbol of backwardness. Its removal, in their view, was essential to the advancement of Iran and its dissociation from Arab-Islamic culture. For the counter-modernists, who wanted to uphold the traditional Islamic social and gender order, the European woman became a scapegoat and a symbol of corruption, immorality, genealogical confusion, secularization, feminization of power, and deviation from the straight path of Islam.

In the Iranian "body politic," the imagined European woman thus provided the subtext for political maneuvers over women's rights and appearance in the public space. These encounters transformed the notion of womanhood (*zanānegī*) from the opposite of masculinity (*mardānegī*) into new conceptions of gender identity. Reżā Shah's coerced unveiling of women in 1936 and Khomeini's compulsory re-veiling of women in 1979 were both influenced by different perceptions of the European woman. The following pages will analyze Persian travelers' recounting of their experience in eighteenth and nineteenth-century Europe and the consequent shaping of two competing discourses on European women.

"Plunderers of Heart and Religion"

Fascination with non-Muslim women has a long history in Perso-Islamic literary culture. The mystical "Story of Sheikh Ṣanʿān" by Farīd-al-Dīn ʿAṭṭār (540-618/1145-1221) is one of the most famous and often narrated tales expressing the Persian imagination on the erotic and the exotic.[1] Sheikh Ṣanʿān, the keeper of Mecca's holy shrine and an accomplished mystic with four hundred disciples, had fallen in love with a Rūmī (Roman/Greek) Christian girl whose beauty "was like the sun in splendor."[2] Her eyes "were a lure for lovers," her face "sparkled like a living flame," and "the silver dimple of her chin was as vivifying as the discourses of Jesus."[3] The Christian woman set forth four difficult demands before she would agree to marry the mystic: "prostrate yourself before idols, burn the Koran, drink wine, and shut your eyes to your religion."[4] After he had fulfilled these conditions and converted to Christianity, the woman requested, instead of the usual dowry, "Now, for my dowry, O imperfect man, go and look after my herd of pigs for the space of a year, and then we shall pass our lives in joy or sadness."[5] Deeply in love, Shaikh Ṣanʿān accepted this task: "Without a protest the sheikh of the Kaaba, this saint, resigned himself to becoming a hog-ward."[6] At the end of the tale, Sheikh Ṣanʿān reconverted, and his Christian beloved also accepted Islam. This and

---

[1] The "Story of Shaikh Ṣanʿān" is a story within the chain of narratives known as *Manṭeq al-ṭayr*. For the Persian original, see *Šayḵ-e Sanʿān*, ed. Ṣādeq Gowharīn (Tehran, 1345 Š./1967); also see *Manṭeq al-ṭayr*, ed. Aḥmad Ḵūhnevīs (Isfahan, 1978), 66-85. English translations include *The Conference of the Birds, Mantiq ut-Tair: A Philosophical Religious Poem in Prose*, tr. C. S. Nott (London, 1961; repr. New York, 1974), 34-44, and *The Conference of the Birds*, tr. Afkham Darbandi and Dick Davis (New York, 1984), 57-75. For futher information on ʿAṭṭār and his mystical poetry see Margaret Smith, *The Persian Mystic Attar* (London, 1932); Badīʿ-al-Zamān Forūzānfar, *Šarḥ-e aḥvāl va naqd o taḥlīl-e āṯār-e Šayḵ Farīd-al-Dīn Moḥammad ʿAṭṭār Nīšābūrī* (Tehran, 1940 Š./1961); Neʿmat-Allāh Qāšī, *Bīsū-ye Sīmorḡ* (Tehran, n.d.).

[2] ʿAṭṭār/Nott, *Conference of the Birds*, 34.

[3] ʿAṭṭār/Nott, *Conference of the Birds*, 34, 35.

[4] ʿAṭṭār/Nott, *Conference of the Birds*, 37.

[5] ʿAṭṭār/Nott, *Conference of the Birds*, 39.

[6] ʿAṭṭār/Nott, *Conference of the Birds*, 39.

other similar stories provide a glimpse of how exotic and erotic Christian women figured in the philosophical and religious formation of identities in pre-modern South and Southwest Asia.

Persian travelers' accounts of their journeys to Europe frequently followed the narrative plot of the "Story of Sheikh Ṣanʿān." While enthusiastically reporting on the liberty of European women, their mixing with men in masquerade and dancing parties, and their sexual laxity, at the same time they often sought forgiveness for deviating from the straight path during their journey to infideldom (*kofrestān*). For example, Mīrzā Abū Ṭāleb Laknawī Eṣfahānī (1752-1806), who traveled to Europe during the years 1799-1803, confessed to having abandoned his cherished goal of learning "English sciences" (*ʿelm-e engelīs*) in favor of "love and gaiety" in London. On his return journey home, he visited the shrines of the Shiʿite Imams ʿAlī, Ḥosayn, and Zayn-al-ʿAbedīn and sought their forgiveness for his sins in Europe. He also composed two elegies in praise of ʿAlī and Ḥosayn:

> Whilst at Baghdad, I had them beautifully transcribed on gold paper and suspended them near the tombs of those illustrious saints at Karbela and Najaf. These elegies were much approved by both the superintendents; and they promised me to take care they were not removed, but they should be preserved, a testimony of my zeal.[7]

Not all the travelers visited Muslim shrines repenting for their experiences in Europe like Mīrzā Abū Ṭāleb, but they often assumed the posture of objective observers in their recounting of Europe and Europeans. This objectivist posture, like repentance, enabled the travelers to reintegrate themselves into their own society by making the European an exotic Other.

The early Persian travelers described Europe as "heaven on Earth" (*behešt-e rū-ye zamīn*),[8] "the birth-place of beauty" (*zād būm-e ḥosn*),[9]

---

[7] Mīrzā Abū Ṭāleb Khan, *Masīr-e ṭālebī yā safar-nāma-ye Mīrzā Abū Ṭāleb Ḵān*, ed. Ḥosayn Ḵadīv-jam (Tehran, 1973), 408-20; henceforth, *Masīr*. The Persian text was originally published in Calcutta in 1812 by Mīrzā Abū Ṭāleb's son, Mīrzā Ḥosayn-ʿAlī. For an English translation, see Mīrzā Abū Ṭāleb Khan, *The Travels of Mirza Abu Taleb Khan in Asia, Africa, and Europe during the years 1799, 1800, 1801, 1802, and 1893*, tr. Charles Stewart (2 vols, London, 1810; repr. New Delhi, 1972).

[8] Abu'l-Ḥasan Khan Īlčī, *Ḥayrat-nāma: Safar-nāma-ye Mīrzā Abu'l-Ḥasan Khan Īlčī ba Landan*, ed. Ḥasan Morselvand (Tehran, 1364 Š./1986).

[9] Mīrzā Eʿteṣām-al-Dīn, *Šegarf-nāma-ye velāyat* (MS London, British Library, OR 5848), fol. 83b.

and "the beauty cultivating land" (*molk-e ḥosn ḵīz*).[10] The attraction of Europe paralleled the attraction of the "houri-like" (*ḥūrvaš*),[11] "fairy-countenanced" (*ḥūr-peykar*),[12] and "fairy-mannered" (*ferešta-ḵūy*)[13] women of Europe. The appearance of unveiled women in public parks, playhouses, operas, dances, and masquerades impressed the Persian "voyageurs," who were unaccustomed to the public display of female beauty. For them, the only cultural equivalent to the public display of male-female intimacy was the imaginary Muslim heaven. In the Muslim heaven, all desires could be fulfilled without delay. Unlike the Šarīʿa-bound earthly societies, the pious residents of heaven were to be rewarded with "the fair ones ... whom neither man nor jinni will have touched before them ...."[14] Like many other Persian travelers, Eʿteṣām-al-Dīn, who traveled to England in 1765, was attracted to the spectacle of male-female intimacy in public parks. Recalling the scenes he observed in a public park near the Queen's Palace in London, for example, he wrote:

> On Sunday, men, women, and youths, poor and rich, travelers and natives, resort here. This park enlivens the heart, and people overcome with sorrow, repairing thither, are entertained in a heavenly manner; and grieved hearts, from seeing that place of amusement, are gladdened against their will. On every side females with silver forms, resembling peacocks, walk about, and at every corner fairy-faced ravishers of hearts move with a thousand blandishments and

---

[10] Abū Ṭāleb Khan, *Masīr*, 166.

[11] Reżāqolī Mīrzā Qājār, *Safar-nāma-ye Reżāqolī Mīrzā Nāyeb-al-Īāla, nava-ye Fatḥ-ʿAlī Šāh*, ed. Aṣḡar Farmānfarmāʾī Qājār (Tehran, 1982), 418.

[12] Abū Ṭāleb Khan, *Masīr*, 169.

[13] Reżāqolī Mīrzā, *Safar-nāma*, 322.

[14] Koran, 55:72-74. According to the Koran 76:12-19: "And [Allah] hath awarded them for all that they endured, a Garden and silk attire. Reclining therein upon couches, they will find there neither (heat of) a sun nor a bitter cold. The shade thereof is close upon them and the clustered fruits thereof bow down. Goblets of silver are brought round for them, and beakers (as) of glass. (Bright as) glass but (made) of silver, which they (themselves) have measured to the measure (of their deeds). There are they watered with a cup whereof the mixture of Zanzabīl. (The water of) a spring therein, named Salsabīl. There wait on them immortal youths, whom, when thou sees, thou wouldst take for scattered pearls." On the houris, see also Koran 2:25; 37:48-49; 44:54; 52:20; 55:56-61, 70-76; 56:22-23, 35-38. For a valuable study of paradise in the Koran, see Fatna Ait Sabbah, *La femme dans l'inconscient musulman: desir et pouvoir* (Paris, 1982).

coquetries; the plain of the earth becomes a paradise from the resplendent foreheads, and heaven (itself) hangs down its head for shame at seeing the beauty of the loves. There lovers meet their fairy-resembling sweethearts: they attain their end without fear of the police or of rivals, and gallants obtain a sight of rosy cheeks without restraint. When I viewed this heavenly place I involuntarily exclaimed:

If there is a paradise on earth,
It is this, oh! It is this.
(*Agar ferdowsī bar rū-ye zamīn ast*
hamīn ast o hamīn ast o hamīn ast)[15]

Seeing women unveiled in the public sphere, the Muslim travelers recalled the male-constructed promised heaven where all earthly limitations were to be obliterated. For example, Mīrzā Abu'l-Ḥasan Khān Īlčī, who had traveled to Europe in 1809-10, made a remarkably similar statement about Hyde Park and St. James's Park:

If a sorrowing soul traverses these heavenly fields, his head is crowned with flowers of joy, and looking on these saffron beds—luxurious as Kashmir's—he smiles despite himself. In the gardens and on the paths, beauteous women shine like the sun and rouse the envy of the stars, and the houris of paradise blush with shame to look upon the rose-cheeked beauties of the earth below. In absolute amazement, I said to Sir Gore Ouseley:

If there be paradise on earth
It is this, oh! it is this![16]

---

[15] Mīrzā Eʿteṣām-al-Dīn, *Šegarf-nāma-ye velāyat*, tr. James Edward Alexander as Mirza Itesa Modeen, *Shigurf namah i Velaet, or Excellent Intelligence Concerning Europe* (London, 1827), 45-46; when necessary, all translated materials have been edited. For my modifications I have consulted the Persian manuscripts (National Archives of India, Oriental Collections, and the British Library, OR 5848).

[16] Abu'l-Ḥasan Khan Īlčī, *Ḥayrat-nāma*, tr. Margaret Cloake, as *A Persian at the Court of King George: The Journal of Mirza Abul Hasan Khan*, 1809-10 (London, 1988), 78 (henceforth Īlčī, *A Persian at the Court*). Textual evidence indicates that Mīrzā Abu'l-Ḥasan had access to Mīrzā Eʿteṣām-al-Dīn's *Šegarf-nāma*. In a recently published Persian edition of Abu'l-Ḥasan Khan's travelogue, Ḥasan Morselvand has edited out this verse and a few other sentences, noting that "a few phrases which offer an immoral description of the moon-faced ones of London [*māhrīyān-e landanī*] have been taken out"; see Īlčī, *Ḥayrat-nāma*, 144.

Such physical proximity among women and men would have aroused instant public condemnation and moral indignation in a Muslim society. The acceptance of male-female physical intimacy in public places differentiated the "land of heavenly ordinances" (*sar zamīn-e behešt ā'īn*)[17] from an actual Muslim society where such a behavior was thought to be indecent, a sign of moral and social disorder. But what was only imaginable in the promised heaven was reported to exist on earth by Persian travelers returning from Europe.

Conscious of the religious implication of reporting the mixing of men and women in Europe, Prince Reżāqolī Mīrzā Qājār, who visited England in 1836 along with his brothers Tīmūr and Najafqolī Mīrzā, recalled a Hadith that "The world is a prison for a believer and a paradise for an unbeliever."[18] Elaborating on this saying, he assured himself that: "All conveniences that the Lord of the universe has promised to His special servants in the hereafter is available for their [European] view in this world. But the difference is that these intoxicants and pleasures are temporary and those conveniences are permanent."[19] With the accumulation of eroticized narratives of self-experience, Europe became a bifurcated landscape both inviting and threatening. It was at the same time both an utopia and dystopia, heaven on earth and "infideldom" (*kofrestān*).

Persian "voyageurs" often used the conventional symbols and metaphors of women from classical Persian poetry in describing European women. European women were compared to various beauties who had had been sources of temptation, irrationality, or madness, such as ʿAḏrā' (beloved of Vāmeq), Vīs (beloved of Rāmīn), Belqīs (the queen of Sheba who visited Solomon), Zolayḵā (who tempted Joseph), Laylā (beloved of Majnūn), or Shīrīn (beloved of Farhād).[20] Mīrzā Abū Ṭāleb, for instance, compared Lady Palm with such important women characters and observed: "I would be an imposter, if I claimed to have seen a woman like Lady Palm in Europe and Asia. While such great women [*māh-bānūvān*] have been mentioned in ancient myths, I had never seen one [in real life]."[21] In another poem, dedicated to a "Miss Garden," he said he found in London the promised Muslim's heaven: "While I have heard the description of the garden

---

[17] Eʿteṣām-al-Dīn, *Šegarf-nāma*, fol. 66a.

[18] Reżāqolī Mīrzā, *Safar-nāma*, 393.

[19] Reżāqolī Mīrzā, *Safar-nāma*, 393.

[20] For the best example of such an intercultural reading, see the poem written for Lady Palm [Pālm]: Abū Ṭāleb Khan, *Masīr*, 243-44.

[21] Abū Ṭāleb Khan, *Masīr*, 244.

of paradise enough times, in London I have seen better than it many times."[22] He thought the real fairies of London were much more attractive than the imaginary fairies of paradise. In the same poem while addressing the Muslim ascetics, he stated, "In every street a hundred fairies appear in blandishment; for how long would you babble about the houris, it's enough!"[23]

> To you, the ascetic, marry the houris!
> I am content with the face of Miss Garden.
> With honey and apple, you deceive me like a child,
> But I am content with the gem and apple of the chin.[24]

Mīrzā Abū Ṭāleb, informed by Persian aesthetic values, viewed beauty and nature as synonymous and so compared female beauty to the moon, sun, flowers, trees, and animals. Natural beauty was to be appreciated, and human intervention was thought of as deceptive. For example, narrating the differences between French and English women, he remarked:

> Although the French women are tall, corpulent, and rounder than the English, they are not comparable to the beauty and excellence of the English women. Because of their lack of simplicity, girlish shyness, grace, and good behavior, [the French women] appear rather ugly.[25]

He found the French women's hair styles contrary to his standards of female beauty and equated them with those of "the base and whorish women of India."[26] Unlike the idealized silent and immobile Muslim women, French women were viewed as "fast walkers, big talkers, rapid speakers, loud-voiced, and quick responders."[27] Mīrzā Abū Ṭāleb disapproved the behavior of French women, and while in Paris, he claimed to have abandoned voyeurism:

> Although I am by nature amorous and easily affected by the sight of beauty, I have lost the desire for the profession of voyeurism that I had in London. Now, my heart desires a different profession.

---

22 Abū Ṭāleb Khan, *Masīr*, 160.
23 Abū Ṭāleb Khan, *Masīr*, 160.
24 Abū Ṭāleb Khan, *Masīr*, 160.
25 Abū Ṭāleb Khan, *Masīr*, 315.
26 Abū Ṭāleb Khan, *Masīr*, 315.
27 Abū Ṭāleb Khan, *Masīr*, 315.

> In the Palace Royal I encountered thousands of women day and night,
> but I was not at all impressed and none were attractive to me.[28]

Other Persian travelers were infatuated by the women that they met, and their poems, while conventional in their meter and imagery, were expressive of genuine desire. For instance, Mīrzā Abu'l-Ḥasan Khan Īlčī, in a party at the residence of Lady Buckinghamshire[29] held on 15 January 1810, "noticed groups of sunny-faced girls and houri-like ladies chatting together, their beauty illuminated by the candle light."[30] On that night Īlčī talked to many women whose beauty dazzled him. He was talking to a "rare beauty" when "another fairy creature," attracted him. He then met another young lady, "Miss Pole," who "inflamed" his heart. Inspired by this "girl of noble birth," who shyly distanced herself from him after a short conversation, Īlčī recited this quatrain:

> *Like a cypress you proudly stand, but when did a cypress walk?*
> *Like a rosebud your ruby lips, but when did a rosebud talk?*
> *Like a hyacinth's blooms are the ringlets of your sweet hair—*
> *But when were men's hearts enslaved by a hyacinth's stalk?*

Īlčī was so infatuated with Miss Pole that he did not notice the presence of the Princess of Wales at that gathering.[31] The story of his love even circulated around the high circles of London. For example, the Queen is reported to have asked Sir Gore Ouseley, Īlčī's official *mehmāndār*: "I have heard that the Iranian Ambassador is so enamoured of a certain young lady that the affairs of Iran are far from his thoughts!"[32]

One day's fairies, however, would on other occasions be denigrated. For example, writing about his observations at a party at the house of the Marquis of Douglas and his wife Susan Euphemia, Īlčī wrote that the Marquis "has recently married a lady whose flawless beauty makes

---

[28] Abū Ṭāleb Khan, *Masīr*, 315.

[29] Albinia, Dowager Countess of Buckinghamshire (d. 1816).

[30] Īlčī, *A Persian at the Court*, 98-99.

[31] According to Margaret Cloake (Īlčī, *A Persian at the Court*, 100), Miss Pole was a daughter of William Wellesley-Pole, brother of the Marquis Wellesley.

[32] Īlčī, *A Persian at the Court*, 136. Īlčī mentions 'Miss Pole' many times throughout his travelogue. For examples, see pp. 104, 138, 148, 157, 262 [*Ḥayrat-nāma*, 332], 283, 288 [352], 332. *Ḥayrat-nāma*, 166 deletes the remarks about the ambassador's love.

other women look like witches. She has a matchless singing voice: the nightingale's song is like a crow's compared to hers!" Having met her for the first time, he wrote:

> I lamented that—just on the eve of my departure—I should be ensnared by the curve of a straying lock:
> *It is not only I whom your ringlets ensnare,*
> *There's a captive tied up by each lock of your hair.*[33]

Īlčī reported that one night he was so absorbed by "the beauty of that fairy-faced girl" that he had no interest in eating and drinking.[34] In a Sufi-style poem where Susan was the beloved, he declared, "This I is not I; if there is an I, it is you" (*īn man nah manam, agar manī hast tōʾī*).[35]

Infatuated with the unveiled feminine beauties witnessed in Europe, a few Persian travelers like Īlčī and Mīrzā Abū Ṭāleb uttered poems and statements which would be of the same type as those of the "intoxicated" or unconventional Sufis (the *šaṭaḥīyāt*). Classical Sufi poems were basically ambiguous, leaving unclarified the identity of the beloved and the nature of the love. Yet in the poetic utterances of travelers, heaven was occasionally compared with parks, European women to fairies, and Islam was abandoned in favor of the religion of love. It was no wonder that Reżāqolī Mīrzā referred to some European women as "plunderers of heart and religion" and noted that thousands would abandon their religion like Sheikh Ṣanʿān.[36]

Dancing in Public

The pioneering Persian "voyageurs" were often invited to ballrooms, theaters, concerts, and masquerade parties. They found the level of male-female intimacy at these gatherings to be radically different from anything at public gatherings in India and Iran. A Persian who was used to seeing women veiled in social gatherings was shocked by the dancing in public of unveiled women with men. They interpreted this proximity of the sexes as a collapse of the moral into the immoral, the decent into the indecent. The observed/imagined irregularities and differences in female social space provided the loci for imagining the life and power of *farangī* women.

---

[33] Īlčī, *A Persian at the Court,* 290; *Ḥayrat-nāma,* 354.

[34] Īlčī, *A Persian at the Court,* 290-91; *Ḥayrat-nāma,* 354.

[35] Īlčī, *Ḥayrat-nāma,* 354. This verse does not appear in the English translation.

[36] Reżāqolī Mīrzā, *Safar-nāma*, 360-361.

Playhouses, operas, dances, and masquerades impressed the Persian "voyageurs" and provided important sites for the acquisition of knowledge about European customs and manners. Abū Ṭāleb viewed the visit to playhouses as an "occupation of sensuality" (*mašġala-ye nafs*) and wrote a detailed description of a playhouse in Dublin, explaining the arrangement of the stage, seats, spectacles, and spectators. He even drew a detailed blueprint of the playhouse.[37] Miss Garden occasionally went to the playhouses with Mīrzā Abū Ṭāleb, and he described her as a "fanatic in religion and used to the habits of old London."[38] During his stay in England, Īlčī was also invited to many plays and operas. He noted after attending the opera of "Sidagero" at King's Theater in December 1809: "Dancers and sweet-voiced singers appeared one after the other to entertain us, acting and dancing like Greeks and Russians and Turks. It is amazing that although five thousand people may gather in the theater, they do not make a loud noise ...."[39] On that night a historical ballet entitled "Pietro il Grande" by Signor Rossi was performed. Īlčī commented that "the dancers imitated the Emperor and the Empress of Russia and the Pasha of Turkey and his wife and other Turks." Lord Radstock described Īlčī's reaction to the historical ballet in a letter:

> He laughed heartily at the folly of bringing forward Peter the Great and his Empress as dancing to divert the throng. 'What!' exclaimed he, 'is it possible that a mighty monarch and his queen should expose themselves thus? How absurd! How out of nature! How perfectly ridiculous!' Were I to translate the look that followed these words it would be thus: 'Surely a nation that can suffer so childish and preposterous an exhibition, and be pleased with it, can have little pretensions either to taste or judgement.'

Radstock further reported that Īlčī had jokingly said, "When I get back to my own country, the King shall ask me, 'What did the English do to divert you?' I will answer, Sir, they brought before me your Majesty's great enemies, the Emperor and Empress of Russia, and made them dance for my amusement." Radstock added, "This he repeated with the highest glee, as if conscious of saying a witty thing."[40]

---

[37] Abū Ṭāleb Khan, *Masīr*, 74.

[38] Abū Ṭāleb Khan, *Masīr*, 163.

[39] Īlčī, *A Persian at the Court,* 76.

[40] William Waldegrave Radstock, "A Slight Sketch of the Character, Person, &c. of Aboul Hassen, Envoy Extraordinary from the King of Persia to the Court of Great Britain, in the Years 1809 and 1810," *The Gentleman's*

Īlčī also attended a few plays including an improved version of King Lear at the Royal Opera House. Walking around the theater, he noted that "my companions and I saw beautiful ladies, beautifully dressed, casting flirtatious glances from their boxes."[41] He attended the performances of Angelica Catalan (1789-1849), the famous Italian soprano, saying that "[her] performance was superb and her talent was highly praised by those who attended the Opera regularly."[42] He was astonished by her salary: "a high ranking general is said to receive a salary of 1,000 tomans a year, yet a female entertainer is paid 5,000 tomans for three nights' work!"[43] After seeing Mlle Angiolini's performance of the "Persian Wedding Dance," he remarked that it "bore no resemblance at all to the real thing. Such novelties are mounted to attract the money of the idle rich who are forever seeking new diversions."[44]

Most Persian travelers thought of theaters as respectable and entertaining places. But Mīrzā ʿAbd-al-Fattāḥ Garmrūdī, who visited England in 1839, viewed them as "the gathering places of whores and adulteresses and the rendezvous of well experienced pimps."[45] He took the intermission between performances to be an occasion for sex between the performers and their customers.[46] Such misunderstandings played an important role in shaping the popular opinion about Europe and European style theaters.

Masquerade parties were another attraction for Persian travelers. Mirzā Abū Ṭāleb viewed masquerades as a way of "testing the limits of each other's cleverness."[47] "Maximum freedom for a short period of time" was listed as a benefit masquerades.[48] "Since the identities of individuals are not apparent," according to Mīrzā Abū Ṭāleb, "they can behave in any manner."[49] He found the diversity of nations represented in the

---

Magazine (February 1820):119-122, quotes on p. 120. Quoted in part in Īlčī, *A Persian at the Court,* 76-77.

41 Īlčī, *A Persian at the Court,* 92; idem, *Ḥayrat-nāma*, 159.

42 Īlčī, *A Persian at the Court,* 165; idem, *Ḥayrat-nāma*, 159.

43 Īlčī, *A Persian at the Court,* 165; idem, *Ḥayrat-nāma,* 228-29.

44 Īlčī, *A Persian at the Court,* 263; idem, *Ḥayrat-nāma,* 333.

45 Mīrzā ʿAbd-al-Fattāḥ Khan Garmrūdī, "Šāb-nāma," in *Safar-nāma-ye Mīrzā Fattāḥ K̲ān Garmrūdī be-Orūpā, mawsūm ba Čahār faṣl va do resāla-ye dīgar be-nām-e Šab-nāma va Safar-nāma-ye Mamasānī dar zamān-e Moḥammad Šāh Qājār*, ed. Fatḥ-al-Dīn Fattāḥī (Tehran, 1347 Š./1968), 970.

46 Garmrūdī, "Šāb-nāma," 970.

47 Abū Ṭāleb Khan, *Masīr*, 189.

48 Abū Ṭāleb Khan, *Masīr*, 189.

49 Abū Ṭāleb Khan, *Masīr*, 189.

masquerades appealing and noted, "since the English have traveled all over the world and are more familiar with the conditions of most other nations, London masquerades are perfect. In their masquerades Iranians, Indians, Arabs, Turkomans, Hindus, ... and a hundred other types can be found. Some mimic to the extent that it affects their language and bodily movement."[50] The most attractive aspect of the masquerade for Mirzā Abū Ṭāleb, who was called the "Persian Prince,"[51] was the masking of class distinctions so that "the nobility wear the clothing of the artisans and appear like barbers, flower-sellers, and bakers, imitating them so well that it is not possible to distinguish the original from the imitated."[52] Among the memorable masquerades described by Īlčī, "a lady unknown to me [Lady William Gordon], who was disguised as a priest, introduced herself to me: The English call such behavior 'forward.'"[53]

Comparing Women

Women figured prominently in the travelers' understanding of the political hegemony of Europe. They often established a causal relation between education of women and progress of Europe. For them the public appearance and behavior of European women symbolized a different order of politics and gender relations. Eʿteṣām-al-Dīn, for example, recognized the significance of schooling in the shaping of social and gender relations:

> In England it is usual for the people of rank to send both their sons and daughters to a distant place of education .... The people of wealth in England, commencing at the age of four years, keep their sons and daughters constantly employed in writing, reading, and acquiring knowledge; they never permit them to be idle. If a man or woman not be acquainted with the musical art, be unable to dance or ride, he

---

[50] Abū Ṭāleb Khan, *Masīr*, 189.

[51] Concerning the title of the "Persian Prince," Abū Ṭāleb wrote: "When I went to Court, or paid my respects to one of the princes or ministers of the state, the circumstance was always reported by the newspapers of the following day. In all these advertisements, they did me the honour of naming me the Persian Prince. I declared I never assumed the title; but I was so much better known by it than by my own name, that I found it in vain to contend with godfathers (Abū Ṭāleb Khan, *Travels*, 111; *Masīr,* 195).

[52] Abū Ṭāleb Khan, *Masīr*, 189.

[53] Īlčī, *A Persian at the Court,* 274; idem, *Ḥayrat-nāma,* 339.

> or she is accounted by people of substance as descended from a mean parentage, and taunts and reproaches are not spared ....The ladies, particularly, who can neither dance nor sing, are considered in a very inferior light; they will never get well married.[54]

Eʿteṣām-al-Dīn reprimanded his own people for retaining tutors as house servants.[55] Like many nineteenth century reformers, he praised the European devotion to education and the search for knowledge, contrasting it to the Perso-Indian quest for the beloved:

> They are not like the people of this country, who repeat Hindi and Persian poems in praise of a mistress's face, or descriptive of the qualities of the wine, of the goblet, and of the cup-bearer, and who pretend to be in love.[56]

Mīrzā Abū Ṭāleb, like Eʿteṣām-al-Dīn, was interested in the European educational system, especially that for women. Commenting on the "apparent freedom" (*āzādī-ye ẓāherī*) and education of English women, Mīrzā Abū Ṭāleb noted that through education the English "have cleverly restrained them [women] from deviant deeds."[57] He viewed educating and veiling as two diverse methods of disciplining women. He observed that "the institution of the veil as a form of restraining is an instigator of sedition and corruption."[58] Mīrzā Ṣāleḥ Šīrāzī, who resided in England from 1815-19, explained that English women, while unveiled, as a result of education "do not have the propensity for committing wicked acts."[59] Disciplining women through education was more appealing to Persian travelers who viewed the veil as a instigator of moral depravation. Īlčī, for instance, in a conversation with Mrs. Perceval in January 1810, contrasted European and Persian women, remarking: "Your custom is better indeed. A veiled woman with downcast eyes [*zan-e masṭūra-ye čašm basta*] is like a caged bird: when she is released she lacks even the strength to fly around the rose garden."[60] Likewise, in a Persianized English letter

---

[54] Eʿteṣām-al-Dīn, *Šegarf-nāma*, tr. Alexander, 157-59.

[55] Eʿteṣām-al-Dīn, *Šegarf-nāma*, tr. Alexander, 159.

[56] Eʿteṣām-al-Dīn, *Šegarf-nāma*, tr. Alexander, 168.

[57] Abū Ṭāleb Khan, *Masīr*, 226.

[58] Abū Ṭāleb Khan, *Masīr*, 226.

[59] Mīrzā Ṣāleḥ Šīrāzī, *Gozāreš-e safar-e Mīrzā Ṣāleḥ Šīrāzī*, ed. Homāyūn Šahīdī (Tehran, 1362 Š./1983), 333-34.

[60] Īlčī, *A Persian at the Court*, 98; idem, *Ḥayrat-nāma,* 163.

published in the London Morning Post (29 May 1810) and reprinted in many other newspapers and journals, Īlčī observed:

> English ladies [are] very handsome, very beautiful.... I [have] see[n] the best Georgian, Circassian, Turkish, and Greek ladies—but nothing so beautiful as English ladies—all very clever—speak French, speak English, speak Italian, play music very well, sing very good—very glad for me if Persian Ladies [were] like them....[61]

On another occasion Īlčī wished that Iranian women could become like British women.

> As God is my witness, I wish the women of Iran could be more like the women of England. Iranian women are chaste because they are forced to be—they are shut away from men; but the English women are chaste by choice. They are free and independent and responsible only to their husband, whom they look upon as the only man in the world. They do not hide themselves away but appear veil-less in society.[62]

Such arguments became fashionable among modernist men who linked the unveiling of women to the progress of the nation. Likewise, women such as Bībī K̲ānom Astarābādī in her *Vices of Men* utilized the same rhetoric in their struggle for suffrage and participation in public life.[63]

Persian travelers were also conscious of the legal order that made women's participation in the public sphere less restrictive. Eʿteṣām-al-Dīn explained the sexual liberty of Europeans in contrast to Muslim women in terms of the different legal systems:

> The courts have nothing to do with cases of simple fornication, unless a woman complains that she was forcibly violated .... If a man and woman commit fornication in a retired house, or even in any place whatever, they may do so with impunity, and neither

[61] "Letter from the Persian Envoy, Mirza Abul Hassan to the Lord, or Gentleman, without name, who lately write Letter to him and ask very mush to give Answer [sic]," *The Morning Post* (29 May 1810); reprinted in Īlčī, *A Persian at the Court*, 246-47; Denis Wright, *The Persians Amongst the English* (London, 1985), 226-27.

[62] Īlčī, *A Persian at the Court*, 135.

[63] Bībī K̲ānom Astarābādī, *Maʿāyeb al-rejāl: dar pasūk̲ ba Taʾdīb al-nisvān*, ed. Afsaneh Najmabadi (Chicago, 1992), 57.

> the police [*kūtvāl*] nor the censor [*moḥtaseb*] can take any notice of it; for it is a common saying, 'what business has the superintendent inside a house?' [*moḥtaseb-rā dar darūn-e ḵāna cheh kār?*] In England it is completely the reverse of what it is in this country, for there the police and the censor have little or nothing to do [with it], and don't have the power of seizing either a fornicator or a fornicatress, what ever the people may say.[64]

Eʿteṣām-al-Dīn further observed that "the King of England is not independent in matters of government ... and can do nothing without first consulting with his ministers and nobles and a few selected men."[65] By focusing on the relative freedom of women and the restriction on the power of sovereign, he shifted the meaning of freedom (*āzādī*):

> In England every one is free [*āzād*]; no one can lord it over another, and there is no such thing known as master and slave, which is totally different from other countries, in which all are slaves of the king. In England, both great and small would be greatly ashamed at the term slave.[66]

Such observations on freedom of citizens and education of women became important elements in forming modern political imagery and giving rise to the notion of "citizen" in Persian. For example, Ebrāhīm Ṣaḥḥāfbāšī, who visited Europe and North America in 1896-97, praised the education of women in Europe and criticized the position of women in Iran: "We raise our girls in a cage and would not teach them anything besides eating and sleeping .... Unfortunately we comprehend the enjoyment of eating and intercourse more than progress and education."[67] To strengthen the nation, many nineteenth-century Persian travelers, either directly or indirectly, called for the establishment of a constitutional government and the increased participation of women in the public sphere.

Insatiable Lust

Unlike many nineteenth-century Persian travelers, Mīrzā Fattāḥ Garmrūdī, who went to Europe in 1838, developed a distaste for European manners and characteristics and warned against closer contacts

---

64 Eʿteṣām-al-Dīn, *Šegarf-nāma*, tr. Alexander, 149-150.

65 Eʿteṣām-al-Dīn, *Šegarf-nāma*, tr. Alexander, 137-38.

66 Eʿteṣām-al-Dīn, *Šegarf-nāma*, tr. Alexander, 138.

67 Ebrāhīm Ṣaḥḥāfbāšī, *Safar-nāma-ye Ebrāhīm Ṣaḥḥāfbāšī*, ed. Moḥammad Mošīrī (Tehran, 1357 Š./1978), 81.

with them. He called upon the ulema and the political elite to distance themselves from the "wicked group" of Europeans. Aware of the colonization of India, he warned that Europeans should not be trusted. For given the opportunity, they would "damage the religion and the state and will destroy the Šarīʿa traditions."[68] He referred to Europe (Farangestān) as the land of the infidels (*kofrestān*) and concluded his "Šab-nāma" (Night Report) by noting that "due to the emotional depression and immensity of regret and sorrow that resulted from my observation of the state of affairs in Kofrestān, I have been able to narrate no more than a seed from a donkey's burden and a drop in a sea about the obscene acts and indecent behaviors of this malevolent people."[69] The pornographic view of Europe constructed by Garmrūdī was the precursor of the Europhobic view which sought to protect Iran from the feminization of power and European domination by guarding Iranian women from the malady of Europeanization.

Garmrūdī was a member of an Iranian delegation which was dispatched to Europe in 1838 and traveled to Vienna, Paris, and London. The main objective of the mission, led by Mīrzā Ḥosayn Khan Ājūdānbāšī, was to offer condolences to Queen Victoria on the death of William IV, to congratulate her on her accession to power, and to ask the British government to recall John McNeil, its minister plenipotentiary, for being unsympathetic to Iran's political claim on the city of Herat.

This delegation, arriving in London in April 1839, faced a most discourteous reception. Queen Victoria declined to see them. The British government refused to receive them as official guests. Lord Palmerston pointed out that "the Persian Ambassador must be Europeanized" by making him pay for all of his expenses.[70] This was a reversal of the earlier protocol according to which the British government, like its Iranian counterpart, paid all the expenses of diplomatic guests for the duration of their stay. Adding to the insult, the Iranian delegate was asked to revise Moḥammad Shah's letter to Queen Victoria, changing her title from *maleka* to *pādšāh*, for, according to Palmerston "we have no sexual distinction for our sovereign," a distinction which is implied in the concept *maleka* but not in *pādšāh*.[71] This hostility, instead of the expected hospitality,

[68] Garmrūdī, "Šab-nāma," 983.

[69] Garmrudī, "Šab-nāma," 983.

[70] Wright, *Persians Amongst the English*, 49.

[71] Palmerston to Ājūdānbāšī, 11 July 1839 (Iranian Foreign Ministry Archive, document no. 500). My special thanks to Ahmad Hajhosseini of the Iranian Interest Section, Washington, D. C., who made possible the acquisition of this document in 1989 from the Iranian Foreign Ministry archive.

shaped the Iranian delegates' image of Farangestān and perception of *farangīs*. This is clearly illustrated in Garmrūdī's "Šab-nāma" (1258/1842). He recounted about twenty anecdotes and incidents witnessed by him or Eqbāl-al-Dawla, his newly found Perso-Indian friend who was in England at that time.[72] Mīrzā Fattāḥ constructed a pornographic view of Europe by focusing on women and their supposed sexual debauchery.

After discussing the source of his anecdotes, Mīrzā Fattāḥ noted that he would "briefly explain some of the conditions and characteristics of the women and their husbands":

> In this land of diverse persuasions, women and girls generally go without undergarments and without a veil [*čādor*] and have a constant desire for able pummellers. Covered women are rare and unacceptable. Women are masterful in the realization of the wishes of men. They are addicted to pleasure and play and are free from suffering and toil. In actualization of the demands of their partners, they are always daring and exquisite, while in preservation of their own honor they are incompetent and frail.[73]

According to Mīrzā Fattāḥ, "A common characteristic of [European] women is their extreme desire for sexual intercourse." In his view:

> They have escaped from the trap of chastity into freedom and have masterly leapt from the snare of purity. They have extreme desire for union with men and are endlessly coquettish and flirtatious. They glorify freedom and appreciate self-reliance.[74]

He equated European women's freedom with a lack of honor and chastity. This constituted the nodal point of the emerging Europhobic and misogynist discourse. Women and men, according to Garmrūdī, were copulating night and day in ballrooms, theaters, coffeehouses, and whorehouses. To highlight the sexual debauchery of Europeans, he offered an erotic description of how some women satisfied their sexual desires by keeping dogs at home.[75] He explained that this practice was accepted and appreciated by the husbands:

---

[72] Eqbāl-al-Dawla, the author of the bilingual Persian-English book *Eqbāl-e Farang: dar šamma-ye sīar-e ahl-e Farang-e bā farhang* (Calcutta, 1834). He had gone to England to protest the British policy in Awadh.

[73] Garmrūdī, "Šab-nāma," 951.

[74] Garmrūdī, "Šab-nāma," 951.

[75] Garmrūdī, "Šab-nāma," 955-56.

> In this land, due to the enormity of a woman's lust, a man does not have the strength to satisfy and realize her wishes promptly. Consequently, if a woman has an affair with another man and receives from him a payment, or due to her nobility and magnanimity, doesn't receive anything, according to the law of the nation the poor husband has no right to punish her. Under such a condition the zealous husband is thankful that the dog has done the job for her instead of a neighbor or an ignorant rogue in the street. To be just and fair, the poor husband cannot be blamed.[76]

Men's sexual impotence and their inability to punish their wives was viewed as a cause of women's bestiality. To further illustrate the legal restrictions on men and the resultant sexual practices of women, Garmrūdī recounted the story of a wife who was "ugly and bad looking and singularly ill-created and ill-humored."[77] Her husband had become repulsed by her and preferred "living in a cave with a snake" to her companionship:

> But since in their nation it is established that a man cannot have more than one wife, he was compelled to give in to his destiny and persevere, always praying to God for mercy and his liberation from the yoke of damnation.[78]

One day the husband came home to find his wife with another man. He asked the adulterer why he was not looking for a better woman. The adulterer replied, "I do not have such bad taste. I am laboring and getting paid for it."[79] Because of the incompetence of European men and the voracious sexual appetite of European women, Garmrūdī concluded that women had to rely on extra-marital relations or on dildos to satisfy their desires.

Why did Garmrūdī focus on such incidents? One is the obvious fact that the special mission was ill-treated by the British government. But there are a number of other factors which may illuminate his motivation for writing the "Šab-nāma." For example, he says:

> With all these destructive conditions and deplorable actions, if a person in the nations of Farangestān, especially in England, unintentionally (which is the necessary nature, meaning that it is

[76] Garmrūdī, "Šab-nāma," 956.
[77] Garmrūdī, "Šab-nāma," 956.
[78] Garmrūdī, "Šab-nāma," 956.
[79] Garmrūdī, "Šab-nāma," 956.

> the second nature of human beings) mentions chest and breast, or vagina and phallus, or the like among women, they will immediately print and register that in the newspapers and will disseminate it around the world that so and so in such and such gathering had no shame and talked about such and such in front of women.[80]

So Mīrzā Fattāḥ Garmrūdī and his colleagues might well have been victims of such journalistic intrigues, which capitalized on the Persian travelers unfamiliarity with European norms, mocked them, and portrayed them as indecent and uncivilized. This might also explain Mīrzā Fattāḥ's rather negative view of newspapers, which earlier Persian travelers admired. He wrote,

> Since the majority of newspapers print pure lies, and they lie thoroughly, then it is clever of them to clean their posteriors with these papers. There is no better use for them. They believe that with these papers the feces is cleaned from their rears, but this is neither clear nor obvious. It is not clear whether in reality their rears are cleaned by the papers, or whether the newsprint is actually purified by the excrement.[81]

The members of the special mission became extremely sensitive to and angry with journalists who seemed to have reported on all that would appear irregular and unfamiliar to their readers. There are other possible explanations for Mīrzā Fattāḥ's negative image of Europeans. As this same text suggests, Mīrzā Fattāḥ may also have been responding to a denigrating European view of Iran:

> With all these desolate affairs and deplorable conditions, they [Europeans] have written some books to reproach and reprimand Iran. Especially the Englishman [James Baillie] Fraser has denigrated Iran and has gone to extremes in this regard. Among his charges is that the men of Iran have excessive desire for beardless teenagers and some men commit obscene acts with them.... Yes, in the midst of all nations of the world, some fools, due to the predominance of lascivious spirit and temptations of Satan, commit some unacceptable acts. It is far from just that the people of Farangestān, with all of their imperfect attributes and obscene behaviors for which they are characterized and are

[80] Garmrūdī, "Šab-nāma," 959.
[81] Garmrūdī, "Šab-nāma," 961.

> particularly famous, i. e., the establishment of eunuch- and whore-houses, where they go at all times and pay money and commit obscene acts, that they characterize the people of Iran with such qualities and write about them in their books.[82]

After expressing his disapproval of Fraser's generalizations about and condemnation of Iranians,[83] Mīrzā Fattāḥ recounted the story of an Italian lord who copulated with the son of an English gentleman after gaining the consent of the boy's father. He concluded that:

> The above incident, besides indicating unfairness and the engagement [of Europeans] in demeaning behavior, is also an indication of the stupidity and foolishness of this people; but they ignore all these incidents and occurrences amongst themselves and attach their own characteristics to others.[84]

As Mīrzā Fattāḥ saw it, Europeans were attributing their behavior and ways to Iran. Reflecting on the European perception of Iran, Garmrūdī recognized the importance of power in determining the type of relations Europeans establish with other countries:

> Apparently, they always interact on an appropriate and humane basis with strong states and never initiate opposition. With a state which appears weaker, however, they constantly search for excuses, make downright illogical statements, and resist listening to logical views.[85]

Garmrūdī did, however, praise some European political institutions. Concerning the parliamentary arrangements, he remarked, "Individually, the people of Farangestān are not very wise or mature, nor are they endowed with much eloquence or intelligence; but the parliament and the house of consultation [*mašvarat-ḵāna*] that they have established apparently conceal these shortcomings."[86]

Garmrūdī's "Šab-nāma" ends with a warning that the Iranian governmental elite should distance itself from the "wicked" Europeans,

---

[82] Garmrūdī, "Šab-nāma," 962.

[83] It should be noted that James Baillie Fraser (1783-1856) served as *mehmāndār* (host) for this delegation.

[84] Garmrūdī, "Šab-nāma," 964.

[85] Garmrūdī, "Šab-nāma," 982.

[86] Garmrūdī, "Šab-nāma," 982.

for otherwise the foundation of the state and religion would be damaged. During the nineteenth century, pornographic views of Europe provided ammunition for an intensified struggle against the reformists who were idealizing Europe. Such eroticized denunciation of Europe played a pivotal role in the counter-modernist Islamist discourse on the dangers of unveiling and the feminization of power. In the counter-modernist discourse, the "fairy-faced" women of Europe appeared as demonic. Garmrūdī was amongst the originators of such a Europhobic discourse, a discourse in which the political threat of Europe was connected to the sexual debauchery of European women.

The Gazing Spectacle

Misogyny and ethnocentrism were the shared characteristics of both Orientalist and Occidentalist narrations of the Other. European fascination with the imagined Muslim harems, seraglios, and gynaeceums paralleled the Persian view of Europe as an eroticized "heaven on earth" and European women and lascivious and licentious.[87] Woman's body became an object of curiosity and gaze and served as a marker of similarities and differences. Both Occidentals and Orientals constituted the body of the "other" women as a site for sexual and political imagination. Traveling in Iran in 1812, James Morier explained that the residents of the Iranian city of Būšehr showed a "feeling of great wonder" about the women who accompanied the British delegation to Iran: "Above all things, that which excited their curiosity was the circumstance of our ambassador having brought his harem with him; for although the Easterns look upon it as indecorous to make inquiries about each other's women, yet still we could observe how anxious they were to know something about ours."[88] Morier, who had traveled to Iran a few years earlier, explained that this inquisitiveness was reciprocal:

---

[87] On the Western perception of "harem" see: Leila Ahmad, "Western Ethnocentrism and Perceptions of the Harem," *Feminist Studies* 8/3(1982):521-34; Suzanne Rodin Pucci, "The Discrete Charms of the Exotic: Fiction of the Harem in Eighteenth-century France," in G. S. Rousseau and Roy Porter, eds., *Exoticism in the Enlightenment* (Manchester, 1990), 145-74.

[88] James Justinian Morier, *A Second Journey through Persia, Armenia, and Asia Minor, to Constantinople, between the years 1810 and 1816 with a journal of the voyage by the Brazils and Bombay to the Persian Gulf; together with an account of the proceedings of His Majesty's Embassy under His Excellency Sir Gore Ouseley, Bart. K.L.S.* (London, 1818), 39.

> Perhaps their curiosity about the women of Europe is quite as great as that of Europeans about those of Asia. I can state, in confirmation of the last assertion, that one of the first questions put to me by my acquaintances in Europe, has ever been on that subject; and from the conversations I have had with Asiatics upon the same topic, both parties have universally appeared to entertain in their imaginations the highest ideas of beauty of each other's women.[89]

The idealized women of the other became objects of male desire and conquest. Seeking the fulfillment of their fantasies, travelers pursued exotic sex unobtainable at home.[90] Such "pre-programmed expectations" over-determined what travelers sought, saw, and reported.[91]

The Persian travelers narrated the spectacle of Europe, and the European onlookers reported the spectacle of the exotic Persians in their midst. The surveyors of Europe and its cultural differences found themselves surveyed by Europeans. Reflecting on his own experience as a spectacle, Mīrzā Eᶜteṣām-al-Dīn wrote:

> Whenever I went outdoors, crowds accompanied me, and the people in the houses and bazaars thrust their heads out of the windows and gazed at me with wonder. The children and boys took me for a black devil, and being afraid kept at a distance from me.[92]

Mīrzā Abū Ṭāleb recalled happier experiences. Remembering his visit to Dublin, he wrote:

> As I would walk out of the house they would surround me and every one would say nice things about me. Some said that I must be the

---

[89] Morier, *A Second Journey through Persia*, 39-40

[90] Edward Said in his pioneering study of Orientalism concluded that for many Europeans, "the Orient was a place where one could look for sexual experience unobtainable in Europe." Explaining the convergence of the Orient and sex in Orientalist discourse, Said wrote, "In time 'Oriental sex' was as standard as a commodity as any other available in the mass culture, with the result that readers and writers could have it if they wished without necessarily going to the Orient." Edward Said, *Orientalism* (New York, 1978), 190.

[91] G. S. Rousseau and Roy Porter, "Introduction: Approaching Enlightenment Exoticism," in G. S. Rousseau and Roy Porter, eds., *Exoticism in the Enlightenment* (New York, 1989), 1-22, quote on p. 10.

[92] Eᶜteṣām-al-Dīn, *Šegarf-nāma*, fol. 59a.

> Russian General, who had been for some time expected; others guessed that I am a German ruler, and still other would view me as a Spanish noble. But the greater part perceived me as a Persian Prince.[93]

Observing the details of English social and political life, Mīrzā Abu'l-Ḥasan Khan Īlčī, was himself constituted as an object of popular gaze and amazement. According to the *London Literary Gazette:*

> He was so great an object of public curiosity, that he could not leave his hotel without being surrounded by a multitude of gazers. When he attended fashionable parties, the eagerness evinced by the ladies to gain a sight of him, subjected him to a degree of embarrassment the more insupportable, as the people of the East entertain notions very unfavourable to that kind of female curiosity.[94]

Īlčī's appearance provided a signifying surface for the rearticulation of cultural differences and the replaying of European sexual fantasies. Drawing on the culturally available resources, the *Morning Herald* offered a sensationalized description of Īlčī's appearance:

> The Persian Ambassador attracts the particular attention of the Hyde Park belles as an equestrian of a singular order, for he rides in silken pantaloons of such a wide dimension, that, being inflated by the wind makes his Excellency appear [more] like flying to a Turkish Harem, than riding for the pure air in Rotten Row.[95]

The harem, a misrecognized space, had already become an exotic site for the projection of European sexual fantasies. As a symbolic condensation of the Muslim Orient, the harem became a point of reference for culturally placing the Persian travelers, who were often asked about polygamous practices.

The Persian visitors were the objects of intense public voyeurism. To ward off the public eye, they found mimicry and transvestitism a valuable protective shield. By "cross-dressing," that is, by replacing their Persian dress with European costumes, the visitors hoped to de-exoticize themselves and remove the most obvious sign of their other-

---

[93] Abū Ṭāleb Khan, *Masīr*, 83; *Travels*, 64.

[94] "Sketches of Society," *The London Literary Gazette, and Journal of Belles Lettres, Arts, Sciences, etc.* (8 May 1819):299, column 3.

[95] London *Morning Herald* (29 March 1810); Īlčī, *A Persian Prince at the Court,* 188.

ness. Such transvestite protection from public gaze was sought by Moḥammad-Reżā Beyk (d. 1714), a Persian envoy to France, who may have provided Montesquieu with material for the *Persian Letters*. A central episode of the *Persian Letters* terminated with the question "How can one be Persian?" (*Comment peut-on être Persan?*). The Persian Reżā Beyk found the excessive public curiosity to be burdensome and so decided "to give up Persian costume and dress like a European."[96]

The protective shield of transvestitism was occasionally sought by Mīrzā Ṣāleḥ Šīrāzī, a Persian student who lived in England between 1816 and 1819. On the occasion of King George's birthday, Mīrzā Ṣāleḥ was asked by his friends to participate in the public celebration. Worried about the public gaze and harassment, Mīrzā Ṣāleḥ intended to wear a European costume instead of Persian attire. But his friends advised him against it, arguing that he should not be worried since he was to be accompanied by English women and men. Upon their insistence, Mīrzā Ṣāleḥ wore his Persian costume and, holding hands with a certain Sara Abraham, accompanied his friends to the public celebration. But the sight of an "exotic Persian" walking hand-in-hand with a local woman intensified public curiosity: "All of a sudden, the masses, who had not seen a person dressed like me, appeared from all sides and in a short time five hundred people gathered around me."[97] Mīrzā Ṣāleḥ escaped from the scene, went to his apartment, and after changing into European dress, rejoined his friends. According to his own report, no one harassed him after he cross-dressed.[98] Such harassing public curiosity was also reported by European travelers who visited the Middle East in the eighteenth and nineteenth centuries.

Liberties of Women

The stereotypical European views of the Persians provided the subtext for inquiries to which travelers had to respond. Mīrzā Abū Ṭāleb viewed such probing by the English as "a contempt for the customs of other nations" and listed it as one of the twelve defects of the English character.[99] Mīrzā Abū Ṭāleb, for example, commented:

---

[96] Montesquieu, *Lettres persans* (tr. C. J. Betts as *The Persian Letters*, New York, 1973), letter xxx, 83.

[97] Mīrzā Ṣāleḥ Šīrāzī, *Gozāreš-e safar*, 201.

[98] Mīrzā Ṣāleḥ Šīrāzī, *Gozāreš-e safar*, 201.

[99] On Abū Ṭāleb Khan's exposition of the defects and virtues of the English character see *Travels*, 167-85; quote on p. 177. Also see: "Ẕekr-e fażāʾel va rasāʾel-e Engelīs," in *Masīr*, 263-84.

> Some of these, who were otherwise respectable characters, ridiculed the idea of my wearing trousers, and night-dress, when I went to bed; and contended, that they slept much more at ease by going to bed nearly naked. I replied, that I slept very comfortably; that mine was certainly the most decent ...."[100]

Reporting on polemical inquiries about Islam, he wrote:

> In London, I was frequently attacked on the apparent unreasonableness and childishness of some of the Mohammedan customs; but as, from my knowledge of the English characters, I was convinced that it would be folly to argue the point philosophically with them, I contented myself with parrying the subject. Thus, when they attempted to turn into ridicule the ceremonies used by the pilgrims on their arrival at Mecca, I asked them why they supposed the ceremony of baptism by a clergyman requisite for the salvation of a child, who could not possibly be sensible what he was about."[101]

Such a theatrical approach was also adopted by other Persian travelers who were frequently interrogated about polygamy. James Fraser, the *mehmāndār* and translator for the three Persian princes who traveled to England in 1836, recorded such an inquiry about polygamy. Among the questions that the princes were asked, Fraser listed the following: "Ask them do they like England?"; "Is Persia a fine country?"; "Do ask them what they think of English ladies?"; "What do they think of dancing?"; "Do Persian ladies dance?"; "Ask them if the Persian ladies are handsome?"; "Ask him how many wives he has?"[102] Commenting on this last question Fraser reported:

> This being a question which, in Persia, can never be put, and if put would certainly not be replied to, it produced here only a variety of jokes, equivocations, or inventions. 'No, no; no wife; wife gone dead!' (with a mock-melancholy look.) Or, 'One—no more, Wullah!" The last response triggered a protestation: 'Ah, he does not tell truth; tell him it is a very bad custom that of

---

[100] Abū Ṭāleb Khan, *Travels*, 177.

[101] Abū Ṭāleb Khan, *Travels*, 177.

[102] Fraser, *Narrative of the Residence of the Persian Princes in London, in 1835 and 1836*, 2 vols. (London, 1838, repr. New York, 1973), 1:138-39.

> taking so many wives. What do they do with them all? I suppose he cuts off their heads sometimes with the great knife he wears in his girdle?'[103]

Fraser remarked: "On this occasion, in reply to the abuse which was launched against polygamy, he offered one ingeniously devised excuse, which succeeded, as he could see, so well, that he repeated it more than once in the sequel."[104]

> 'Tell these ladies,' said he to me, 'that our Persian women are not like those of England,—educated, accomplished, fitted to be companions to their husbands; they can do little except embroider and look after their slaves, or cook a dinner. Now, your English ladies are as well educated as yourselves, and are full of accomplishments; they retain their beauty so well, that, after having had a large family, they are still lovely and blooming;—Wullah! they are fresher and more lovely after forty, than our women are at twenty-five. Thus, one English woman is worth at least ten Persian women, and so we take quantity to make up for quality; had we English women, then one would suffice.[105]

According to Fraser, "this sort of reasoning amused and delighted his fair auditors."[106] Such theatrical responses were used by other Persianate travelers who wished to silence the inquirers and shield themselves from stereotypical cultural criticisms. But the intended irony in such a reply was often ignored by the European listeners and consequently contributed to the solidification of stereotypes and misrepresentation of Iranian and Indian women. But occasionally such dialogues led to critical and comparative reflection on the status of women. Mīrzā Abū Ṭāleb Khan's "Vindication of the Liberties of the Asiatic Women," translated and published in 1801, was exemplary

---

[103] Fraser, *Narrative of the Residence of the Persian Princes*, 1:139. Commenting on the appearance of the princes, Morier, *Second Journey*, Appendix, 2:401, quoted in Īlčī, *A Persian Prince at the Court*, 31, wrote: "They armed themselves from head to foot with pistol, sword, and each a musket in his hand, as if they were about to make a journey in their own country; and thus encumbered, notwithstanding every assurance that nothing could happen to them, they got into the coach."

[104] Fraser, *Narratives of the Residence of the Persian Princes*, 1:140.

[105] Fraser, *Narratives of the Residence of the Persian Princes*, 1:138-40.

[106] Fraser, *Narratives of the Residence of the Persian Princes*, 1:141.

for both its insights and contribution to comparative reflections.[107] The essay was written as a response to a stereotypical inquiry concerning the Asiatic women:

> One day, in a certain company, the conversation turned upon LIBERTY, in respect of which the English consider their own customs the most perfect in the world. An English lady, addressing herself to me, observed that the women of Asia have no liberty at all, but live like slaves, without honour and authority, in the houses of their husbands; and she censured the men for their unkindness, and the women, also, for submitting to be so undervalued.[108]

In what followed, Mīrzā Abū Ṭāleb attempted "to undeceive her" and to demonstrate that "it is the European women who do not possess so much power."[109] Having "waver[ed] in her own opinion," the English woman asked Mīrzā Abū Ṭāleb "to write something on the subject ...."[110] Explaining his reason for writing the essay, Mīrzā Abū Ṭāleb remarked:

> Since the same wrong opinion is deeply rooted in the minds of all other Europeans, and has been frequently before this held forth, I considered it necessary to write a few lines concerning the privileges of the female sex, as established, both by law and custom, in Asia and in Europe; omitting whatever was common to both, and noticing what is principally peculiar to each, in the manner of comparison, that the distinction may be the more easily made, and the real state of the case become evident to those capable of discernment."[111]

He then articulated six spheres where the liberty of the Asiatic women appeared "less that of Europeans" and eight areas in which Asian women were ranked above Europeans. The European women, according to Mīrzā Abū Ṭāleb, had more liberty than Asian women in

---

[107] Abū Ṭāleb Khan, "Vindication of the Liberties of the Asiatic Women," *Asiatic Annual Register or a View of the History of Hindustan*, 3(1801):100-107 (section on miscellaneous tracts); also in *Travels,* 342-51. It appears that Mīrzā Abū Ṭāleb was familiar with Mary Wollstonecraft's *A Vindication of the Rights of Woman,* which was published in 1792.

[108] Abū Ṭāleb Khan, "Vindication," in *Travels*, 342.

[109] Abū Ṭāleb Khan, "Vindication," in *Travels*, 342.

[110] Abū Ṭāleb Khan, "Vindication," in *Travels*, 342.

[111] Abū Ṭāleb Khan, "Vindication," in *Travels*, 342-43.

these ways: "The little intercourse with men, and concealment from view"; "the privilege of the husband, by law, to marry several wives"; "the power of divorce being in the hands of the husband"; "the little credit the law attaches to the evidence of women in Asia"; "the Asiatic women having to leave off going to balls and entertainment, and wearing showy dresses and ornaments, after their husband's death"; and "the Asiatic daughters not having the liberty of choosing their husbands."[112] The spheres where Asian women had more rights than Europeans included: "Their power over the property and children of the husband, by custom"; "their power, by custom, as to the marriage of their children, and choice of their religious faith"; "their authority over their servants"; "the freedom, by custom, of the Asiatic women from assisting in the business of the husband, or service of his guests"; "the greater deference the Asiatic ladies find paid to their humours, and a prescriptive right of teasing their husbands by every pretext"; "the greater reliance placed by the Asiatic husbands on their wives' virtue, both from law and custom"; "their share in the children, by law"; and "the ease, both by law and custom, with which the wife may separate from her husband, when there may be a quarrel between them, without producing a divorce."[113] Mīrzā Abū Ṭāleb's essay became a seminal text on the comparative study of European and Asian women. As explained below, the influence of Mīrzā Abū Ṭāleb's arguments can be found in a number of early nineteenth-century texts.

Mīrzā Abū Ṭāleb's eyewitness report of Europe influenced his close friend Mīr ʿAbd-al-Laṭīf Šūštarī in writing the *Toḥfat al-ʿālam* (1801).[114] Šūštarī, who corresponded with Mīrzā Abū Ṭāleb, explained that after the French Revolution unveiling had become so prevalent that the institution of marriage was weakened:

> Among the new incubations in France are the spread of immodesty among women and abandonment of nuptials and marriage. For specified amount and with the satisfaction of both sides and with two or three hours of music, they become engaged without an engagement ceremony. It is understood

[112] Abū Ṭāleb Khan, "Vindication," in *Travels*, 343-47.

[113] Abū Ṭāleb Khan, "Vindication," in *Travels*, 348-51.

[114] Mīr ʿAbd-al-Laṭīf [b. Abī Ṭāleb Jazāʾerī] Šūstarī, *Toḥfat al-ʿālam va ẕayl al-toḥfa: Safar-nāma va ḵāṭerat-e Mīr ʿAbd-al-Laṭīf Khan Šūstarī*, ed. Ṣamad Movaḥḥed, Tehran, 1984).

> that after engagement they would stay together for two months. Then, they have the choice of either remaining together or breaking-up, each going his or her own way."[115]

Āqā Aḥmad Behbahānī, a close associate of Šūštarī and a leading Shiʿi scholar who traveled to India in 1220-25/1805-10, had read Mīrzā Abū Ṭāleb's travelogue. He offered his own interpretive scheme for the "facts" reported by Mīrzā Abū Ṭāleb. He devoted a section of his book to the "Rejection of women's virginity, their domination over men and their unveiling" in Europe.[116] Likewise Jahān Begom (1850-1930), the Navvāb of Bhopal, in her *ʿEffat al-moslemāt* (1918) authoritatively cited Mīrzā Abū Ṭāleb in her rhetorical defense of Muslim women and purdah.[117]

A wider familiarity with the work of Mīrzā Abū Ṭāleb is evident from John Malcolm in his *Sketches of Persia*. Malcolm outlined a conversation in 1809 on the general conditions of Iranian women in a "strong contrast with those of the civilized nations of Europe."[118] He enumerated to his Iranian friends that Muslim women are "shut up like wild animals," "travel in curtained carriage," "are enveloped in robes," and "are married while mere children," and he alluded to "the numerous progeny of slaves and others of the harem."[119] Moḥammad-Ḥosayn Khan, Jaʿfar-ʿAlī Khan, and Mīrzā Āqā Mīr refuted these claims. On the last point, Mīrzā Āqā Mīr, citing Mīrzā Abū Ṭāleb's report on illegitimate children produced by the courtesans of London,[120] remarked: "a great proportion of your females and their offspring are in a much more miserable and degraded state than any in our country." He

---

[115] Šūštarī, *Toḥfat al-ʿÂlam*, 267. Abū Ṭāleb Khan corresponded with Šūštarī during his residence in England; see, Šūštarī, *Toḥfat al-ʿālam*, 368. On Abū Ṭāleb Khan's view of Šūštarī, see *Masīr*, 452.

[116] Āqā Aḥmad Behbahānī, *Merʾāt al-aḥwāl-e jahān-nemā*, ed. ʿAlī Davanī (Tehran, 1991), 91. The description of European women appears in Part 3, Chapter 9 of the manuscript.

[117] Solṭān Jahān Begom, *ʿEffat al-moslemāt* (Agra, 1337/1918), 198-201.

[118] Sir John Malcolm, *Sketches of Persia* (London, 1845), 187.

[119] Malcolm, *Sketches of Persia*, 187, 194.

[120] According to Abū Ṭāleb Khan "I was credibly informed, that in the single parish of Mary-la-bonne, which is only a sixth part of London, there reside sixty thousand courtezans; besides which, there is scarcely, a street in the metropolis where they are not to be found." See Mīrzā Abū Ṭāleb, *Travels*, 175.

immediately added that perhaps "Aboo Talib has exaggerated, which travelers are in the habit of doing."[121]

Sir Walter Scott summarized this dialogue on the condition of women in his review of Malcolm's *Sketches of Persia*. He granted that "Mirza Aga Meer justly remarks, in regard to the seclusion of women, that the free admission to society so prized in England would, from the difference of habit and feeling, be deemed discreditable and inconvenient by women characters in Persia."[122] Scott further added, "in fact, when we compare the allusions of Meerza and his companions, to the shrill tone of command often heard in a Persian family, with the description of the domestic life of the king's physician in Hajji Baba,[123] the autocracy of the Mohamedan husband does seem to be reduced almost to the level of marital authority in Europe."[124] The cultural relativism prefigured in such an exposition was a product of conversations between Europeans and Asians. Such relativism was also evident in the work of James Atkinson. Informed by Mīrzā Abū Ṭāleb's essay, Atkinson wrote, "Like many enthusiasts, who fancy England as the only land of liberty and happiness, because other countries do not act and feel in the same way, we think the women of Persia or India oppressed and degraded, because they do not possess and exercise exactly the same rights and privileges as our own."[125] Drawing upon Mīrzā Abū Ṭāleb's argument, he realized that: "whilst Europeans generally think them treated in the most barbarous and monstrous manner, with regard to their liberty and rank in society, the Persians themselves look upon their women as virtually invested with more power and liberty, and greater privileges, than the women of Europe."[126]

---

[121] Malcolm, *Sketches of Persia*, 194. Also partly quoted by Judy Mabro, *Veiled Half-Truths: Western Traveller's Perceptions of Middle Eastern Women* (London and New York, 1991), 25-26.

[122] Sir Walter Scott, "Sketches of Persia," *The Quarterly Review* 36 (June-October 1827):353-91, quote on p. 375.

[123] Written by James Morier, *The Adventures of Hajji Baba of Ispahan* and *The Adventures of Hajji Baba of Ispahan in England* (repr., New York, 1982), were based on his close interaction with Mīrzā Abu'l-Ḥasan Khan Īlčī, the Iranian ambassador to England, 1809-1810. Morier had accompanied Mīrzā Abu'l-Ḥasan to and from England. Ḥājjī Bābā was the name of an Iranian student who was sent to England in 1811 to study medicine.

[124] Scott, "Sketches of Persia," 375.

[125] James Atkinson, tr., *Customs and Manners of the Women of Persia and their Superstitions* (London:, 1832), Preface, vii-viii.

[126] Atkinson, "Preface," xi.

Frederick Shoberl, an American traveler who visited Iran, was also influenced by Mīrzā Abū Ṭāleb. Shoberl, writing on the condition of Persian women, noted: "We never think of Asia, without deploring the severity of their lot."[127] He then summarized Mīrzā Abū Ṭāleb who "endeavored to prove, in his work, that these women, who are the object of our pity, enjoy a condition far preferable to that of European females."[128] After noting that "there is really and truly no such a thing as liberty" for Asiatic women, he concluded:

> We judge in general of things by comparing them with our own customs, manners, and opinions; and hence the erroneous notions and ideas that we form. Pleasure and pain depend much on habit; what pleases in one country, disgusts in another. We are unable to conceive a more wretched condition than that of a woman whose life is passed in [a] harem. But this woman, who from disposition and habit is fond of repose, who has never known the pleasure of attracting the attention of the other sex, and eclipsing her own in personal charms, and in splendor and elegance of dress, cannot imagine that in other countries a female would compromise her honour, her dignity, and her modesty, by exposing her face unveiled to the public eye, and mingling among crowds of pedestrians.[129]

Although Shoberl understood different cultural practices, he yet found Persian women "totally devoid of delicacy" as judged by his own cultural standards:

> Their language is often gross and disgusting, nor do they feel less hesitation in expressing themselves before men, than they would before their female societies. Their terms of abuse or reproach are indelicate to the highest degree: it may safely be averred that it is not possible for the imagination to conceive, or language to express, more indecent or grosser images.[130]

The language of expression which seemed gross and indecent by Puritan standards was unproblematic in gender segregated communities of men and women. With the appearance of Iranian women in the public

---

[127] Frederic Shoberl, *Persia* (London, 1822), 116.
[128] Shoberl, *Persia*, 116; summary in pp. 116-19.
[129] Shoberl, *Persia*, 119.
[130] Shoberl, *Persia,* 115.

sphere the sanitizing of female language became a cultural necessary. The unveiling of women in public was balanced with the veiling of their language.[131]

With the emergence of a new class of intellectuals educated in Europe and in European style schools, the Farangī ways of life became a serious threat to the position of the ulema, the religious intellectuals. In the struggle between the traditional and the modern intellectuals, the image of Europe became an important component of political and cultural contention. The reformist and revolutionary discourses articulated a positive and idealized image of the West. On the other hand, the anti-reformist and Islamist discourses chose the European woman as a scapegoat to reconstitute the Islamic nation's sense of boundaries, which it was feared would disintegrate with increased Europeanization and the feminization of power.

Scapegoating Women

In the course of the nineteenth century, pornographic views of European women became popular. Ṣaḥḥāfbāšī's observation that in Europe "virgin women are rare, and womanizing is like eating bread and yogurt in Iran and is not offensive,"[132] became a prevalent view. These views provided the Iranian ulema with rhetorical ammunition to attack the modernists who were questioning their moral and intellectual leadership. An early example of clerical scapegoating of European women is evident in the writings of Ḥājjī Moḥammad-Karīm Khan Kermānī (1810-71), a leading Šayḵī theologian.[133] Writing in 1856/1273, Kermānī believed that Iran was becoming infected with a "new malady" which was the result of "pleasure-seeking individuals, who refuse to associate with the ulema, and would no longer abide by religious principles."[134] Relying on the eyewitness account of Europe narrated to him by "a leading Iranian notable" who had taken refuge in England,[135] he warned of the ensuing feminization of power in Iran:

---

[131] Afsaneh Najmabadi, "Introduction," in Bībī Ḵānom Astarābādī, *Maʿāyeb al-rejāl*, 16-21, quote on p. 21.

[132] Ṣaḥḥāfbāšī, *Safar-nāma*, 62.

[133] For a detailed study of Karīm Khan's thought see: Mangol Bayat, *Mysticism and Dissent: Socio-religious Thought in Qajar Iran* (Syracuse, 1982), 63-86. See also Abbas Amanat, *Resurrection and Renewal: The Making of the Babi Movement in Iran, 1844-1850* (Ithaca, 1989), 286-94.

[134] Quoted in Bayat, *Mysticism and Dissent*, 85.

[135] The above mentioned individual appears to be either Reżāqolī Mīrzā or his brothers Najafqolī or Tīmūr Mīrzā, who settled in Iraq where Ḥājjī

> Can any Muslim allow incompetent women to have affairs in their hands so that they could go wherever they choose, sit with whomever they desire, leave the house whenever they wish? They [Europeans] have not yet gained firm control of Iran, but they are already ordering our women not to cover themselves from men. Would any Muslim consent to women wearing makeup, sitting in the squares and at shops, going to theaters? Can any Muslim consent to the independence and beautification of his wife and allow her to go to the bazaar and buy wine and drink it and get intoxicated ... and sit with rogues and ruffians [*alvāṭ va awbāš*] and do whatever she chooses? God forbid! Would anyone consent to allowing freedom and loosing charge of one's daughter, wife, slave, and housekeeper? And allow them to go wherever they please and do whatever they like and sit with whomever they choose and have available in their gatherings any kind of wine they desire and mingle with rogues, and not be able to protest because an unbeliever has ordered the establishment of a land of freedom (*velāyat-e āzādī*)?[136]

Kermānī described his antagonists as "ignorant, conceited youth who, upon hearing the call of freedom, immediately make themselves look like Europeans, adopting European customs and betraying Islam and Islamic values."[137] He warned:

> When they hear the call to freedom they would shape themselves like the Farangīs, organize their assemblies and associations patterned after Europeans, model their behaviors on the bases of European customs, and turn away from Islam and Islamic traditions.[138]

Fearing the de-differentiation of gender and religious identities which could result from freedom and the feminization and Europeanization of power in Iran, Kermānī warned Muslim men:

> Then if your wife abstains from you, if she choses to convert to Armenianism, she would go to a church, and after she is baptized in

---

Moḥammad-Karīm Khan Kermānī was attending seminars offered by his master Sayyed Kāẓem Raštī (d. 1844).

[136] Kermānī, *Resāla-ye naṣīrīya*, 388-89; For an alternate rendering see Bayat's *Mysticism and Dissent*, 85-86.

[137] Quoted in Bayat, *Mysticism and Dissent*, 85.

[138] Kermānī, *Resāla-ye naṣīrīya*, 389.

> public, she would enter the Christian religion.... If the deviant women wish to become apostates, no one can protest. Due to freedom, a large number of people would become apostates, and the ulema and others would have no power to speak out. In conclusion, they would establish schools, and classes would be taught by European teachers ... and then the simple minded people would send their children to European schools and they would become totally Christianized.[139]

He further warned the male believers that if Iranian women mingled with European women, they would be tempted to dress like Europeans, dance in public celebrations and gatherings, drink wine, and sit with men on benches and chairs, and joke with strangers.[140] If Iran became

[139] Kermānī, *Resāla-ye naṣīrīya*, 390. It is important to note that Europeanization of education led to a different anxiety among European clerics. For example a certain Rev. A. Duff, addressing the General Assembly of the Church of Scotland, supporting the establishment of English in India as 'the grand medium by which all our knowledge is conveyed" remarked, "This naturally leads me to refer to a crisis in the history of India, which seems now approaching ... Already, in Calcutta, Allahabad, Delhi, and other stations, there are government seminaries established, where English is taught without religion. And the demand for English is likely soon to increase ten-fold, if not a hundred-fold. The reason is obvious. Till very recently, the language universal in India, as the language of government business, political, financial, and judicial, has been the Persian; the attainment of which will not enlighten, though it may greatly darken, the mind, and vitiate the heart. At the present, there is a strong disposition to abolish it altogether, and to substitute the English in its place. About two years ago, it was abolished in the political department of government. This change has already begun to work. In the great native courts, instead of Persian, must in the future be supported an English secretary: and the next step is to send for an English schoolmaster. In some instances, these two offices have been conjoined; so that, in several of the places of the rajahs, there is now an English school." After claiming that from "the Burman empire to the banks of the Indus, there has been more or less a demand for English books and English teachers," Rev. Duff rhetorically asked: "Once we let these leaders of the people become thorough English scholars, what will they be? Here upon us the glimpse of a dreadful crisis. Give the knowledge without religion, according to the government plan, and they will become a nation of infidels! So that, instead of having to content with the abominations of idolatry, you will have to content with the wildest forms of European infidelity!" ("The Rev. A. Duff['s] ... address to the General Assembly of the Church of Scotland," *The Asiatic Journal and Monthly Register* 18(1836): 86-88, quotes on pp. 87-88).

[140] Kermānī, *Resāla-ye naṣīrīya*, 391.

a "land of freedom" (*velāyat-e āzādī*) women would copulate with Europeans and no one would dare to protest.[141] Kermānī declared that "anyone who befriends a European would be considered a European himself . . . and thus has apostatized and adopted the religion of the Europeans."[142] This line of argument was later followed by Sheikh Fażl-Allāh Nūrī (d. 1909) in his pronouncements against the revolutionary constitutionalists of 1905-9, whom he viewed as "Paris worshipers" (*Parīs parasthā*).[143]

To preserve the Islamic social and gender orders and maintain the moral and intellectual leadership of the Muslim clergy, the Iranian counter-modernists made European women their scapegoat—a metaphor for secularization and deviation from Islam. In the decades after the Constitutional Revolution of 1905-9, woman's body became a terrain for an intensified cultural and political contest. The bodies of women were an important metaphor for delineating self and "other," Iran and Europe, Islam and Christianity. Veiled and unveiled women became symbols of two antagonistic views of social, political, and gender relations. Veiled women provided the organizing element of an Islamic and anti-reformist discours; unveiled women became a marker of secular-modernist discourse. In both discourses women's dress were symbols for the integrity, independence, and progress of the nation (*mellat*).

The antagonistic discourses constructed around the veil had as their subtext two conflicting images of Europe. One viewed Europe as *Farang-e bā farhang* ("the cultured Frank") and the other as *Kofrestān* (the land of the infidels). One was grounded in a positive notion of freedom (*āzadī*) anchored to the memories of the French Revolution and called for the refinement (*tarbīyat*) and unveiling of Iranian women. The other was grounded in a negative notion of freedom discursively connected to the presumed "indecency" and "corruption" of European women and sought to protect Iranians and the "nation of Islam" (*mellat-e Eslām*) from the maladies of Europeanization. The imagined Farangī woman was often a displacement and a simulacrum for Iranian women.

The centrality of the veil in twentieth-century Iranian political discourse conditioned the emergence of a particular Islamic genre focusing on the dangers of unveiling and the Europeanization of Iran.

---

141 Kermānī, *Resāla-ye naṣīrīya*, 389.

142 Kermānī, *Resāla-ye naṣīrīya*, 382-83; cited in Bayat, *Mysticism and Dissent*, 86.

143 Sheikh Fażl-Allāh Nūrī, *Lavā'eḥ-e Āqā Šayḵ Fażl-Allāh Nūrī*, ed. Homā Reżvānī (Tehran, 1362 Š./1983), 62.

Two exemplars of this genre are Moḥammad-Ṣādeq Fak̲r-al-Eslām's *Vojūb-e neqāb va ḥormat-e šarāb* ("The necessity of the veil and the prohibition of wine"), written in 1911, and Ẕabīh-Allāh Maḥallātī's *Kašf al-ğorūr yā mafāsed-e sofūr* ("Exposition of deceit or the depravity of unveiling"), written in 1932.[144] The authors of these texts developed a genre in which the dangers of unveiling and the indecency of European women were anchored to Islamic textual, sexual, and political strategies. Fak̲r-al-Eslām argued that the veiling of women was sanctioned in Judaism, Christianity, and Islam and that the unveiling of European women was against divine law. He further noted that Christian priests and missionaries would be burned in the fire of hell for allowing singing and dancing in churches. Fak̲r-al-Eslām concluded by arguing that those who called for the unveiling of women were simply pimping for free.[145]

To demonstrate the dangers of unveiling, Sheikh Ẕabīh-Allāh used diverse narrative and poetic strategies in which modernists and Islamicists clashed with one another. The *Kašf* ended with an Islamic novella, "The Tale of Mollā Solaymān and His Two Daughters." In this tale the veiled daughters of Mollā Solaymān successfully debated with two unveiled women activists who advocated unveiling in front of the shrine of Emām Reżā in Mašhad, the most holy city of Iran. The novella ends with the activists' confession that as a result of their prostitution they were suffering from syphilis. After repenting for having gone to a modern secular school, they decided to veil themselves again. These debates changed the meaning of the veil (*ḥejāb/čādor*) and transformed the notion of femininity (*zanānegī*) from a polar opposite of masculinity (*mardānegī*) into a signifier of Western-mediated gender identity.

Thus for Islamists and for many other anti-imperialist/anti-shah activists of the 1960s and 1970s, the "European doll" (*ʿarūsak-e farangī*), the simulacrum of Iranian woman mindlessly imitating Europeans, became a symbol for all social and political evils brought about by the shah's regime. To eradicate the shah and Western influence on Iran, the post-revolutionary Islamic government set itself the task of eradicating the "European dolls" of Iran by establishing the veil as a compulsory uniform, removing the makeup from women's faces, and closing night clubs and all other institutions modeled on an imagined Europe.

---

[144] Moḥammad-Ṣādeq Fak̲r-al-Eslām, *Resāla-ye vojūb-e neqāb* (Tehran, 1329/1911); Ẕabīh-Allāh Maḥallātī, *Kašf al-ğorūr* (Tehran, 1338 Š./1959).

[145] Fak̲r-al-Eslām, *Vojūb-e neqāb*, 38.

Mīrzā Abu'l-Ḥasan Khan Šīrāzī Īlčī's *Safar-nāma ba Rūsīya*: The Persians Amongst the Russians

Anna Vanzan

The *Safar-nāma ba Rūsīya* is the account of the Persian ambassador Mīrzā Abu'l-Ḥasan Khan Šīrāzī's expedition to Russia, although the diary was actually written by his secretary, Mīrzā Moḥammad-Hādī ʿAlavī Šīrāzī. As I will try to show, the chronicle is not merely the scribe's transcription of what the ambassador dictated; on the contrary, it is almost entirely ʿAlavī Šīrāzī's own production and reflects his own *Weltanschaung*. However, the ambassador's ideas are occasionally presented as well, thus offering an interesting example of "dual" authorship.

After the Treaty of Golestān (14 October 1813), the Qajars tried to renegotiate the terms of the treaty under which the Caucasian territories were lost after the wars against Russia. The treaty was rather humiliating for the Persians, who were also prohibited from maintaining any warships on the Caspian Sea. In addition, the clauses regarding the border between Russia and Iran were so vague as to give rise to misunderstanding and abuse. In order to obtain a rectification of the frontier, the Persian government sent a mission to Russia headed by Mīrzā Abu'l-Ḥasan Khan Šīrāzī, a nephew of Āgā Moḥammad Shah Qajar's prominent vizier, Ḥājjī Ebrāhīm, who had taken part in the Treaty of Golestān negotiations.

The mission left Tehran for Russia via Tiflis in June 1814 and returned to the Persian capital two years later with nothing tangible in hand except a diary of the expedition which Mīrzā Abu'l-Ḥasan Khan Šīrāzī had kept during its journey.[1]

[1] The mission cannot be held responsible for this diplomatic failure: Crucial events (the war against France that led Alexander I as far as Paris and then

Mīrzā Abu'l-Ḥasan Khan Šīrāzī, nicknamed the Īlčī, was not new to this kind of experience: In the years 1809-10, he had been sent to Great Britain, where he had become a "darling of London high society."[2]

The Īlčī had fascinated the British, so much so that the most popular local newspapers often reported on the Persian envoy's activities, and two well-known English painters painted the ambassador.[3] It also seems that the Īlčī was the inspiration for James Morier's character of Mirza Firouz, which satirizes the eccentric Persian ambassador in Morier's famous book *The Adventures of Hajji Baba of Ispahan*.[4]

As for the Īlčī, he was so impressed by his English experience that he partially narrated it in his *Ḥayrat-nāma* or "Book of Wonders," which offers a "limited vision of the West," probably as a result of the Īlčī's "egotistic and essentially hedonistic character."[5] However, the diary related to his second journey, the *Safar-nāma ba Rūsīya*, written by his secretary Mīrzā Moḥammad Hādī ʿAlavī Šīrāzī, is a thoughtful and exhaustive description of the places he visited, of the people he met, and of the ideas with which he was confronted. Probably due to the fact that he was officially charged with narrating his Russian experience, this time the Īlčī was not preoccupied with impressing the readers with the wonders he had seen: Rather, he described with clarity and precision scientific discoveries and technological devices (which required the use of words which did not exist in the Persian vocabulary); the czar's way of ruling; the royal family and the court; Russian customs and pastimes. The result was a witty portrait of not only events the mission took part in, but also of visits to museums, factories, schools

---

the defeat of Napoleon and the Congress of Vienna) kept the Czar far from Russia for a long time.

[2] Denis Wright, *The Persians Amongst the English* (London, 1985), 53.

[3] Sir William Beechey and Sir Thomas Lawrence, who both portrayed the Īlčī in 1810. The first portrait is hosted in Whitehall, the second one is in the Fogg Art Museum (Boston). These paintings are reproduced respectively in Wright, *Persians Amongst the English*, 53 and in the *Safar-nāma ba Rūsīya*, ed. Moḥammad Golbon (Tehran, 1357 Š./1978), 65, 292.

[4] See, for example, A. Bausani, "Un manoscritto persiano inedito sull'ambasceria di Ḥusein H̱ān Moqaddam Āǧūdānbāšī in Europa negli anni 1254-1255 H. (=1839-39 A.D.)," *Oriente Moderno* 33(1953):493; Hasan Javadi, "James Morier and his Hajji Baba of Isfahan," in *Persian Literary Influence on English Literature* (Calcutta, 1970), 123-25; Wright, *Persians Amongst the English*, 68-69.

[5] M. R. Ghanoonparvar, *In a Persian Mirror* (Austin, 1993), 21. The *Ḥayrat-nāma* has been edited by Ḥasan Morselvand (see bibliography).

and other institutions. It was certainly one of the most extensive and informative documents on Russian society that the Qajar court had at that time.[6]

The style is simple and direct, so much so that the diary can be placed among the examples of *sāda-nevīsī* of the last century. It is also interesting to note that the text is rich in Russian (and French) words which were imported into Iran perhaps for the first time through this diary and which later became part of the Persian language.

The text can be divided into two parts. The first one (about one third of its length) is devoted to the journey from Tehran to Tiflis and the stay in the Caucasus region, which lasted about eight months. The second one concerns the cities of Moscow, where the Īlčī stayed for a few months, and of St. Petersburg, where the mission remained from May 1815 to January 1816. During the stay in the Russian capital, the Īlčī wrote, or rather ordered his secretary to write, a report on "the Russian emperor's rules and manners and [on] St. Petersburg's construction and its buildings."[7] The scribe had plenty of time to accomplish this task. In fact, the mission, which reached St. Petersburg in May 1815, had to wait until the following December for Czar Alexander to return from Paris.

Mīrzā Moḥammad Hādī ʿAlavī Šīrāzī reported on the following ten issues (*dah maqāla*):[8] (1) The foundation of the Russian Empire and its kings; (2) the creation of St. Petersburg and the characteristics of the great river which runs through it; (3) the position of buildings, houses, and streets on the south bank of the river; (4) the houses, furniture, and equipment, and women's and men's apparel; (5) the food and the way of sleeping, the way of receiving guests and piety, the way of having sexual intercourse and ablutions, and how women deal with menstruation; (6) the people, marriage, religion and state, and habits and behaviors; (7) the emperor and what is related to him, his counselors, senators, and ministries; (8) how the printed paper called "banknote" circulates, the government expenses, allowances, and transactions with the royal treasury and so forth; (9) the system and

[6] Another contemporaneous description of Russian society is by Mīrzā Ṣāleḥ, *Gozāreš-e safar,* ed. Homāyūn Šahīdī (Tehran, 1363 Š./1985). Mīrzā Ṣāleḥ was sent to England by ʿAbbās Mīrzā with other Persian students in order to study sciences. He traveled via Russia and sojourned in St. Petersburg, where he met the Īlčī; this meeting is recorded in the *Safar-nāma ba Rūsīya*, 213.

[7] *Safar-nāma ba Rūsīya*, 132.

[8] *Safar-nāma ba Rūsīya*, 132-81.

equipment of the army, cavalry and infantry, the soldiers and their reputation, the way they serve the state, the salary, clothes, and food with which the state provides them, their horses, weapons and military stores, the mounted and foot soldiers who were always in the emperor's arsenal, their uniforms and equipment, their reverence toward the emperor, the quality of their artillery and their arsenal and of the other war equipment and their rules, and so forth; (10) the laws and rules [the Russians] observe in every manner and so forth.

The last part of the diary relates the unsuccessful conclusion of the Īlčī's mission. The czar's return to St. Petersburg coincided with the marriage ceremony of one of his sisters. That event so completely absorbed the Russian emperor that he had no time to discuss the Persians' requests! Even the British, who had previously supported Persian claims, disappointed the Īlčī when their ambassador in St. Petersburg revealed his skepticism about the possibility of the Persians regaining some of the Caucasian territories.[9] With the czar eluding the Īlčī's petitions and the British withdrawing their patronage, Mīrzā Abu'l-Ḥasan Khan Šīrāzī had nothing to do but return empty-handed to Tehran (April 1816).

In many respects, the diary is in the full tradition of Persian nineteenth-century travel literature. It abounds in statistical details such as the distances traversed, the size of buildings and bridges, and the population of the places visited. The diary becomes very precise—and sometimes tedious—especially in the ten chapters on St. Petersburg.[10] Here the intent on pedantically describing data and memorabilia is evident and plausible since the author's purpose was to offer as accurate a picture of Russian society as possible. The author, like the majority of nineteenth-century Persian travelers, was impressed by the minutia and concern for details in the daily work of his European counterparts—he reports, for example, on the European custom of recording births and deaths[11]—and tried to imitate them.

---

[9] *Safar-nāma ba Rūsīya*, 252. The Īlčī's mission had been strongly encouraged by Sir Gore Ouseley, English ambassador in Tehran in 1810. Great Britain was, of course, much interested in the Persians regaining their lost Caucasian territories. But after Napoleon's defeat and the new alliances due to the Congress of Vienna, the English withdrew their support: Iran was becoming a pawn in what was later styled the "Great Game."

[10] See, for example, the meticulous report on one of the bridges in St. Petersburg, *Safar-nāma ba Rūsīya*, 138.

[11] *Safar-nāma ba Rūsīya*, 85.

Another feature common to many *safar-nāma*s was the fascination with superior European (in this case Russian) technology. Much space is devoted to the textile factories that the Īlčī visited on more than one occasion. Our author stresses the fact that the Russian cotton mills were larger and were able to produce more rapidly than the Persian ones. This, by the way, should have sounded an alarm for the Persians, who were about to face a dramatic decrease in their textile exports to Russia in the second half of the nineteenth century.[12]

As usual, great attention was devoted to the army—now more than ever, since to inspect the Russian army could have been a key to understanding the Persians' recent defeat in the Caucasus. The author revealed that the Russian soldiers (*sāldāt*) were well-dressed, well-equipped, well-armed and well- (or at least regularly) paid.[13] Curiously, he also stressed the importance of trumpeters and drummers in the vanguard of the Russian army: Their presence encouraged the troops so much so that they faced death happily.[14] Morale, however, was the most important ingredient: and it was well known that the Russian soldiers were the most courageous in Europe, although France had the best generals and officers.[15]

Even so, the writer is not generous about praising Russian morals. On the contrary, while showing admiration for Russian scientific, political, administrative, and financial organization, he did not miss a single occasion to underline Russian debauchery and moral corruption. As soon as the mission crossed the threshold of Persian territory, the author discovered a world of depravity that also had a contaminating influence on Muslim ethics. An example was Āġā Beg Darbandī, the Persian interpreter in the retinue of the general of Tiflis, who forgot his Muslim principles and behaved like a Russian, that is to say:

> drinking wine and committing all sorts of sins.... He is so involved in the Russian habits and doctrine that he has no limit; he has abandoned any apparent purity and piety so much so that he was repeatedly seen with his trousers open while urinating by standing dog-like or Russian-like; and once relieved, he set forth into the street.[16] In addition, he does not use water in his privy, but instead

---

[12] See Charles Issawi, ed., *The Economic History of Iran 1800-1914* (Chicago and London, 1971), 300-310.

[13] *Safar-nāma ba Rūsīya*, 168-74.

[14] *Safar-nāma ba Rūsīya*, 169.

[15] *Safar-nāma ba Rūsīya*, 170.

[16] As is well know, the general custom among Muslims was to squat while urinating, and when finished to wash themselves.

> he keeps in his hat a piece of paper, like the Russians do, and cleans himself with it.[17]

Russian perversions contaminated the people as well by means of the Russian soldiers quartered in peoples' homes who deprived women of their honor and chastity. Russians and local women even went to the public bath (*ḥammām*) together, but it was the Russians who were blamed. They had already contaminated the Georgians and the Armenians with their customs, and now they were corrupting the Muslims too.[18] By watching women and girls walking in the streets and markets, it became evident that only a few of them were honest and chaste. They used heavy make-up and followed Russian customs; that is, they gathered with men at every corner, drank wine, and committed every sort of sin. Even the wife of the general of Tiflis openly cheated on her husband, and he could not help it.[19] This situation was mainly due to the ethics of the Russians, whose women enjoyed absolute power: They did whatever they desired, they went wherever they wanted, they spoke with whomever they wanted, and no man had the authority to reproach them. Women had complete liberty.[20]

Thus, if women were a kind of barometer according to which one could evaluate the moral level of a society, Russian society was highly depraved. Even institutions of social usefulness, such as an asylum for unmarried mothers in Moscow, were described as a consequence of moral depravity. The author visited and carefully described the foundation, financed by the czar's mother, where unmarried girls could deliver their children, who were subsequently raised and taught a vocation in that very place.[21] He meticulously records that by the beginning of that year (Rabīʿ I 1230/March 1815) four hundred women

---

[17] *Safar-nāma ba Rūsīya*, 29.

[18] *Safar-nāma ba Rūsīya*, 28. This part is undoubtedly written by Mīrzā Moḥammad Šīrāzī, whose warning sounds as an early call for Muslim solidarity (Pan-Islamism).

[19] *Safar-nāma ba Rūsīya*, 28. Curiously, the anecdote reminds one of that about the (Muslim) general of Erevan who was notorious for his lust for Armenian women. One of the many versions of this narrative is the "Story of Yousuf and Mariam" in *The Adventures of Hajji Baba*. In the *Safar-nāma*, on the contrary, it is the (Russian) general of Tiflis who becomes a victim of his wife's lust. Is it the counter-myth of the story as seen from the perspective of "the Other" (i.e., the Muslim) side?

[20] *Safar-nāma ba Rūsīya*, 29.

[21] *Safar-nāma ba Rūsīya*, 107-11.

had entered the shelter, and all of them had given birth. Even more extraordinary was the fact that the night before the visit of the Persian delegation, twelve women arrived, gave birth to twelve children, and left.[22] "Anyway, one should not wonder about it," adds our author, "if one considers the fact that the word 'virginity' among the Russians has no meaning. 'Virginity, what does it mean?' they say. 'A young girl bleeds when she has intercourse, an older woman does not.'"[23] Russian women did not need virginity in order to get married, the only thing they needed was money and property. As a result, there was no woman or girl who was not lost or who was not engaged in reproachful actions.[24]

The author stressed several times the fact that virginity was meaningless among the Russians,[25] and that the kind of freedom women got from this situation led to moral degeneracy. Furthermore, he seems to include the whole of Russian society in his harsh sentence. While he was rather prudent when he examined other matters (financial, administrative, legal, military issues, and so on) and avoided pronouncing any judgment, perhaps in order to appear impartial and objective to the readers, when it came to morality, and especially to women's morality, he became hyper-critical and even rude.

Another confirmation of this attitude was the fact that, while he usually made a distinction among the social classes when he talked about manners and habits, he lumped everything together when he wrote about Russian women or about Russian sexual behavior. For instance, he described at length the way Russians set a table, giving details on the silverware and crystal, and later also mentioned that the poor used only wooden plates and utensils.[26] But in the chapter on how women dealt with menstruation, although the source of his information was probably a prostitute with whom he had been intimate, he associated all Russian women in general in this disdainful analogy:

> Women do not use any kind of binding when they menstruate. And since they have neither pants or under garments, the blood

[22] *Safar-nāma ba Rūsīya*, 108.

[23] *Safar-nāma ba Rūsīya*, 110.

[24] *Safar-nāma ba Rūsīya*, 110.

[25] For example, *Safar-nāma ba Rūsīya*, 153, where he also repeats that "they [the Russians] say that a very small woman bleeds a little bit during her first intercourse, while a big one does not." See also p. 154.

[26] *Safar-nāma ba Rūsīya*, 149-50.

> flows from them and soils their petticoat. Although the blood sticks, they do not change their petticoat until their period is over.[27]

Frankness bordering almost on vulgarity sometimes characterized the author's descriptions of the relationship between the two genders, not only in Russia, but in Europe in general. After explaining that Russian women did not shave their genitals in order to please their men, he reinforced this notion with a licentious story. A bald English gentleman was traveling in the Ottoman territories[28] where he had an affair with a local (and, naturally, shaved) lady. Since Europeans did not like shaved women, he used his wig to supply the lady's deficiency.[29] Moral and physical uncleanliness went together: Russian men and women go simultaneously to the baths (*ḥammām*), but this seems to be only a pretext for a promiscuous rendezvous since they do not have the custom of washing themselves with water.[30]

Although our author's attitude towards Russian women was severely negative, one could nevertheless say he was sometimes ambiguous and contradictory (another aspect of nineteenth-century Persian travel literature[31]). Especially during the long and ineffective sojourn in Moscow, the Persian mission was very often invited to promenades, tea-parties, soirees, dances, and masquerades that were attended by women of the Russian aristocracy. The narrative of these social gatherings is almost always favorable to women: They danced graciously, they knew how to entertain their guests, they played some instruments, they spoke French;[32] furthermore (and now the author's praise even turned into exaggeration), there were many Russian girls and women who spoke five or six languages.[33] All the Russians, be they rich or poor, gave an early education to their daughters, who later could read and write, sing and dance, speak several foreign languages, make drawings and portraits, and read and understand books on Russian history. It was unusual to find illiterate women or those who could not dance or sing, and even among the poor peasants literacy was frequent among girls. The main reason lay in the fact that Europeans, and especially Russians, favored their daughters rather than their sons. In

[27] *Safar-nāma ba Rūsīya*, 150.

[28] *Rūm* in the text, *Safar-nāma ba Rūsīya*, 155.

[29] *Safar-nāma ba Rūsīya*, 155.

[30] *Safar-nāma ba Rūsīya*, 150-51.

[31] On this point, see Ghanoonparvar, *In a Persian Mirror*, 24-35.

[32] *Safar-nāma ba Rūsīya*, 90-100, *passim*.

[33] *Safar-nāma ba Rūsīya*, 156.

addition, if a girl was not educated, she would not find a husband.[34] When they grew up and got married, Russian women enjoyed social respect—so much so that when husband and wife walked together in the street, the woman preceded her man. And when women and men met in public, men kissed women's hands and made them sit first, as the author wrote in his chapter on people and marriage.[35] And then he continued by repeating some concepts stated before: Russian men had no power over their women, who went wherever they wanted, brought home whomever they wanted, did whatever they liked, and men could not prohibit them because women normally had complete freedom.[36] Then the author turned again to moral critique. This freedom led to transgression, such that the majority of women and girls, from upper or lower classes, had two or three sexual encounters before getting married. As stated earlier, virginity was not worthy of consideration.[37]

All this criticism about European/Russian women and morals was common to many nineteenth-century Persian travelogues; but in this case, it raises a question: How was it that a person like the Īlčī, who had already traveled and sojourned in Europe and who was fascinated, above all, by English women and the freedom they enjoyed, now turned into a bitter Savonarola?

The possible answer involves the authorship of the diary. How much of the journal was due to the Īlčī, and how much was due to the secretary's own observations and opinions? Probably, the large space dedicated to the female universe was due to the Īlčī's interest in women, but, undoubtedly, the diary was primarily Mīrzā Moḥammad-Hādī ʿAlavī Šīrāzī's work, and it principally reflected the secretary's comments and ideas. It seems inconceivable, for instance, that the Īlčī would wonder at the Russian ladies curtseying when they were introduced to someone,[38] or that he—a habitué of concerts and operas in London—would describe what a theater was.[39]

Mīrzā Moḥammad-Hādī ʿAlavī Šīrāzī's pessimistic impression of Russian moral behavior cannot only be the product of a general negative conception that Persians had about the Russians, who recently had been victorious over the Qajars in the Caucasus. At the beginning of

---

[34] *Safar-nāma ba Rūsīya*, 156.

[35] *Safar-nāma ba Rūsīya*, 153.

[36] *Safar-nāma ba Rūsīya*, 153. The author repeats almost exactly the terms used before, 29.

[37] *Safar-nāma ba Rūsīya*, 153-54. See note above.

[38] *Safar-nāma ba Rūsīya*, 91.

[39] *Safar-nāma ba Rūsīya*, 87.

the expedition—and of the diary as well—the writer was full of interest for the world he was about to visit and full of hope of a positive resolution about the Caucasian territories. However, as stated above, he formulated his condemnation of' Russian behavior as soon as he crossed the Iranian border into lands which had been of Islamic culture until recently. Evidently, the shock provoked by the different concept of morality among the Russians did not enable him to appreciate some of the positive features of that society.

One also wonders whether the writer's bias against Russian women was not a result of his misogynist attitude in general; in fact, on the only occasion in which he compared Russian women to Persian, he denigrated even his female compatriots. Commenting upon the fact that Russian women would use a precious shawl for ten or twenty years, the author says:

> They do not behave like Persian women who dissipate a lot of money for their apparels ...which they would use only for three or fourth months, and for which they make their husbands bankrupt.[40]

Another question is whether the Īlčī revised his secretary's chronicle and, if he did, whether he agreed with what the Mīrzā wrote. Perhaps this time the Īlčī was ordered not only to write something more substantial than the account of his affairs with women, but also to give an image of himself more appropriate to his status, i.e., an official envoy of an Islamic country. We have also to consider the fact that the diary was bound to go into royal hands or, more probably, into the hands of the hereditary crown prince, ʿAbbās Mīrzā, who was the most interested of the Qajar leaders in accounts about the West.

In any case, the chronicle is an official document. As a result, although the core of the diary concerns official institutions and gives an altogether favorable impression of the Russian empire, the numerous observations concerning Russian manners and customs must have negatively influenced the opinion Persians had of their powerful neighbors.

---

[40] *Safar-nāma ba Rūsīya*, 148.

BIBLIOGRAPHY

Primary Sources

Mīrzā Abu'l-Ḥasan Khan Šīrāzī Īlčī. *Ḥayrat-nāma: Safar-nāma-ye Abu'l-Ḥasan K̲ān Šīrāzī Īlčī ba Landan.* Edited by Ḥasan Morselvand. Tehran, 1364 Š./1986.

Mīrzā Moḥammad-Hādī ʿAlavī Šīrāzī. *Safar-nāma ba Rūsīya.* Edited by Moḥammad Golbon. Tehran, 1357 Š./1978.

Secondary Sources

Bausani, Alessandro. "Un manoscritto persiano inedito sul'ambasceria di Ḥusein H̯ān Moqaddam Āğūdānbāšī in Europa negli anni 1254-1255 H. (=1838-39 A.D.)." *Oriente Moderno* 33(1953):485-505.

Farmayan, Hafez. "The Forces of Modernization in Nineteenth Century Iran: A Historical Survey." In William Polk and Richard Chambers, eds., *Beginnings of Modernization in the Middle East: The Nineteenth Century*. Chicago, 1968. Pp. 119-51.

Ghanoonparvar, M. R. *In a Persian Mirror*. Austin, 1993.

Javadi, Hasan. "James Morier and His Hajji Baba of Isfahan." In *Persian Literary Influence on English Literature*. Calcutta, 1970. Pp. 113-26.

—. "Abu'l-Ḥasan Khan Īlčī." In *Encyclopaedia Iranica* (London, etc. 1985-), 1:308-10.

Polimeno, Massimiliano. "Il *Safarname ye Mirzā Abu'l-Hasan Khan Shirāzi Ilchi be Rusiye*: una relazione di viaggio persiana nella Russia di Alessandro I." M.A. thesis, University of Bologna, 1994.

Wright, Denis. *The Persians Amongst the English: Episodes in Anglo-Persian History*. London, 1985.

British Travelers in Qajar Persia and Their Books

Denis Wright

English literature is richer than that of any other country in travel books about Qajar Persia.[1] The reason is not far to seek and lies mainly in the fact that throughout the period Britain, with the defense of her expanding Indian empire in mind, was more interested in Persia than any other Power with the possible exception of Tsarist Russia. The East India Company and its successor the Government of India watched Persia with eagle eyes from their headquarters in Calcutta and Bombay. They sought information about the country, its rulers, and its topography. Many of their officials, civil and military, served in Persia or traveled through the country, as did adventurous independent individuals. Some were well versed in Persian history and language, then used by Indian officialdom. Several wrote books which today provide a valuable source for the historian in many fields.[2]

One of the earliest such books was that of the scholarly E. Scott Waring of the East India Company's Bengal Civil Establishment who, for reasons of "ill health and curiosity" spent four months in and around Shiraz in 1802. His book, published in 1807, was the first serious study of Persia by an Englishman during the Qajar period. Its lengthy title speaks for itself:

> *A Tour of Sheeraz, by the route of Kazroon and Feerozabad; with various remarks on the Manners, Customs, Laws, Language and*

---

[1] See E. Ehlers, *Iran: A Bibliographic Research Survey* (Munich, 1980), 43-68 and Shōkō Okazaki and Kinji Eura, *Bibliography on Qajar Persia* (Osaka, 1985).

[2] See, for example, J. A. Lerner, "British Travellers' Accounts as a Source for Qajar Shiraz," *Bulletin of the Asia Institute, Pahlavi University, Shiraz* nos. 1-4(1976):205-73.

Literature of the Persians, to which is added A History of Persia from the death of Kureem Khan to the subversion of the Zund Dynasty.

Fear of a French threat to India in the very early days of Qajar rule led to John Malcolm's first mission to Persia in 1800 and Sir Harford Jones' arrival in Tehran in February 1809 to establish permanent diplomatic relations with the Qajar Court and negotiate a treaty of alliance. Both men wrote about their travels and experiences.[3]

James Morier, son of a naturalized British subject and without a drop of British blood in his veins, had traveled to Tehran with Harford Jones as his secretary. They had spent four months on the journey by what in those days was the normal route—sailing round the Cape of Good Hope to Bombay, then up the Persian Gulf to Būšehr followed by a long and arduous march by way of Shiraz and Isfahan to Tehran. At the end of 1809, Morier broke new ground when he accompanied the Persian envoy Mīrzā Abu'l-Ḥasan Šīrāzī to London, traveling overland via Tabriz to Turkey and then sailing through the Mediterranean to Falmouth. Morier and the Mīrzā returned to Tehran in 1811 in company with Jones' successor Sir Gore Ouseley—this time by the long sea route. Morier describes these journeys in his two magnificent travel books, packed with information about the country and its people and illustrated with his own drawings—one of them entitled "Tomb of Madre Suleiman," which he all but identified as the tomb of Cyrus, for which the hunt was on.

Morier was a shrewd observer and drew heavily on his Persian experiences for his two Hajji Baba novels. He did not like the Persians and poked fun at them in both books, not least at his friend Mīrzā Abu'l-Ḥasan, thinly disguised as "Mirza Firouz." Prophetically, he noted that the influence of the leading mullah in Qom was such that "many believe he could even subvert the authority of the Shah himself and make his subjects look upon his firmans as worthless."[4] His later novels with a Persian setting make heavy reading these days.

Two other members of Ouseley's staff wrote about their travels—William Price and Ouseley's brother William, an erudite orientalist. From Shiraz, the latter went to Fāsā in the mistaken belief that it was the site of Pasargadae and that he would find there traces of Cyrus's

---

[3] See the appended bibliography, which lists all travel and other books with a Persian background by authors mentioned in the text.

[4] James Morier, *The Adventures of Hajji Baba of Ispahan* (London, 1897), 333.

tomb. A few years later, another Englishman, Robert Ker Porter, after a close study of all available classical sources, positively identified Pasargadae and thus confirmed Morier's speculations.

Ker Porter was married to a Russian princess and while painting in Russia had been encouraged to visit Persia and make drawings at Persepolis and elsewhere. Leaving St. Petersburg in 1817, he spent the next two years in Persia and made careful drawings at Persepolis and other ancient sites. He is credited with having identified Darius I's tomb at Naqš-e Rostam and with being the first European to notice and sketch the Sasanian bas-reliefs of Ṭāq-e Bostān and visit the remote Sasanian and Il-Khanid site of Taḵt-e Solaymān, built round a spectacular volcanic lake in Kurdish country.

The illustrated tomes of Morier, Ouseley, and Porter stimulated public interest in Persia's ancient past; they also provide an invaluable record of monuments, some now lost. In contrast, slim, rare volumes by half-forgotten travelers sometimes reveal nuggets for the specialist—e.g. accounts by R. C. Money of his meetings with Mīrzā Abu'l-Ḥasan in 1824, and by Thomas Alcock and T. B. Armstrong, master and servant, of the murder of Griboyedov, the Russian ambassador, and his staff in Tehran in 1828 a few days before their arrival there. This dramatic event is described in more detail by the mysterious adventurer George Fowler who was in Tabriz at the time.

A few years earlier, another independent traveler, the twenty-eight year old James Baillie Fraser, had visited Persia. Failing to find satisfactory employment in India, he decided in 1821 to return home slowly by way of Būšehr and Tehran. At Qom, he entered the shrine in disguise. but in Mašhad, with the help of high-ranking clerical friends, he became a Muslim—*pro tempore* at least—and was able to enter the shrine and sketch there unmolested. After six weeks in Mašhad, he turned west, traveling through little known and lawless Turkoman country to Astarābād (Gorgān), then along the Caspian littoral to Ardabīl, Tabrīz, and Orūmīya (Urmia). After some eight months in the country, he reached his Scottish Highland home in 1823. He then spent the next ten years between Scotland and London, writing seven lengthy books of travel and fiction, all but one with a Persian or Turkoman background. His *Narrative of a Journey in Khorasan in the Years 1821 and 1822* and *Travels and Adventures in the Persian Provinces of the Southern Banks of the Caspian Sea* contained much information about a region then almost unknown to the outside world, as did his two later travel books, *A Winter's Journey (Tatar) from Constantinople to Tehran etc*. and *Travels in Koordistan, Mesopotamia etc*, written after his second visit to Persia. These books won high praise from Lord Curzon many years later for their "faithful portraiture of every aspect of modern Persian life."[5] Fraser's first two novels, *The Kuzzilbash: A Tale of Khorasan* and its sequel *The Persian Adventurer*, were woven round the life of Nāder Shah and allegedly based on Fraser's translation of the memoirs of one of the shah's entourage.

In 1833, the British Foreign Secretary, Lord Palmerston, alarmed by Russia's expansionist policies, invited Fraser to visit Persia and Mesopotamia and report secretly on Russian activities and influence there. Fraser spent nearly eighteen months on this exhausting mission, during which he covered some ten thousand miles, mostly on horseback. On his return in 1835, he wrote the two travel books mentioned above and two very long romantic novels with a Persian background, in addition to a detailed account of his attendance on the three exiled Qajar princes who had come to London in 1836.

Henry Layard, who was to achieve fame as the excavator of Nimrud and Nineveh, resembled Fraser in many ways, being an adventurous yet careful traveler, gifted with intelligence and curiosity about both the past and present. Bored with life in a London solicitor's office, he decided at the tender age of twenty-two to seek his fortune in Ceylon, where he had relatives, traveling there slowly through the Near and Middle East in company with an older friend, Edward Mitford. Layard's interest in the East had, he tells, been stirred by his childhood reading of the *Arabian Nights*. As he grew older, he read every book he could find on eastern travel—those by Fraser (whom he met), Malcolm, Morier, and others, such as James Buckingham, founder of the *Calcutta Journal*, and Claudius Rich, the East India Co.'s brilliant young Resident in Baghdad, who died of cholera in Shiraz in 1821, Fraser reading the burial service over his grave.

Layard never reached Ceylon. On arriving in Hamadān from Baghdad in mid-1840, he and Mitford parted company. The latter went on to Ceylon, where he joined the Civil Service and many years later, when retired, wrote an interesting account of his Persian travels, while Layard traveled to Isfahan. There, he met some Ba<u>k</u>tīārī khans and with their help spent over a year deep in Ba<u>k</u>tīārī country, where the chieftains of both branches of that great tribe treated him as an honored guest. He then returned to Baghdad and concentrated on excavating the great mounds he had noticed close to the Tigris on his way to Persia. Later, he was to become both a Member of Parliament (for Aylesbury) and ambassador (to Turkey). His *Early Adventures in Persia, Susiana and Babylonia* provides a unique account of life among the Ba<u>k</u>tīārīs.

---

[5] George N. Curzon, *Persia and the Persian Question,* 2 vols. (London, 1892), 1:24.

The perceived French threat to India led, as already mentioned, to an Anglo-Persian alliance finally enshrined in the Treaty of Tehran (1812). One consequence was the dispatch from India and England of military missions and advisers to train the Persian army and collect topographical information about the country. Lieutenant H. Pottinger (who as Sir Henry Pottinger became Hong Kong's first governor in 1843), disguised as an Indian horse dealer, traveled through Baluchistan and wrote about these unknown regions in his four-hundred page *Travels in Baloochistan and Sinde*, while Captain John Macdonald Kinneir (better known as Sir John Macdonald, British Minister to Persia, 1826-30) collated in his *Geographical Memoir of the Persian Empire* the information gathered by various members of Malcolm's third mission to Persia in 1810.

In 1829, under the terms of the Treaty of Adrianople, the Turks had reluctantly opened their Black Sea ports to foreign shipping, thus providing a relatively short overland route to Tabriz and Tehran from Trebizond (Trabzon) on the Black Sea. Henry Ellis went this way when sent from London in 1835 to offer congratulations to Moḥammad Shah on his accession. Charles Stuart, a member of his staff, has described the journey, the personalities they met, etc. in his *Journal of a Residence in Northern Persia*. Their ship, *HMS Pluto,* was probably the first British steamer to anchor off Trebizond. A year later, the last British military mission to Persia under the terms of the Treaty of Tehran, consisting of eight riflemen sergeants under Captain Richard Wilbraham, followed this same route to Tabriz. Both Wilbraham and Robert Macdonald, one of his sergeants, subsequently wrote about their travels. Macdonald, like Fraser and most of those who wrote about the Persians, took a poor view of the national character and customs, which they criticized freely with scant thought for Persian feelings. Nevertheless, in the eyes of a recent Persian critic, the humble sergeant's *Personal Narrative of Military Travel in Turkey and Persia* is "vastly better than many books written by the author's superiors in the nineteenth century."[6]

Fraser's 1834 mission to Persia was an early move in the Great Game. Others involved in it at this time who published accounts of their Persian travels were two of the East India Co.'s up and coming officers—Arthur Conolly (later murdered in Bokhara) and Alexander Burnes (murdered in Kabul in 1841). Both concentrated on Persia's northeastern frontier and, like Fraser, wrote about the Turkoman tribes

---

[6] Cyrus Ghani, *Iran and the West: A Critical Bibliography* (London, 1987), 232.

there. Interest in this strategic area remained keen throughout the Qajar period, and in the 1870s and 1880s other intelligence-gathering officers traveled there. Among those who later wrote books were H. C. Marsh, V. Baker, C. M. MacGregor, and C. Stewart. MacGregor's *Narrative of a Journey through the Province of Khorasan* etc. is particularly noteworthy for its topographical details and description and sketches of the great natural fortress of Qalʿa-ye Nāderī which Fraser had described without seeing and where Curzon was refused entry in 1889.

One traveler more interested in the Persians as people than in their country's topography and antiquities was E. G. Browne, later renowned as a great Persian scholar who was to win the affection and esteem of the Persians as no other Englishman has done. His interest, like Curzon's, had first been stimulated when an Eton schoolboy. At Cambridge, he studied both medicine and Oriental languages before, aged twenty-six, traveling to Persia in 1887. His *A Year amongst the Persians* is unlike any other travel book about the country for its insight into Persian thinking and literature and was a fitting prelude to his later books on the country's literature, history, press, and politics.

A year after Browne's departure, George Curzon, then a young member of the House of Commons, arrived in Persia. The previous year he had been one of the first to travel on the newly-built Trans-Caspian railway and came to the conclusion that it gave Russia practical control of Khorasan. Now, in order to study the Persian situation for himself (and write some articles for the London *Times*), he entered the country by its back door—once again traveling on the railway from its terminus on the Caspian to Ashkhabad deep in Russian-occupied Turkoman country, where he hired horses and rode across the frontier to Qūčān, Mašhad, and Tehran. His *Persia and the Persian Question* is indispensable reading for all students of Qajar Persia, not only as a well illustrated travelogue but for its meticulous account of the country's history, government, and monuments.

Percy Sykes was another keen and friendly observer of the Persian scene. As a young British cavalry officer stationed in India, he had traveled widely in Persia in 1893 and again in 1894, collecting information for Military Intelligence in India. The decision to open a British consulate in Kermān and appoint Sykes as the first consul there was part of the game of stealing a march on the Russians in an area of both strategic and commercial interest to the Government of India. Abandoning active soldiering, Sykes arrived in Kermān early in 1895 and remained there for ten years before being sent to take charge of the consulate-general in Mašhad, Britain's main listening post on Russia's Central Asian border. Sykes remained in Mašhad until 1913. He traveled widely at both posts and describes his travels and much more besides in his *Ten Thousand Miles in Persia,* which was followed by two other books about the country—*The Glory of the Shia World* and *A History of Persia*, since revised and reprinted a number of times and still a useful introduction to the country's long history. Sykes, in contrast to so many of his fellow countrymen, liked and admired the Persians.

His sister, Ella, accompanied Sykes to Kermān and acted as his hostess for two years. She traveled with him everywhere and was one of the very few, though not the first, women travelers in Persia to go into print. Her *Through Persia on a Side-Saddle* contains vivid descriptions of life in and around Kermān, where she was probably the first European lady ever seen.

The first female to write about Persia was the Irish-born Leonara Sheil who traveled there in 1849 as the newly-wed wife of the British minister, Justin Sheil. Her shrewd and informative *Glimpses of Life and Manners in Persia* contains an interesting account of the couple's journey to Tehran through Germany, Poland, and Russia to Tiflis, Erevan, and Tabrīz by train, carriage, and *ta<u>k</u>t-e ravān*—accompanied by two Irish maids, a French chef, and a Scotch terrier. Best of all, though, is the indomitable, middle-aged, and widowed Mrs. Bishop (Isabella Bird)'s account of her winter's ride in January 1890 from Baghdad to Tehran, then on to Isfahan and across wild Ba<u>k</u>tīārī and Kurdish mountains to Lake Van before sailing home from Trabzon.

By way of contrast, the reader should dip into Lady Durand's account of *An Autumn Tour in Western Persia* nine years later with her husband, then British Minister to Persia. A personal maid and an army of cooks and servants attended their every want.

There were many others not mentioned in this short essay who wrote about their Persian travels—army officers from India like T. Lumsden and J. Johnson; Indian civilians such as R. B. M. Binning (author in Curzon's view of "the last really good book that has been written on Persia"[7]) and Edward Stack; missionaries such as J. Wolff and H. A Stern, both naturalized British subjects; the diplomat E. B. Eastwick; men involved in frontier-making and the erection of the Indo-European telegraph line, F. J. Goldsmid and E. A. Floyer; and enterprising independent travelers like J. H. Stocqueler (J. H. Siddons), A. Arnold and A. H. Savage-Landor.

These and many others not mentioned contributed much to the West's knowledge of Persia and, for all their prejudices, remain an invaluable source of information about Qajar Persia.

---

[7] Curzon, *Persia,* 2:22.

BIBLIOGRAPHY

Travel and Other Books about Persia by Authors Mentioned in the Article

Alcock, Thomas. *Travels in Russia, Persia, Turkey, and Greece, in 1828-9*. London, 1831.

Armstrong, T. B. *Journal of Travels in the Seat of War during the Last Two Campaigns of Russia and Turkey*. London, 1831.

Arnold, Arthur. *Through Persia by Caravan*. 2 vols. London, 1877.

Baker, Valentine. *Clouds in the East*. London, 1876.

Binning, Robert B. M. *A Journal of Two Years' Travel in Persia, Ceylon, etc*. 2 vols. London, 1857.

Bishop, Mrs. J. F. [Isabella Bird]. *Journeys in Persia and Kurdistan*. London, 1891.

Browne, Edward G. *A Brief Narrative of Recent Events in Persia*. 2 vols. London, 1909

—. *A Literary History of Persia*. 4 vols. Cambridge, 1902-24.

—. *A Year amongst the Persians*. London, 1893.

—. *The Persian Revolution 1905-09*. Cambridge, 1910.

—. *The Press and Poetry of Modern Persia*. Cambridge, 1914.

Brydges, Harford Jones. *An Account of the Transactions of His Majesty's Mission to the Court of Persia in the years 1807-11*. London, 1834.

Buckingham, James Silk. *Travels in Assyria, Media and Persia*. London, 1829.

Burnes, Alexander. *Travels into Bokhara*. 3 vols. London, 1834.

Conolly, Arthur. *Journey to the North of India overland from England, through Russia, Persia, and Affghaunistaun*. 2 vols. London, 1834.

Curzon, George N. *Persia and the Persian Question*. 2 vols. London, 1892.

Durand, Ella R. *An Autumn Tour in Western Persia*. London, 1902.

Eastwick, Edward B. *Journal of a Diplomate's Three Years' Residence in Persia*. 2 vols. London, 1864.

Floyer, Ernest A. *Unexplored Baluchistan*. London, 1882.

Fowler, George. *Three Years in Persia with Travelling Adventures in Koordistan*. 2 vols. London, 1841.

Fraser, James Baillie. *A Winter's Journey (Tatar) from Constantinople to Tehran etc*. 2 vols. London, 1838.

—. *Allee Neemroo, the Buchtiaree Adventurer: A Tale of Louristan*. 3 vols. London, 1842. [Fiction].

—. *An Historical and Descriptive Account of Persia from the Earliest Ages to the Present Time*. Edinburgh, 1834.

Fraser, James Baillie. *Narrative of a Journey into Khorasan in the Years 1821 and 1822 etc*. London, 1825.
—. *Narrative of the Residence of the Persian Princes in London and Subsequent Adventures*. 2 vols. London, 1838.
—. *Tales of the Caravenserai: The Khan's Tale*. London, 1833. [Fiction].
—. *The Dark Falcon: A Tale of the Attruck*. 4 vols. London, 1844. [Fiction].
—. *The Kuzzilbash: A Tale of Khorasan*. 3 vols. London, 1828. [Fiction].
—. *The Persian Adventurer*. 3 vols. London, 1830. [Fiction].
—. *Travels and Adventures in the Persian Provinces of the Southern Banks of the Caspian Sea*. London, 1826.
—. *Travels in Koordistan, Mesopotamia etc., including an Account of Parts of those Countries hitherto Unvisited by Europeans*. 2 vols. London, 1840.
Goldsmid, Frederic John (ed.) *Eastern Persia, an Account of the Journeys of the Persian Boundary Commission, 1870-72*. 2 vols. London, 1876.
—. *Telegraph and Travel: A Narrative of the Formation and Development of Telegraphic Communications between England and India*. London, 1874.
Johnson, John A. *Journey to England, through Persia, Georgia, Russia, Poland, and Prussia, in the Year 1817*. London, 1818.
Jones, H. See Brydges, Harford Jones.
Kinneir, John M. *A Geographical Memoir of the Persian Empire*. London, 1813.
Layard, Austen Henry. *Early Adventures in Persia, Susiana and Babylonia*. 2 vols. London, 1887.
Lumsden, Thomas. *A Journey from Merut in India to London through Arabia, Persia, Armenia, Georgia, Russia, Austria, Switzerland, and France, during the Years 1819 and 1820*. London, 1822.
MacDonald, J. K. See Kinneir, John M.
MacDonald, Robert. *Personal Narrative of Military Travel and Adventure in Turkey and Persia*. 1859.
MacGregor, Charles M. *Narrative of a Journey through the Province of Khorasan and on the N.W. Frontier of Afghanistan in 1875*. 2 vols. London, 1879.
Malcolm, John. *The History of Persia*. 2 vols. London, 1815.
—. *Sketches of Persia*. 2 vols. London, 1828.
Marsh, Hippisley Cunliffe. *A Ride through Islam, being a Journey through Persia and Afghanistan to India via Meshed, Herat, and Kandahar*. London, 1877.

Mitford, Edward L. *A Land March from England to Ceylon Forty Years Ago*. 2 vols. London, 1884.

[Money, Robert Cotton], R. C. M. *Journal of a Tour in Persia during the Years 1824 and 1825*. London, 1828.

Morier, James. *A Journey through Persia, Armenia, and Asia Minor, to Constantinople, in the Years 1808 and 1809*. London, 1812

—. *A Second Journey through Persia, Armenia, and Asia Minor, to Constantinople, between the Years 1810 and 1816*. London, 1818.

—. *Misselman, A Persian Tale*. London, 1847. [Fiction].

—. *The Adventures of Hajji Baba of Ispahan in England*. 2 vols. London, 1828. [Fiction].

—. *The Adventures of Hajji Baba of Ispahan*. 3 vols. London, 1824. [Fiction].

—. *The Mirza*. 3 vols. London, 1841. [Fiction].

—. *Zohrab the Hostage*. 3 vols. London, 1832. [Fiction].

Ouseley, William. *Travels in Various Countries of the East, more Particularly Persia*. 3 vols. London, 1819-23.

Porter, Robert Ker. *Travels in Georgia, Persia, Armenia, Ancient Babylonia, etc. etc. during the Years 1817, 1818, 1819 and 1820*. 2 vols. London, 1821-22.

Pottinger, Henry. *Travels in Baloochistan and Sinde*. London, 1816.

Price, William. *Journal of the British Embassy to Persia*. London, 1832.

Rich, Cladius J. *Narrative of a Residence in Koordistan ... and an Account of a Visit to Shirauz and Persepolis*. 2 vols. London, 1836.

Savage-Landor, Arnold H. *Across Coveted Lands*. 2 vols. London, 1902.

Sheil, Mary Leonora. *Glimpses of Life and Manners in Persia*. London, 1856.

Stack, Edward. *Six Months in Persia*. 2 vols. London, 1882.

Stern, Henry A. *Dawnings of Light in the East, with Biblical, Historical, and Statistical Notices of Persons and Places Visited during a Mission to the Jews in Persia, Coordistan, and Mesopotamia*. London, 1854.

Stewart, Charles Edward. *Through Persia in Disguise*. London, 1911.

Stocqueler, Joachim Hayward. *Fifteen Months' Pilgrimage through Untrodden Tracts in Khuzistan and Persiąin the Years 1831 and 1832*. 2 vols. London, 1832.

—. *Memoirs of a Journalist*. London, 1873.

Stuart, Charles. *Journal of a Residence in Northern Persia and the Adjacent Provinces of Turkey*. London, 1854.

Sykes, Ella Constance. *Persia and its People*. London, 1910.

—. *The Story Book of the Shah; or, Legends of Old Persia*. London, 1901.

—. *Through Persia on a Side-Saddle*. London, 1898.

Sykes, Percy Molesworth. *A History of Persia*. 2 vols. London, 1915.

—. *Ten Thousand Miles in Persia, or Eight Years in Iran*. London, 1902.

—. *The Glory of the Shia World*. London, 1910.

Waring, Edward S. *A Tour to Sheeraz by the Route of Kazroon and Feerozabad etc*. London, 1807.

Wilbraham, Richard. *Travels in the Trans-Caucasian Provinces of Russia, and along the Southern Shores of the Lakes of Van and Urumiah, in the Autumn and Winter of 1837*. London, 1839.

Wolff, Joseph. *Narrative of a Mission to Bokhara in the Years 1843-45*. 2 vols. London, 1845.

—. *Travels and Adventures of the Rev. Joseph Wolff*. Edited by Alfred Gatty. 2 vols. London, 1860-61.

About the Contributors

Iraj AFSHAR, University of Tehran (emeritus), is editor of the journal *Āyanda* and has published numerous works, including editions of Persian texts and various comprehensive bibliographies such as the *Fehrest-e maqālat-e fārsī*.

Elena ANDREEVA, Virginia Military Institute, received her doctoral degree from New York University.

James CLARK, American Institute of Iranian Studies, is completing research for his doctoral degree from the University of Texas.

Elton L. DANIEL, University of Hawaii at Manoa, is author of *The Political and Social History of Khurasan under Abbasid Rule* and *The History of Iran*.

Layla S. DIBA, independent curator (New York), received her doctoral degree from the Institute of Fine Arts and is author of *Lacquerwork of Safavid Persia* and co-editor of *Royal Persian Paintings: The Qajar Epoch*.

Maryam EKHTIAR, independent scholar (New York), received her doctoral degree from New York University and is co-editor of *Royal Persian Paintings: The Qajar Epoch*.

Mansureh ETTEHADIEH, University of Tehran, is founder of Našr-e Tārīḵ-e Īrān, has edited numerous Persian historical sources, and is the author of *Aḥzāb-e sīāsī dar Majles-e Sevvom* and *Īnjā Tehrān ast*.

M. R. GHANOONPARVAR, University of Texas, is author of *In a Persian Mirror: Images of the West and Westerners in Iranian Fiction*, *Translating the Garden*, and *Prophets of Doom: Literature as a Socio-Political Phenomenon in Modern Iran*.

William L. HANAWAY, University of Pennsylvania (retired), is author of *Persian Popular Romances* and co-editor of *Studies in Pakistani Popular Culture*.

Shireen MAHDAVI, independent scholar (Salt Lake City), received her doctoral degree from the University of London and is the author of *For God, Mammon, and Country: A Nineteenth Century Persian Merchant*.

Hashem RAJABZADEH, Osaka University of Foreign Studies, is co-editor of *55 Sanad-e fārsī az dawra-ye Qājār*, author of *Tārīḵ-e Žāpon*, and translator of numerous works from Japanese to Persian, including the travel account of Yoshida Masaharu.

Roger SAVORY, University of Toronto (emeritus), is translator of Eskandar Beg Monšī's *Tārīḵ-e ʿālamāra-ye ʿAbbāsī* and author of *Iran under the Safavids* and *Studies on the History of Safawid Iran*.

Mohammad TAVAKOLI-TARGHI, Illinois State University-Normal, is author of *Refashioning Iran: Orientalism, Occidentalism, and Historiography*.

Farzin VAHDAT, Tufts University, is author of *God and Juggernaut: Iran's Intellectual Encounter with Modernity*.

Anna VANZAN, Università IULM Milano-Feltre, is translator of the *Memoirs* of Taj-al-Saltana and author of *Parole svelate: racconti di donne persiane*.

Denis WRIGHT, former ambassador of Great Britain to Iran and member of the British Institute of Persian Studies, is author of *The English amongst the Persians: Imperial Lives in Nineteenth-Century Iran* and *The Persians amongst the English: Episodes in Anglo-Persian History*.